BARRON'S

MW00803249

NEW YORK CITY
SHSAT

SPECIALIZED HIGH SCHOOLS ADMISSIONS TEST

5TH EDITION

BARRON'S

The 5th edition of *Barron's NYC SHSAT* was extensively revised and updated through the tireless efforts of Young Kim, Bronx High School of Science, and Patrick Honner, Brooklyn Technical High School. Barron's Test Prep editors are grateful for all of their hard work in making this edition ready in time for students preparing for the SHSAT this coming October.

*The views expressed in this book are those of the authors and not necessarily those of the City of New York (NYC).

All inquiries should be addressed to:
Barron's Educational Series, Inc.
250 Wireless Boulevard
Hauppauge, New York 11788
www.barronseduc.com

ISBN: 978-1-4380-1239-1

ISSN: 2168-8249

Printed in the United States of America
→ 9 8 7 6 5 4 3 2 1

Contents

The Barron's Advantage v

Preface vii

INSIDE THE SHSAT

Introduction 3

Diagnostic Minitest 1 19

TEST-TAKING STRATEGIES

General Advice 41

Skillbuilder A: Stand-Alone Revising/Editing 45

Skillbuilder B: Passage-Based Revising/Editing 74

Skillbuilder C: Reading 97

Skillbuilder D: Mathematics 111

    Section 1. Mathematical Problem Analysis 111

    Section 2. The Math Skills Diagnoser 127

    Section 3. Some Basic Terms and Concepts You Should Know 155

PRACTICE TESTS

Minitest 2 167

Minitest 3 189

Minitest 4 209

Practice Test 1 231

Practice Test 2 269

Practice Test 3 309

NINTH-GRADE MATHEMATICS SUPPLEMENT

Practice Problems 349

Appendix: Progress on Math Workouts and Follow-Ups 359

The Barron's Advantage

You have already made TWO very good decisions!
You have decided to attend one of the best high schools in the country, and you have chosen the right test prep book.

Here's why Barron's *SHSAT* for New York City Specialized High Schools gives you the ADVANTAGE.

- **More than 600 practice problems** cover every aspect of the actual test.
- **Three full-length** practice tests and **four minitests** written in the style and at the level of the actual test offer plenty of practice to test what you know.
- **Detailed solutions to every practice test problem are given.** These solutions feature useful TIPS and FACTS that provide topical review as you go.
- **Study guides**, powerful and productive **test-taking strategies**, and lots and lots of **practice problems** solved and analyzed in detail let you proceed at your own pace.
- **Skillbuilders** that carefully guide you through each type of test question with additional practice exercises give you even more opportunities to test your knowledge. The unique **Math Diagnosers** find and correct any weaknesses while reinforcing your strengths.

Students have told us that much of the other test prep materials they have used in the past was too easy—that when it came time for the actual test, they were in for a big surprise. The questions you find in Barron's test prep materials accurately reflect the level of difficulty of the actual test. The Barron's authors are experts in their fields, with more than forty years of experience.

Preface

Admission to the New York City Specialized High Schools has become increasingly competitive. Now more than ever, good test preparation is essential.

The Admissions Test is a challenging test that calls for logical thinking and strong ability in both English and mathematics. To be successful, you must be very well prepared. That means you must have your mathematical and reading skills in top working order, you should be thoroughly familiar with the test format and types of questions that will be asked, and you should be aware of test-taking tips that will help you score well. A major approach to all of this is practicing with well-written, comprehensive test prep materials.

This book has been written with these aims in mind. You will find a wealth of carefully crafted material to help you achieve your goal. In addition to practice tests with detailed solutions and explanations, there are sections devoted to strengthening your skills in each of the four major areas covered by the test. The design of the book allows you to work at your own pace. Care has been taken to ensure accuracy, especially regarding mathematical concepts and terminology. Topical review is actually contained within the solutions and the Skillbuilders, where important information, facts, and tips have been highlighted and explained.

Inside the SHSAT

Introduction

AN OVERVIEW

The specialized high schools of New York City offer a wide range of excellent academic programs. Whereas some emphasize mathematics, science, technology, and engineering, others stress social science and the humanities.

Admission to these schools is based entirely on one single exam—the New York City Specialized High Schools Admissions Test, often referred to as the SHSAT. Basing admission on a single exam may seem unfair, but it is prescribed by New York State law. Nearly 30,000 students compete for the limited number of places available in these specialized schools each year, so to have a real advantage, you must adequately prepare for this annual test. Even if you are the best and the brightest, and many of you are, you can significantly enhance your chances of admission to the school of your choice with good test prep and guided practice and review.

When Should You Begin to Prepare? What Do You Have to Do?

The sooner you begin, the more time you will have to prepare. Some students begin more than a year in advance. This book allows you to proceed at your own pace and provides you with all the material you need to perform well on the exam.

What's on the Test?

The test consists of two major sections.

English Language Arts	(three parts)
	Stand-Alone Revising/Editing
	Passage-Based Revising/Editing
	Reading Comprehension
Mathematics	(two parts)
	Grid-In Questions
	Multiple-Choice Questions

All questions are worth the same number of raw points. No one question is worth more than another. There is a time limit of 180 minutes, with no break. It is recommended that you allow 90 minutes for each of the two sections, but you are permitted to allocate the time however you wish. There is no penalty for wrong answers or omissions (questions left blank), so it is to your advantage to bubble in an answer to every question, even if you must guess. Detailed descriptions of each section are found on pages 6–12.

The number of correct answers you get is converted into a scaled score that is used to determine your standing. The conversion formulas vary from year to year.

When Is the Test Administered?

The test has traditionally been given in late October. It is for admission in the following September. For example, you would take the October 2018 exam for admission in September 2019. Be sure to verify this year's test dates and locations. The test is administered to current eighth graders seeking admission to the ninth grade, and another form of the test is given to current ninth graders seeking admission to the tenth grade. The overwhelming number of applicants are eighth graders.

How and When Do I Obtain Information and Application Forms?

You must get information regarding applications and test sites from your guidance counselor. Do this early in September. In addition, you should obtain a copy of the *Specialized High Schools Student Handbook*. This is available from your guidance counselor or online from the Department of Education Office. The *Handbook* contains additional current information regarding the test sites and any special rules that may apply.

All procedures and dates are subject to change. Be sure to obtain current information from your counselor or the handbook.

What Decisions Do I Have to Make?

You have to decide, in advance, which will be your first, second, etc., choice of schools. Where you actually take the exam does not affect your indicated choice of schools. You may take the exam only once in any given year. Violation of this rule will disqualify you from attending any of the specialized schools.

> **IMPORTANT:** If your score on the exam is high enough to gain admission to your first-choice school, you are fully expected to attend that school.

What Score Do I Need?

Your total number of correct answers is your raw score. The raw score is converted to a scaled score by means of a special formula. This process converts your raw score into an integer between 200 and 800. (The Department of Education does not publicly release the conversion formulas.) The scaled scores are not directly proportional to the raw scores. For example, at the middle range of scores, a difference of one correct answer may change the scaled score by only a few points, whereas at higher and lower ranges, a difference of one correct answer may change the scaled score by 10 to 20 points. The cut-off score (minimum scaled score needed) for each of the schools is determined by how many places each school has available.

Although we can prepare you for the test, there are some things we cannot do. We cannot predict the cut-off scores and we cannot tell you precisely how many questions you have to answer correctly to achieve a particular cut-off score.

Trends over the years indicate that the number of students taking the test is increasing and that cut-off scores are rising.

The Summer Discovery Program

Certain applicants whose scores are just short of the cut-off score may qualify for the Summer Discovery Program. Successful completion of this program allows qualifying students to gain admission. The eligibility requirements for admission to this program include

- scoring just below the cut-off score.
- recommendation from counselor, and documentation of special circumstances and needs. See your counselor and the DOE Handbook for details.

THE SPECIALIZED HIGH SCHOOLS

Bronx High School of Science
75 West 205th Street; Bronx, New York 10468
Telephone: (718) 817-7700   Website: *www.bxscience.edu*

Brooklyn Latin School
325 Graham Avenue; Brooklyn, New York 11206
Telephone: (718) 366-0154   Website: *www.brooklynlatin.org*

Brooklyn Technical High School
29 Fort Greene Place; Brooklyn, New York 11217
Telephone: (718) 804-6400   Website: *www.bths.edu*

High School for Mathematics, Science and Engineering at City College
240 Convent Avenue; New York, New York 10031
Telephone: (212) 281-6490   Website: *www.hsmse.org*

High School of American Studies at Lehman College
2925 Goulden Avenue; Bronx, New York 10468
Telephone: (718) 329-2144   Website: *www.hsas-lehman.org*

Queens High School for the Sciences at York College
94-50 159th Street; Jamaica, New York 11451
Telephone: (718) 657-3181   Website: *www.qhss.org*

Staten Island Technical High School
485 Clawson Street; Staten Island, New York 10306
Telephone: (718) 667-3222   Website: *www.siths.org*

Stuyvesant High School
345 Chambers Street; New York, New York 10282-1099
Telephone: (212) 312-4800   Website: *www.stuy.enschool.org*

THE TEST: A DETAILED DESCRIPTION

The SHSAT consists of two major sections: English Language Arts and Mathematics. The time limit is 180 minutes total for both sections with no break. The suggested time is 90 minutes for each section.

English Language Arts Section: 57 multiple-choice questions

- Up to 8 Stand-Alone Revising/Editing questions
- Up to 8 Passage-Based Revising/Editing questions
- 5 to 6 Reading passages, each followed by 5 to 7 related questions

Mathematics Section: 5 grid-in questions and 52 multiple-choice questions

- Total 57 questions covering a range of topics and testing a variety of skills and abilities

There is no penalty for wrong or omitted answers.

Stand-Alone Revising/Editing

DESCRIPTION

Part A of the Revising/Editing section includes up to eight questions, each of which is based on its own sentence or paragraph and measures your ability to identify an error, correct an error, or improve the quality of a given text.

Each question directs you to read a sentence, a list of sentences, or a paragraph with numbered sentences. Then you must address issues associated with language or punctuation.

DIRECTIONS

The usual directions instruct you to read the sentence or paragraph and identify an error or to select an option that fixes an existing error.

➡ Example _____

1. Read this paragraph.

> (1) People often associate monosodium glutamate, or better known as MSG, with headaches and nausea, but there was no evidence to substantiate that link. (2) In fact, the compounds associated with MSG are commonly found in beef, pork, or chicken. (3) Scientists believe the sicknesses might be the result of a "nocebo effect." (4) The nocebo effect, like the placebo effect, isn't caused by an actual substance, but merely by suggestion.

Which sentence in this paragraph contains an error in verb tense?

    A. sentence 1
    B. sentence 2
    C. sentence 3
    D. sentence 4

The Answer
The correct answer is A. The paragraph is written in present verb tense; however, the use of *was* in sentence 1 is past tense.

Passage-Based Revising/Editing

DESCRIPTION

Part B includes questions that are based on one or two passages. Each Revising/Editing passage may have up to eight questions. Revising/Editing items assess students' ability to recognize and correct language errors and to improve the overall quality of a piece of writing. The passages are approximately 400 words long and may be either informative or argumentative. An argument presents evidence to persuade the reader of its claim, while an informative passage introduces an idea and presents supporting examples to illustrate that idea. Subjects range from history to the sciences.

Passages may contain errors that are typical in student writing, such as errors in language usage, irrelevant or insufficient details, inappropriate transitions, and problematic introductory/concluding statements. Each sentence is numbered for your convenience.

DIRECTIONS

The usual directions instruct you to read the passage and identify an error or to select an option that fixes an existing error from a given sentence.

 Example

The Harmful Effects of Acid Rain

(1) An ecosystem is a community of plants, animals and other organisms along with their environment including the air, water and soil. (2) Everything in an ecosystem is connected.

(3) The ecological effects of acid rain are most clearly seen in aquatic environments, such as streams, lakes, and marshes where it can be harmful to fish and other wildlife. (4) As it flows through the soil, acidic rain water can be harmful to the environment. (5) The more acid that is introduced to the ecosystem, the more aluminum is released.

(6) Some types of plants and animals are able to tolerate acidic waters and moderate amounts of aluminum. (7) Others are acid-sensitive and will be lost as the pH declines. (8) Generally, the young of most species are more sensitive to environmental conditions than adults. (9) At pH 5, most fish eggs cannot hatch, while at lower pH levels, some adult fish die. (10) Even if a species of fish or animal can tolerate moderately acidic water, the animals or plants it eats might not. (11) For example, frogs have a critical pH around 4, but the mayflies they eat are more sensitive and may not survive pH below 5.5.

1. Which sentence can best follow and support sentence 2?

   A. If something harms one part of an ecosystem—one species of plant or animal, the soil, or the water—it can have an impact on everything else.
   B. Likewise, humans create connections primarily through technology, such as telephones and the Internet.
   C. The government currently manages 58 national parks around the country, each with its unique needs.
   D. The consequences of overdevelopment and pollution are apparently manageable precisely because of the redundancies built into these interconnections.

The Answer
The correct answer is A. This sentence best explains how an ecosystem can be connected, which supports sentence 2.

Reading

DESCRIPTION

You are presented with a prose passage of about 350 to 450 words in length. The subject matter may include descriptions of historical events, information about natural or scientific phenomena, discussions of topics relating to music, art, or sports, and so on. In each passage, there is a central unifying theme, and points of view are often expressed or implied. Following each passage there is a set of 5–7 multiple-choice questions. The first question asks you to identify the central theme or main idea of the passage. Other questions pertain to factual information contained in the passage, inferences that may be drawn, the meaning of words and phrases, points of view expressed or implied, and so on.

DIRECTIONS

The usual directions instruct you to read the passage and answer the 5–7 questions following that passage. You are cautioned to base your answers **only on what is contained in the passage**. Choose, from among the answer choices, the **best** answer for each question.

➡ Example _____

Antonio Stradivari was born in 1644 in Cremona, Italy, a town noted for the production of excellent violins. Although Stradivari made cellos and violas as well as violins, it is violins for which he is renowned. His teacher, Nicolo Amati, passed on to him the techniques of violin making as these were practiced in Cremona. The pupil Stradivari employed these techniques but went on to surpass his teacher, making violins whose excellence has never been exceeded or even fully understood.

What makes a Stradivarius such a fine instrument? Stradivari did alter the proportions of the violin, but this change alone does not explain their superiority. Some think that the special varnish he used is responsible for the wonderful sound of the instruments, but not every expert agrees with this idea. A relatively recent theory concerns the unusually cold weather in Europe during this period of history. Lower-than-usual temperatures would have slowed the growth rate of the trees whose wood was used in the violins, resulting in a very dense wood. Perhaps the magnificent Stradivarius sound derives from the density of the wood rather than from the composition of the varnish.

The only violin maker whose instruments rival those of Antonio Stradivari is Giuseppe Antonio Guarneri, who lived at the same time. This fact does not give conclusive proof, but it does seem to bolster the cold-weather theory of the secret of the Stradivarius.

21. Which of the following best expresses the purpose of the author of the passage?

    A. To discuss the excellence of the violins produced by Stradivari
    B. To indicate a surprising result of climate change
    C. To explain what makes a violin superior
    D. To compare the violins of Stradivari and Guarneri

22. Which of the following is **not** mentioned as a possible factor influencing the quality of a Stradivarius violin?

    E. Special varnish
    F. Dense wood
    G. Experience gained through making violas and cellos
    H. Changes in proportions

The Answers

The correct answers are 21 A and 22 G. This example is fully discussed in Skillbuilder C: Reading.

The Reading questions test your ability to read carefully and understand what you have read. This is gauged by your ability to distinguish between stated fact and implication, as well as your ability to draw valid inferences based on the passage.

Mathematics

DESCRIPTION

There are 52 multiple-choice questions and 5 grid-in questions covering a broad range of topics and assessing a wide range of abilities. Topics include arithmetic, basic algebra, elementary geometry, probability, and statistics. On the ninth year version of the test, there is also some trigonometry. Many questions assess your knowledge of basic concepts. Others test your ability to think creatively and apply what you know in what may be new or unfamiliar situations.

> **IMPORTANT:**
> - Calculators are **not** permitted.
> - No formulas are provided.

POINT VALUE

There are 57 questions in the Mathematics section: 52 multiple-choice questions and 5 grid-in questions. Only 47 preselected questions of the 57 questions will actually be scored. (There will be 10 unidentified "field test items" on the test that will not be scored.) Since you will not know which questions are field items, it is to your advantage to answer all items in each section.

DIRECTIONS

The usual directions instruct you to solve each problem and choose the **best** answer from among the given choices. You are directed to do your work in the test booklet or on scratch paper (if provided). Formulas and definitions of technical terms are not given. Diagrams are not necessarily drawn to scale, but graphs are drawn to scale. You are told that lines that appear to be straight are indeed straight and lines that appear to be parallel or perpendicular may be assumed to be so, and so on. Reduce fractions to lowest terms when appropriate and do not do any figuring on your answer sheet.

Multiple-choice Questions

51. The value of $\frac{9090}{90}$ is

   A. 11
   B. 100
   C. 101
   D. 111

52. For positive numbers x and y, define $x \circledR y$ to mean $x^2 - 2y$. Find the value of $5 \circledR 3$.

   E. 69
   F. 19
   G. 16
   H. 13

53. The sides of a square are each multiplied by 3 to form a new square. If the area of the original square was K, then the area of the new square is

   A. K^3
   B. $3K$
   C. $6K$
   D. $9K$

The Answers

The correct answers are 51 C, 52 F, and 53 D. These examples are fully discussed in Skillbuilder D, Section 1 on page 111.

Grid-In Questions

A "grid-in question" requires that you solve a problem by computing a numerical answer and placing that answer on an answer grid. This is different from a "multiple-choice question," which requires that you select the correct answer from among a given set of choices.

For example, if a problem asks you to compute the product of -3×0.4, then the answer, -1.2, would be correctly entered as shown on the grid on the right.

The official directions that you will see on the actual exam appear as follows:

Directions: Solve each problem. On the answer sheet, write your answer in the boxes at the top of the grid. Start on the left side of each grid. Print only one number or symbol in each box. **DO NOT LEAVE A BOX BLANK IN THE MIDDLE OF AN ANSWER.** Under each box, fill in the circle that matches the number or symbol you wrote above. **DO NOT FILL IN A CIRCLE UNDER AN UNUSED BOX.**

GENERAL TIPS

(1) *No calculators are permitted, so do not practice with them!*

(2) *Immediately after solving (and checking) a problem:*

- Enter the answer in the boxes in the top line of its grid.
- If you skip a problem, be sure to also skip the grid for that problem.

(3) *When entering your answer in the top line of the grid, note that:*

- The first box is **only** used if the answer has a minus (–) sign.
- For accuracy and consistency, the rest of your answer should be entered starting at the second box, with each box you use getting either a digit (from 0 to 9) or a decimal point (.).
- Do not leave any blank boxes **within** the answer.

(4) *Under each box in the top line:*

- Fill in the circle that matches the number or symbol you entered at the top.
- If you change the top boxes later, be sure to erase and correct the filled in circles below.
- **If there is no entry in a top box, do not fill in any circles below that box.**
- **Be accurate**: Grading is based on the filled in circles, not on your entries in the top line.

(5) *Additional suggestions:*

- Be sure to place your answer in the top line before filling in the circles; this helps ensure accuracy and helps prevent gridding errors.
- There is no penalty for wrong answers, so when you finish the problems you know, go back and enter your best guess for the questions you skipped. **Answer every question!**
- Review the material in the Mathematics "Skillbuilder" section in this book.

SAMPLES OF CORRECT AND INCORRECT GRIDDING

Suppose the answer is –3.2:

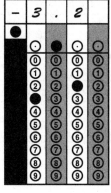

acceptable

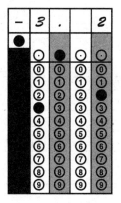

not acceptable
(has blank box
within answer)

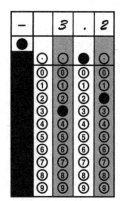

not acceptable
(has blank box
within answer)

Suppose the answer is 602:

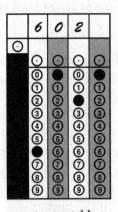

acceptable

not acceptable
(the filled in 0 in
the last column
changes the
answer to 6020)

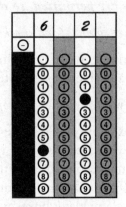

not acceptable
(has blank box
within answer)

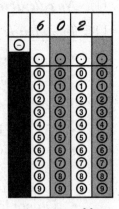

not acceptable
(column numbers
not filled in)

SUMMARY OF THE NUMBERS AND TYPES OF QUESTIONS ON THE SHSAT

The ELA and Mathematics sections of the test will each contain 57 questions, distributed as follows:

English Language Arts Section	
Type of Question	**Number of Questions***
Stand-Alone Revising/Editing questions	5–8 multiple-choice questions (with 4 answer choices)
Passage-Based Revising/Editing questions	2 reading passages each with 6–8 associated multiple-choice questions (with 4 answer choices)
Reading Comprehension Passages with associated questions	6 reading passages each with 5–7 associated multiple-choice questions (with 4 answer choices)

*There will be 20 Revising/Editing questions and 37 Reading Comprehension questions.

Mathematics Section	
Type of Question	**Number of Questions**
Multiple-choice questions	52 questions
Grid-in questions	5 questions

Marking the Answer Sheet

Bring to the test three to five well-sharpened #2 pencils, a good eraser, and a noncalculator watch to keep track of time.

When you bubble in an answer on the answer sheet, make sure your mark is clear and dark and completely fills the circle.

Be careful where you bubble in each answer. If you enter answers on the wrong line, you not only lose credit for those answers, but you waste a tremendous amount of time because you must eventually erase those answers and enter them correctly. This is a costly mistake, yet it is an **easily avoidable error**. *Each time* you bubble in an answer, say the question number to yourself and be sure the grid number matches it. Make this automatic. This is especially important if you skip a question.

If you change an answer, erase the old mark **completely**. Do not bubble in more than one answer to a problem, or no credit will be given for either answer.

A few minutes before the test ends, look over your answer sheet to be sure **every** question has some answer bubbled in. You cannot get credit for an empty space, so simply guess if necessary. On this test you do not lose credit if an answer is wrong, but you do get credit for a correct guess.

Make sure there are no stray marks on the answer sheet. Do not fold or tear that sheet.

> The test information in this book is accurate as of the date of publication. However, some aspects of the test have varied over the years. It is important that you check with your school counselor for the latest information and instructions.

HOW TO USE THIS BOOK

This book is designed to help you improve your score on the SHSAT by

- Providing you with sample tests in the style and at the level of the actual test.
- Providing detailed solutions featuring TIPS AND FACTS. Review of material is provided through the solutions.
- Helping you find and correct weaknesses while sharpening your skills. "Skillbuilders" for each part of the exam provide you with detailed analyses and methods for solving each type of question.
- Providing you with test-taking strategies and suggestions that will bring you to peak performance.

The successful test taker should follow several important principles.

- **Know your basics.**
  You already have basic math and verbal skills. Practice will sharpen them to the degree needed to help you attain a high score.

- **Know the test format.**
  This includes types of questions, time limits, directions, and gridding procedures.

- **Know the strategies.**
  Familiarity with general test-taking techniques, as well as strategies that are specific to each type of question, will give you the test-taking advantage.

- **Practice!**
  Taking the actual test is like preparing for a performance, or getting ready for the big game of the season. A good performance depends on good rehearsals. You want to give a **great** performance on test day.

> **EXTREMELY IMPORTANT:** Whenever you practice, work under test-like conditions.

- **Do practice exams under strict time limits.**
- **Review solutions in detail.** These contain important and informative review material.
- **Don't cram.**

A Suggested Plan of Study

The time necessary to accomplish this plan will vary from individual to individual. Some students will spread this over months; others may do it in much less time. However, we suggest that you set up a regular schedule of study and try to do some practice every day.

1. Be sure you have read the detailed description of the test beginning on page 6 in order to acquaint yourself with the test format.
2. Next, take Minitest 1 under strict test-like conditions. This will give you an idea of what the actual test is like.
3. Now grade the test (there is an answer key following the minitest). Then carefully review the Answer Explanations to this minitest (they follow the answer key). Look at the Analysis that follows the Answer Explanations.
4. Begin with the opening section ("General Advice"), which is followed by the Skillbuilders. Skillbuilders are detailed "how-to" sections; the Revising/Editing, Reading, and Mathematics portions of the test are each treated in a separate Skillbuilder. You may do these Skillbuilders in any order you choose. In fact, it is advisable to start with your weakest area, especially if the time you have to prepare before the exam is limited.

   Skillbuilder D, Section 2 contains a Math Skills Diagnoser, which consists of six "Workouts" focused on specific areas of math skill such as arithmetic, algebra, geometry, and graphs. After you grade each "Workout" (the Solutions immediately follow the Workout), enter the results on the Math Workouts and Follow-ups page in the back of the book. Then review those Solutions. After you finish each "Follow-Up," grade it (the answers appear after Follow-Up F) and enter those results as well..
5. Do the rest of the sample tests. For maximum benefit, leave ample time between taking these practice tests. It is best not to do and review more than one test on any given day. *It is absolutely necessary that each practice test be done in a single sitting, under strict time limits.* After each test, check the answer key. Then study the solutions. Return to the appropriate Skillbuilders for any needed review.

6. If you are a ninth-grade student applying for admission to the tenth grade, do the ninth-grade math supplement.

7. When you have completed all the tests in the book, redo each one, beginning with Minitest 1. Review those problems that were answered incorrectly both times.

8. For additional practice, redo the math Workouts and Follow-Ups in Skillbuilder D, Section 2.

9. *Be sure to make a photocopy of the answer sheets in case you retake any of the tests.*

ANSWER SHEET
Diagnostic Minitest 1

Part I   English Language Arts

Revising/Editing Part A

1. Ⓐ Ⓑ Ⓒ Ⓓ
2. Ⓔ Ⓕ Ⓖ Ⓗ
3. Ⓐ Ⓑ Ⓒ Ⓓ
4. Ⓔ Ⓕ Ⓖ Ⓗ
5. Ⓐ Ⓑ Ⓒ Ⓓ
6. Ⓔ Ⓕ Ⓖ Ⓗ

Revising/Editing Part B

7. Ⓐ Ⓑ Ⓒ Ⓓ
8. Ⓔ Ⓕ Ⓖ Ⓗ
9. Ⓐ Ⓑ Ⓒ Ⓓ
10. Ⓔ Ⓕ Ⓖ Ⓗ
11. Ⓐ Ⓑ Ⓒ Ⓓ
12. Ⓔ Ⓕ Ⓖ Ⓗ
13. Ⓐ Ⓑ Ⓒ Ⓓ

Reading

14. Ⓐ Ⓑ Ⓒ Ⓓ
15. Ⓔ Ⓕ Ⓖ Ⓗ
16. Ⓐ Ⓑ Ⓒ Ⓓ
17. Ⓔ Ⓕ Ⓖ Ⓗ
18. Ⓐ Ⓑ Ⓒ Ⓓ
19. Ⓔ Ⓕ Ⓖ Ⓗ

20. Ⓐ Ⓑ Ⓒ Ⓓ
21. Ⓔ Ⓕ Ⓖ Ⓗ
22. Ⓐ Ⓑ Ⓒ Ⓓ
23. Ⓔ Ⓕ Ⓖ Ⓗ
24. Ⓐ Ⓑ Ⓒ Ⓓ
25. Ⓔ Ⓕ Ⓖ Ⓗ

Part II   Mathematics

26.

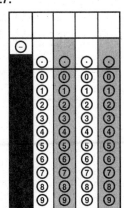

27.

28. Ⓐ Ⓑ Ⓒ Ⓓ
29. Ⓔ Ⓕ Ⓖ Ⓗ
30. Ⓐ Ⓑ Ⓒ Ⓓ
31. Ⓔ Ⓕ Ⓖ Ⓗ
32. Ⓐ Ⓑ Ⓒ Ⓓ
33. Ⓔ Ⓕ Ⓖ Ⓗ
34. Ⓐ Ⓑ Ⓒ Ⓓ
35. Ⓔ Ⓕ Ⓖ Ⓗ
36. Ⓐ Ⓑ Ⓒ Ⓓ

37. Ⓔ Ⓕ Ⓖ Ⓗ
38. Ⓐ Ⓑ Ⓒ Ⓓ
39. Ⓔ Ⓕ Ⓖ Ⓗ
40. Ⓐ Ⓑ Ⓒ Ⓓ
41. Ⓔ Ⓕ Ⓖ Ⓗ
42. Ⓐ Ⓑ Ⓒ Ⓓ
43. Ⓔ Ⓕ Ⓖ Ⓗ
44. Ⓐ Ⓑ Ⓒ Ⓓ
45. Ⓔ Ⓕ Ⓖ Ⓗ

46. Ⓐ Ⓑ Ⓒ Ⓓ
47. Ⓔ Ⓕ Ⓖ Ⓗ
48. Ⓐ Ⓑ Ⓒ Ⓓ
49. Ⓔ Ⓕ Ⓖ Ⓗ
50. Ⓐ Ⓑ Ⓒ Ⓓ
51. Ⓔ Ⓕ Ⓖ Ⓗ
52. Ⓐ Ⓑ Ⓒ Ⓓ

Diagnostic Minitest 1

PART 1—ENGLISH LANGUAGE ARTS

25 QUESTIONS

SUGGESTED TIME: 30 MINUTES

Revising/Editing

QUESTIONS 1–13

Revising/Editing Part A

Directions: Read and answer each of the following questions. You will be asked to recognize and correct errors in sentences or short paragraphs. Mark the **best** answer for each question.

1. Read this paragraph.

> (1) Aquaculture, also known as fish farming or shellfish farming, refers to the breeding of plants and animals in water environment. (2) Researchers of this exciting field are "farming" all different kinds of aquatic species. (3) The work by thousands of scientists and engineers has made remarkable progress throughout the years. (4) Continued advances in this technology is expanding aquaculture's role in both conservation and commercial efforts.

Which sentence in this paragraph contains an error in subject-verb agreement?

  A. sentence 1
  B. sentence 2
  C. sentence 3
  D. sentence 4

2. Read this sentence.

> The Civil War of the 19th century was one of the most brutal deadly wars and claimed more American lives than the two world wars combined.

Which edit should be made to correct this sentence?

  E. insert a comma after *War*
  F. insert a comma after *century*
  G. insert a comma after *brutal*
  H. insert a comma after *lives*

3. Read this paragraph.

> (1) The combination of hydraulic fracking and horizontal drilling is mostly responsible for the recent increase in U.S. oil production. (2) However, the drilling methods by the fracking industry had come under heavy scrutiny. (3) Some critics looking at the environmental impact point to exploding faucets and the increasing frequency of sinkholes. (4) Others examining the economy suggest that these methods make minimal contributions to overall growth.

Which sentence should be revised to correct an inappropriate shift in verb tense?

A. sentence 1
B. sentence 2
C. sentence 3
D. sentence 4

4. Read these sentences.

> (1) The SHSAT is offered to all New York City students.
> (2) Students in 8th and 9th grade take the exam.
> (3) Students from all the boroughs are encouraged to take the exam.

What is the best way to combine these sentences?

E. The SHSAT is offered to all New York City students, who are in the 8th and 9th grade to take the exam, although students from all the boroughs are encouraged to take the exam.
F. When the SHSAT is offered to all New York City students in the 8th and 9th grade, they are all encouraged to take the exam.
G. While the SHSAT is offered to all 8th and 9th grade students in New York City, students from all boroughs are encouraged to take the exam.
H. 8th and 9th grade students from all boroughs of New York City are encouraged to take the SHSAT.

5. Read this sentence.

> Due to the rising costs of materials, people interested in arts and crafts get their stuff from other countries.

Which of these is the most precise revision for the words *people interested in arts and crafts get their stuff*?

A. people interested in arts and crafts obtain resources
B. people who are interested in arts and crafts purchase fabrics and wood
C. arts and crafts enthusiasts get fabrics and wood
D. arts and crafts enthusiasts purchase fabrics and wood

6. Read this paragraph.

> (1) The dramatic decline of bee populations has perplexed scientists, who attribute it to numerous factors. (2) One study examined the impact of neonicotinoids in a laboratory setting and concluded that it has a significant influence on the health of a beehive. (3) Another study examined the radiation of cell phones and found that it reduced honey production. (4) Neither is the magical bullet that solves the mystery, but both studies suggest that there may be multiple factors that help explain it.

Which sentence should be revised to correct an inappropriate shift in pronoun?

E. sentence 1
F. sentence 2
G. sentence 3
H. sentence 4

Revising/Editing Part B

Directions: Read the passage below and answer the questions following it. You will be asked to improve the writing quality of the passage and to correct errors so that the passage follows the conventions of standard written English. You may reread the passage if you need to. Mark the best answer for each question.

Tombs of the Egyptian Dynasty

(1) For many years, various European collections of Egyptian antiquities have contained a certain series of objects, which gave certain people great difficulty. (2) There were vases of a peculiar form and color, greenish plates of slate, many of them in curious animal forms, and other similar things. (3) It was known, positively, that these objects had been found in Egypt, but it was impossible to assign them a place in the known periods of Egyptian art.

(4) Egyptian art has long served an important role in museums all over the world. (5) The first light was thrown on this question in two places on the west bank of the Nile. (6) A lucky man found many important objects. (7) Many findings that help us understand the basic foundation of life can be found in the Nile. (8) Containing pottery and the slate tablets that did not seem to be Egyptian, the newly found necropolis and the puzzling objects were assumed to represent the art of a foreign people who had temporarily resided in Egypt in the time between the old and the middle kingdoms. (9) British archaeologists gave this unknown people the name "New Race."

(10) The bold assertion of this appellation made headlines in academia. (11) This theory met with little approval, least of all from German Egyptologists. (12) In spite of much discussion, the question could not then be decided.

7. Which revision of sentence 1 uses the most precise language?

   A. For many years, various European collections of Egyptian antiquities have contained a certain series of objects, which gave certain people great difficulty.

   B. For many years, various collections of Egyptian antiquities have contained a certain series of objects, which gave scientists great difficulty.

   C. For more than 100 years, various collections of Egyptian antiquities have contained a certain series of objects, which gave archaeologists great difficulty.

   D. For more than 100 years, various European collections of Egyptian antiquities have contained a certain series of objects, which gave archaeologists great difficulty.

8. Which sentence should replace sentence 4 to more clearly introduce the topic of this passage?

   E. Learning more about art enhances not only one's understanding of the world but also the very essence of what it means to be human.

   F. The strange style of the objects, as well as the difficulty in situating their composition, led many investigators to question their origins.

   G. Egypt has always been a source of mystery and wonder for both the adventurer and the homebody.

   H. It might certainly be productive of unusual emotions to know that the few human bones found in the tomb once belonged to the oldest Egyptian king.

9. Which revision of sentence 6 uses the most precise language?

   A. A lucky investigator found an important discovery that contained numerous objects.

   B. An English investigator found an important discovery that contained numerous graves.

   C. A lucky English investigator discovered a very large necropolis containing about three thousand graves.

   D. A lucky English person came upon an important discovery of about three thousand graves.

10. Which transition word or phrase should be added to the beginning of sentence 9?

    E. In addition,
    F. However,
    G. Nonetheless,
    H. Therefore,

11. Which sentence is irrelevant to the argument presented in the passage and should be deleted?

    A. sentence 2

    B. sentence 5

    C. sentence 7

    D. sentence 11

12. What is the best way to combine sentences 10 and 11 to clarify the relationship between ideas?

    E. The bold assertion of this appellation made headlines in academia, and this theory met with little approval, least of all from German Egyptologists.

    F. Because the bold assertion of this appellation made headlines in academia, the theory met with little approval, least of all from German Egyptologists.

    G. Whereas the bold assertion of this appellation made headlines in academia, the theory met with little approval, least of all from German Egyptologists.

    H. The bold assertion of this appellation made headlines in academia, but this theory met with little approval, least of all from German Egyptologists.

13. Which sentence could best follow sentence 12 and support the main point of the third paragraph?

    A. Scientists today, however, have new technology that can easily date and locate artifacts by examining the composition of their organic materials.

    B. The disagreement between the Germans and the British often extended outside of academia and into politics.

    C. It would take another decade and another fortunate discovery to address the controversial claim.

    D. Many valuable facts about history and the ancient world are the result of disagreements.

Directions: Read each passage and answer the questions that follow it. Base your answers **only on the material contained in the passage.** Select the one **best** answer for each question. Bubble in the letter corresponding to that answer on the answer sheet.

I. Today a growing number of parents are practicing infant massage and finding it a rewarding experience. To give infant mas-
Line sage, the parent usually lays the baby on a
(5) blanket on the floor. Having rubbed a little canola oil onto his or her index finger, the parent begins lightly stroking the baby's skin. Parents report that infants usually lie quiet, seeming to enjoy the experience.
(10) Furthermore, they claim that massaged infants are less colicky—that is, less tense and fussy.

Just a few decades ago in this country medi-tation was seen as a practice only for monks
(15) and other recluses; hypnotism was viewed as a parlor trick; and acupuncture was con-sidered Far Eastern quackery. Today these "alternative health" methods are recognized by the medical community as valuable tools
(20) for maintaining wellness and for managing health problems. Now comes infant mas-sage. In other cultures it has been used for hundreds of years as a way to promote the emotional and physical health of babies. In
(25) the United States, however, it is still in the process of gaining general acceptance as a useful technique.

Proponents of infant massage say that mas-saged babies are more relaxed and less irrita-
(30) ble. Such babies, they maintain, sleep better and even tend to be healthier. Studies support these claims. Research data indicate that massage improves digestion, aids brain and muscle development, and boosts immune
(35) function. Premature and drug-addicted babies who are massaged have fewer motor difficulties, better neurological development, more favorable weight gain, and fewer hospi-

talizations. There is even some evidence that
(40) massage may improve IQ.

With minimum instruction anyone can successfully practice this valuable tech-nique. The ideal person to administer the massage, however, is the child's parent. The
(45) reason for this is that a major benefit of this shared experience is a closer bonding. The gentle, loving touch administered to the tiny body communicates caring and pro-motes a sense of security. Moreover, the
(50) communication is two-way. The parent learns to interpret and respond to the baby's cues—for example, which are the baby's favorite massage spots, and whether the baby would prefer not to be massaged at a
(55) given time. Thus, the interpersonal bond is strengthened even more.

14. Which of the following best expresses the topic of the passage?

  A. Resistance to change in the American medical community
  B. A treatment for colic in infants
  C. Nonverbal communication—a key to physical and emotional well-being
  D. The benefits of infant massage

15. According to the passage, which of the following is **not** a possible benefit of infant massage for the parents?

  E. They may have fewer medical bills.
  F. They may be more rested.
  G. They may learn about other alternative health practices.
  H. They build a stronger bond with their babies.

16. The passage suggests that

    A. infant massage guarantees a healthy baby.

    B. doctors do not approve of infant massage.

    C. hypnotism is best reserved for purposes of entertainment.

    D. the skin is an important medium of nonverbal communication.

17. With which of the following would the author of the passage **not** agree?

    E. Parents should take their babies to professional massage therapists.

    F. Most babies can benefit from massage.

    G. A baby may not always want massage when it is convenient for the parent.

    H. Massage can make a parent and infant emotionally closer to each other.

18. In the context of this passage, what is the significance of meditation, hypnotism, and acupuncture?

    A. They are "alternative" and thus not practiced by health professionals in this country.

    B. Like massage, they rely on touch.

    C. They are useful in promoting infant well-being.

    D. They are examples of health practices that had slow acceptance in this country.

19. All of the following are mentioned as possible benefits of infant massage **except**

    E. improved brain development.

    F. higher IQ.

    G. better motor skills.

    H. addiction cure.

II. Earthworms are familiar creatures, although most people don't encounter them every day. Fishing enthusiasts use them for *Line* bait, and biology students dissect them in (5) the laboratory. But most of the time they stay out of sight unless rain has soaked the soil, driving them above ground. Squeamish gardeners probably wince when their bare hands suddenly feel a telltale cool wiggle, (10) but they have ample reason to appreciate the little reddish dirt dwellers.

There are five families of earthworms (class *Oligochaeta* of phylum *Annelida*) distributed across every continent except Antarctica. (15) Although most of the species found in North America are only a few inches in length, some tropical areas boast worms 11 feet long. Earthworms have no eyes or ears, but the lack is no hindrance, as vision and (20) hearing are unnecessary for finding food— these underground dwellers can actually eat their habitat! And they can even communicate with each other in a limited way. When disturbed, their bodies exude an oily film (25) that serves as a warning to nearby fellows.

The cylindrical bodies of earthworms bear tiny external structures called *setae*. In combination with an elongated, tapered shape and an efficient muscular system, these tiny (30) bristles enable earthworms to burrow easily through soil. As they burrow, they stir up and loosen the soil, creating tiny pockets of air that they breathe through their skin. This tilling makes for a healthy medium for (35) vegetative growth. Underground cultivation is not their only service, for these helpful creatures also process and excrete decaying vegetation called humus, which directly fertilizes the earth. And when they die, their (40) decomposing bodies perform a last act of service.

A healthy acre of land may contain up to three million earthworms, which together can till about eighteen tons of soil per year. (45) Regrettably, modern farming methods often decrease earthworm population through the

overuse of pesticides. Persistent heavy applications of toxins over a period of years can
actually result in "dead" soil, which no
(50) longer contains the earthworms necessary to
make it productive. By contrast, land that
is farmed with earthworm-friendly methods
can continue its optimum productivity for
thousands of years—and then thousands
(55) more after that.

20. Which of the following is the best title for
this passage?

A. "How to Have a Healthy Garden"
B. "Annelids Worldwide"
C. "Meet a Friend of the Soil"
D. "Pesticides and the Death of the Soil"

21. What is the "last act of service" that an
earthworm provides?

E. It warns its neighbors by exuding an
oily film.
F. It excretes processed humus.
G. It aerates the soil.
H. Its decaying body fertilizes the soil.

22. What is the most likely reason why
earthworms come to the surface when it
rains?

A. They are attracted to the moisture
above.
B. Their air supply is replaced by water.
C. Raindrops striking the ground trigger
their "warning" systems.
D. The underground temperatures drop
too low.

23. What is the meaning of the word "setae"
(line 27)?

E. Setae are the earthworm's rudimentary
lungs.
F. It refers to the shape of the
earthworm's body.
G. It is the name of the earthworm's
projecting bristles.
H. It refers to the peculiarly shaped mouth
of the earthworm.

24. Which of the following best explains the
earthworm's beneficial effect on the soil?

A. The earthworm cultivates and enriches
the soil.
B. The earthworm digs burrows that
provide air passages.
C. The earthworm is a scavenger that
cleans the soil.
D. Dwindling numbers of earthworms can
warn of toxic conditions in the soil.

25. According to the passage, which of the
following statements is true concerning
pesticide use?

E. It is "earthworm friendly."
F. Too much can kill off earthworms.
G. It is an essential part of modern
farming.
H. Properly applied, pesticides guarantee
productive land for thousands of years.

90° 180° 360°

PART 2—MATHEMATICS

QUESTIONS 26–52

SUGGESTED TIME: 45 MINUTES

Grid-In Problems

Directions: Solve each problem. On the answer sheet, write your answer in the boxes at the top of the grid. Start on the left side of each grid. Print only one number or symbol in each box. **DO NOT LEAVE A BOX BLANK IN THE MIDDLE OF AN ANSWER.** Under each box, fill in the circle that matches the number or symbol you wrote above. **DO NOT FILL IN A CIRCLE UNDER AN UNUSED BOX.**

26. What is the value of x in the given equation?

$$\frac{162 - x}{11} = 13$$

27. Two straight lines intersect at point B. A ray extends from B making a right angle as shown. What is the value of y?

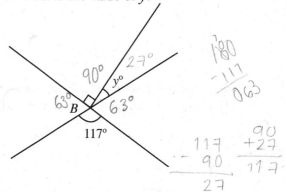

Multiple-Choice Problems

Directions: For each of the following questions, select the **best** answer from the given choices. Bubble in the letter corresponding to your answer on the answer sheet. **DO NOT PUT ANY OTHER WORK ON THE ANSWER SHEET.** All necessary work can be done in your test booklet or on scrap paper that is provided.

NOTE: Diagrams other than graphs might not be drawn to scale. Do not assume any relationships that are not specifically stated unless they are implied by the given information.

28. $\frac{1}{2} + \frac{1}{3} - \frac{1}{4} =$

A. $\frac{1}{20}$

B. $\frac{7}{12}$

C. $\frac{3}{4}$

D. 1

29. In the diagram, $AC = BD = 17$ and $BC = 3$. The length of segment $\overline{AD}$ is

E. 20
F. 24
G. 28
H. 31

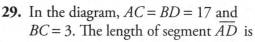

30. What is the value of $|x - y| + |y - x|$ if $x = -3$ and $y = -7$?

 A. −14
 B. −6
 C. 0
 D. 8

(handwritten: $|-3 + 7| + |-7 + 3|$ $+4 + 4 = 8$)

31. The product of the first ten prime numbers must be divisible by

(handwritten: 1 3 5 7 9 11 13 15 17)

 E. 16
 F. 18
 G. 20
 H. 22

32. $4^3 + 4^3 + 4^3 + 4^3 =$ *(handwritten: 4×4^3)*

 A. 4^4
 B. 4^9
 C. 4^{12}
 D. 16^3

33. If the mean of 4 and x is the same as the mean of 4, 10, and x, what is the value of x?

 E. 16
 F. 10
 G. 7
 H. No value of x will make this true.

34. If $x = 3$, what is the value of $\dfrac{5(4 + x)}{2x}$?

 A. 15
 B. $\dfrac{25}{2}$
 C. 10
 D. $\dfrac{35}{6}$

(handwritten: $\dfrac{5(4+3)}{2(3)}$ $\dfrac{35}{6}$)

35. $.\overline{3} \times .\overline{3} =$

 E. $.09$
 F. $.\overline{09}$
 G. $.\overline{1}$
 H. $.\overline{6}$

36. In the diagram, figure I is a square, and figures II and III are equilateral triangles. What is the value of x?

 A. 10
 B. 15
 C. 30
 D. 45

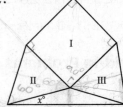

37. Two years ago, Esther was 3 years younger than Miguel is now. Let Miguel's present age be represented by M. Esther's age 10 years from now will be

 E. $M + 7$
 F. $M + 9$
 G. $M + 10$
 H. $M + 11$

38. All of the students in Mr. Jacobs's class are taking either French or algebra or both subjects. Exactly 16 students are taking French, exactly 18 students are taking algebra, and exactly 6 are taking both subjects. What is the total number of students in Mr. Jacobs's class?

 A. 22
 B. 28
 C. 31
 D. 34

39. Which of the following could be the sum of exactly three consecutive integers?

 E. 98
 F. 198
 G. 298
 H. 398

40. Five hamburgers and one order of fries together cost $10.24, whereas one hamburger and five orders of fries together cost $5.84. What is the total cost of three hamburgers and three orders of fries?

 A. $13.20
 B. $12.72
 C. $8.04
 D. $3.30

(handwritten: $5H + 1F = \$10.24$ $1H + 5F = \$5.84$ $= 2(6H + 6F = \$16.08)$ $3H + 3F = ?$)

less greater
> <

41. Circles A and B touch but do not overlap, as shown. The area of circle A is 9π and the area of circle B is 16π. What is the area of the smallest circle that can contain the entire shaded figure?

4.5 + 8 = 12.5 / 2

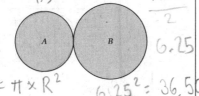

6.25

    E. 25π
    F. 36π
    G. 49π
    H. 64π

$A = \pi \times R^2$ *$6.25^2 = 36.50\pi$*

42. Which of the following numbers is closest to 1?

    A. $\dfrac{49}{50}$

    B. $\dfrac{99}{100}$

    C. $\dfrac{197}{200}$

    D. $\dfrac{499}{500}$

43. Referring to the diagram, find the value of $(x + y)$.

$120° - 180° = 60$
$180° - 40° = 140°$

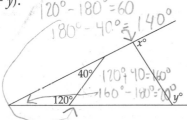

$120 + 40 = 160$
$160° - 180° = 0°\ y°$

    E. 200
    F. 180
    G. 160
    H. Cannot be determined from the information given

44. If the notation $q*r$ means $\dfrac{q+r}{2}$, then $(a*b)*c$ will be equal to $a*(b*c)$

    A. always
    B. never
    C. only if $a = b$
    D. only if $a = c$

45. $X: \dfrac{3}{7} > \dfrac{11}{24}$ $Y: \dfrac{2}{5} < \dfrac{9}{22}$ $Z: (.1)^2 > .1$

$0.01 > .1$

    E. X, Y, and Z are all true
    F. Z is true
    G. X, Y, and Z are all false
    H. X is false

46. Let n be a fixed integer between 1 and 50. If the number 100 is decreased by $n\%$, and this result is then increased by $n\%$, the final value obtained

    A. must be more than 100
    B. must be exactly 100
    C. must be less than 100
    D. will sometimes be less than 100 and sometimes more than 100, depending on the value of n

47. If x is a positive number, then $\dfrac{12+x}{2+x}$ *$= 6-X$*

    E. must be less than 6
    F. must equal 6
    G. must be greater than 6
    H. is sometimes less than 6 and sometimes greater than 6, depending on the value of x

48. One of the following numbers is the product of a three-digit number and a four-digit number. Which is it?

    A. 22,146
    B. 745,691
    C. 10,000,001
    D. 803,024,559

49. If p is a prime, which one of the following *could* be a prime also?

    E. $23p + 45$
    F. $23p + 46$
    G. $23p + 47$
    H. $23p + 48$

50. Which of the following is equivalent to the inequality $9 - x < 7 < 15 - x$?

A. $x > 2$
B. $x < 8$
C. $1 < x < 4$
D. $2 < x < 8$

51. When the spinner shown in the diagram is spun once, the probability that the arrow will land on any one of the numbers 1, 2, 3, 4, or 5 is $\frac{1}{5}$. (Assume that the arrow never lands on a line.) The spinner is spun exactly twice. What is the probability that the *product* of the two numbers that occur is a prime number?

E. $\frac{4}{25}$

F. $\frac{5}{25}$

G. $\frac{6}{25}$

H. $\frac{7}{25}$

52. The area of trapezoid *ABCD* is

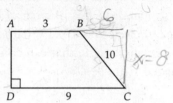

A. 48
B. 36
C. 30
D. cannot be determined from the information given

$$x = \sqrt{(10)^2 - (6)^2}$$
$$x = \sqrt{100 - 36}$$
$$x = \sqrt{64}$$
$$x = 8$$

Revising/Editing Part A

1. D
2. G
3. B
4. H
5. D
6. F

Revising/Editing Part B

7. D
8. F
9. C
10. H
11. C
12. H
13. C

Reading

14. D
15. G
16. D
17. E
18. D
19. H
20. C
21. H
22. B
23. G
24. A
25. F

Mathematics

26. **19**
27. **27**
28. B
29. H
30. D
31. H
32. A
33. E
34. D
35. G
36. B
37. F
38. B
39. F
40. C
41. G
42. D
43. E
44. D
45. H
46. C
47. E
48. B
49. H
50. D
51. G
52. A

ANSWER EXPLANATIONS
MINITEST 1

Revising/Editing Part A

1. **(D)** Examine the subject noun and predicate verb pairings for each sentence. The incorrect pairing is *italicized*.

   (1) <u>Aquaculture</u>, also known as fish farming or shellfish farming, <u>refers</u> to the breeding of plants and animals in water environment. (2) <u>Researchers</u> ~~of this exciting field~~ <u>are</u> "farming" all different kinds of aquatic species. (3) The <u>work</u> ~~by thousands of scientists and engineers~~ <u>has</u> made remarkable progress throughout the years. (4) Continued *advances* ~~in this technology~~ *is* expanding aquaculture's role in both conservation and commercial efforts.

2. **(G)** The words *brutal deadly* are coordinate adjectives. You can use them interchangeably with the word *and* to modify *wars*. *The most deadly and brutal wars* would make sense.

   "The Civil War of the 19th century was one of the most *brutal, deadly* wars and claimed more American lives than the two world wars combined."

   Choice E is wrong because a comma between a word and its preposition is unnecessary.

   Choice F is wrong because a comma between a subject and its predicate verb is unnecessary.

   Choice H is wrong because a comma between two correlative conjunctions (more *x* than *y*) is unnecessary.

3. **(B)** Examine all the predicate verbs underlined below.

   (1) The combination of hydraulic fracking and horizontal drilling <u>is</u> mostly responsible for the recent increase in U.S. oil production. (2) However, the drilling methods by the fracking industry <u>had</u> come under heavy scrutiny. (3) Some critics looking at the environmental impact <u>point</u> to exploding faucets and the increasing frequency of sinkholes. (4) Others examining the economy <u>suggest</u> that these methods <u>make</u> minimal contributions to overall growth.

   The paragraph is written in the present tense and the predicate verb that doesn't agree is the past tense verb *had*.

4. **(H)**

   E. "The SHSAT is offered to all New York City students, who are in the 8th and 9th grade to take the exam, although students from all the boroughs are encouraged to take the exam."

   This sentence contains an independent clause and two dependent clauses. In addition, it unnecessarily sets up a contrast with the word *although*.

   F. "When the SHSAT is offered to all New York City students in the 8th and 9th grade, they are all encouraged to take the exam."

   This sentence creates an illogical relationship between the two clauses.

   G. "While the SHSAT is offered to all 8th and 9th grade students in New York City, students from all boroughs are encouraged to take the exam."

   This sentence creates an illogical relationship between the two clauses.

   H. "8th and 9th grade students from all boroughs of New York City are encouraged to take the SHSAT."

   This sentence contains only one clause. It combines information from all three sentences without changing the meaning.

5. **(D)**

Least Precise (cross out)	Most Precise
people interested in arts and crafts — people who are interested in arts and crafts	arts and crafts enthusiasts
obtain — get	purchase
resources	fabrics and wood

6. **(F)** Examine the pairings of <u>antecedents</u> and **pronouns** below.

(1) The dramatic <u>decline</u> of bee populations has perplexed scientists, who attribute **it** to numerous factors. (2) One study examined the impact of <u>neonicotinoids</u> in a laboratory setting and concluded that **it** has a significant influence on the health of a beehive. (3) Another study examined the <u>radiation</u> of cell phones and found that **it** reduced honey production. (4) Neither is the magical bullet that solves for the <u>mystery</u>, but both studies suggest that there may be multiple factors that help explain **it**.

Sentence 1: The correct antecedent to the singular pronoun **it** is <u>decline</u>.

Sentence 2: The singular pronoun **it** is an inappropriate replacement for the plural antecedent <u>neonicotinoids</u>. **It has** should be revised to **they have**.

Sentence 3: The correct antecedent to the singular pronoun **it** is <u>radiation</u>.

Sentence 4: The correct antecedent to the singular pronoun **it** is <u>mystery</u>.

Revising/Editing Part B

7. **(D)**

Least Precise (cross out)	Most Precise
many years	more than 100 years
certain people, scientists	archaeologists

8. **(F)** Sentence (5) contains the phrase *this question*. This phrase connects best with the phrase *to question* in choice B.

9. **(C)** *A lucky English investigator* provides the most detailed information about the person who made the discovery. The phrase *a very large necropolis containing about three thousand graves* provides the most detailed information about the discovery itself.

10. **(H)** The assumption in sentence (8) led the archaeologists to give the people a new name. Therefore, the most logical relationship is cause and effect. The transition word *Therefore* best connects the two sentences.

11. **(C)** Sentence 7 provides a general statement about the importance of art. It has no relevance to the topic about the question of the object's origins. Sentence 2 is necessary because it provides details on the *difficulty* that archaeologists encountered. Sentence 5 is necessary because it introduces how the mystery of the objects were explored. Sentence 11 is necessary because it concludes the main idea of the paragraph.

12. **(H)** The two sentences need a transition word to reveal a contrast. Choice H uses the word *but* to reveal that contrast.

13. **(C)** This answer choice concludes the paragraph by addressing how *the question* would later be resolved.

Reading

Passage I

14. **(D)** Main Idea   All of the other choices are too narrow because they involve only small parts of the passage. Every paragraph discusses the benefits of massage, so D is correct.

15. **(G)** Detail and Inference   The wording of the question (a "possible" benefit) does not require a direct statement. E is suggested by the indication of improved health (line 31), and F is stated in line 30. The last paragraph states H. G is not suggested or stated in the passage.

16. **(D)** Inference   A is too extreme. Claims are made that massaged babies "tend to be healthier" (line 31). B also is too extreme. The passage says that the procedure is "gaining general acceptance" (line 26) in the medical community, which indicates that at least some doctors approve of it.

17. **(E)** Detail   The last paragraph names the parent as the ideal infant massager (lines 43–44). The passage is clearly promoting infant massage as a generally beneficial practice, so F is incorrect. The last paragraph says that a baby may not want to be massaged at a particular time, so the author would agree with G (line 54). H is stated in the passage.

18. **(D)** Detail   None of the other choices are stated or suggested in the passage. The second paragraph states the slow acceptance of these practices and likens it to the slow acceptance of infant massage.

19. **(H)** Detail   All of the other choices are mentioned in the third paragraph.

Passage II

20. **(C)** Main Idea   A and D are too narrow. B is too broad, as the passage discusses only earthworms, not all Annelida (line 13). C is broad enough and accurate, for the passage introduces the reader to the earthworm and indicates its benefits to the soil.

21. **(H)** Inference   E, F, and G are all inaccurate since the "last act of service" (lines 40–41) occurs after death, and these choices concern actions of the living worm. The last two sentences in the third paragraph link decaying matter with fertilization (line 39) and attribute the "act of service" to the worm's "decomposing" body (lines 40–41). Thus H is the correct choice.

22. **(B)** This question involves information from two paragraphs. The third paragraph states that the worms breathe air in soil pockets (lines 32–33). The first paragraph states that they come to the surface when driven above ground by a rain that has soaked, or filled, the soil (lines 6–7). B is the correct choice. None of the other choices is suggested or stated in the passage.

23. **(G)** Detail   The first two sentences of the third paragraph define *setae*.

24. **(A)** Detail   The beneficial cultivation and enriching, or fertilization, are directly stated in the passage. B and D are not presented as directly beneficial effects on soil. C is not stated or suggested in the passage.

25. **(F)** Detail   The last paragraph says that pesticides can kill off earthworms (line 47). None of the other choices are stated or suggested.

Mathematics

26. **(19)** Multiply both sides of the equation $\frac{162 - x}{11} = 13$ by 11 to get $(162 - x) = 143$, and so $x = 162 - 143 = 19$.

27. **(27)** Right angles measure 90 degrees. Since vertical angles formed by intersecting lines are congruent, we know that $117 = 90 + y$. So $y = 117 - 90 = 27$.

28. **(B)** Getting a common denominator of 12 produces $\frac{6}{12} + \frac{4}{12} - \frac{3}{12} = \frac{7}{12}$.

29. **(H)** Adding AC and BD counts the over-lapped segment BC twice. Therefore we subtract it once, getting $17 + 17 - 3 = 31$.

30. **(D)**

> **TIP:** Combine the terms inside the absolute value signs before you compute the absolute value.

We have $|-3 + 7| + |-7 + 3| = |4| + |-4| = 4 + 4 = 8$.

31. **(H)** Two of those ten primes are 2 and 11, so the correct answer is 22. Each other choice contains some prime factor at least twice.

32. **(A)** This is 4×4^3, which is 4^4.

33. **(E)**

> **TIP:** If the mean of n numbers is A, then the numbers add up to $n \times A$.

$\dfrac{4 + x}{2} = \dfrac{4 + 10 + x}{3}$, leading to $3(4 + x) = 2(14 + x)$. This gives us $x = 16$.

34. **(D)** After substituting 3 for x, combine terms in the parentheses:

$$\frac{5(4 + 3)}{2(3)} = \frac{5(7)}{6} = \frac{35}{6}$$

35. **(G)** Changing the repeating decimals to fractions, we have $\dfrac{1}{3} \times \dfrac{1}{3} = \dfrac{1}{9}$. Changing $\dfrac{1}{9}$ back to a decimal results in $.\overline{1}$.

> **FACT:**
> $$\frac{1}{9} = .\overline{1},\ \frac{2}{9} = .\overline{2},\ \frac{3}{9} = .\overline{3}\left[= \frac{1}{3}\right],$$
> and so on. Surprisingly,
> $$.\overline{9} = \frac{9}{9} = 1$$

36. **(B)** The angles around the central point must add up to 360°, so the vertex angle of the bottom isosceles triangle is 150°. Each base angle is then 15°.

37. **(F)** Two years ago, Esther's age was $M - 3$. Her age now is $(M - 3) + 2 = M - 1$. Ten years from now, her age will be $(M - 1) + 10 = M + 9$.

38. **(B)** Draw a Venn diagram, one circle representing students who take French and the other representing students who take algebra. The overlapping section represents students who take both. In the overlap, put the number 6. That leaves $16 - 6 = 10$ for the other part of the French circle, and $18 - 6 = 12$ for the other part of the algebra circle. We can now add the numbers in these three separate sections, getting the final answer

$$10 + 6 + 12 = 28.$$

39. **(F)** Think of the consecutive integers as being represented by k, $k + 1$, and $k + 2$. Notice that the sum of these, $3k + 3$, must be divisible by 3. Now check the choices for divisibility by 3. Only choice F works.

> **TIP:** An even nicer representation for three consecutive integers is $k - 1$, k, and $k + 1$, because their sum is so simple.

40. **(C)** Using single letters to represent the types of food, we have $5H + 1F = 10.24$ and $1H + 5F = 5.84$. We can find $3H + 3F$ very easily by adding the two equations and then dividing by 2. This gives $3H + 3F = 8.04$.

> **TIP:** It is not always necessary to solve for H and F individually. See if the problem requires the individual values or not.

41. **(G)** Since the radii of the small circles are 3 and 4, the diameter of the enclosing circle is 14. Since its radius is 7, its area is 49π.

42. **(D)** Convert each fraction to an equivalent fraction with a denominator of 1000. The choices then become:

$$\frac{980}{1000},\ \frac{990}{1000},\ \frac{985}{1000},\ \text{and}\ \frac{998}{1000}$$

The closest to 1 is $\dfrac{998}{1000}$ or $\dfrac{499}{500}$.

43. **(E)** In the small triangle, the missing angle must be 20°. Then in the large triangle, the sum of the other two interior angles must be 160°. Those last two angles plus x and y form two straight angles, which total $180° + 180° = 360°$. Therefore we have $160 + x + y = 360$, so $x + y = 200$.

> **TIP:** It is not always possible to obtain x and y individually (and problems may not call for that).

44. **(D)** According to the * notation, $(a*b)*c$

means $\dfrac{\frac{a+b}{2}+c}{2}$, and $a*(b*c)$ means

$\dfrac{a+\frac{b+c}{2}}{2}$. Equating the two expressions, then

multiplying both sides by 2 produces

$\dfrac{a+b}{2}+c=a+\dfrac{b+c}{2}$.

Again multiplying both sides by 2, we get $a + b + 2c = 2a + b + c$. This leads to $c = a$. The fact that the position of the parentheses is important here means that this new operation is not associative. This is not an easy problem.

45. **(H)**

> **FACT:** For positive numbers a, b, c, and d, $\frac{a}{b}>\frac{c}{d}$ if and only if $ad > bc$. Also, for positive numbers a, b, c, and d, $\frac{a}{b}<\frac{c}{d}$ if and only if $ad < bc$.

Inequality X is equivalent to $72 > 77$, which is false. Inequality Y is equivalent to $44 < 45$, which is true. After squaring (.1), inequality Z produces $.01 > .1$, which is false. Thus the answer is H.

46. **(C)**

> **TIP:** It is sometimes easiest to choose a simple but specific value of a variable to work with.

For example, let $n = 10$. Note that 10% of 100 is 10. Subtracting that from 100 leaves us with 90. Now 10% of 90 is 9. Adding that to 90 brings the total to 99, which is less than the original 100. Other choices for n will produce a similar result. Use of algebra would prove that this result is always true.

47. **(E)** One possible beginning is to try a convenient number for x, such as 8; this produces the value $\dfrac{20}{10} = 2$. That eliminates all but E

and H as possible answers (good progress so far), but now only guessing or trying lots of other values for x seems to finish the problem. The problem can be fully solved without guessing by actually dividing $12 + x$ by $2 + x$ using algebraic long division. This gives a quotient of 6 and a remainder of $-5x$. Therefore $\dfrac{12+x}{2+x}=6+\dfrac{-5x}{2+x}$. Since x is positive, this is always less than 6.

48. **(B)** The product of the smallest three-digit and four-digit numbers is $100 \times 1{,}000 = 100{,}000$. The product of the largest three-digit and four-digit numbers is *less than* $1{,}000 \times 10{,}000 = 10{,}000{,}000$. Thus, the answer is between these results, so it must have at least six digits and *fewer than* 8 digits. The only possible choice is 745,691. Notice that the problem does not ask for the factors of that number. Finding those factors in a limited time period could be a very difficult problem.

49. **(H)**

> **FACT:** The product of two odd numbers is odd. The sum of two odd numbers is even.

If p is an odd prime, answers E and G will be even numbers. These could not be primes. Answer F must be a multiple of 23, since 23 is a factor of both terms. Therefore $23p + 46$ is not prime. The only possible choice is H (which actually becomes prime, for example, when $p = 5$).

> **FACT:** The number 2 is a prime (the smallest prime, and the only even one).

Checking to see if E, F, or G becomes prime when $p = 2$, we see that this does not occur.

50. **(D)** We can work with all three parts of the inequality at the same time, being sure to do the same thing to *all* parts (never to only two of the parts). Adding x to each of the three parts gives $9 < 7 + x < 15$. Subtracting 7 from each part gives $2 < x < 8$.

51. **(G)** There are $5 \times 5 = 25$ possible outcomes. (It is instructive to draw a tree or make a list to see them all.) The only products that are prime numbers come from 1×2, 2×1, 1×3, 3×1, 1×5, and 5×1. Thus the desired probability is $\dfrac{6}{25}$.

> **FACT:** A prime number is a positive integer greater than 1 whose only factors are itself and 1.

52. **(A)** Drop a perpendicular line from B, meeting $\overline{DC}$ at E. Then $DE = 3$, so $EC = 6$. Now in right triangle BEC, BE must equal 8 (by the Pythagorean theorem).

> **FACT:** The area of a trapezoid is $\frac{1}{2}h(b_1 + b_2)$, where h is its height, and b_1 and b_2 are the lengths of its bases.

We now have the area of the trapezoid = $\left(\dfrac{1}{2}\right)(8)(3+9) = 48$.

Test-Taking Strategies

General Advice

The suggestions that follow apply to the overall test. Special tips that apply to the individual sections of the test are given in the Skillbuilders.

Know the Test Site

Be sure you know how to get there. Perhaps you should try going there once to be familiar with the travel route.

Know the Format of the Test

Verbal Section	
Stand-Alone Revising/Editing	8–10 questions
Passage-Based Revising/Editing	8–10 questions
Reading	37 questions
(6 passages with 5–7 questions about each passage)	
Mathematics Section	
Mathematics	57 questions

There is a 180-minute time limit for the entire test. Try not to spend more than 90 minutes on either the Math section or the (entire) Verbal section. You may take the parts of the test in any order. Read on for more details.

Know the Test Directions

Look over the practice tests in this book. Completely familiarize yourself with the directions for each part of the test. There is no reason to lose time on the actual exam by having to carefully reread directions. On the actual test, just spend a few seconds glancing at the directions to be sure there are no changes.

Remember, for the Mathematics section, that no reference formulas are given and calculators are **not** permitted.

Develop a Plan

Choose the order in which you wish to do the different parts of the test.

1. If you are especially good in English, choose Revising/Editing, Reading, Mathematics.
2. If you are especially good in Math, choose Mathematics, Revising/Editing, Reading.

To find the best approach for you, try using different orders when doing the practice tests in this book.

Pace Yourself

Don't spend too much time on any one question. Getting bogged down on a single question is one of the greatest time wasters. You are aiming to get as many correct answers as possible, so **keep moving**. To help you do this, use the **? X** system.

The ? X System

As you do each test, you may find some questions that you are unsure of and some that you cannot do at all. This system keeps track of those problems, making it easier to find them and return to them later. When using the **? X** system, put these marks only in your test booklet, never on the answer sheet.

1. If you try a problem but are not sure of the answer, put a **?** next to the problem number **in your test booklet**. Because you have already spent some time analyzing the problem, choose an answer now and mark it on the grid, even if it is a guess. (See the next section for suggestions on eliminating choices.) You will go back to these problems later.

2. If you have no idea how to do a problem, put an **X** next to the problem number **in your test booklet**. Do not grid in an answer at this time. You may go back to these problems later if you have time.

3. When you finish the problems you are sure of, go back to the **?** problems. That mark in your test booklet makes them easy to locate. You may find that you now remember things that will help with the solution.

4. When you finish looking over the **?** problems, try your **X** problems. Because there is no penalty for guessing, enter some answer for **every** question, even if it is a random guess! But try to eliminate some of the choices first.

Eliminating Choices: If you must guess at an answer, try to reduce the number of choices first. If you can eliminate choices that are obviously wrong, your chances of guessing correctly are improved. Lightly cross out the choices that you eliminate. That way, when you return to the problem later, you need only concentrate on the reduced set of choices.

Timing: Try to get an idea of how much time you spend on each part of the test. This will identify those parts on which you may be going too slowly. In particular, for the Reading part, determine how much time it takes you to read a single passage. To do this, go to a test you have done previously, such as Minitest 1, and reread a passage. Note the time it takes to read the **passage**, not the questions. Do this for several passages. You should aim for about 3 to 4 minutes per passage on average to allow for ample time to answer the 5–7 associated questions.

Tracking: Keep track of the question numbers and the corresponding answer numbers on the answer sheet. **Each time** you bubble in an answer, say the question number to yourself and be sure the grid number matches it. Make this automatic. This is especially important if you skip a question.

Skipping: **Leave no blanks.** Use the last few minutes of the test to look over your answer sheet and simply **fill in answers for any skipped questions**. At this point, do not even look back at the test booklet itself. Remember that there is no penalty for incorrect answers.

Read the Questions with Focus and Purpose

Focus on the words of each question. Always determine precisely what is being called for.

More specific tips and strategies for each type of question appear in the Skillbuilder sections of this book.

Rehearse for the Test: Be in Control

Familiarity instills confidence. Good rehearsals make good performances. If you follow a good plan of study, you will be prepared. This confidence will allow you to be more relaxed during the test. Don't panic if there are questions you cannot do at first. Remember that you don't have to get every question right. (See page 4 for information regarding scoring and scaling.) Of the nearly 30,000 students taking the test, probably no one will get a perfect score.

Simulate test conditions by strictly adhering to the time limits and working under test-like conditions. Work for the **full time** and check your work if you finish early, just as you would on the actual exam.

Maintain a steady pace. Don't rush. Don't skip around wildly.

Concentrate on what you are doing at the moment. Don't think about what's coming up later in the test. Focus on one question at a time.

Do all of the practice tests in this book carefully. Working under the proper time limits and test conditions will make you ready for the actual test. You will then have a plan and a sense of self-assuredness that will enable you to do your best.

Anxiety control: It is likely that there will be some questions you cannot answer. Don't let this make you panic. Everyone feels nervous at times. Don't let this take control of you. If you start to get anxious, close your eyes for a moment and take a few slow, deep breaths to help you relax. Remind yourself that you need think about only one question at a time. Remember that each individual question you answer adds to your total score. Then open your eyes and continue with the test, one question at a time.

Use the Test Booklet and Scratch Paper Wisely

Work in the test booket and on scratch paper if provided. Be **neat** and **organized**. This helps keep you focused and provides a means for checking. Organize your scrap work. If you are all over the place, you leave yourself open to careless errors and are less likely to be mentally focused.

Number the scrap work for each problem by putting the problem number in a circle at the start of the work. It is very difficult to go back over any work you have done if that work is not orderly and numbered according to each problem.

Use the **?** **X** system.

Mark the test booklet in any way that is comfortable for you. The test booklet is not graded. Only your answer sheet will be graded. For example, on the Math section of the test, make helpful marks directly on diagrams, graphs, and charts.

THE NIGHT AND MORNING BEFORE THE TEST

- Prepare your supplies: admission ticket, 3 to 5 well-sharpened #2 pencils, a good eraser, and a noncalculator watch.
- Review directions for getting to the site.
- Get a good night's sleep.
- Get up early and have a good breakfast.
- Take all your supplies.
- Leave home extra early. That way, if any mishaps occur, you will still be on time and not feel rushed.

You have done your practicing. You're very well prepared for this test! All the past hints and skills will come to you automatically.

SOME ADDITIONAL IDEAS AND SUGGESTIONS

Read

Read regularly and read a wide variety of works. Be an alert, focused reader. Try to be aware of the writer's purpose and tone. Look up and learn new words. Try to improve your reading speed without sacrificing comprehension.

Write

Practice writing. Write often and write with care. Widen your vocabulary. Incorporate new words and phrases into your writing. Don't be sloppy or haphazard. Be careful not to practice poor habits.

Do Challenging Math Problems

If your school has a math team, try to join or attend practices and math contests. Do extra math problems on a daily basis. Try to add nonroutine problems to your daily practice.

Write Your Own Problems

Try writing your own test-style questions. This task can provide great insight and dramatically improve your own problem-solving skills. Write some multiple-choice style questions, but be sure to include the best wrong answers. Be precise. Try the problems out on friends.

Design your own Scrambled Paragraphs using passages from books and articles that you read. Write some reading comprehension questions based on a passage from a book or article.

Don't Cram!

Spread out your practice over time. Cramming for this exam will not be beneficial because it is unlikely to improve your score. Some students begin their preparation more than a year in advance.

Stand-Alone Revising/Editing: Subject-Verb Agreement

Every sentence contains something called a **subject noun** and a **predicate verb**. These two words always share a relationship, where if the noun is singular or plural, then the predicate verb must also agree in its form. The subject noun is in parenthesis and the predicate verb is underlined.

The (dog) is barking.
The (dog) bites the shoe.

Notice that if you change the "dog" into "dogs" the verbs "is" and "bites" must change as well.

The (dogs) are barking.
The (dogs) bite the shoe.

Now, the SHSAT won't make it this easy. To make it more difficult, the SHSAT includes a series of filler words between the subject noun and the predicate verb. They hope that you will lose track of the original subject noun and choose the seemingly correct but actually incorrect answer choice. Examine the following incorrectly constructed sentence.

The books is not on sale.

Set this way, you should be able to see that the verb "is" is clearly wrong. However, the SHSAT will insert words between the subject noun and the predicate. Consider the following sentence.

Wrong: The books, written by Mr. Monkey, is not on sale.

Notice that there is a singular noun, "Mr. Monkey," placed right next to the singular verb "is." Because of its location, your brain might not really register an error because it processes the singular noun with a singular verb. However, this sentence is wrong because the thing that accompanies the verb "is" is not Mr. Monkey but the books.

Right: The **books**, written by Mr. Monkey, **are** not on sale.

Examine the following examples.

Wrong: My friend, who is commended by all the teachers, are working hard.
Right: My **friend**, who is commended by all the teachers, **is** working hard.

Wrong: The angry group of students were thinking about escaping school.
Right: The angry **group** of students **was** thinking about escaping school.

Hint 1: If you see an auxiliary verb (is/was, are/were, has/have) in the answer choice, always trace it back to the subject noun.

Hint 2: Prepositions are words that typically indicate position (thus the word PRE-POSITION). If you see a preposition followed by a series of words, it's almost NEVER the subject. They're placed between the subject noun and the predicate verb to trick you. Prepositions to look out for are as follows:

of, at, in, for, on, with, by, from, to, about, over, below, above, between

If you see prepositions, follow these steps.

1. Cross out the preposition and all the words that appear after them UP to the verb.
2. Circle the subject noun and the predicate verb.
3. Change subject noun or predicate verb.

➡ Example _____

The dog in the house of my brothers bark really loud.

Step 1: The dog ~~in the house of my brothers~~ bark really loud.
Step 2: The dog ~~in the house of my brothers~~ bark really loud.
Step 3: The dogs ~~in the house of my brothers~~ bark really loud.

OR

Step 3: The dog ~~in the house of my brothers~~ barks really loud.

Hint 3: If you see a comma to the left of the predicate verb, cross out all the words between that comma and the other comma. You should be able to connect the subject nouns and the predicate verbs.

➡ Example _____

My four yachts, which were constructed by my dad, travels very slow.

Step 1: My four yachts~~, which were constructed by my dad,~~ travels very slow.
Step 2: My four yachts~~, which were constructed by my dad,~~ travels very slow.
Step 3: My four yachts~~, which were constructed by my dad,~~ travel very slow.

SUBJECT-VERB AGREEMENT EXERCISES

1. Read this sentence.

> In the fourteenth century, jobs in farming was abundant, because the bubonic plague drastically reduced the labor supply.

Which edit should be made to correct this sentence?

A. change *farming* to *farmings*
B. change *jobs* to *job*
C. change *was abundant* to *were abundant*
D. change *reduced* to *reduce*

2. Read this sentence.

> A distinguished and respected organization of students and teachers have met with the administration to voice concerns about plans for the new program.

Which edit should be made to correct this sentence?

E. change *organization* to *organizations*
F. change *have* to *has*
G. change *met* to *meetings*
H. change *voice* to *voices*

3. Read this sentence.

> Studying the effects of different types of poisons help toxicologists understand how different combinations of molecules can lead to deadly, yet interesting outcomes.

Which edit should be made to correct this sentence?

A. change *Studying* to *To study*
B. change *effects* to *affects*
C. change *help* to *helps*
D. change *understand* to *understanding*

4. Read this sentence.

> Many readers in today's society consider complex intricacy to be the hallmark of quality writing, but the most sophisticated writings by Ernest Hemingway is marked by an austere simplicity.

Which edit should be made to correct this sentence?

E. change *readers* to *reader*
F. change *society* to *societies*
G. change *consider* to *considers*
H. change *is* to *are*

(Answers are on page 65.)

Stand-Alone Revising/Editing: Pronouns

Pronouns are a class of words that almost everyone knows and uses. You learn to use pronouns before you learn to form sentences. Here's a list of pronouns.

I, me, mine, my, you, your, yours, he, him, his, she, her, hers, we, us, our, ours, they, them, their, it, its, that, this, these, those, who, whom, one

To solve pronoun antecedent problems, you must trace the pronoun's antecedent. The antecedent is a fancy word for the word that the pronoun is supposed to replace. Examine the following sentence.

<u>The book</u> was so popular that **it** was turned into a movie.

The pronoun **it** replaces the word <u>book</u>, so the antecedent to **it** is <u>book</u>.

Now this is what an error looks like:

<u>The book</u> was so popular that **they were** turned into a movie.

You can see here that the plural pronoun **they** replaces the singular noun <u>book</u>. This is wrong because a plural pronoun cannot replace a singular noun.

To make this more difficult, the SHSAT may ask you to find a "vague pronoun." The word "vague" simply means unclear. A vague pronoun question is a sentence in which the antecedent cannot be identified. For instance, if I were to tell you "Give me that," you would be confused. In real life, I can point to something or we might have been talking about something to help you know what "that" is. In text, however, pronouns are difficult to identify unless there are clues.

To solve the vague pronoun problems, first apply the same method. Trace the pronoun to its antecedent. However, unlike the pronoun antecedent agreement question types, you will find either TWO equally acceptable antecedents or none at all.

Examine the following sentence:

<u>Charlie and Robert</u> both swore to be best friends forever, but **he** changed his mind after graduating college.

The pronoun here is **he**, and the antecedent is <u>Charlie and Robert</u>. The problem here is that **he** can refer to either Charlie OR Robert. Therefore, the pronoun is vague.

There will also be times when there is no antecedent. Examine the following sentence.

<u>Charlie</u> took the train to see the movie, but the instructions **they** gave **him** were unclear.

In this sentence, there are two pronouns. The antecedent to the pronoun **him** can be traced to <u>Charlie</u>, but what about the pronoun **they**? We can assume many things, but unless the sentence clearly contains an antecedent, this pronoun remains a problem and, therefore, would be committing a "vague pronoun" error.

PRONOUNS EXERCISES

1. Read this paragraph.

> (1) In 1692, the people in the town of Salem, Massachusetts, were wracked by a fear and paranoia that paralyzed them to the very core. (2) Poor and wealthy people alike were accused of witchcraft, regardless of how many times they protested. (3) Two of the more affluent men were John Proctor and Giles Corey. (4) He was executed by "pressing," which involved the placement of heavy weights on top of a person.

Which sentence should be revised to correct a vague pronoun?

A. sentence 1
B. sentence 2
C. sentence 3
D. sentence 4

2. Read this paragraph.

> (1) Many people are growing alarmed about conventionally grown food products and believe that organic food is better for their health. (2) However, studies show that their fears may be unwarranted. (3) If Betty ate organic apples while Jody ate conventionally grown apples, she would have to eat 700 more apples to exceed the EPA safety limit on harmful chemicals. (4) For some reason though, organic fruits seem to taste better, possibly because people believe they are better.

Which sentence should be revised to correct a vague pronoun?

E. sentence 1
F. sentence 2
G. sentence 3
H. sentence 4

3. Read this paragraph.

> (1) My mother was looking over a lamp and a table from the yard sale and praised their beauty. (2) Although the lamp was chipped and the table was splintered, she said that they reminded her of her happy childhood home. (3) When she brought them home, my father was less than excited. (4) In fact, he examined the cracked lamp and the splintered table and exclaimed that it was filled with bedbugs.

Which sentence should be revised to correct a vague pronoun?

A. sentence 1
B. sentence 2
C. sentence 3
D. sentence 4

4. Read this paragraph.

> (1) The Loch Ness Monster, an aquatic creature allegedly living in the Scottish Highlands, resembles a brontosaurus, but many claim that its neck is a lot longer. (2) Photographs suggest that Nessie's neck reaches a maximum length of about 6 to 10 feet long, while that of the brontosaurus reach about 70. (3) While there is no doubt that Nessie is no brontosaurus, Loch Ness specialists claim that Nessie's size is due to the size of its environment. (4) The smaller the area in which an organism lives, the smaller it gets.

Which sentence should be revised to correct a vague pronoun?

E. sentence 1
F. sentence 2
G. sentence 3
H. sentence 4

(Answers are on page 65.)

Stand-Alone Revising/Editing: Verb Tense

There are three basic tenses: the past, the present, and the future. As a general rule on the exam, all predicate verbs should be in the same tense. If three sentences contain past tense verbs and one uses a present tense verb, then that will usually be the incorrect verb. To identify the incorrect verb usage, identify all the predicate verbs, and then select the one that doesn't look like the others.

➡ **Example** _____

(1) Prairie dogs **are named** dogs because their habitat and warning calls **resemble** a dog's bark. (2) However, the prairie dog **is** not really a dog. (3) In fact, it **was** more a squirrel than dog. (4) It **belongs** to the Sciuridae family, which **includes** squirrels, chipmunks, and marmots.

The list of predicate verbs in the sentence above is as follows.

1. are named (always use the helping verb rather than the verb that follows to determine tense)
2. resemble
3. is
4. was
5. belongs
6. includes

All verbs are in the present tense, except the verb "was," which is in the past tense. Therefore, "was" is used incorrectly. It should be "is."

Hint: Watch out for participles and gerunds. They should NOT be used to identify the tense of the sentence. Participles are verbs that end with *–ed* or *–ing*. Participles are more like adjectives than they are verbs. Gerunds are verbs that are transformed into nouns by adding *–ing* to the end of the verb.

Examine the sentence below.

John, tired of running the race, went home.

You'll notice three verbs here: *tired, running,* and *went.* The word *tired* describes John, while the word *running* is a gerund. The verb *went* is the predicate verb.

VERB TENSE EXERCISES

1. Read this sentence.

> After the air force destroyed the critical infrastructure, the rebels decided to retreat to their bunkers because there is nowhere to go.

Which edit should be made to correct this sentence?

A. change *destroyed* to *destroys*
B. change *decided* to *will decide*
C. change *retreat* to *retreated*
D. change *is* to *was*

2. Read this sentence.

> Although doctors recommend a minimum of seven hours of sleep per day, many people believed that they can operate with less sleep and neglect the advice.

Which edit should be made to correct this sentence?

E. change *recommend* to *recommending*
F. change *believed* to *believe*
G. change *operate* to *operated*
H. change *neglect* to *will neglect*

3. Read this sentence.

> In the 1860s, George Washington Carver was born into slavery, but he goes on to become one of the greatest scientists, devising more than 100 products through the humble peanut.

Which edit should be made to correct this sentence?

A. change *was* to *is*
B. change *goes* to *went*
C. change *become* to *becoming*
D. change *devising* to *devises*

4. Read this sentence.

> The biggest problem I faced when I took the test is identifying verb tenses.

Which edit should be made to correct this sentence?

E. change *faced* to *face*
F. change *took* to *take*
G. change *is* to *was*
H. change *identifying* to *identified*

(Answers are on page 67.)

Stand-Alone Revising/Editing: Misplaced Modifiers

Modifiers are words that add more information to another word. They can be a single word or a group of words, but generally they are placed right next to the word that is being modified. Examine the modifiers added to each sentence below and notice how each modifier adds more information to the first sentence. Modifiers will be underlined.

> The dog barked at Joey.
> The ugly dog barked at Joey.
> The very ugly dog barked at Joey.
> The very ugly dog barked loudly at Joey.
> Louder than thunder, the really ugly dog barked loudly at Joey.

It is very important to note that the modifiers typically have to be adjacent to (next to) the word that they are modifying (object modified).

The SHSAT will rearrange words so that the object modified is placed away from the modifier. Examine the following sentence.

> Louder than thunder, Joey was barked at by the really ugly dog.

In this sentence, the modifier *Louder than thunder* is placed next to Joey, so the sentence suggests that Joey is louder than thunder. To fix this, *the really ugly dog* should be placed right next to the modifier *Louder than thunder*.

A lot of times, the misplaced modifiers are quite comical if you imagine them. Try to imagine how the modifiers add information to the **modified object** in the following sentences.

1. The rat was chased by **mom** hiding behind a box of cereal.
2. Having cheated on the test, **the teacher** punished Jimmy.
3. The magician amazed **the crowd** wearing a mysterious, shape-shifting cape.

In the following incorrect sentences, the modifiers appear in the beginning of the sentence right before the comma and the **modified object** appears away from the position it is supposed to be in. The correct sentences place the modifiers and **modified object** next to each other.

Incorrect: <u>Located deep in the Amazonian jungle</u>, the explorers found **the Lost City**.
Correct: <u>Located deep in the Amazonian jungle</u>, **the Lost City** was discovered by the explorers.

Incorrect: <u>Eaten by millions in the United States</u>, Americans love **pizza**.
Correct: <u>Eaten by millions in the United States</u>, **pizza** is loved by Americans.

Incorrect: <u>Eating millions every year</u>, pizza is loved by **Americans**.
Correct: <u>Eating millions every year</u>, **Americans** love pizza.

Incorrect: <u>A woman of many talents</u>, the trombone can be played masterfully by **Kimberly**.
Correct: <u>A woman of many talents</u>, **Kimberly** can play the trombone masterfully.

Incorrect: <u>Dried up and brown</u>, we decided to throw away the **Christmas tree**.
Correct: <u>Dried up and brown</u>, **the Christmas tree** was thrown away.

MISPLACED MODIFIERS EXERCISES

1. Read this paragraph.

> (1) The Bronx High School of Science was a product of its time founded in 1938. (2) Considered unfit for rigorous academic programs, girls were excluded from specialized high schools. (3) In 1946, the school's principal, Dr. Morrie Meister, and the Parents Association spearheaded the efforts to open the school to girls. (4) Stuyvesant and Brooklyn Tech soon followed suit, making their program accessible to both boys and girls.

Which sentence should be revised to correct a misplaced modifier?

A. sentence 1
B. sentence 2
C. sentence 3
D. sentence 4

2. Read this paragraph.

> (1) In the early nineteenth century, rivers served as primary conduits that linked the major hubs in interstate commerce. (2) Dewitt Clinton, governor of New York, played an instrumental role by securing $7 million, equivalent to $100 billion today, to develop the Erie Canal. (3) Reducing the cost of shipping from $100 per ton to $8, creating jobs for thousands, and providing revenue for the state government, New Yorkers received many economic benefits from the Erie Canal. (4) Soon, however, the canal gave way to the railroad, which made the glorious canal obsolete.

Which sentence should be revised to correct a misplaced modifier?

E. sentence 1
F. sentence 2
G. sentence 3
H. sentence 4

3. Read this paragraph.

> (1) While money may not grow on trees, scientists have found that gold does. (2) Examining eucalyptus trees near gold prospecting sites, scientists observed that gold gets sucked up with other nutrients in the soil. (3) As a dissolved mineral, the tree transports the element throughout its leaves. (4) Trace amounts of the mineral found on leaves is not enough to make anyone rich, but it does provide a new way to find hidden sources of gold.

Which sentence should be revised to correct a misplaced modifier?

A. sentence 1
B. sentence 2
C. sentence 3
D. sentence 4

4. Read this paragraph.

> (1) To improve upon a skill, people typically train one skill at a time. (2) It would make sense that one should learn to walk before learning to run to someone who is learning a new skill. (3) Psychologists, however, are finding that this is not always the case. (4) Practicing several skills together, a process called interleaving, produces much better results than working one skill at a time.

Which sentence should be revised to correct a misplaced modifier?

E. sentence 1
F. sentence 2
G. sentence 3
H. sentence 4

(Answers are on page 68.)

Stand-Alone Revising/Editing: Punctuation I

This is a very broad topic, and it's impossible to cover all the rules of punctuation, but there are five basic sets you need to know. In this section, we will cover three: coordinate adjectives, modifiers, and serial commas.

COORDINATE ADJECTIVES

Adjectives are a class of words that describe nouns. A noun can take an infinite number of adjectives, but for convenience sake we usually use one or two, maximum three, adjectives to describe a noun. There are two ways to use these adjectives. One is to use the word "and" to modify a noun. Examine the adjectives in the sentence below.

We want **passionate** and **talented** people to sing *Mary Had a Little Lamb*.

The other is to replace the "and" with a comma, like so.

We want **passionate**‿ **talented** people to sing *Mary Had a Little Lamb*.

Simple enough. However, there are some cases in which commas should not be used. To test this, do two things. First, switch the order of the adjectives and insert the word. If it makes sense, then the commas should be used. If it doesn't make sense and distorts the meaning, then a comma should not be used. Examine the following sentences.

Jill bought a **pink polyester** sweater.

In this sentence, the phrase "a polyester pink sweater" or the phrase "a polyester and pink sweater" would not make sense because the object is not just a sweater but a polyester sweater.

Here's another example.

The president flew to Davos in an **expensive supersonic** jet.

Again, you should notice that "a supersonic expensive jet" is awkward. If you add an "and" between the two adjectives "an expensive and supersonic jet," again, you should see that it makes it awkward.

MODIFIERS

Remember that a modifier is a group of words that provides extra information about the word next to it. If the modifier appears at the beginning of the sentence, then place a comma right before the object being modified. If the modifier appears after the word being modified, then it needs commas around it.

The skinny man⊙ **an intimidating figure on his own**⊙ picked up a stick.

Using nothing but a stick⊙ the man beat the bear.

The bear⊙ **beaten by the man**⊙ retaliated.

Afraid of the retaliation⊙ the man ran away.

The bear⊙ **watching the man run**⊙ laughed.

SERIAL COMMAS

If there is a list of more than two words or phrases, the items in the list need to be separated by a comma. This is called an Oxford comma, or a serial comma. Your teacher may have told you that you do not need a comma before the "and." On the SHSAT, the commas are necessary.

Incorrect: The dog ate a shoe, a pie and a peach.
Correct: The dog ate a shoe, a pie, and a peach.

Incorrect: Jill found that the key to life consisted of taking long walks finding close friends, and making good dinners.
Correct: Jill found that the key to life consisted of taking long walks, finding close friends, and making good dinners.

Incorrect: Teachers and psychologists have both found that successful students make concerted efforts to create a routine, stick to their schedule and approach difficulties with a good attitude.
Correct: Teachers and psychologists have both found that successful students make concerted efforts to create a routine, stick to their schedule, and approach difficulties with a good attitude.

Commas and Prepositional Phrases
Commas should not be placed before prepositional phrases.

> **Incorrect:** The king, of the jungle, is the lion.
> **Correct:** The king of the jungle is the lion.
>
> **Incorrect:** We stayed at my grandma's house, in Miami.
> **Correct:** We stayed at my grandma's house in Miami.
>
> **Incorrect:** I went to school, with the actress, in that movie.
> **Correct:** I went to school with the actress in that movie.

PUNCTUATION I EXERCISES

1. Read this sentence.

> John Brown, an ardent abolitionist launched an attack on Harper's Ferry, West Virginia.

Which edit should be made to correct this sentence?

A. delete the comma after *Brown*
B. insert a comma after *abolitionist*
C. insert a comma after *attack*
D. delete the comma after *Ferry*

2. Read this sentence.

> After poring over the problem John felt that his spirit, body, and mind were frazzled with all the energy spent on thinking.

Which edit should be made to correct this sentence?

E. insert a comma after *problem*
F. delete the comma after *spirit*
G. delete the comma after *body*
H. insert a comma after *spent*

3. Read this sentence.

> Jerry, unfazed by anything, jumped headlong into the messy, formidable task of cleaning his bedroom, and the kitchen.

Which edit should be made to correct this sentence?

A. delete a comma after *Jerry*
B. delete a comma after *anything*
C. delete a comma after *messy*
D. delete a comma after *bedroom*

4. Read this sentence.

> Traveling at a slow and deliberate pace, massive alien, spaceships hovered over the Pentagon, the White House, and the Empire State Building.

Which edit should be made to correct this sentence?

E. delete a comma after *pace*
F. insert a comma after *massive*
G. delete a comma after *alien*
H. insert a comma after *spaceships*

(Answers are on page 68.)

Stand-Alone Revising/Editing: Punctuation II

In order to properly punctuate two clauses, you'll need to identify key words that separate clauses. A clause, in its most basic form, is a subject noun and a predicate verb. Here are the rules.

1. When you see two clauses (what look like two sentences) separated by FANBOYS (For, And, Nor, But, Or, Yet, So), then a comma needs to be inserted before the FANBOYS.

   Examine how the comma and FANBOYS separate the two clauses in the following.

   John drank the dirty water, **for** he was thirsty.
   John drank the dirty water, **and** he got sick.
   John didn't take medicine, **nor** did he go to the doctor.
   John stayed home, **but** he got better.
   He knew he had to leave, **or** he would go crazy.
   He was feeling better, **yet** he wasn't well enough to run.
   John wasn't strong enough, **so** he stayed home.

2. Beware of FANBOYS connecting two phrases. A sentence that uses a FANBOYS conjunction to connect two different phrases does NOT take a comma before FANBOYS.

   Examine the following. You will notice that following the FANBOYS, the series of words is a phrase and cannot stand alone as a sentence.

   John drank the dirty water **and** got sick.
   John stayed home **but** got better.
   He knew he had to leave **or** would go crazy.
   He was feeling better **yet** wasn't well enough to run.

3. When you see two clauses separated by subordinate conjunctions (because, while, when, after, if, since, that, though), then they do not take a comma.

Examine how the non-FANBOYS subordinate conjunctions separate the two clauses in the following.

John drank the dirty water **because** he was thirsty.
John drank the dirty water **when** he got sick.
John didn't take the medicine **while** he was sick.
John stayed home **after** he got sick.
John was feeling better **since** he took some medicine.

4. If a sentence begins with a subordinate conjunction to start off the sentence with a subordinate clause, then it must take a comma before the beginning of a new clause.

Examine the following.

Because he was thirsty, John drank the dirty water.
When he got sick, John drank the dirty water.
While he was sick, John didn't take the medicine.
After he got sick, John stayed home.
Since he took some medicine, John was feeling better.

PUNCTUATION II EXERCISES

1. Read this sentence.

> John Brown, an ardent abolitionist, launched an attack on Harper's Ferry, because he believed that slavery was wrong.

Which edit should be made to correct this sentence?

A. delete the comma after *Brown*
B. delete the comma after *abolitionist*
C. insert a comma after *believed*
D. delete the comma after *Ferry*

2. Read this sentence.

> After John pored over the problem he felt that his spirit, body, and mind were frazzled with all the energy spent on thinking.

Which edit should be made to correct this sentence?

E. insert a comma after *problem*
F. delete the comma after *spirit*
G. delete the comma after *body*
H. insert a comma after *spent*

3. Read this sentence.

> Jerry, unfazed by anything, jumped headlong into the messy, but formidable task of cleaning his bedroom, the living room, and the kitchen.

Which edit should be made to correct this sentence?

A. delete a comma after *Jerry*
B. delete a comma after *anything*
C. delete a comma after *messy*
D. delete a comma after *bedroom*

4. Read this sentence.

> Traveling at a slow and deliberate pace, the massive alien spaceships hovered over the Pentagon, the White House, and the Empire State Building and caused a lot of understandable, panic.

Which edit should be made to correct this sentence?

E. insert a comma after *slow*
F. delete the comma after *pace*
G. insert a comma after *Building*
H. delete the comma after *understandable*

(Answers are on page 69.)

Stand-Alone Revising/Editing: Run-ons

Note: It is very important that you complete both Punctuation I and Punctuation II exercises to understand the section on run-ons. It will be very difficult to understand the terminology without completing these sections first.

A run-on is a sentence that connects two clauses without a conjunction.
Examine the examples below.

➡ **Example 1**_____

Although it was feared that the storm might persist until the dawn, a time understood as the time of the leprechauns, the rain, as fierce as it was, stopped at the witching hour, reassuring those of us who feared the worst.

➡ **Example 2** _____

I walked, John ran.

To the untrained eye, Example 1 would seem to run-on, drawing out a lot of information (running on and on and on and on). Example 2, in contrast, appears short, direct, to the point. However, Example 1 properly uses conjunctions and supporting phrases to connect different ideas. In contrast, Example 2 connects two ideas with nothing but a comma. A conjunction like *but, and, because,* or *while* is necessary to correct the sentence. Therefore, Example 2 commits the run-on error.

To identify run-ons, you must learn to identify independent clauses, dependent clauses, and phrases/modifiers. Independent clauses look like sentences. They can stand by themselves. Dependent clauses begin with a FANBOYS or subordinate conjunction or a relative pronoun (*who, when, which, whose*). Phrases or modifiers are groups of words that do not complete a full thought.

Examine the following sentences, which contain a mixture of an independent clause, a dependent clause, and a phrase/modifier.

I walked,	**and** John ran.
Independent Clause	Independent Clause

While I walked,	John ran.
Dependent Clause	Independent Clause

One of the fastest kids in class	John ran	**because** he could.
Noun phrase/modifier	Independent Clause	Dependent Clause

One of the fastest kids in class	John ran to his home in Elmhurst	**because** he could run like the wind.
Noun phrase/modifier	Independent Clause	Dependent Clause

IDENTIFYING RUN-ONS EXERCISES

For each sentence:

1. Add a set of parentheses around the clauses, both dependent and independent.
2. If two independent clauses are combined in one sentence, then it is a run-on.
3. Correct the sentence by inserting an appropriate conjunction OR by replacing a word for a relative pronoun (*who, which, that, when, where, whom, whoever, whose*).

➥ **Example** _____

The doctor, fearful of a mass epidemic, decided to place her patient under quarantine it would stop the spread of the disease.

(The doctor, fearful of a mass epidemic, decided to place her patient under quarantine) **because** (it would stop the spread of the disease.)

OR

(The doctor, fearful of a mass epidemic, decided to place her patient under quarantine) (i̶t̶, **which** would stop the spread of the disease.)

1. During the 1980s, personal computers were never expected to change the world, they did.

2. When I was a child, I believed in Santa, he would bring me presents.

3. With nothing but a hammer, Abraham Lincoln nailed down an entire house it stayed erect for centuries.

4. George Washington, one of the richest men of the American colonies, had a very strong interest in leading a military unit, he became a general during the fateful war.

5. The incessant rain, unforgiving in its intensity, saw to it that I would be drenched, I was waiting for the bus.

6. Before President Truman met Joseph Stalin, he believed that the two countries would cooperate, their relationship soon led to the beginning of the Cold War.

7. As more people "cut their cord" and turned to the Internet for entertainment, the format of entertainment changed people, did not have the time to sit through a thirty-minute episode.

8. John Quincy Adams was forced to take a trip with his father, his mother, sensing his unhappiness, wrote a letter to inspire him.

(Answers are on page 70.)

RUN-ON EXERCISES

1. Read this paragraph.

> (1) Never the one to back down, Harry fought against the crowd full of people from all walks of life. (2) These people who existed solely to put Harry down couldn't accept the fact that he was different. (3) Because he was so filled with rage, he never considered the possibility that it might be all in his head, it could have been a dream. (4) Then in the blink of an eye, Harry woke up, and it was, indeed, a dream.

Which sentence should be revised to correct a run-on?

A. sentence 1
B. sentence 2
C. sentence 3
D. sentence 4

2. Read this paragraph.

> (1) Thomas Jefferson was a polymath, a man skilled in numerous subjects. (2) A philosopher, artist, scientist, and architect, Jefferson represented the ideal academic in a New World filled with possibilities. (3) Accordingly, it seemed fit that Jefferson should draft the Declaration of Independence because he was the right man for the job. (4) His words laid the foundation for a nation, they were the foundation for the future as well.

Which sentence should be revised to correct a run-on?

E. sentence 1
F. sentence 2
G. sentence 3
H. sentence 4

3. Read this paragraph.

> (1) When Jimmy Johnson decided to run for class president, he knew that it would be a long shot. (2) Not many people knew what he was about, nor did many people believe that he could make a difference. (3) However, his mother believed otherwise, Jimmy could make a difference. (4) She urged him to run, and he ran because he believed in a person who believed in him.

Which sentence should be revised to correct a run-on?

A. sentence 1
B. sentence 2
C. sentence 3
D. sentence 4

4. Read this paragraph.

> (1) Hidden deep in the farthest reaches of Edwards Air Force Base, Area 51 is one of the most intriguing military bases in the United States. (2) Many UFO enthusiasts believe the base to be a secret labyrinth, storing secret alien spaceships. (3) Others believe that the base is a communications lab it has been in contact with aliens since the 1950s. (4) Whatever it may be, it serves as an important source of stories in the public imagination.

Which sentence should be revised to correct a run-on?

E. sentence 1
F. sentence 2
G. sentence 3
H. sentence 4

(Answers are on page 70.)

Stand-Alone Revising/Editing: Precision

The best way to approach the precise revision questions is to divide the answer choices into two segments. For each segment, eliminate the answer choice that comparatively contains the least precise element.

For example, look at the following sentence.

1. The subway is a good way for people to get to places.

   A. great option for New Yorkers to get to where they need to go
   B. superior method of transportation for people to get to places
   C. speedy form of transportation for New Yorkers
   D. great method for people to get to places where they need to go

Here are the steps.

1. Look for common elements and compare them.

Least Precise (cross out)	Most Precise
great option	superior method of transportation
great method	speedy form of transportation
people	New Yorkers

2. Eliminate the choices that contain the least precise information.

   A. ~~great option~~ for ~~people~~ to get to where they need to go
   B. superior method of transportation for ~~people~~ to get to places
   C. speedy form of transportation for New Yorkers
   D. ~~great method~~ for ~~people~~ to get to places where they need to go

3. Select the remaining answer. In this case, the remaining answer is choice C.

PRECISE REVISION EXERCISES

1. Read this sentence.

   > During the winter break, my family decided to do something that was interesting in the community.

   Which of these is the most precise revision for the words ***do something that was interesting in the community?***

   A. engage in a community activity that was interesting
   B. participate in something that's interesting
   C. volunteer for an interesting community activity
   D. do an interesting community activity

2. Read this sentence.

> Our class felt that it was important to work very hard for the test that was coming up.

Which of these is the most precise revision for the words ***work very hard for the test that was coming up***?

E. study all day for the upcoming test
F. make sure that the test coming up was studied very hard for
G. review the chapter for the upcoming test
H. do our best for the future test

3. Read this sentence.

> In light of a possible epidemic, the scientists made recommendations in order to prevent the disease from spreading further.

Which of these is the most precise revision for the words ***the scientists made recommendations***?

A. the scientists told people about the virus
B. the scientists cautioned against sharing glasses
C. the scientists shared their thoughts
D. the scientists brought up their ideas for consideration to the public

4. Read this sentence.

> Anthropologists believe that culture is one of the characteristics that make humans different from other types of life.

Which of these is the most precise revision for the words ***is one of the characteristics that make humans different from other types of life***?

E. differentiates humans from other animals
F. is a reason that makes humans different from other types of life
G. makes humans different from other types of life
H. is precisely the reason that makes humans different from other animals

(Answers are on page 73.)

Answer Explanations

SUBJECT-VERB AGREEMENT EXERCISES (PAGES 46–47)

1. **(C)** Choice C correctly changes the predicate verb "was" to "were" so that the predicate verb agrees with the subject noun "jobs."

   ~~In the fourteenth century~~, <u>jobs</u> ~~in farming~~ <u>was</u> abundant, because the bubonic plague drastically reduced the labor supply.

2. **(F)** Choice E makes the subject noun *organizations* agree with the verb *have*, but the phrase *A . . . organizations* is incorrect. Choice F correctly changes the plural predicate verb "have" to "has" so that it agrees with the singular subject noun *organization*.

   A distinguished and respected <u>organization</u> ~~of students and teachers~~ <u>have</u> met with the administration to voice concerns about plans for the new program.

3. **(C)** In this question, the word "Studying" is the subject. Now you might be saying to yourself that studying is a verb, but a verb can be turned into a noun (called a gerund) by adding an *–ing* to a verb. For example, look at the following sentence. "Studying is hard." Studying, or the act of studying, now functions as the subject noun. Here's another example. "Cleaning my house is hard work." Notice again. What is "hard work?" Hard work would be "Cleaning," and not "my house." Gerunds are almost ALWAYS singular and therefore take a singular verb. Choice C correctly changes the predicate verb "help" to "helps" so that the predicate verb agrees with the subject noun "Studying."

   <u>Studying</u> ~~the effects of different types of poisons~~ <u>help</u> toxicologists understand how different combinations of molecules can lead to deadly, yet interesting outcomes.

4. **(H)** The incorrect pairing is *italicized*.

   Many <u>readers</u> ~~in today's society~~ <u>consider</u> complex intricacy to be the hallmark of quality writing, but the most sophisticated *writings* ~~by Ernest Hemingway~~ *is* marked by an austere simplicity.

   The subject noun "readers" correctly agrees with the predicate verb "consider." The subject noun "writings" does not agree with the predicate verb "is."

PRONOUNS EXERCISES (PAGES 49–50)

1. **(D)** Examine the pairings of <u>antecedents</u> and **pronouns** below.

   (1) In 1692, the <u>people</u> in the town of Salem, Massachusetts, were wracked by a fear and paranoia that paralyzed **them** to the very core. (2) <u>Poor and wealthy people</u> alike were accused of witchcraft, regardless of how many times **they** protested. (3) Two of the more affluent men were <u>John Proctor and Giles Corey</u>. (4) **He** was executed by "pressing," which involved the placement of heavy weights on top of a person.

   Sentence 1: The correct antecedent to **them** is <u>people</u>.

Sentence 2: The correct antecedent to **they** is <u>Poor and wealthy people</u>.

Sentence 3: There is no pronoun, but <u>John Proctor and Giles Corey</u> serve as the antecedent to the pronoun in sentence 4.

Sentence 4: The pronoun **He** indicates a singular antecedent, but it is impossible to determine whether the pronoun replaces <u>John Proctor and Giles Corey</u>. Therefore, the pronoun should be revised to **John Proctor** or **Giles Corey** to clearly indicate who was executed.

2. **(G)** Examine the pairings of <u>antecedents</u> and **pronouns** below.

    (1) Many <u>people</u> are growing alarmed about conventionally grown food products and believe that organic food is better for **their** health. (2) However, studies show that **their** fears may be unwarranted. (3) If <u>Betty</u> ate organic apples while <u>Jody</u> ate conventionally grown apples, **she** would have to eat 700 more apples to exceed the EPA safety limit on harmful chemicals. (4) For some reason though, <u>organic fruits</u> seem to taste better, possibly because people believe **they** are better.

    Sentence 1: The correct antecedent to the plural pronoun **their** is <u>people</u>.

    Sentence 2: The correct antecedent to the plural pronoun **their** is <u>people</u> from sentence 1 (yes, this is allowed).

    Sentence 3: The pronoun **she** indicates a singular antecedent, but it is impossible to determine whether the pronoun replaces <u>Betty</u> or <u>Jody</u>. Therefore, the pronoun **she** should be revised to either **Betty** or **Jody** in order to indicate who would have to eat 700 more apples.

    Sentence 4: The correct antecedent to the plural pronoun **they** is <u>organic fruits</u>.

3. **(D)** Examine the pairings of <u>antecedents</u> and **pronouns** below.

    (1) My mother was looking over <u>a lamp and a table</u> from the yard sale and praised **their** beauty. (2) Although the <u>lamp</u> was chipped and the <u>table</u> was splintered, she said that **they** reminded her of her happy childhood home. (3) When she brought **them** home, my father was less than excited. (4) In fact, he examined <u>the cracked lamp and the splintered table</u> and exclaimed that **it** was filled with bedbugs.

    Sentence 1: The correct antecedent to the plural pronoun **their** is <u>a lamp and a table</u>.

    Sentence 2: The correct antecedent to the plural pronoun **they** is <u>lamp and table</u>.

    Sentence 3: The plural pronoun **them** can be traced back to the two items, lamp and table, in sentence 2.

    Sentence 4: The pronoun **it** indicates a singular antecedent, but it is impossible to determine whether the pronoun replaces the <u>lamp</u> or the <u>table</u>. Therefore, pronoun **it** should be revised to **the lamp** or **the table** to indicate which object was filled with bedbugs.

4. **(E)** Examine the pairings of <u>antecedents</u> and **pronouns** below.

(1) The <u>Loch Ness Monster</u>, an aquatic creature allegedly living in the Scottish Highlands, resembles a <u>brontosaurus</u>, but many claim that **its** neck is a lot longer. (2) Photographs suggest that Nessie's <u>neck</u> reaches a maximum length of about 6 to 10 feet long, while **that** of the brontosaurus reaches about 70. (3) While there is no doubt that <u>Nessie</u> is no brontosaurus, Loch Ness specialists claim that Nessie's size is due to the size of **its** environment. (4)The smaller the area in which an <u>organism</u> lives, the smaller **it** gets.

Sentence 1: The antecedent to the pronoun **it** can refer to <u>brontosaurus</u> or the <u>Loch Ness Monster</u>. Therefore, the pronoun **it** should be revised to <u>the brontosaurus</u> to indicate which creature possessed a longer neck.

Sentence 2: The antecedent to the pronoun **that** is <u>neck</u>. The phrasing *that of* indicates possession in the same way *Nessie's* neck indicates possession.

Sentence 3: The correct antecedent to the pronoun **it** is <u>Nessie</u>.

Sentence 4: The correct antecedent to the pronoun **it** is <u>organism</u>.

VERB TENSE EXERCISES (PAGES 51–52)

1. **(D)** Examine all the predicate verbs underlined below.

After the air force <u>destroyed</u> the critical infrastructure, the rebels <u>decided</u> to retreat to their bunkers because there <u>is</u> nowhere to go.

All predicate verbs are in the past tense except *is*. Choice D correctly revises the predicate verb to the past tense.

2. **(F)** Examine all the predicate verbs underlined below.

Although doctors <u>recommend</u> a minimum of seven hours of sleep per day, many people <u>believed</u> that they <u>can</u> operate with less sleep and neglect the advice.

All predicate verbs are in the present tense except *believed*. Choice F correctly revises the predicate verb to the past tense.

3. **(B)** Examine all the predicate verbs underlined below.

In the 1860s, George Washington Carver <u>was</u> born into slavery, but he <u>goes</u> on to become one of the greatest scientists, devising more than 100 products through the humble peanut.

Choice B correctly revises the verb to the appropriate past tense. The verb *to become* is an infinitive and *devising* is a gerund. Neither is a predicate verb, so they do not need to be changed.

4. **(G)** Examine all the predicate verbs underlined below.

The biggest problem I <u>faced</u> when I <u>took</u> the test <u>is</u> identifying verb tenses.

The verb tense in this sentence is primarily in the past tense. The verb *is* should be changed to the past tense. The verb *identifying* is a participle, so it should not be changed.

MISPLACED MODIFIERS EXERCISES (PAGES 53–54)

1. **(A)** Examine the pairings of <u>modifiers</u> and **modified object**s below.

   Incorrect: The Bronx High School of Science was a product of its time <u>founded in 1938</u>.

   Correct: <u>Founded in 1938</u>, **the Bronx High School of Science** was a product of its time.

2. **(G)** Examine the pairings of <u>modifiers</u> and **modified object**s below.

   Incorrect: <u>Reducing the cost of shipping from $100 a ton to $8, creating jobs for thousands, and providing revenue for the state government</u>, New Yorkers received many economic benefits from **the Erie Canal**.

   Correct: <u>Reducing the cost of shipping from $100 a ton to $8, creating jobs for thousands, and providing revenue for the state government</u>, **the Erie Canal** provided many economic benefits for New Yorkers.

3. **(C)** Examine the pairings of <u>modifiers</u> and **modified object**s below.

   Incorrect: <u>As a dissolved mineral</u>, the tree transports **the element** throughout its leaves.

   Correct: <u>As a dissolved mineral</u>, **the element** is transported by the tree throughout its leaves.

4. **(F)** Examine the pairings of <u>modifiers</u> and **modified object**s below.

   Incorrect: It would make **sense** that one should learn to walk before learning to run <u>to someone who is learning a new skill</u>.

   Correct: It would make **sense** <u>to someone who is learning a new skill</u> that one should learn to walk before learning to run.

PUNCTUATION I EXERCISES (PAGES 56–57)

1. **(B)** The phrase *an ardent abolitionist* is a noun phrase modifier that provides more information about John Brown. Commas around the phrase are necessary:

   John Brown₃ *an ardent abolitionist*₃ launched an attack on Harper's Ferry, West Virginia.

   Choice C is wrong because it violates the rule about prepositions. Choice D is wrong because a comma is necessary to separate a city and state.

2. **(E)** *After poring over the problem* is a participle phrase that modifies *John*. A comma right after the phrase is necessary.

   *After poring over the problem*₃ John felt that his spirit, body, and mind were frazzled with all the energy spent on thinking.

   Choice F is wrong because the comma is necessary for the list. Choice G is wrong because the serial comma is necessary before the word *and*. Choice H is wrong because a comma is not necessary before a preposition.

3. **(D)** There are only two places he needs to clean: *his bedroom* and *the kitchen.* If there are two objects, then you do not need to insert a serial comma.

Jerry, unfazed by anything, jumped headlong into the messy, formidable task of cleaning his *bedroom and* the kitchen.

Choices A and B are wrong because *unfazed by anything* is a participle phrase that modifies *Jerry.* It appears to the right of *Jerry* so the phrase needs commas around it. Choice C is wrong because *messy* and *formidable* are coordinate adjectives. You can say *formidable and messy kitchen.* Therefore, the comma is necessary.

4. **(G)** A comma is never placed between a noun and the adjective right next to it. You would rarely say *the happy, boy.*

Traveling at a slow and deliberate pace, massive *alien spaceships* hovered over the Pentagon, the White House, and the Empire State Building.

Choice E is wrong because *Traveling at a slow and deliberate pace* is a participle phrase that modifies the *massive circular disks* and therefore needs the comma to break it off from the modified object. Choice F is wrong because the words *massive alien* are not coordinate adjectives. They cannot be used interchangeably. You cannot say *alien and massive spaceships.* Choice H is wrong because *spaceships* is the subject and *hovered* the predicate verb. You cannot separate those two with a comma when they are directly next to each other. For example, *John, walks* would be wrong because a comma is between the subject noun and predicate verb.

PUNCTUATION II EXERCISES (PAGES 58–59)

1. **(D)** Rule number 3. Subordinate conjunction *because* doesn't take a comma.

John Brown, an ardent abolitionist, launched an attack on Harper's Ferry *because* he believed that slavery was wrong.

2. **(E)** Rule number 4. The sentence begins with the subordinate clause, *After John pored over the problem.* After this clause, a comma is necessary to begin the following independent clause.

After John pored over the *problem,* he felt that his spirit, body, and mind were frazzled with all the energy spent on thinking.

3. **(C)** Rule number 2. A phrase, not a clause, follows the FANBOYS conjunction *but.* Therefore, a comma is unnecessary.

Jerry, unfazed by anything, jumped headlong into the *messy but* formidable task of cleaning his bedroom, the living room, and the kitchen.

4. **(H)** A phrase, not a clause, follows the FANBOYS conjunction *and.* Therefore, a comma is unnecessary.

Traveling at a slow and deliberate pace, the massive alien spaceships hovered over the Pentagon, the White House, and the Empire State Building, and caused a lot of *understandable* panic.

IDENTIFYING RUN-ONS EXERCISES (PAGES 60–61)

1. (During the 1980s, personal computers were never expected to change the world), **but** (they did.)

2. (When I was a child), (I believed in Santa), (~~he~~ **who** would bring me presents.)

3. (With nothing but a hammer, Abraham Lincoln nailed down an entire house)**,** (**which** ~~it~~ stayed erect for centuries.)

4. (George Washington, one of the richest men of the American colonies, had a very strong interest in leading a military unit)**,** **and** (he became a general during the fateful war.)

5. (The incessant rain, unforgiving in its intensity, saw to it that I would be drenched) **while** (I was waiting for the bus.)

6. (Before President Truman met Joseph Stalin), (he believed that the two countries would cooperate), **but** (their relationship soon led to the beginning of the Cold War.)

7. (As more people "cut the cord" and turned to the Internet for entertainment), (the format of entertainment changed people), **who** (did not have the time to sit through a thrity-minute episode.)

8. **When** (John Quincy Adams was forced to take a trip with his father), (his mother, sensing his unhappiness, wrote a letter to inspire him.)

RUN-ON EXERCISES (PAGES 61–62)

1. **(C)** Sentence 1 contains a modifier and an independent clause. This is not a run-on.

Never the one to back down,	Harry fought against the crowd full of people from all walks of life.
Phrase	Independent Clause

Sentence 2 contains an independent clause and a dependent clause. This is not a run-on.

These **people** *who existed solely to put Harry down* **couldn't** accept the fact	that he was different.
Independent clause with a *relative clause* inserted between the **subject noun** and the **predicate**	Dependent Clause

Sentence 3 contains an independent clause at the end of the sentence. The independent clause requires a conjunction to correct it. This is a run-on.

Because he was so filled with rage,	he never considered the possibility	that it might be all in his head	it could have been a dream.
Dependent Clause	Independent Clause	Dependent Clause	Independent Clause

Correction: Because he was so filled with rage, he never considered the possibility that it might be all in his head *and that* it could have been a dream.

Sentence 4 contains a modifier, independent clause, and a dependent clause. This is not a run-on.

Then in the blink of an eye,	Harry woke up,	and it was, indeed, a dream.
Phrase	Independent Clause	Dependent Clause

2. **(H)** Sentence 1 contains an independent clause and a modifier. This is not a run-on.

Thomas Jefferson was a polymath,	a man skilled in numerous subjects.
Independent Clause	Modifier

Sentence 2 contains a modifier and an independent clause. This is not a run-on.

A philosopher, artist, scientist, and architect	Jefferson represented the ideal academic in a New World filled with possibilities.
Modifier	Independent Clause

Sentence 3 contains an independent clause, a dependent clause, and a dependent clause. This is not a run-on.

Accordingly, it seemed fit	that Jefferson should draft the Declaration of Independence	because he was the right man for the job.
Independent Clause	Dependent Clause	Dependent Clause

Sentence 4 contains two independent clauses. This is a run-on.

His words laid the foundation for a nation	they were the foundation for the future as well.
Independent Clause	Independent Clause

Correction: His words laid the foundation for a nation, *and* they were the foundation for the future as well.

3. **(C)** Sentence 1 contains a dependent clause and an independent clause. This is not a run-on.

When Jimmy Johnson decided to run for class president,	he knew that it would be a long shot.
Dependent Clause	Independent Clause

Sentence 2 contains an independent clause followed by two dependent clauses. This is not a run-on.

Not many people knew what he was about,	nor did many people believe	that he could make a difference.
Independent Clause	Dependent Clause	Dependent Clause

Sentence 3 contains two independent clauses. *However* is not a conjunction. It is instead called a "conjunctive adverb." Conjunctive adverbs are used to connect two sentences but not two clauses. Here is an example:

John likes cheese. However, Jill like apples.

This is, therefore, a run-on.

However, his mother believed in Jimmy,	Jimmy could make a difference.
Independent Clause	Independent Clause

Correction: However, his mother believed in Jimmy, *who* could make a difference.

Sentence 4 contains two independent clauses followed by two dependent clauses. This is not a run-on.

She urged him to run,	and he ran	because he believed in a person	who believed in him.
Independent Clause	Independent Clause	Dependent Clause	Dependent Clause

4. **(G)** Sentence 1 contains a modifier and an independent clause. This is not a run-on.

Hidden deep in the farthest reaches of Edwards Air Force Base,	Area 51 is one of the most intriguing military bases in the United States.
Modifier	Independent Clause

Sentence 2 contains an independent clause and a modifier. This is not a run-on.

Many UFO enthusiasts believe the base to be a secret labyrinth,	storing secret alien spaceships.
Independent Clause	Modifier

Sentence 3 contains an independent clause, a dependent clause, and an independent clause. This is a run-on.

Others believe	that the base is a communications lab	it has been in contact with aliens since the 1950s.
Independent Clause	Dependent Clause	Independent Clause

Correction: Others believe that the base is a communications lab *and that* it has been in contact with aliens since the 1950s.

Sentence 4 contains a dependent clause and an independent clause. This is not a run-on.

Whatever it may be,	it serves as an important source of stories in the public imagination.
Dependent Clause	Independent Clause

PRECISE REVISION EXERCISES (PAGES 63–64)

1. **(C)**

Least Precise (cross out)	Most Precise
engage participate do	volunteer
community activity that was interesting something that's interesting	interesting community activity

2. **(G)**

Least Precise (cross out)	Most Precise
study all day make sure do our best	review the chapter
the test coming up the upcoming test the future test	the chapter for the upcoming test

3. **(B)**

Least Precise (cross out)	Most Precise
told people shared their thoughts brought up their ideas	cautioned against sharing glasses

4. **(E)**

Least Precise (cross out)	Most Precise
is makes	differentiates
types of life	animals

Passage-Based Revising/Editing: Introductory Sentences

In the introductory sentence questions, you are asked to find the best introductory sentence or the main claim. To tackle these questions, first read the information that follows and identify how the details fit into a larger category. Examine the following.

> (1) Baseball begins in the spring and ends in the fall. (2) Football picks up in the fall and ends in the winter. (3) Basketball starts around the same time as football but ends in the spring. (4) Hockey, in contrast, begins in the fall but extends even further into the summer.

You should notice that this paragraph discusses a variety of sports and the seasons in which the sports are played. Therefore, the main claim, or the sentence that best introduces the topic of the passage, should discuss those two elements.

Note: You should do these introductory/main claim questions last because you will need to read the entire passage to fit the details into a larger category.

INTRODUCTORY/MAIN CLAIM EXERCISES

(1) For some students, nothing causes more panic than the due date for an essay quickly approaching the deadline. (2) On the night before the due date, students frantically cobble together a mishmash of words, hoping that it somehow makes sense. (3) However, writing doesn't always have to be associated with stress. (4) Writing can also cause sadness and depression.

(5) One of the strongest benefits is that writing can reduce stress. (6) Researchers at Humboldt University devised an experiment where an experimental group wrote 15 minutes about their day for a period of six weeks. (7) They found that the subjects who wrote for 15 minutes a day reported better organization of their thoughts and a clearer idea of their future. (8) The subjects' level of cortisol, a hormone triggered by stress, was significantly lower than that of the control subjects. (9) Desco University reported similar results, where people who kept diaries reported a higher satisfaction in life.

1. Which sentence should replace sentence 4 to more clearly introduce the topic of the passage?

   A. Writing provides a wide variety of benefits, and it might be wise to rethink one's attitude toward writing.
   B. People should abandon writing essays because doing so can reduce stress.
   C. If people try hard enough, people can become excellent essay writers.
   D. Writing can help a person reach professional success, so people should consider majoring in English.

(1) The great events in history are those where a man or a people have made a stand against tyranny and have preserved or advanced freedom for the people. (2) Sometimes tyranny has taken the form of the oppression of the many by the few in the same nation, and sometimes it has been the oppression of a weak nation by a stronger one. (3) Tyranny is a scourge that needs to be eradicated to preserve the future of democracy.

(4) At that time nearly all of Europe was inhabited by rude barbarous tribes. (5) In all that broad land the arts and sciences had made their appearance only in the small and apparently insignificant peninsula of Greece, lying on the extreme southeast border adjoining Asia. (6) The numerous harbors and bays which subdivide Greece invited a maritime life, and at a very early time, the descendants of the original shepherds became skillful navigators and courageous adventurers.

2. Which sentence should replace sentence 3 to more clearly introduce the topic of the passage?

   E. Barbarians were one of the first forms of social organization that gave rise to the civilizations in Europe.
   F. One of the earliest and notable of these conflicts took place in Greece twenty-four hundred years ago.
   G. Regardless of the oppression, people have always emerged as the losers in these conflicts.
   H. As populations increase to unmanageable levels, oppression becomes an inescapable facet of life throughout the history of civilization.

(1) Way, way off, in the distance, far beyond the yellow sands of the desert, you will see something green and shimmering. (2) It is a valley situated between two rivers. (3) It is a land that many people can easily recognize if they had paid attention in history class.

(4) The names of the two rivers are the Euphrates and the Tigris. (5) They begin their course amidst the snows of the mountains of Armenia where Noah's Ark is said to have found a resting place and slowly they flow through the southern plain until they reach the muddy banks of the Persian Gulf. (6) They perform a very useful service, turning the arid regions of western Asia into a fertile garden.

3. Which sentence should replace sentence 3 to more clearly introduce the topic of the passage?

   A. It is a place that is mentioned in classrooms all over the world.
   B. It is the land of mystery and wonder which the Greeks called Mesopotamia— the "country between the rivers."
   C. It is a land that exists in the dreams of explorers who wish to unlock the mysteries of the Bible.
   D. It is the land where agriculture and civilization were born.

(1) The birth of democracy can be traced back to Greece. (2) However, the Greeks were not a monolithic bloc that was made up of a homogeneous group. (3) Take the Athenians and the Spartans for example. (4) They were the true founders of democracy.

(5) Athens rose high from the plain. (6) It was a city exposed to the fresh breezes from the sea, willing to look at the world with the eyes of a happy child. (7) Sparta, on the other hand, was built at the bottom of a deep valley, and used the surrounding mountains as a barrier against foreign thought. (8) Athens was a city of busy trade, whereas Sparta was an armed camp where people were soldiers for the sake of being soldiers. (9) The people of Athens loved to sit in the sun and discuss poetry or listen to the wise words of a philosopher. (10) The Spartans, on the other hand, never wrote a single line that was considered literature, but they knew how to fight, they liked to fight, and they sacrificed all human emotions to their ideal of military preparedness.

4. Which sentence should replace sentence 4 to more clearly introduce the topic of the passage?

  E. Their geographical differences led to sharp differences in manners.
  F. Political aspirations clearly aggravated the conflict between the two powerful states.
  G. We should all aspire to celebrate their diversity.
  H. They might have spoken a common language but were different in every other respect.

(Answers are on page 89.)

Passage-Based Revising/Editing: Concluding Sentence

In this section, you are asked to find the concluding sentence or the main claim. These questions are very similar to the introductory sentence questions except that you place the summary or main idea sentence at the end of the passage. Examine the following paragraph from the previous section.

(1) Baseball begins in the spring and ends in the fall. (2) Football picks up in the fall and ends in the winter. (3) Basketball starts around the same time as football but ends in the spring. (4) Hockey, in contrast, begins in the fall but extends even further into the summer.

In finding the best concluding sentence, the same principles apply. This paragraph discusses a variety of sports and the seasons in which the sports are played. Therefore, the main claim, or the sentence that best concludes the topic of the passage, should discuss those two elements. Here's another example.

(1) The traditional account describes Lady Guinevere as King Arthur's wife. (2) In another account, Lady Guinevere is a sorceress who helps the kingdom in various ways. (3) Some stories characterize her as Sir Lancelot's love, while others completely dismiss any evidence of the sort. (4) She can be of Roman, British, or even Greek origin.

In this paragraph, the subject is Lady Guinevere and the details provide several different character traits of Lady Guinevere. Therefore, the concluding sentence should discuss these two ideas.

CONCLUDING SENTENCE EXERCISES

(1) Madagascar is the home to over 10,000 different species of unique plants. (2) Such diversity, however, is in danger because of the growing needs of the people who live there. (3) Agriculture is the primary form of subsistence, and farmers, clearing the land for agriculture, are destroying the rich variety of vegetation. (4) Moreover, climate change is distorting seasonal rainfall patterns, making it very difficult for plants to adapt. (5) The diversity is very important.

1. Which concluding sentence should replace sentence 5 to better support the information presented in the passage?

   A. Madagascar's primary export is coffee, and this is also another problem that conservationists have to deal with.
   B. People must learn more about conservation so that they can make a difference in the world.
   C. Madagascar's economy is growing at an alarming speed, which may help spur modernization.
   D. Scientists are concerned about the consequences of such losses because once these species are gone, they can never be studied again.

(1) Over 200 years ago, Thomas Malthus predicted that the world's population would be unsustainable. (2) The rate of population would overtake the rate of food production, and millions would inevitably suffer from hunger and famine. (3) Malthus, however, didn't count on the ingenuity of mankind. (4) Agricultural innovations, technological advancements, and industrial food production have helped the population grow by more than sevenfold. (5) Today, people waste about 3.5 million pounds of food each day.

2. Which concluding sentence should replace sentence 5 to better support the information presented in the passage?

   E. The new problems now are pollution and overproduction.
   F. The biggest problem today is whether we can feed all of them.
   G. People should encourage, not criticize, new forms of technology.
   H. It would seem, then, that Malthus's claims about humans, and not human claims to existence, are unsustainable.

(1) Once upon a less technologically connected time, talking to yourself was considered a sign of madness. (2) However, times have certainly changed. (3) Today, people casually gesture to no one in particular, as they walk down the aisle of a shopping mall. (4) Drivers can be seen irately arguing with their poor innocent windshields that have no other choice but to listen. (5) Others seem to laugh and giggle as they stare down at their cell phone, completely oblivious to a pole or a hole that awaits their unsuspecting faces and bodies. (6) Who knows what technology will bring in the future?

3. Which concluding sentence should replace sentence 6 to better support the information presented in the passage?

    A. Obviously, people need their cell phones more than ever before.

    B. Despite such changes in behavior, the desire to remain connected to other people, regardless of how silly one may appear to an outsider, is unmistakably something that makes us human.

    C. The telecommunications industry, however, seems interested only in producing profits and cell phone zombies.

    D. The health risks of cell phone use are well documented in numerous research studies.

(1) Gardens are more than just places to pluck the ingredients for a quick snack. (2) They are a living and natural pharmacy. (3) The roots, leaves, and fruits of various plants can treat a number of conditions. (4) Garlic, for example, has often been used as an antibiotic to ward off infections, while cayenne peppers can be used to treat the flu and bronchitis. (5) People continue to acknowledge the benefits of these natural medicines.

4. Which concluding sentence should replace sentence 5 to better support the argument presented in the passage?

    E. The cost effectiveness of growing these natural medicines can harm the biotechnology industry.

    F. Starting a garden in your backyard today might help you fill your belly with a nutritious dinner and your immune system with natural remedies.

    G. Educating the public about the benefits of a garden can be difficult for people living in cities.

    H. Finally, chamomile tea can also help people who suffer from anxiety or insomnia.

(Answers are on page 91.)

Passage-Based Revising/Editing: Transitions

In this section, you are asked to find a word that best fits the logical relationship between two sentences or two clauses. There are five basic categories of logical transition you need to be familiar with.

CAUSAL TRANSITIONS

This transition connects causal relationships between two sentences. Examine the following sentences.

1. My dog Max barked very loudly.
2. He woke up the neighbors.

The list of causal transition words below can be used to connect the causal relationship between the two sentences.

as a result, for this reason, therefore, thus, because,
due to the fact, consequently, hence, accordingly, since

ADDITIVE TRANSITIONS

This transition is used to link additional information or similarities with another set of information. Examine the following sentences.

1. The SHSAT is a difficult exam for middle school students.
2. The SAT is a difficult exam for high school students.

The list of additive transition words below can be used to link a sentence that provides more information.

and, also, furthermore, moreover, in addition, additionally,
similarly, in the same way, by the same token, likewise

CONTRASTING TRANSITIONS

This transition is used between sentences that suggest contrary or conflicting ideas. Examine the following sentences.

1. My sister loves school.
2. I hate school.

The list of contrasting transition words below can be used to emphasize the contrast between the two sentences.

but, in contrast, conversely, however, still, nevertheless, nonetheless,
yet, on the other hand, on the contrary, in spite of this, actually,
notwithstanding, although, despite, while, regardless

ILLUSTRATIVE TRANSITIONS

This transition is used to link a general statement and an example or detail that supports the statement. Examine the following sentences.

1. Specialized high schools are notorious for the amount of work assigned.
2. Students attending the High School for Specialized Programs typically spend three to four hours on their homework each day.

The list of illustrative transition words below can be used to support the claim in sentence 1.

for example, for instance, in particular, to illustrate, to be specific, specifically, such as, in this case, for this reason, for one thing

INTENSIFYING TRANSITIONS

This transition is used to emphasize a certain aspect of a given sentence. Examine the following sentences.

1. Americans are in a love-hate relationship with debt.
2. The average American household carries over $120,000 in debt.

The list of intensifying transition words below can be used to build upon the claim in sentence 1.

indeed, of course, without a doubt, in fact, surely, more importantly, as a matter of fact, in other words, in short

However, to tackle these problems, DO NOT plug in each of the transition words to "see if it makes sense." Doing so can actually work against you. Your brain is designed to make sense of any relationships, so this method will work about half of the time. Instead, read the two sentences without looking at the transitions. Then identify the relationship before selecting the transition word.

TRANSITION EXERCISES

(1) Prior to the twentieth century, most people believed that germs arose from a theory called "spontaneous generation." (2) Louis Pasteur felt that the idea was absurd, and attributing life to such random speculation was tantamount to superstition. (3) He began a series of experiments that would conclusively explain the process of putrefaction.

1. Which transition should be added to the beginning of sentence 2?

    A. In addition,
    B. Therefore,
    C. However,
    D. For example,

(1) The r/K selection theory attempts to describe two modes of evolutionary strategies. (2) The theory holds that "r-selected" organisms produce numerous offspring expecting only a few to survive into adulthood. (3) Spiders lay between 100 and 200 eggs but only a few survive the first week.

2. Which transition should be added to the beginning of sentence 3?

    E. In fact,
    F. For example,
    G. Likewise,
    H. Thus,

(1) High school is a time marked by notable changes. (2) Changes in location, friends, beliefs, and value systems, as well as one's own physical self, lead to a considerable amount of stress that some adolescents are unprepared to handle. (3) Many high schools provide both teachers and guidance counselors with training to ensure that students seek help when they are overwhelmed.

3. Which transition should be added to the beginning of sentence 3?

    A. In particular,
    B. On the other hand,
    C. Indeed,
    D. Due to this fact,

(1) As long as our society remains technology reliant, the demand for energy will continue to soar unabated. (2) Due to this trend, job prospects in the energy sector are promising. (3) Job prospects for petroleum engineers are anticipated to be three times the average rate for all other jobs.

4. Which transition should be added to the beginning of sentence 3?

    E. In particular,
    F. Conversely,
    G. Similarly,
    H. Thus,

(Answers are on page 92.)

Passage-Based Revising/Editing: Organization

In organization-based questions, you are asked to reorder the sentence to improve the organization of the paragraph. There are three things you need to look for in order to reorganize these sentences correctly.

1. Transition words (additive, causal, contrasting, illustrative, intensifying)
2. Pronouns
3. Key words

TRANSITION WORDS

Look for transition words to help you organize the sentences logically. Examine the following sentences.

(1) Unless one is up close to see the creature, it is easy to dismiss the magnitude of a creature's size.

(2) However, at 300,000 pounds, the blue whale, easily the largest creature on this planet, is as long as a jumbo jet.

(3) For example, the elephant, the largest land creature on the surface of this blue marble we call Earth, is as tall as a bus.

The transitions words *For example* and *However* can help you organize these sentences. Sentence (2) begins with a contrasting transition, so the sentence before sentence (2) must provide some information that contrasts with the blue whale. Sentence (3) should, therefore be placed between sentence (1) and (2), since the elephant is an example of the claim of the previous sentence.

(1) Unless one is up close to see the creature, it is easy to dismiss the magnitude of a creature's size.

(3) **For example**, the elephant, the largest land creature on the surface of this blue marble we call Earth, is as tall as a bus.

(2) **However**, at approximately a length of 85 feet, the blue whale, easily the largest creature on this planet, is as long as a jumbo jet.

PRONOUNS

Look for a pronoun and connect it to a sentence containing its antecedent. Examine the following sentences.

(1) Snapping shrimps are the loudest animals in the deep blue sea.

(2) Shrimp are delicious sautéed, fried, or in pasta, but they're more than a mouthwatering item in the finest restaurants.

(3) They are so loud that navy submarines hide in their presence to mask their location from sonar.

Sentence (3) contains the pronoun *They*, which needs to be placed before a sentence that describes what *They* refers to. To correct this sentence, sentence (1) needs to be placed between sentences (2) and (3) so the pronoun *They* correctly follows its antecedent *Snapping shrimps*.

(2) Shrimp are delicious sautéed, fried, or in pasta, but they're more than a mouthwatering item in the finest restaurants.

(1) Snapping shrimps are the loudest animals in the deep blue sea.

(3) They are so loud that navy submarines hide in their presence to mask their location from sonar.

KEY WORDS

Look to connect key words. They are typically in the form of "A (noun)" or "The (noun)." Structurally they will look like this.

(1) Words words words [KEY WORD] words words.
(2) Chicken chicken chicken chicken chicken.
(3) [KEY WORD] pizza pizza pizza pizza.

You will just need to connect sentences (1) and (3) so that the KEY WORDS are next to each other. Examine the following sentences.

(1) The movie adjusted for inflation actually made $3.4 billion, making it the highest grossing film ever.
(2) Today, the standard blockbuster movie brings in millions of dollars.
(3) By that standard, the film *Gone with the Wind*, grossing $189 million at the box office in 1939, easily qualifies as a blockbuster.

Sentence (1) contains the key words *The movie.* Therefore, the sentence should be placed after a sentence that describes that movie. Sentence (1) should be placed after sentence (3).

(2) Today, the standard blockbuster movie brings in millions of dollars.
(3) By that standard, *the film Gone with the Wind*, grossing $189 million at the box office in 1939, easily qualifies as a blockbuster.
(1) *The movie* adjusted for inflation actually made $3.4 billion, making it the highest grossing film ever.

ORGANIZATION EXERCISES

(1) Most people are more familiar with butterflies than moths, because butterflies are diurnal and moths are nocturnal, but there are key differences between the two. (2) They are similar insects, but there are ways to distinguish between them on sight. (3) Another difference is that the resting butterfly folds its wings up, closing them, while the wings of the resting moth are held straight out or folded down. (4) One obvious difference is the antennae, which in butterflies are slender, long, and knobbed and in moths are thicker and furry looking. (5) Distinguishing between these two insects is, therefore, not a difficult task.

1. Where should sentence (3) be moved to improve the organization of the first paragraph (sentences 1–5)?

   A. To the beginning of the paragraph
   B. Between sentences 1 and 2
   C. Between sentences 4 and 5
   D. After sentence 5

(1) Living in the harsh Southwest, the Navajo Indians have survived the deprivation of the desert as well as the violent persecution of the United States government. (2) In spite of these hardships, they have managed to retain their language as well as many of their customs and much of their native tradition. (3) On the other hand, the Navajo have proved adaptable, incorporating over the years valuable aspects of other cultures, Indian and non-Indian. (4) Many Navajos speak English, and from other Indian tribes these former warriors have learned trades that have given them a measure of prosperity. (5) For example, the weaving of blankets and rugs is one tradition that has been passed on from mother to daughter for hundreds of years. (6) The Navajo tribe's main source of wealth, however, is the reservation's abundant resources of coal, oil, and uranium; these riches make them the wealthiest American Indian tribe.

2. Where should sentence (5) be moved to improve the organization of the first paragraph (sentences 1–6)?

   E. To the beginning of the paragraph
   F. Between sentences 1 and 2
   G. Between sentences 2 and 3
   H. Between sentences 3 and 4

(1) In the nineteenth century, a French fabric called *serge de Nimes*, after Nimes, its city of origin, became a favorite material for work trousers. (2) A dry-goods wholesaler named Levi Strauss sold the fabric to Gold Rush miners in California, so he was already familiar with its strength and comfort when inventor Jacob Davis suggested using rivets to reinforce the pockets of work pants. (3) The first Levi's riveted work pants, called "waist overalls," were an immediate success and sold well for several decades with only minor changes. (4) Other companies began making similar work pants from denim, and in the 1940s denim pants called "dungarees" became the popular casual wear called *jeans*. (5) They became a symbol of teenage rebellion in the 1950s, but today, they can be found on anybody, almost anywhere. (6) It was exported to other European countries and also to the United States, where it came to be called by the shorter name *denim*.

3. Where should sentence (6) be moved to improve the organization of the first paragraph (sentences 1–6)?

   A. To the beginning of the paragraph
   B. Between sentences 1 and 2
   C. Between sentences 2 and 3
   D. Between sentences 3 and 4

(1) Europe hopes to achieve a first in space exploration when the European Agency lands a spacecraft on the comet Wirtanen in 2022. (2) The rendezvous will take place when the comet is approaching the sun but is still 420 million miles from it. (3) At that great distance from the sun, Wirtanen will be a frozen mass that is not yet trailed by the characteristic comet's tail. (4) *Rosetta* will orbit Wirtanen for about a month as it hurtles toward the sun at 81,000 miles per hour. (5) The spacecraft *Rosetta* will rendezvous with Wirtanen and begin its mission of matter collection from the surface of the comet.

4. Where should sentence (5) be moved to improve the organization of the first paragraph (sentences 1–5)?

   E. To the beginning of the paragraph
   F. Between sentences 1 and 2
   G. Between sentences 2 and 3
   H. Between sentences 3 and 4

(Answers are on page 93.)

Passage-Based Revising/Editing: Irrelevant Sentence

In irrelevant sentence questions, you are asked to identify a sentence that seems out of place within a paragraph. In one type, you will have to select a sentence that seems out of place. You can often tell because it does not follow the sequence or purpose of the paragraph. Examine the following.

(1) Dolphins are remarkably intelligent creatures, whose intelligence "mirrors" that of our own.
(2) Researchers devised an experiment in which dolphins demonstrated the ability to recognize the concept of themselves.
(3) Dolphins also possess a blowhole and sonar-like abilities.
(4) By identifying themselves in the mirror, dolphins revealed that they too possess the advanced cognitive ability of self-awareness.

In these four sentences, the main purpose is to explain the dolphin's intellect. Sentence (3) discusses other physical characteristics, so it should be deleted.

Another way to identify the irrelevant sentence is to use transition words, pronouns, and key words. Examine the following sentences.

(1) The white-nose syndrome poses a major threat to bat populations, killing off more than 5 million bats within the first year of its discovery.
(2) Scientists and government agencies have both made a concerted effort to stem the catastrophic disease.
(3) White-nose syndrome is a fungal disease that causes eccentric behavior.
(4) They have worked with the public to raise awareness of the issues so that tourists would minimize behaviors that can harm their environment.

Sentence (4) contains the pronoun *They*. The antecedent to the pronoun is *Scientists and government agencies* located in sentence (2). Although sentence (3) might be relevant, it is irrelevant at that location. Therefore, it should be deleted. The same principle applies to sentences containing transitions.

(1) The sharing economy refers to peer-to-peer-based sharing of goods and services through advances in technology.

(2) Various industries have arisen within the last ten years, capitalizing on the capacities of mobile technology.

(3) It is becoming increasingly more difficult to subsist on one job, so people use sharing economies to supplement their income.

(4) Ride-share companies, for example, use GPS and a mobile app platform to help riders connect with drivers who are willing to share their cars.

Sentence (4) contains the transition words *for example*, which introduces an example of a company that uses mobile technology mentioned in sentence (2). Sentence (3) breaks the connection between the sentences linked by the transition *for example*.

IRRELEVANT SENTENCE EXERCISES

(1) The tin can for preserving food was a revolutionary invention of the early nineteenth century. (2) For more than a hundred years, however, it was difficult and sometimes even dangerous to get at the stored food. (3) In 1930, an efficient and convenient can opener became available, and this design continues to be used today. (4) Meats, vegetables, and fruits retain their flavor and nutrients through the canning process. (5) This useful machine has a sharp circular blade that cuts into the lid of the can as a toothed wheel under the lip of the can moves the can around in a smooth, continuous cut.

1. Which sentence is irrelevant to the argument presented in the passage and should be deleted?

   A. sentence 1
   B. sentence 2
   C. sentence 3
   D. sentence 4

(1) The *Rails to Trails* movement has become an influential force in many communities. (2) The purpose of the movement is to transform useless eyesores into useful and attractive spaces. (3) The amount of trash in the world has been accumulating to unsustainable levels. (4) The transformation requires an initial investment to pay for the removal of unused railroad tracks. (5) Then only minimal maintenance is required to ensure a usable pathway for hiking, running, or biking.

2. Which sentence is irrelevant to the argument presented in the passage and should be deleted?

   E. sentence 1
   F. sentence 2
   G. sentence 3
   H. sentence 4

(1) Ranging in length from 18 to 25 inches and with a wingspread of 36 to 60 inches, the great horned owl is indeed one of the "greatest" North American owls. (2) The North American owl is a highly adaptive species whose population has stabilized. (3) However, while the greatness might be justified, the "horned" is not, for the bird's head bears not horns, but prominent ear tufts. (4) These giant appendages give it a fearsome appearance that is not at all deceiving, as this species is one of the most ferocious predators of the bird world. (5) Aided by its size and strength, extremely acute hearing, and flying speeds of up to 40 miles per hour, this owl preys not only on small animals but also on larger ones.

3. Which sentence is irrelevant to the argument presented in the passage and should be deleted?

   A. sentence 1
   B. sentence 2
   C. sentence 3
   D. sentence 4

(1) The main function of leaves is photosynthesis, which takes place in a leaf tissue called *mesophyll*, where cells absorb carbon dioxide from air in the surrounding spaces, replacing it with expelled oxygen. (2) Food produced by this process is circulated to other parts of the plant by a vascular system, which also transports water to the leaf. (3) Some plants have modified leaves that help the plant in special ways. (4) Many gardeners prefer cactus to leafy plants. (5) Some plants use leaves to trap insects, while others use them to deter predators.

4. Which sentence is irrelevant to the argument presented in the passage and should be deleted?

   E. sentence 1
   F. sentence 2
   G. sentence 3
   H. sentence 4

(Answers are on page 94.)

Passage-Based Revising/Editing: Supporting Details

In supporting details questions, you are asked to support the ideas of a given paragraph. To answer these questions, identify the main idea or the topic. Then select the sentence that best provides an example of that idea.

   (1) Most people believe that the best way to improve their performance is to train one skill at a time.
   (2) Studies, however, have shown that this is not always the case.
   (3) Called "interleaving," the practice mixes up different skills during a given session.

The sentence that follows sentence (3) should provide a supporting or relevant detail that helps the reader gain more information about the practices involved in "interleaving."

SUPPORTING DETAILS EXERCISES

(1) For centuries, sleep was often so steeped in mystery that it required an explanation. (2) Some cultures believed that sleep was a gateway into the spirit world, while other cultures believed that it released the soul to travel the world. (3) Psychoanalysts believe it is the window to one's inner psyche, while other scientists believe that it's simply an evolutionary holdover from our primate ancestor. (4) The most recent research from neuroscientists suggests a less fantastical explanation.

1. Which sentence should be added to follow and support sentence (4)?

    A. Sleep is something that most people need to ensure a productive day.
    B. It usually takes about 10 to 15 minutes for a person to fall asleep.
    C. Sleep functions as a cleaning mechanism that removes toxins that are associated with dementia.
    D. The problem with sleep research is that it is extremely difficult to establish an objective measure of sleepiness.

(1) The urgent care industry is one of the fastest growing healthcare industries in the country today. (2) Each year, more than 150 million people go to urgent care centers, resulting in about two urgent care centers opening every day. (3) The reason for this explosion can be attributed to several factors. (4) One of the most important factors is customer demand.

2. Which sentence should be added to follow and support sentence (4)?

    E. In order to better evaluate what people need, the term "customer demand" is better defined as a customer "want."
    F. Urgent cares provide shorter wait times, comparatively lower prices, and more attentive physicians that make their services an attractive alternative to the emergency room.
    G. "Customer demand" means something different in the healthcare industry than it does in other industries.
    H. The most successful business industries are the ones that have their ear to the ground, listening for the demands of their customers.

(1) Nitrogen is a vital element that plants need to produce chlorophyll, the compound by which sunlight is converted into usable energy. (2) Soil rich in nitrogen can drastically improve the agricultural yield of any given plant. (3) However, although nitrogen is one of the most abundant elements on earth, it is inaccessible to living organisms in its atmospheric form. (4) Thanks to the ingenious research of chemist Fritz Haber, today we can create fertilizer literally from thin air.

3. Which sentence should be added to follow and support sentence (4)?

    A. The Haber-Bosch process combines nitrogen from the air with hydrogen under extreme pressures and temperatures.
    B. Hydrogen is also an important element but not nearly as important as nitrogen.
    C. Creating fertilizer from thin air can cause numerous problems in the environment.
    D. Soil rich in nitrogen can also enhance the flavor and nutrition of a crop.

(1) The octopus, lacking the physical apparatus that most land animals use to perceive color, appears to be color-blind. (2) However, their tendency to change color during courtship rituals has made scientists reluctant to claim that they were, in fact, color-blind. (3) Nature, it would seem, need not conform to human expectations. (4) Rather than using pigments in the eye, octopus possess a pair of strangely shaped pupils, which acts like a prism breaking up light in its cephalopod head.

4. Which sentence should be added to follow and support sentence (4)?

    E. A prism is a triangular glass that is commonly used to break up light.

    F. The giant squid, like the octopus, may also have the ability to break up light in its gigantic head.

    G. Once light is divided into separate wavelengths, the octopus then processes each wave, allowing for color discrimination.

    H. Many animals have strangely shaped body parts that make for a unique and interesting world.

(Answers are on page 95.)

Answer Explanations

INTRODUCTORY/MAIN CLAIM EXERCISES (PAGES 74–76)

1. **(A)**

    A. Writing provides a wide variety of benefits, and it might be wise to rethink one's attitude toward writing.

The sentence introduces the benefit of reduced stress in the following paragraph.

    B. People should abandon writing essays because doing so can reduce stress.

This sentence introduces the idea of abandoning the writing of essays, which is not discussed in the following paragraph.

    C. If people try hard enough, people can become excellent essay writers.

This sentence claims that working hard leads to better skills in essay writing, which is not discussed in the following paragraph

    D. Writing can help a person reach professional success, so people should consider majoring in English.

This sentence attempts to persuade the reader to major in English, which is not discussed in the following paragraph.

2. **(F)**

    E. Barbarians were one of the first forms of social organization that gave rise to the civilizations in Europe.

This sentence introduces barbarians and early forms of social organization, and the following paragraph mentions barbarians in the first sentence. However, the following paragraph primarily discusses the geographical environment of the Greeks. The mentioning of the *barbarous tribes* is a detail used to contextualize the Greek environment.

F. One of the earliest and notable of these conflicts took place in Greece twenty-four hundred years ago.

This sentence is the best introduction because it introduces the topic of the Greeks. Also, the phrase *twenty-four hundred years ago* in the answer choice connects with the phrase *At that time* in sentence (4).

G. Regardless of the oppression, people have always emerged as the losers in these conflicts.

This sentence introduces the consequence of conflicts for *people* in the general sense.

H. As populations increase to unmanageable levels, oppression becomes an inescapable facet of life throughout the history of civilization.

This sentence introduces the impact of oppression on the history of civilization, not specifically the Greeks.

3. **(B)**

A. It is a place that is mentioned in classrooms all over the world.

This is a tempting answer, since it uses a similar structure "It is." However, the phrase "two rivers" in sentence 4 needs an introduction, which choice A does not provide.

B. It is the land of mystery and wonder which the Greeks called Mesopotamia— the "country between the rivers."

This is the best answer choice as the phrase *the rivers* in the answer choice introduces the *two rivers* mentioned in sentence (4).

C. It is a land that exists in the dreams of explorers who wish to unlock the mysteries of the Bible.

Although a biblical reference is made in sentence (5), it is a minor detail. The other sentences discuss geography associated with the two rivers, not the Bible.

D. It is the land where agriculture and civilization were born.

This sentence introduces *the land,* so it is not an appropriate introduction.

4. **(H)**

E. Their geographical differences led to sharp differences in manners.

This is a very tempting answer choice but fails to introduce the main idea. While sentences (5) through (8) make references to geography, sentences (9) and (10) discuss preferences and values rather than manners.

F. Political aspirations clearly aggravated the conflict between the two powerful states.

The following paragraph does not discuss the conflict between Athens and Sparta.

G. We should all aspire to celebrate their diversity.

The following paragraph does not discuss diversity at all.

H. They might have spoken a common language but were different in every other respect.

This is the best answer because the paragraph that follows outlines several ways in which the Athenians and Spartans are different.

CONCLUDING SENTENCE EXERCISES (PAGES 77–78)

1. **(D)**

   A. Madagascar's primary export is coffee, and this is also another problem that conservationists have to deal with.

   Discussion of the economy is outside the scope of the paragraph's discussion on the loss of diversity.

   B. People must learn more about conservation so that they can make a difference in the world.

   This answer choice unnecessarily advocates a course of action. The course of action may be implied, but the paragraph is primarily intended to describe the loss of diversity and its impact.

   C. Madagascar's economy is growing at an alarming speed, which may help spur modernization.

   Discussion of the economy is outside the scope of the paragraph's discussion on the loss of diversity.

   D. Scientists are concerned about the consequences of such losses because once these species are gone, they can never be studied again.

   This sentence further elaborates on the main claim of the topic, which is the loss of diversity.

2. **(H)**

   E. The new problems now are pollution and overproduction.

   The paragraph discusses not problems but human responses to a prediction.

   F. The biggest problem today is whether we can feed all of them.

   This sentence would seem to contradict the main idea of the passage.

   G. People should encourage, not criticize, new forms of technology.

   This sentence advocates a course of action, which is not the intended purpose of the passage.

   H. It would seem, then, that Malthus's claims about humans, and not human claims to existence, are unsustainable.

   This sentence is the best concluding sentence since it combines expectations and reality of population and resources.

3. **(B)**

   A. Obviously, people need their cell phones more than ever before.

   The paragraph illustrates people's preoccupation with cell phones, but the phrase *than ever before* suggests that the passage was discussing the importance of phones today.

B. Despite such changes in behavior, the desire to remain connected to other people, regardless of how silly one may appear to an outsider, is unmistakably something that makes us human.

The phrase *such changes in behavior* connects the previous descriptions and ties it into a claim about how the practices are normal and acceptable human behavior to support the idea that *times have . . . changed*.

C. The telecommunications industry, however, seems interested only in producing profits and cell phone zombies.

This sentence focuses on the interests of the telecommunications industry, which was not discussed at all in the passage.

D. The health risks of cell phone use are well documented in numerous research studies.

Although there may be risks associated with using cell phones, the main idea in the passage is not to emphasize the dangers of using a cell phone.

4. **(F)**

E. The cost effectiveness of growing these natural medicines can harm the biotechnology industry.

While growing your own plants in a garden might be cost-effective, the biotechnology industry is never discussed in the passage, so it is an inappropriate concluding sentence.

F. Starting a garden in your backyard today might help you fill your belly with nutritious dinner and your immune system with natural remedies.

This sentence is the best answer choice because it captures the idea that gardens can be used for both food and medicine.

G. Educating the public about the benefits of a garden can be difficult for people living in cities.

This sentence is a judgment on the difficulties of educating people. The purpose of this passage is not to outline the difficulties.

H. Finally, chamomile tea can also help people who suffer from anxiety or insomnia.

This is an additional detail, which does not serve to capture the main idea.

TRANSITION EXERCISES (PAGES 80–81)

1. **(C)** Louis Pasteur's belief stands in contrast to what most people believed, so a contrasting transition best introduces the contrasting belief.

   A. In addition, (Additive)
   B. Therefore, (Causal)
   C. However, (Contrasting)
   D. For example, (Illustrative)

2. **(F)** Spiders are an example of an r-selected organism, so an illustrative transition best introduces the example.

    E. In fact, (Intensifying)
    F. For example, (Illustrative)
    G. Likewise, (Additive)
    H. Thus, (Causal)

3. **(D)** Sentence 2 discusses a cause (*considerable amount of stress*) that leads to the effect in sentence 3 (*schools provide both teachers and guidance counselors with training*).

    A. In particular, (Illustrative)
    B. On the other hand, (Contrasting)
    C. Indeed, (Intensifying)
    D. Due to this fact, (Causal)

4. **(E)** Sentence 2 introduces the idea that job prospects are promising. Sentence 3 provides an illustrative example of such an instance (*for petroleum engineers*). Choice G is a tempting choice, but the specificity of petroleum engineers makes E the better choice.

    E. In particular, (Illustrative)
    F. Conversely, (Contrasting)
    G. Similarly, (Additional)
    H. Thus, (Causal)

ORGANIZATION EXERCISES (PAGES 83–85)

1. **(C)** The phrase *Another* is a transition word, which suggests that the preceding sentence talked about one difference.

(1) Most people are more familiar with butterflies than moths, because butterflies are diurnal and moths are nocturnal, but there are key differences between the two. (2) They are similar insects, but there are ways to distinguish between them on sight. (4) *One obvious difference* is the antennae, which in butterflies are slender, long, and knobbed and in moths are thicker and furry-looking. (3) *Another difference* is that the resting butterfly folds its wings up, closing them, while the wings of the resting moth are held straight out or folded down. (5) Distinguishing between the two insects is, therefore, not a difficult task.

2. **(G)** The transition words *For example* lead into an example of *one tradition that has been passed down*. Sentence (2) best introduces this example with the phrase *retain their . . . native tradition.*

(1) Living in the harsh Southwest, the Navajo Indians have survived the deprivation of the desert as well as the violent persecution of the United States government. (2) In spite of these hardships, they have managed to *retain their* language as well as many of their customs and much of their *native tradition.* (5) For example, the weaving of blankets and rugs is *one tradition that has been passed on from mother to daughter for hundreds of years.* (3) On the other hand, the Navajo have proved adaptable, incorporating over the years valuable aspects of other cultures, Indian and non-Indian. (4) Many Navajos speak English,

and from other Indian tribes these former warriors have learned trades that have given them a measure of prosperity. (6) The Navajo tribe's main source of wealth, however, is the reservation's abundant resources of coal, oil, and uranium; these riches make them the wealthiest American Indian tribe.

3. **(B)** Sentence (6) begins with the pronoun *It*. Sentence (1) contains the antecedent *a French fabric*, which would logically be *exported to other European countries and also the United States*.

(1) In the nineteenth century, *a French fabric* called *serge de Nimes*, after Nimes, its city of origin, became a favorite material for work trousers. (6) It was *exported to other European countries and also to the United States*, where it came to be called by the shorter name *denim*. (2) A dry-goods wholesaler named Levi Strauss sold the fabric to Gold Rush miners in California, so he was already familiar with its strength and comfort when inventor Jacob Davis suggested using rivets to reinforce the pockets of work pants. (3) The first Levi's riveted work pants, called "waist overalls," were an immediate success and sold well for several decades with only minor changes. (4) Other companies began making similar work pants from denim, and in the 1940s denim pants called "dungarees" became the popular casual wear called *jeans*. (5) They became a symbol of teenage rebellion in the 1950s, but today, they can be found on anybody, almost anywhere.

4. **(F)** Here you can link two words. Link the key word *spacecraft* of sentence (5) with *spacecraft* in sentence (1) and link the key word *rendezvous* in sentence (5) with *The rendezvous* in sentence (2).

(1) Europe hopes to achieve a first in space exploration when the European Agency lands *a spacecraft* on the comet Wirtanen in 2022. (5) *The spacecraft Rosetta* will *rendezvous* with Wirtanen and begin its mission of matter collection from the surface of the comet. (2) *The rendezvous* will take place when the comet is approaching the sun but is still 420 million miles from it.

IRRELEVANT SENTENCE EXERCISES (PAGES 86–87)

1. **(D)** Sentence (4) interrupts the connection between *an efficient and convenient can opener* and the pronoun and keyword *This useful machine*.

(1) The tin can for preserving food was a revolutionary invention of the early nineteenth century. (2) For more than a hundred years, however, it was difficult and sometimes even dangerous to get at the stored food. (3) In 1930, *an efficient and convenient can opener* became available, and this design continues to be used today. (4) Meats, vegetables, and fruits retain their flavor and nutrients through the canning process. (5) *This useful machine* has a sharp circular blade that cuts into the lid of the can as a toothed wheel under the lip of the can moves the can around in a smooth, continuous cut.

2. **(G)** Sentence (3) interrupts the flow of ideas connected by the key word *transform* in sentence (2) and *The transformation* in sentence (4).

(1) The *Rails to Trails* movement has become an influential force in many communities. (2) The purpose of the movement is to *transform* useless eyesores into useful and attractive spaces. (3) The amount of trash in the world has

been accumulating to unsustainable levels. (4) *The transformation* requires an initial investment to pay for the removal of unused railroad tracks. (5) Then only minimal maintenance is required to ensure a usable pathway for hiking, running, or biking.

3. **(B)** Sentence (2) interrupts the transition relationship between sentences (1) and (3). The transition word *However* introduces the idea that there is a problem with the name of the great horned owl.

   (1) Ranging in length from 18 to 25 inches and with a wingspread of 36 to 60 inches, the great horned owl is indeed one of the *"greatest"* North American owls. (2) The North American owl is a highly adaptive species whose population has stabilized. (3) *However*, while the *greatness* might be justified, the "horned" is not, for the bird's head bears not horns, but prominent ear tufts. (4) These giant appendages give it a fearsome appearance that is not at all deceiving, as this species is one of the most ferocious predators of the bird world. (5) Aided by its size and strength, extremely acute hearing, and flying speeds of up to 40 miles per hour, this owl preys not only on small animals but also on larger ones.

4. **(H)** Sentence (4) introduces the preferences of gardeners, which is not relevant to the topic of plant leaves.

   (1) The main function of leaves is photosynthesis, which takes place in a leaf tissue called *mesophyll*, where cells absorb carbon dioxide from air in the surrounding spaces, replacing it with expelled oxygen. (2) Food produced by this process is circulated to other parts of the plant by a vascular system, which also transports water to the leaf. (3) Some plants have modified *leaves* that help the plant in special ways. (4) Many gardeners prefer cactus to leafy plants. (5) Some plants use *leaves* to trap insects, while others use them to deter predators.

SUPPORTING DETAILS EXERCISES (PAGES 88–89)

1. **(C)** Sentence (4) introduces the explanation from the most recent findings. Choice C provides an explanation that best resembles a scientific explanation.

   A. Sleep is something that most people need to ensure a productive day.

   This answer choice is out of scope and irrelevant.

   B. It usually takes about 10 to 15 minutes for a person to fall asleep.

   This answer choice elaborates on the way people fall asleep and not on the explanation.

   C. Sleep functions as a cleaning mechanism that removes toxins that are associated with dementia.

   This is the best answer.

   D. The problem with sleep research is that it is extremely difficult to establish an objective measure of sleepiness.

   This touches upon scientific studies of sleep, but it describes a drawback that is not discussed in the previous sentence.

2. **(F)** Choice F provides several reasons that help provide more information about the customer demand that contributes to the rising popularity of urgent cares.

E. In order to better evaluate what people need, the term "customer demand" is better defined as a customer "want."

Although this answer choice links the term *customer demand*, the sentence is irrelevant as it looks to redefine a term unnecessarily.

F. Urgent cares provide shorter wait times, comparatively lower prices, and more attentive physicians that make their services an attractive alternative to the emergency room.

This answer choice best illustrates the factors that constitute "customer demand."

G. "Customer demand" means something different in the healthcare industry than it does in other industries.

The definition of customer demand is irrelevant here.

H. The most successful business industries are the ones that have their ear to the ground, listening for the demands of their customers.

This sentence introduces what may be important for business industries.

3. **(A)** Choice A links *Fritz Haber* with *The Haber-Bosch process* and provides more details on how the fertilizer is created.

A. The Haber-Bosch process combines nitrogen from the air with hydrogen under extreme pressures and temperatures.

This answer choice best supports sentence 4 by explaining how fertilizer is created from air.

B. Hydrogen is also an important element but not nearly as important as nitrogen.

This answer choice deals with important elements, which is irrelevant.

C. Creating fertilizer from the thin air can cause numerous problems in the environment.

This answer choice brings up environmental problems, which are not discussed in the passage.

D. Soil rich in nitrogen can also enhance the flavor and nutrition of a crop.

This answer choice brings up the impact of nitrogen on food, which is not discussed in the passage.

4. **(G)** Choice G further explains what happens after light breaks up in a cephalopod's head.

E. A prism is a triangular glass that is commonly used to break up light.

An explanation of a prism's use is unnecessary in this paragraph.

F. The giant squid, like the octopus, may also have the ability to break up light in its gigantic head.

There is no indication that the passage needs to discuss squids.

G. Once light is divided into separate wavelengths, the octopus then processes each wave, allowing for color discrimination.

This is the best answer.

H. Many animals have strangely shaped body parts that make for a unique and interesting world.

The passage discusses cephalopods, not other animals or their traits.

SKILLBUILDER C: READING

Reading questions test your ability to read with understanding and to answer questions based on your reading. The reading section of the SHSAT consists of five passages of 350–450 words followed by six multiple-choice questions for each passage. The questions in this section are arranged in order of difficulty. They are not presented in the order in which the correct answer appears in the passage. The content of the passages is varied, with subject matter including (but not limited to) science, history, biography, anthropology, and the arts.

This Skillbuilder will provide you with techniques for more efficient reading, and will teach you what kinds of questions to expect and how to find their answers. By practicing the suggested methods, you will gain skill and confidence.

WHAT'S BEING TESTED?

A Reading question usually asks you to find a **main idea,** to answer a specific question about the **facts** of a passage, or to draw an **inference**—that is, to perceive an idea that is suggested rather than stated.

What Do I Do?

- Follow an **orderly procedure** that gives you a **purpose** in reading and a way to **focus** on important points in the passage.
- Identify the **key elements** in each question. Determine the **type of information** the question requires.
- **Find the answer** by using the **clues** provided by your focused method of reading.

Your first challenge is to master the best approach to reading the passages. If you learn and practice an orderly, efficient way to read, answering the questions will be easier.

Reading for Purpose and Focus

When you are reading a relatively short passage that you know you are going to be tested on, your reading technique should be different from the way you read a magazine article or a long chapter in a textbook. You want to read quickly, spending just two or three minutes on each passage, but you should read with purpose, and you should mark the passage to highlight major ideas and topics.

- *Reading the question.* Some people prefer to glance at the questions (ignoring the answer choices) before reading the passage. Others prefer to start by reading the passage. You are free to choose whichever strategy works best for you; however, you should try both before you decide.
- *Reading the passage.* Read the passage quickly, circling important words and phrases. Try to jot down the main idea of the passage. Don't reread any part of the material more than once—you will have a chance to go back and reread relevant portions again.

PURPOSE AND FOCUS EXERCISES

Read and mark the following passage for **purpose** and **focus**.

The French Revolution, which began in 1789, ended the control of France by monarch and aristocracy, and launched the era of middle-class control. Business and financial leaders maintained their power even after a counter-revolution restored the monarchy in 1814. Although it regained its status and even some privilege, the aristocracy no longer dominated the affairs of the country.

1. Which of the following best tells what the passage is about?

    A. The history of the French Revolution
    B. The causes and results of the French Revolution
    C. The end of the monarchy in France as a result of the French Revolution
    D. Middle-class power as an outcome of the French Revolution

2. What does the passage suggest about the Revolution?

    E. Changes brought about by the revolution were all reversed.
    F. Some of the French people were dissatisfied with the outcome of the French Revolution.
    G. The French Revolution was mainly a struggle of monarchy against aristocracy.
    H. The French Revolution was influenced by the American Revolution.

Look at the sample marked passage below. Note that no attempt has been made to mark *every* detail.

The (French Revolution), which began in 1789, ended the control of France by monarch and aristocracy, and launched the (era of middle-class control.) Business and financial leaders maintained their power even after a counter-revolution restored the monarchy in 1814. Although it regained its status and even some privilege, the (aristocracy no longer dominated) the affairs of the country.

The student who marked this passage circled what seemed most important. Another student might have circled different facts. Don't worry if your markings are different from this sample. *Marking the passage helps you to focus.* It also helps you find answers, but you can't expect to spot every answer on the first reading!

Try Another. Follow the same procedure to read this passage.

The transfer of power from aristocracy to middle class also occurred in England, but through a gradual evolution rather than a revolution. Although royalty and aristocracy held the high positions in early English history, the middle class in that country was important even in the Middle Ages. By the seventeenth century it was strong enough to unseat King Charles I in the Civil War. And even after the English Parliament restored the monarchy, placing Charles II on the throne, the power of the middle class continued to grow at the expense of the aristocracy and monarchy.

3. What is the main idea of the passage?

    A. The outcome of the English Civil War
    B. The evolution of the middle class
    C. The growth in power of the English middle class
    D. Social changes in Europe after the seventeenth century

4. What does the passage suggest about England's middle class?

    E. It had little power before the Civil War.
    F. It gained power mainly by peaceful means.
    G. It was politically dominant during the Middle Ages.
    H. It wished to restore the monarchy after the Civil War.

5. Which of the following statements about Charles II is supported by the details of the passage?

    A. He took power after a counter-revolution restored the monarchy.
    B. He took the throne after his father died.
    C. He passed laws that strengthened the middle class.
    D. He was the next king after Charles I.

6. Which of the following is **not** stated in the passage?

    E. The middle class was responsible for the overthrow of Charles I.
    F. Royalty and aristocracy had elevated status in early England.
    G. Charles I influenced Parliament to restore the monarchy.
    H. The English Civil War took place in the 1600s.

Check the passage below to see the way one student marked it.

The transfer of power from aristocracy to middle class also occurred in England, but through a gradual evolution rather than a revolution. Although royalty and aristocracy held the high positions in early English history, the middle class in that country was important even in the Middle Ages. By the seventeenth century it was strong enough to unseat King Charles I in the Civil War. And even after the English Parliament restored the monarchy, placing Charles II on the throne, the power of the middle class continued to grow at the expense of the aristocracy and monarchy.

Notice that the student who worked on this passage did more marking than the one who worked on the first passage. You may have circled different words and phrases. You may have marked more or fewer. That's okay. The important things are that you were reading attentively and that your markings will help you find the answers.

Now that you've had some practice reading and marking passages, let's move on to the paydirt part of the Reading test.

Key Elements

As you learned early in this Skillbuilder, Reading questions can be classified as **main idea** questions, **fact** questions, or **inference** questions. Knowing how to recognize the question types will make it easier for you to find the correct answers.

MAIN IDEA QUESTIONS

The first question on every passage asks for the main idea of the passage. It may ask

- what the passage is about, or
- what best states the author's purpose, or
- what is the best title for the passage.

Another kind of main idea question asks you

- to summarize some of the details in the passage, or
- to state a reason, or
- to make a generalization of some kind.

If you are not sure about the passage's main idea yet, you may wish to skip over the question for a moment and return to it after doing the other questions for the passage.

FACT QUESTIONS

A specific question about the content of the passage usually asks

- for a particular fact or detail stated in the passage, or
- what is or is **not** stated or is or is **not** true according to the passage.

Don't expect the correct answer to be stated in the exact words of the passage. Answers are more likely to be paraphrased—that is, worded differently.

INFERENCE QUESTIONS

Inference questions are unique in that they do not ask you directly about the material in the passage; instead, they ask you to make a leap or assumption from the information in the passage to a new conclusion—in other words, to *infer*. Be sure, though, that you do not leap too far—a correct answer to an inference question will still be supported or suggested by specific evidence in the passage.

An inference question most frequently asks

- what the passage suggests (implies),
- what a word means in a particular context (setting), or
- what the author's tone or attitude is. It may also ask you to
- infer a reason for some fact stated in the passage.

KEY ELEMENTS EXERCISES

Label the following questions *main idea, fact,* or *inference.*

1. What is the most likely reason that crows congregate at nightfall?
2. Which of the following best tells what the passage is about?
3. All of the following are properties of a liquid **except**
4. What are the favorite foods of the Baltimore Oriole?
5. What does the passage suggest about the origins of acupuncture?
6. What is the best title for the passage?
7. Which of the following best sums up the motivations of the Samurai warriors?
8. At what temperature will freezing water begin to sink?
9. What is the meaning of the word *arcane* as it is used in the passage?
10. Which of the following is a medical use of hypnotism?

(Answers are on page 108.)

Now let's move on to the crucial part of your test-taking method.

Find the Answer

If you have read the passage quickly, you should have a minute or more to work on each question. It's important here to work carefully and not to rush yourself. Take one question at a time. Reread the question, and then go back to the passage and find the answer. Select the correct answer choice and record it. Do all this for each question before going on to the next.

Follow This Procedure

1. **Reread the question carefully, circling key words and phrases.** Circling the words and phrases that specify what you have to find in the passage will help you quickly determine the type of question, and it will also make it easier for you to locate the necessary information.

2. **Label the question according to the type of information it requires—main idea, detail, or inference.** After you have practiced with several passages, you may decide to omit the label. As a beginner, it may help to jot down the question type next to the question.

3. **Choose the answer.** First try to answer the question without looking at the choices. Remember, the incorrect answer choices are designed to look correct. They often contain, for example, a group of words taken directly from the passage. It is, therefore, very important to know what answer you are looking for **before** you look at the answer choices. This way you will not be tempted by incorrect choices and can more easily focus on the correct answer. Once you have your answer in mind, go through the answer choices and eliminate those that do not match up with it.

> Exceptions: Some questions ask you which of the choices is *not* mentioned in the passage. Some require that you examine each choice for some purpose. In these cases, you cannot formulate any answer without looking at the choices first.

If you cannot formulate an answer without looking at the choices, see if looking at the choices helps.

If looking at the choices does not help, return to the passage and find the answer. Your markings will help you. In some cases, you may have circled all or part of the answer. But even if the answer is not already neatly packaged for you, the markings should help steer you to the information you need.

If a question provides a line number, always read at least a few lines above and a few lines below the line referenced. The correct answer will rarely appear in the line specified in the question.

PRACTICE

Go back to the passages you marked on page 98. Reread and answer the questions, following the preceeding method. On the actual test, you will record your answers by blackening a bubble on the answer sheet, but right now just circle the correct answer. The answers are on page 108.

PITFALLS

The preceding practice points out four pitfalls you may encounter on the SHSAT Reading test. Some incorrect answers may seem okay at first glance and so may trick you into a wrong choice. These bad answers include choices that say too much or too little and choices that are not actually stated or suggested in the passage.

Watch out for these kinds of incorrect choices.

- **Too broad.** This kind of wrong choice is most common in a main idea question but can be associated with the others also. It is an answer that includes, or covers, more than the passage does. 3B is an example of this type because it does not limit the subject enough.

- **Too narrow.** This type is also most likely to occur in a main idea question. Be sure that your choice for a main idea response is a subject that is important throughout the passage. 1C illustrates a response that includes only a minor aspect of the passage's content and so is too narrow.

- **Exaggerated.** Sometimes an answer would be okay if it didn't overstate the facts. Overstated choices are usually incorrect. For example, 4G errs in overstating the power of the middle class. Be wary when a choice uses strong language—especially words like *all, always,* and *every.* These words often indicate an exaggerated incorrect choice.

- **True but not given in the passage.** The instructions on the Reading test will tell you to base your answers only on the content of the passage. You need to be careful not to select an answer just because it seems true. Always look back at the passage to make sure it is mentioned (or, for an inference question, suggested) in the passage. 2H might trick an unwary student who has learned that ideas involved in the American Revolution did indeed influence the French Revolution. But H is an incorrect answer because the *passage* makes no such suggestion. It may seem strange to reject an answer that is factually correct! You must remember that you are being tested only on what is in the passage.

Apply what you know about bad answer types as you practice with the next passage and its questions.

First, review the steps for reading with purpose and focus and the steps for rereading and answering the questions. Then use the procedures in the following practice.

PITFALLS EXERCISES

Read the short passage below and carefully answer the questions that follow it. Be alert for answer choices that are too broad, too narrow, exaggerated, and true but not given in the passage. Solutions follow the passage.

Antonio Stradivari was born in 1644 in Cremona, Italy, a town noted for the production of excellent violins. Although Stradivari also made cellos and violas, it is his violins for which he is renowned. His teacher, Nicolo Amati,
Line
(5) passed on to him the techniques of violin making as it was practiced in Cremona. The pupil Stradivari employed these techniques but went on to surpass his teacher, making violins whose excellence has never been exceeded or even fully understood.

What makes a Stradivarius such a fine instrument? Stradivari did alter the proportions of the violin, but this change alone does not explain their supe-
(10) riority. Some think that the special varnish he used is responsible for the wonderful sound of the instruments, but not every expert agrees with this idea. A relatively recent theory concerns the unusually cold weather in Europe during this period of history. Lower-than-usual temperatures would have slowed the growth rate of the trees whose wood was used in the vio-
(15) lins, resulting in a very dense wood. Perhaps the magnificent Stradivarius sound derives from the density of the wood rather than the composition of the varnish.

The only violin maker whose instruments rival those of Antonio Stradivari is Giuseppe Antonio Guarneri, who lived at the same time. This
(20) fact does not give conclusive proof, but it does seem to bolster the cold-weather theory of the secret of the Stradivarius.

1. Which of the following best expresses the purpose of the author of the passage?

   A. To discuss the excellence of the violins produced by Stradivari
   B. To indicate a surprising result of climate change
   C. To explain what makes a violin superior
   D. To compare the violins of Stradivari and Guarneri

2. Which of the following is **not** mentioned as a possible factor influencing the quality of a Stradivarius violin?

   E. Special varnish
   F. Dense wood
   G. Experience gained through making violas and cellos
   H. Changes in proportions

3. Which of the following is suggested in the passage?

    A. The cellos and violas of Stradivari are of inferior quality.
    B. The violins of Guarneri are even more excellent than those of Stradivari.
    C. There was an ice age in Europe during Stradivari's lifetime.
    D. The wood in a Guarneri violin is very dense.

4. According to the passage, how might a denser-than-usual wood affect a violin?

    E. It would be more compact.
    F. The bow would be stronger.
    G. It would produce a deeper sound.
    H. It would improve the quality of the sound.

(Answers are on page 109.)

WHAT IF A PASSAGE IS DIFFICULT TO READ?

You may find some of the passages on the SHSAT, especially the scientific ones, hard to read. Don't let difficult subject matter throw you. Remember, you don't have to master all the information in a passage. Your job is to answer the questions correctly. And you can do this by reading the passage with purpose and focus, and by answering the questions carefully and methodically.

Work on one more short passage, one that you may find a little difficult because of its technical subject matter.

DIFFICULT TO READ PASSAGE EXERCISES

Use your orderly reading and answering procedures to find the correct answers to questions on the following passage. Be on guard for bad answer types, and remember that you may sometimes have to look in more than one place to find the correct answer.

        The majority of our most familiar plants reproduce by means of seeds. There are two types of seed-bearing plants, angiosperm and gymnosperm. Angiosperms, the flowering plants, produce seed enclosed in an ovary that *Line* eventually grows into a fruit. The seeds of gymnosperms, cone-bearers, and
(5) related plants, lie naked on the scales of cones.

        In both groups, a structure called an ovule produces an egg cell, and a structure called the pollen tube contains two sperm cells. Fertilization occurs after the plant's pollen tube passes through a small opening in the ovule called the micropyle. One sperm nucleus unites with the egg cell to form a one-celled
(10) body called a *zygote*. This grows into the embryo, which develops an enclosing sac. In angiosperms two nuclei present in the embryo sac combine with the other sperm nucleus to form one nucleus that eventually produces a nutritive substance, endosperm tissue, around the embryo. Gymnosperm embryo sacs produce the endosperm from their own tissue, without the contribution of a
(15) second sperm nucleus.

The fertilized and mature ovule is called a seed. It is relatively tender, but it is surrounded by a strong, hard seed coat, called a *testa*, that develops from the outer covering of the ovule. In flowering plants the tegmen, a thin membrane, forms a second seed coat within the testa; gymnosperms lack (20) this second coat as well as the surrounding fruit of the angiosperm seeds.

1. Which of the following best tells what this passage is about?

   A. Differences between two categories of plants and how they are fertilized
   B. How fertilization occurs in seed-bearing plants
   C. How a seed becomes a new plant
   D. The structure and production of seeds

2. What does the passage suggest about the testa?

   E. It is not present in gymnosperm seeds.
   F. It protects the mature ovule.
   G. It develops from the embryo sac.
   H. It is surrounded by the tegumen.

3. What structure contains the micropyle?

   A. The embryo sac
   B. The pollen tube
   C. The sperm nucleus
   D. The ovule

4. All of the following are given as parts of the reproduction process **except**

   E. production of an egg cell.
   F. micropyle serving as passageway.
   G. pollen tube entering ovule.
   H. production of ovary by gymnosperms.

(Answers are on page 110.)

WRAP-UP EXERCISES

Before you leave the Reading Skillbuilder, let's have a final review, a few extra hints, and one full-length passage. Try timing yourself on this passage: Aim to read it in two to three minutes, and to spend about one minute answering each question.

Remember

- Set a goal.
- Read quickly, with purpose and focus.
- Circle key words and phrases.
- Read each question, circling key points.
- Answer each question, returning to the passage when necessary.
- Record your answer.

As you did for the short passages, circle the correct answer. When you are working the full Practice Tests, of course, you will record your answers on the answer sheet.

What If None of the Choices Match My Answer?

Lightly cross out clearly incorrect choices.

Select the best choice of those remaining.

Quickly double-check the passage to confirm your choice.

What If I Still Don't Have a Match?

In this case, make your best guess and move on. It doesn't pay to get hung up on one answer.

What If Time Is Running Short?

This is another situation where you should make an educated guess and move on.

Now try this full-length passage. The solutions are at the end of this Skillbuilder.

The wild dogs of Africa, like New World wolves and eagles, have suffered a sustained human assault based in part on prejudice. Farmers and ranchers once sought to eradicate all three species because of their occasional raids
Line on livestock, not understanding the importance of predators in controlling
(5) rodents and other pests. All three species have approached the edge of extinction because of this ill-founded human hatred. African wild dogs, however, have endured an especially virulent extermination campaign based on their undeserved reputation as vicious creatures whose demise would do the world good.

(10) *Lycaon pictus,* a species distantly relative to the wolf, used to flourish on much of the African subcontinent, but eradication efforts have reduced its huge former range to a few widely scattered remnants. Only a few thousand of the dogs remain, and they face overwhelming threats to survival in spite of the fact that recent studies have restored to them the respect that they
(15) deserve.

It used to be thought that African wild dogs were brutal killing machines. They were thought of as hunters who preferred to kill slowly. Furthermore, they supposedly killed and ate indiscriminately not only their natural prey but humans and even their own kind. But recent first-person and filmed observa-
(20) tions have proved that a wild dog kill is just as clean and quick as the kill of most other predators. Furthermore, observers in close contact with the dogs report virtually no aggression against human beings—or each other.

With some exceptions, cooperative rather than competitive behavior is the norm within African wild dog packs. Young adults lavish attention on
(25) puppies and willingly stay home to babysit while mothers hunt. Feeding the young is a cooperative effort also, as adults will provide them with meals of regurgitated food. Even gorging on a fresh kill, which in some other species is punctuated by snarls and nips, is a quiet, orderly process. In feeding, a hierarchy is observed without having to be enforced. And although there are
(30) sometimes special circumstances that result in one pack member killing oth-ers, cannibalism is nonexistent among these animals.

Even with the tide of opinion running in its favor, *Lycaon pictus* faces a perilous future. Lions and other predators kill large numbers of the dogs every year, as do humans, especially farmers trying to protect their live- (35) stock. Recent large-scale commercial cattle ranching poses an even greater threat to the survival of this threatened species. As ranchers fence off huge parcels of land, it becomes harder and harder for predators to survive. The few remaining African wild dogs may not be able to overcome this last onslaught against their existence.

1. Which of the following is the best title for this passage?

    A. "The Wild Dog—Misunderstood and Endangered"
    B. "Why Humans Hate Predators"
    C. "The Attractive Qualities of the Wild Dog"
    D. "Rash Judgment and Encroachment—Humans against Nature"

2. Which of the following is **not** mentioned in the passage as a fact of *Lycaon pictus* life?

    E. The consuming of partially digested food
    F. Caregiving by pack members other than parents
    G. Infant care by both parents
    H. A system of organization by rank

3. Which of the following most precisely explains the function served by the mention of wolves and eagles in the passage?

    A. A sobering reminder of how various human activities can endanger other creatures
    B. Pointing out that wolves and eagles have been hated even more than wild dogs
    C. Comparison and contrast of New World species and *Lycaon pictus*
    D. Showing how misunderstanding causes unreasoning hatred of humans against predators

4. Which of the following is the greatest present threat to the African wild dog?

    E. Unreasoning human hatred
    F. Predators, including lions
    G. Farmers protecting their livestock
    H. Reduction of open range

5. Which of the following best expresses the author's attitude toward behaviors within the dog pack?

    A. Disapproval of the killing within the pack
    B. Admiration of the pack members' mutually supportive behaviors
    C. Amusement at the idea of wild dog babysitters
    D. Relief to know that cannibalism does not exist

6. According to the passage, which of the following best sums up the place of young in a pack of African wild dogs?

    E. An unwelcome burden on younger pack members
    F. Creatures to be protected, loved, and nurtured
    G. Welcome but essentially disposable features of pack life
    H. Creatures to be supported by any means, even by an adult's starvation

(Answers are on page 110.)

You're now ready for the Reading Practice Tests. As you work through them, you may find yourself making some alterations to the procedure recommended in the Skillbuilder. This is fine! The techniques presented here work well for most test-takers, but you are an individual, and through practice you will find what works best for you.

Answer Explanations

KEY ELEMENTS EXERCISES (PAGE 101)

    1. Inference. Words and phrases like *probable* and *most likely* usually indicate inference questions.
    2. Main Idea. This wording is frequently used in the question asking for the main idea of a passage.
    3. Fact. This question asks for a specific detail stated in the passage.
    4. Fact. This question asks for a specific detail stated in the passage.
    5. Inference. The question asks for something that has been *suggested* or inferred—not stated.
    6. Main Idea. A good title refers to the main idea.
    7. Main Idea. This question asks not for the main idea of the entire passage, but rather for the main idea of several separate pieces of information.
    8. Fact. Like 3 and 4, this questions asks for a specific detail.
    9. Inference. A word-definition question usually requires you to use stated information to figure out, or infer, the meaning of a word.
    10. Fact. The question asks for a specific detail.

PURPOSE AND FOCUS EXERCISES (PAGES 98–99)

    1. Main idea. **(D)** A is inaccurate because the paragraph explains a result of the revolution. It does not tell of events making up a history. B is also inaccurate because the paragraph says nothing about causes and mentions only one result. C is incorrect because the paragraph says that the monarchy was later restored. Even if C were accurate, though, it would be an incorrect choice because it is too narrow. Most of the content concerns the middle class, not the monarchy. D is both accurate and complete.

    2. Inference. **(F)** E is incorrect because it is exaggerated. Only one reversal is mentioned. **Hint:** An exaggerated answer is always incorrect. G is inaccurate because the passage actually suggests that the monarchy and aristocracy were allies. H is a correct statement, but nothing in the passage suggests it. F is correct because although dissatisfaction is not stated, it is suggested by the fact of a counter-revolution.

3. Main idea. **(C)** A is inaccurate because no outcome is given except the removal and restoration of the monarchy. B is too broad. Only the English middle class is mentioned, and its evolution only in power. D is too broad; the passage doesn't discuss Europe as a whole, and only one social change. C accurately covers all the information in the passage.

4. Inference. **(F)** A contradicts information given in the passage. G is incorrect because it is exaggerated—"important" does not indicate nearly as much strength as "dominant." H is incorrect because, although Parliament did restore the monarchy, the passage does not suggest that the middle class controlled Parliament. F is correct because of the statement that the English middle class gained power by "evolution rather than revolution."

5. Fact. **(D)** This question requires you to be sure that the passage states supporting information for the choice. A is incorrect because the passage makes no mention of a counter-revolution in England. B is incorrect because although Charles I was the father of Charles II, this fact is not stated in the passage. Also, the death of Charles I is not mentioned. C is not mentioned in the passage. D is correct because Charles I is the king who was removed, and Charles II was installed in the restoration of the monarchy. Therefore, he must have been the next king after Charles I.

6. Fact. **(G)** This is an example of a question that requires you to use the answer choices to find the correct response. A quick rereading of the passage will verify every choice except G. Notice that the answer choices are *paraphrased*. That is, they are not word-for-word repetitions of the statements in the passage.

PITFALLS EXERCISES (PAGES 103–104)

1. Main idea. **(A)** Everything in the passage directly or indirectly concerns the excellence of the violins of Stradivari. B, C, and D are too narrow.

2. Fact. **(G)** Here is a question in which the *incorrect* answers are the ones stated in the passage. It is also an exception to the rule against looking at the answer choices. G is correct because although it is stated that Stradivari made these other instruments, it is not *suggested in the passage* that this experience is a possible factor in the excellence of his violins. The other answers are all stated in the passage. **Hint:** Sometimes you have to look in more than one place to find all the stated facts or suggested ideas.

3. Inference. **(D)** A, B, and C are exaggerated. D is correct because the Guaneri violins, rivals of the Stradivarius instruments, were made during the same period whose weather may have produced a denser wood. C is also an example of an answer that may seem true, but is an incorrect choice. You may remember reading about a "little ice age" in Europe during this period of history. The language of the passage, however, doesn't suggest weather extreme enough to be called an ice age.

4. Fact. **(H)** Although the passage uses the word *perhaps,* this can be considered a fact question because the reader does not have to draw an inference. The answer is stated in lines 15–16.

DIFFICULT TO READ PASSAGE EXERCISES (PAGES 104–105)

1. Main Idea. **(D)** A is inaccurate; the content involves both similarities and differences. B is too narrow because only one part of the passage involves the actual fertilization. C is inaccurate, as the passage describes seed production, not plant production. Only seed-bearing plants are discussed, and every aspect of their reproduction is not included. D is correct, as it includes every part of the passage.

2. Inference. **(F)** This is an example of an inference question that requires you to work from the choices. E is incorrect because although the last paragraph (lines 16–20) says that the second coat is absent in the gymnosperm seed, no such suggestion is made about the testa. F is correct because the word *tender* is used to describe the seed, and the words *strong* and *hard* are used to describe the testa that covers the seed. G and H both contradict information given in the passage. G contradicts the statement (lines 17–18) that the testa develops from the outer covering of the ovule. H contradicts the statement (line 19) that the tegumen is *within* the testa.

3. Fact. **(D)** The correct answer is stated in lines 9–10.

4. Fact/Inference. **(H)** All of the other choices are stated in the second paragraph. The first paragraph mentions ovary production by angiosperms but implies that gymnosperms do not produce ovaries, so H doesn't correctly state the aspect of reproduction. Having verified that the other choices are given, you may have simply chosen H by the process of elimination. In a case like this, though, it's a good idea to double-check before recording the answer. The double-check takes you to a different paragraph from the other choices. Remember, you may have to look at more than one paragraph to find a given answer.

WRAP-UP EXERCISES (PAGES 106–108)

1. Main Idea. **(A)** B and C are too narrow. D is too broad because "nature" involves much more than the subject of the passage, one species only. A involves all the content of the passage and no more than that.

2. Fact. **(G)** All the other choices are stated in the fourth paragraph.

3. Inference. **(D)** A is too broad because the context does not involve "various activities." B is inaccurate according to the last sentence of the first paragraph (lines 6–9). C is too broad, as only one aspect is compared and contrasted—not the entire species. D is correct in the context of the sentences that discuss wolves and eagles.

4. Fact. **(H)** The correct answer is given in lines 36–37.

5. Inference. **(B)** This is an inference question that requires you to recognize the author's tone, or attitude. B is correct because of the positive language used throughout the fourth paragraph, where wild dog behavior is discussed. There is no language expressing disapproval (A) or amusement (C). D is not necessarily untrue, but it is too narrow, involving only the last sentence in the paragraph.

6. Inference. **(F)** E contradicts the word "willingly" in line 25. G is incorrect because there is no suggestion that the young are considered disposable. H is exaggerated—there is no suggestion that the adults who give up food are harming themselves in the process. F is correct because the words "loved" and "nurtured" describe the behavior depicted in lines 25–27.

The SHSAT Mathematics section includes topics from arithmetic, basic algebra, some elementary geometry, and a little probability and statistics. (The ninth-year version also includes some trigonometry.) Many questions test your knowledge of basic concepts. However, there are also some challenging problems that test your ability to think creatively and apply what you know in what may seem to be new and unfamiliar situations.

This Skillbuilder is divided into three sections:

- **Mathematical Problem Analysis**

  Tips and strategies for the Mathematics section of the SHSAT

- **The Math Skills Diagnoser**

  A set of six "Diagnosers" to help you identify, correct, and eliminate some frequently made errors

- **Some Basic Terms and Concepts You Should Know**

  A compact review of important basic terms, concepts, and formulas

SECTION 1
MATHEMATICAL PROBLEM ANALYSIS

Tips and Strategies

The best way to become a confident problem solver is to carefully practice a lot of well-selected problems.

This book contains carefully constructed problems designed to help you succeed. Some problems are very challenging and will require you to really stretch. But like a good athlete in training, you won't improve without pushing yourself beyond what you think are your limits. Sometimes even the best of athletes can benefit from a little coaching. So we provide detailed solutions, tips, strategies, and advice.

In this section you will find practical guidance regarding the Mathematics section of the test, including

- General advice
- How to sharpen your problem-solving skills
- Illustrative problems and solutions

General Advice
WORK CAREFULLY!

It's not only how much you practice, but also the quality of the practice.

A regular practice schedule will permit you to improve steadily. Don't cram! It simply won't work for this type of exam.

Rehearse for the actual test by doing the practice exams in this book *strictly according to the given instructions and time limits.*

When you study, avoid distractions such as TV, radio, and so on. Don't rush. Pay attention to details. Work neatly. Carefully review solutions. For extra practice, redo the problems you get wrong.

BE ORGANIZED—BE NEAT—BE ALERT

Don't be "out of control." Many errors can be avoided by simply being careful about how you write or draw. Be well organized both mentally and on paper. Remember that a careless error is still an error!

Familiarize yourself with the test directions and format. Diagrams may not be drawn to scale. Check the test directions on test day to be sure of this.

Read the questions carefully. Pay particular attention to what each question is asking.

CHALLENGE YOURSELF

The SHSAT is designed to be a challenging test. To really be prepared, practice on challenging problems.

MAKE THAT CALCULATOR DISAPPEAR

As of the date of publication of this book, calculators are NOT permitted on the SHSAT. Therefore, do not rely on your calculator. No test problem will require the use of a calculator.

KNOW THOSE BASIC FORMULAS

Formulas will NOT be provided in the SHSAT test booklet. Commit them to memory. Check Section 3 for a list of some of the basic formulas.

KNOW YOUR MATH VOCABULARY

You have to be familiar with basic math vocabulary. Technical terms such as *consecutive integers, highest common factor, prime number, absolute value, parallel lines, trapezoid,* and many other math terms must be at your fingertips. You are expected to know them. They will NOT be provided in the test booklet. Check Section 3 for some important basic terms and concepts.

USE THE CHOICES WISELY

Learn how to make the most of the given choices.

For many problems, it is best to solve the problem fully before looking at the choices.

For some problems, it is absolutely necessary to look at the choices and make them part of the problem-solving process. Be aware, however, that some choices typically reflect common errors made in problem solving.

More details about using the choices appear later in this section.

IS THE ANSWER REASONABLE?

Always ask yourself whether or not the result that you got makes sense.
More details regarding this appear later in this section.

PACING

During the actual test, follow these general rules:

- When you find the correct choice, STOP! Don't waste time checking the other choices.
- Don't give up too soon on any one question, but also don't dwell on any one question for too long. Keep moving. You're aiming at achieving the greatest number of correct answers.
- Remember that the questions are not arranged in strict order of difficulty. There are some easy questions on the later part of the test.
- Use the **?** **X** system as you go (see page 42). At the end of the test, be sure you have not left any blanks. There is no penalty for wrong answers.

How to Analyze a Problem

There are four basic steps involved in solving problems.

1. **Determine precisely what the problem calls for.** Every problem calls for something specific. What do you have to find? What is the value of x that solves the equation? Which number has the largest value? It helps to *underline it, circle it,* or *write it down.* The value of this simple process cannot be overestimated. This forces you to focus on the specific goal of the problem and prepare a solution strategy.

2. **Determine what information is given.** Note carefully what is given or implied. What do you have to work with? This focuses your attention on the ingredients that will be used in solving the problem.

3. **Think about what additional information or mathematical tools you may need.** For example, do you need a special formula or do you need to know certain properties relating to a geometric figure? Math problem solvers often refer to their collection of facts, formulas, and skills as their "toolbox." In this step you start to think about the tools that may prove useful.

4. **Carry out a plan to solve the problem.** Decide specifically how to bridge the gap between what is given and what is called for.

In short, always think

- What do I want
- What do I have
- What do I need
- What do I do

Knowing the basic problem-solving steps provides you with a structured approach. Of course, your ability to solve problems will only improve with experience and practice.

Be an Active Problem Solver

Problems don't solve themselves. Just looking at a problem won't get it done. You usually have to do something to activate the problem-solving process.

Be an active problem solver. Put your pencil in motion.

Depending on the problem, you could

- use variables to represent unknown quantities
- translate verbal information into mathematical symbols (for example, writing an equation that expresses the words of the problem)
- replace variables with numbers
- try special cases
- note other information that may be needed (for example, formulas)
- mark diagrams (for example, labeling congruent segments or angles)
- transfer numerical information from the text of the problem to the diagram (for example, inserting the given degree measure of an angle)
- draw a well-labeled diagram if none is supplied

Actively doing something can launch thoughts and ideas that get your problem-solving engine started.

Examples

1. READING THE QUESTION

One of the most frequent reasons for making careless and avoidable errors is simply not reading a question or problem carefully.

In this first set of examples, you will see illustrations of how important it is to *determine precisely what the question calls for.* This is the first step in carefully reading, interpreting, and ultimately solving a problem.

➥ Example 1.1 _____

If $x + y = 11$, what is the value of $4x + 4y$?

In this problem it is crucial to determine exactly what is being asked. By doing this, you are alerted to what is NOT being asked.

What do you want to find? It is easy to be distracted and think that you have to find the values of x and y individually before obtaining the sum of $4x$ and $4y$. You don't.

Since $x + y = 11$, simply multiply both sides of this equation by 4. This produces $4x + 4y = 44$. You are done!

That wasn't too difficult. Here is a slight variation on this theme. Remember to use those four basic steps.

➡ Example 1.2_____

If $x + 2y = 5$ and $2x + y = 31$, what is the value of $x + y$?

Once again in this problem it is crucial to determine exactly what is called for. By doing this, you are again alerted to what is NOT asked.

You have to find the value of $x + y$. Does this mean that you must necessarily find the individual values of x and y first? You could. However, it is easier to find the value of $x + y$ in two steps:

since	$x + 2y = 5,$
and	$2x + y = 31,$
adding produces	$3x + 3y = 36$

Dividing both sides by 3, $x + y = 12$. You are finished!

The fact that the problem calls for the value of $x + y$, and not for the value of either x or y, is a clue. Make it work for you.

➡ Example 1.3_____

After completing $\frac{1}{3}$ of a trip, Tony still had 12 miles to go. How long was the trip?

You are asked to find the length of the entire trip.

What do you know?

Tony has 12 miles to go after completing $\frac{1}{3}$ of the trip.

The 12 miles left to go is therefore the remainder of the trip, or $\frac{2}{3}$ of the trip. If 12 miles is $\frac{2}{3}$ of the trip, then 6 miles is $\frac{1}{3}$ of the trip. The entire trip must be 18 miles.

➡ Example 1.4_____

If $12x - 19 = 1999$, what is the value of each of the following?

(a) $12x - 15$
(b) $12x + 19$

(a) The question asks you to find the value of $12x - 15$. Most people would first solve for x and then substitute that value into the expression $12x - 15$. Normally this procedure is fine. But the problem did not call for x. It called for $12x - 15$. This may be a signal that you can find $12x - 15$ directly.

$12x - 15$ can be obtained from $12x - 19$ by simply adding 4. Then $12x - 15 = (12x - 19) + 4 = (1999) + 4 = 2003$.

(b) Notice this time that $12x + 19$ can be obtained from $12x - 19$ by adding 38. Therefore, $12x + 19 = 12x - 19 + 38 = 1999 + 38 = 2037$.

In each of the previous examples, notice how helpful it was to first identify and focus on precisely what was called for.

For extra practice, try these. *Answers are on page 126.*

➡️ **Example 1.5** _____

If $53 - 2x = 1999$, find the value of $65 - 2x$.

➡️ **Example 1.6** _____

If $x + 2y + 3z = 53$ and $3x + 2y + z = 52$, what is the value of $x + y + z$?

➡️ **Example 1.7** _____

Four hot dogs and a soft drink cost $6.30, whereas one hot dog and four soft drinks cost $4.20. What is the total cost of one hot dog and one soft drink?

➡️ **Example 1.8** _____

(a) 30 is 20% of what number?
(b) 20% of 30 is what number?

In examples (a) and (b), accurately determining what is being asked is the key. It is easy to misinterpret the question.

(a) Using x to represent the "number" clarifies the question. "30 is 20% of what number" becomes 30 = 20% of x, or $30 = .2x$. Note that "of" indicates multiplication (see chart on page 159). This equation is equivalent to $300 = 2x$, so $x = 150$.
　　It is wise to do a quick check. Is 30 equal to 20% of 150? A little arithmetic verifies the result.

(b) Use the same technique illustrated in (a). This time we have 20% of 30 is x. $(.2)(30) = x$, so $x = 6$.

As you read each problem, concentrate on what you are actually trying to find. In (a) the number is such that 30 is 20% of that number. We are looking for a number that is LARGER than 30. In (b), the number is 20% of 30, so the number is SMALLER than 30.

2. USING A SPECIAL CASE

Sometimes you find that you have no idea of what to do or where to begin. Perhaps the numbers are too large, or maybe the wording is just too complicated. Frequently it helps to consider a special case. Use some *well-selected* numbers. To get some idea of how to do this, look over the next group of examples.

➡️ **Example 2.1** _____

The sum of an even number of odd numbers is

(A) always even
(B) always odd
(C) sometimes even, sometimes odd

(continued)

First, try some appropriate numbers to get some insight into the problem. Since we want an *even* number of *odd* numbers, consider, for example, the special case $3 + 5 + 9 + 15$. There is no special reason for choosing these particular odd numbers. Just be sure to select an even number of them. Notice that their sum, 32, is even. If you had to guess at this point, you might pick choice A. However, one example may be insufficient for drawing a valid conclusion. Try a few more special cases. In each case, the resulting sum is even. There is mounting evidence that choice **A** is correct.

Here's the math. Recall that the sum of any two odd numbers must be even, and that the sum of any number of even numbers is also even. Therefore, by pairing the odd numbers, we obtain an even sum.

Using a special case quickly suggested what was happening.

TIP: When trying to determine whether some combination of integers is odd or even, you may always use 1 to typify any odd number and 0 to typify any even number. For example, the sum of three odd numbers and an even number is typified by $1 + 1 + 1 + 0 = 3$, which is odd.

➡ Example 2.2

What is 10% of 10^{10}?

A. 1
B. 10
C. 10^5
D. 10^9

Here you may be thinking, "What can I gain by using a special case? The number given is a fixed number—it's already a special case!" The number 10^{10} is a very large number (a 1 followed by 10 zeros), and the presence of the exponent can also prove distracting.

Replace 10^{10} by any reasonably small number. Then let's see what's going on.

What is 10% of 80? What is 10% of 100?

It's easy to find 10% of a number. Just divide the number by 10. Apply this to finding 10% of 10^{10}. Divide 10^{10} by 10.

Since $10^{10} = 10 \times 10 \times 10 \times 10 \times 10 \times 10 \times 10 \times 10 \times 10 \times 10$, the result of dividing 10^{10} by 10 is 10^9 (one of the 10s cancels). The correct answer is **D**.

➡ Example 2.3

The sides of a square are each multiplied by 3 to form a new square. If the area of the original square was K, then the area of the new square is

A. K^3
B. $3K$
C. $6K$
D. $9K$

This example is perfect for using a special case. Try a few values for the side of the square. Don't worry about K at this point. For example, if the original side was 2, the original area was 4. Tripling the side to 6 results in an area of 36, which is 9 times the original area.

Using a starting value of 5 for the original side produces an original area of 25. But tripling 5 to 15 results in an area of 225. Once again this is 9 times the original area.

In each case the new area is 9 times the original area. The answer appears to be choice **D**.

The math goes like this. Let s be the original side. The original area is $K = s^2$. Tripling the side to $3s$ produces a new area of $(3s)^2$, which is $9s^2$ or $9K$.

Example 2.4

The smallest of five consecutive integers is represented by $y - 3$. What is the largest of these integers, in terms of y?

Don't be distracted by the presence of a variable. Look at any set of five consecutive integers. For example 4, 5, 6, 7, and 8, or 23, 24, 25, 26, and 27. The largest integer can always be obtained by simply adding 4 to the first integer. The answer is $y - 3 + 4$, which is $y + 1$.

Example 2.5

N granola bars cost T cents. What is the cost of K of these granola bars?

It can be difficult to solve a problem when many variables are involved. But see how easy it is to do the following similar problem in which the variables have been replaced by numbers.
Three granola bars cost 90 cents. What is the cost of 8 granola bars?

Find the cost of 1 granola bar, $\frac{90}{3}$, and multiply the result by 8.

The answer to the original problem is $(\frac{T}{N})(K)$. When using numbers for a special case, leave all computations in unsimplified form. This reveals the underlying process.

Example 2.6

How many integers are there from 11 to 111 inclusive?

It is surprising how many people get this wrong. The correct answer is 101. The point of using the special case in this problem is to check the soundness of your initial reasoning. Try some easy-to-check numbers. Certainly you can count the number of integers from 11 to 15 inclusive. Subtract 11 from 15, but add back 1 because subtracting fails to include the smaller number. The method that produced this correct answer of 5 will transfer to the original problem.

There is no reason to lose points when you can check using a simple special case.

Try these examples for extra practice. *Answers are on page 126.*

Example 2.7

If a two-digit number is decreased by the sum of its digits, then the resulting difference *must* be divisible by

A. 2
B. 4
C. 5
D. 9

Example 2.8

In the formula $A = bh$, if b is tripled and h is quadrupled, then A is multiplied by N. Compute N.

$A = 2 \times 4 = 8$

$6 \times 16 = 96$

Example 2.9

If y is an even integer, which of the following *may* be an even integer?

A. $\dfrac{y}{2}$
B. $y^2 + 3y + 5$
C. $5y + 11$
D. $6y - 7$

Example 2.10

The original price of an item is discounted by 10% for a sale. A week later the sale price is discounted an *additional* 30% for a clearance sale. What single discount applied to the original price would be equivalent to those two successive discounts?

3. USING THE CHOICES

How should you use the given choices to your best advantage?

- In certain cases, it is best not to look at the choices until you have first worked the problem.
- Sometimes the choices themselves can provide valuable insight into an otherwise difficult problem.
- Finally, there are some questions that require you to try each choice. In these questions, you must actually look at each choice and make decisions.

How can you recognize these different types of situations? When you do use the choices, where should you start? The following examples will answer these questions and provide you with helpful tips.

When It Is Best Not to Try the Choices First

Example 3.1

The mean of 13, 17, and y is the same as the mean of 8, 14, 3, and $3y$. What is the value of y?

A. $\dfrac{2}{3}$
B. $\dfrac{5}{2}$
C. $\dfrac{17}{3}$
D. 9

(continued)

Recall that the mean (average) of a set of values is the sum of the values divided by the number of values. The mean of 13, 17, and y is $\frac{(30+y)}{3}$, and the mean of 8, 14, 3, and $3y$ is $\frac{(25+3y)}{4}$. This leads to the equation $\frac{(30+y)}{3} = \frac{(25+3y)}{4}$. Trying to finish this problem by trying each choice could prove very time consuming and could also lead to arithmetical errors. So it is best here not to check choices first. Solve the equation, producing an answer of $y = 9$. This is choice **D**.

> **TIP:** When a problem involves a lot of computation, or the offered choices are not simple to use, or one of the choices is "none of these," it may be wise to do the problem first before looking at the choices.

When It May Be Helpful to Try the Choices

➥ Example 3.2

The sum of five consecutive multiples of 7 is 350.
The smallest of these is

A. 28
B. 35
C. 42
D. 56

You want to find the smallest of five consecutive multiples of 7 such that their sum is 350. An algebraic solution would solve the problem. However, in this problem, it is fastest to simply try the choices. Pick a choice, list the next four consecutive multiples of 7, add, and see if the result is 350. The computations are quick and easy.

What guidelines should be followed when trying choices? Where should you begin?

> **TIP:** The choices are generally arranged in either increasing or decreasing order of size. When trying the choices, it is often best to begin with choice B or C.

Let's start with choice C. If 42 were the smallest of the five multiples of seven, then the others would be 49, 56, 63, and 70. Their sum is 210. Choice C is incorrect. But we can learn much from this incorrect answer! It is too small. Try larger values. Thus, choices A and B are immediately eliminated. Try choice D. $56 + 63 + 70 + 77 + 84 = 350$. Choice **D** is the correct answer.

Here's one method using algebra. Let the smallest of the five consecutive multiples of 7 be represented by s. The next four are $s+7$, $s+14$, $s+21$, and $s+28$. The sum of all five is $5s + 70$. Setting $5s + 70 = 350$ and solving for s, we have $s = 56$.

When It Helps to Preview the Choices

➥ Example 3.3

The product $5 \times 6 \times 7 \times 8 \times 9 \times 10 \times 11 \times 12$ is divisible by

A. 2^{10}
B. 2^{9}
C. 2^{8}
D. 2^{7}

In this example, previewing the choices provides insightful clues. Without looking at the choices, we really have no idea of what to do.

The choices direct us to look for the indicated power of 2 that is a factor of the given product. We look at those numbers that contribute twos. In the original product, 6 contributes one factor of 2. 8, being $2 \times 2 \times 2$, contributes three factors. 10 contributes one, and 12 contributes two. All together, there is a net contribution of seven twos. Therefore 2^7, choice **D**, is the correct answer. Notice that no higher power of 2 will divide the original product.

When You Must Check the Choices

➥ Example 3.4_____

X: $.5 < (.5)^2$

Y: $\frac{3}{11} > \frac{8}{29}$

Z: $\frac{111}{333} = \frac{1}{3}$

E. X, Y, and Z are all true.
F. Z is true.
G. X, Y, and Z are all false.
H. X and Y are true.

This example actually requires that you check the choices. Previewing the choices alerts us to the fact that we will have to test the validity of each numerical statement X, Y, and Z. Once this is done, we can select the appropriate choice. Doing the math reveals that

X is false. $(.5)^2 = .25$, and .5 is more than .25.

Y is false.   If a, b, c, and d are positive numbers, then $\left(\frac{a}{b}\right) > \left(\frac{c}{d}\right)$ only if $ad > bc$. In this case 3×29 is *less than* 11×8. Notice how much easier it is to compare the sizes of fractions using this method rather than trying to express each fraction using a common denominator.

Z is true. $\frac{111}{333} = \frac{111(1)}{111(3)} = \frac{1}{3}$

The correct answer is choice **F**.

Try these for extra practice. *Answers are on page 126.*

➥ Example 3.5_____

Which of the following is *closest* to .14?

A. $\frac{1}{6}$

B. $\frac{1}{7}$

C. $\frac{1}{8}$

D. $\frac{1}{9}$

The smallest positive integer value of N such that $\frac{3}{11} > \frac{8}{N}$ is

A. 33
B. 32
C. 31
D. 30

4. ESTIMATION

In some problems it is helpful to actually approximate numerical values.

➡ **Example 4.1**

Which of the following is *closest* to .18?

A. $\frac{10}{61}$

B. $\frac{10}{71}$

C. $\frac{10}{81}$

D. $\frac{10}{91}$

You have to find some reasonable way to estimate the given values. Try to approximate each of the choices. In each case, the denominators of the given fractions are close to multiples of 10. To efficiently estimate the value of the fractions, use the following approximations:

A. $\frac{10}{60}$ or $\frac{1}{6}$

B. $\frac{10}{70}$ or $\frac{1}{7}$

C. $\frac{10}{80}$ or $\frac{1}{8}$

D. $\frac{10}{90}$ or $\frac{1}{9}$

Now look at the value .18, which is just a little less than .20 or $\frac{1}{5}$. The best choice appears to be A, which is close to $\frac{1}{6}$. The other choices are all smaller values, and therefore are not as close. Double-check, by expressing $\frac{1}{6}$ as .1666 . . . .

➡ **Example 4.2**

Let $P = \sqrt{3} + \sqrt{5}$, $Q = \sqrt{5} + \sqrt{3}$, and $R = \sqrt{10} - \sqrt{2}$, then

A. $P < Q < R$
B. $P < R < Q$
C. $Q < P < R$
D. $R < Q < P$

This example looks more ferocious than it actually is. Let's do some estimation. First note that $\sqrt{5}$ is a little more than 2. Write this as $\sqrt{5} = 2+$. Similarly, we approximate $\sqrt{3}$ as 1+, and $\sqrt{2}$ as 1+. Keep in mind that $\sqrt{3}$ is greater than $\sqrt{2}$. With these we can write

$$P = \sqrt{5+}, \; Q = \sqrt{6+}, \text{ and } R = \sqrt{8+}.$$

The answer is then **A**. $P < Q < R$

5. IS THE ANSWER REASONABLE?

When you finally arrive at what you think is the answer to a problem, you should always ask yourself whether that answer makes sense. This simple but critical part of problem solving is a powerful way to avoid careless wrong answers.

➥ **Example 5.1** _____

The value of $4^5 + 4^5 + 4^5 + 4^5$ is

A. 4^{20}
B. 16^5
C. 16^{20}
D. 4^6

This particular problem invites error! Let's first look at a commonly occuring wrong answer, namely choice A. We apply the "is the answer reasonable" test to choice A as follows:

$$4^5 = 4 \times 4 \times 4 \times 4 \times 4 = 16 \times 16 \times 4$$

which is about 1000 (actually 1024). The expression in the question is $4^5 + 4^5 + 4^5 + 4^5$, which is about 4000. Now consider the value of 4^{20}. This is an extremely large number, far more than 4000. It is not a reasonable answer.

Can you now determine which other choices are also not reasonable?

Here's the math. The expression $4^5 + 4^5 + 4^5 + 4^5$ is the sum of 4^5 four times. Therefore $4^5 + 4^5 + 4^5 + 4^5 = 4 \times 4^5 = 4^6$. The answer is choice **D**.

➥ **Example 5.2** _____

The value of $\frac{9090}{90}$ is

A. 11
B. 100
C. 101
D. 111

This relatively simple arithmetic problem can easily lead to careless mistakes, especially if you are in a hurry. A common error is illustrated by choice A. Before you commit to choice A, ask yourself whether 11 is really a reasonable answer.

$\frac{9090}{90}$ is about $\frac{9090}{100}$, which is approximately 90. Choice A must be incorrect.

The actual answer obtained by dividing 90 into 9090 is 101. Be careful when cancelling. Don't neglect the middle zero. The correct answer is choice **C**.

6. PSEUDO-OPERATIONS

To test your ability to deal with new mathematical situations, a special type of question is often present. In this type of question, a new definition, symbol, or set of symbols is introduced.

The typical question appears more difficult than it actually is because there is something unfamiliar present.

➡ **Example 6.1** _____

For positive numbers x and y, define $x \circledR y$ to mean $x^2 - 2y$. Find the value of $5 \circledR 3$.

   A. 69
   B. 19
   C. 16
   D. 13

Simply compute $5 \circledR 3 = 5^2 - (2)(3) = 25 - 6 = 19$. This is choice **B**.

A variation on this theme employs a slightly more complicated set of options.

➡ **Example 6.2** _____

For all positive integers a and b, define $<a, b>$ to mean

  I. ab if a and b are *both* even or *both* odd.
  II. $a^2 - b^2$ if *one* is even and the *other* is odd.

Which of the following has the *largest* value?

   A. $<4, 4>$
   B. $<5, 4>$
   C. $<6, 4>$
   D. $<7, 2>$

You must evaluate each choice and compare. To compute the value of each choice, first decide which of the two rules applies.

   $<4,4>$ requires rule I and has a value of $4 \times 4 = 16$
   $<5,4>$ requires rule II and has a value of $25 - 16 = 9$
   $<6,4>$ requires rule I and has a value of $6 \times 4 = 24$
   $<7,2>$ requires rule II and has a value of $49 - 4 = 45$
   The answer is choice **D**.

SUMMARY OF BASIC TIPS AND STRATEGIES

When Studying

- Practice under conditions that are similar to the actual test conditions. Good rehearsals make for good performances.
- Make your study time count. Be focused, alert, and attentive. Do your work in a neat, organized manner.
- Familiarize yourself completely with the test format, directions, and question types. Know your basics and math vocabulary. Do not use a calculator when you practice.
- Read problems with care. Use the four-step approach to problem solving. What do I want? What do I have? What do I need? What do I do? When you think you have solved a problem, ask whether your answer is reasonable.
- Practice under time limits. Learn to pace yourself.
- Practice challenging problems and repeat them to sharpen skills. Don't give up too soon. Persistence can inspire creative, productive thinking.
- For extra practice, redo problems you got wrong.
- Be confident! With proper study, you will be well prepared for the test.

When Taking the Test

- Work carefully. Be neat and well organized. Use the test booklet and the scratch paper for your work. Be in control.
- Do all calculations carefully the first time. Don't waste time correcting avoidable mistakes. It's sometimes helpful to quickly estimate before actually calculating to give yourself an idea of an approximate value.
- Read the questions carefully. Determine precisely what the problem calls for, what is given, what you may need, and what you have to do to answer the question. Always ask yourself whether the answer is reasonable.
- Be an active problem solver. Combine thought and action. Actively mark diagrams, use variables to represent unknown quantities, try numbers, look at a special case, and so on. Do something to get your problem-solving engine started.
- Remember that on this test, diagrams might not be drawn to scale.
- The questions are not necessarily in order of difficulty. Easy questions may appear in the later part of the test.
- Use the choices advantageously. Make the choices work for you.

    Many problems should first be solved completely. Then find your answer among the choices. This is often better and faster than testing each choice to determine if it can fit the question.

    Some problems actually require you to check the choices and/or use the choices as part of the problem-solving process. For some easy questions, checking the choices may prove the fastest. Quickly eliminate choices that are obviously unreasonable.

    In some questions, previewing the choices can offer a clue about how to approach the problem.

When you have found the correct choice, STOP! Don't waste time checking the other choices.

- Don't give up too soon. Some seemingly difficult questions may require extra concentration or insight. In many cases, complex problems combine several simpler steps. Give yourself a chance to fully think, try, and analyze. But don't dwell too long on any one question. Pace yourself. You want to answer as many questions as possible.

- Use the **? X** system as you go. When you have finished the test, be sure you have not left any blanks. Remember that there is no penalty for wrong answers. A guess may yield a correct answer, but a blank cannot.

ANSWERS TO THE EXTRA PROBLEMS

Example 1.5   2011

Example 1.6 $\dfrac{105}{4}$

Example 1.7 $2.10

Example 2.7   Choice **D**

Example 2.8 $N = 12$

Example 2.9   Choice **A**

Example 2.10   37%

Example 3.5   Choice **B**

Example 3.6   Choice **D**

Frequently Made Errors

The Workouts in this section will help you identify, correct, and eliminate some frequently made errors. There are six Workouts and accompanying Follow-ups for extra practice. The Workouts cover some of the basic skills you should know. Workout F contains some additional material for those currently in the ninth grade.

Workout A Arithmetic I
Workout B Arithmetic II
Workout C Algebra
Workout D Geometry
Workout E Graphs and Charts
Workout F 9th Grade Topics

After each Workout you will find detailed solutions that enable you to diagnose and correct any errors. You will then find a set of Follow-up exercises. Use these to check your progress and for additional practice.

Get Ready

For the Workouts to be effective, you must pay careful attention to the time limits. You should not do all of the Workouts in one session.

Get Set

Set proper study conditions.

Work quickly! Don't linger over any one problem. Since these workouts are diagnostic, *avoid random guessing*. Leave out questions you cannot do and return to them later when you review the solutions.

Be sure not to look at the solutions until after you have completed the Workout!

Arithmetic I

Directions for Workout A: 10 Questions   15-Minute Time Limit
Place your answer (A, B, or C) in the answer space provided.

1. $\frac{1}{2} + \frac{1}{3} = \frac{5}{6}$ A. $\frac{2}{5}$ B. $\frac{5}{6}$ C. $\frac{2}{6}$

2. $(7)(5) - 5(5 - 8) =$ A. 50   B. –90   C. 20

   $35 + 15$

3. $\sqrt{16} + \sqrt{9} =$ A. $\sqrt{25}$ B. 25   C. 7

   $4 + 3$

4. $(2^3)(3^3) =$ A. 6^3 B. 6^6 C. 6^9

   $8 \times 27 =$

5. In scientific notation, $387 \times 100{,}000$ is represented as   A. 3.87×10^3 B. 3.87×10^7 C. 387×10^5

6. $(-12)(-6) \div (-3) =$ A. –24   B. 8   C. –6

   $2^3 \cdot 3^3 = 6^3$

7. $(.\overline{3})(.\overline{6})$ A. $.\overline{18}$ B. $.\overline{2}$ C. 1

8. N granola bars cost 84 cents. At this price, 21 granola bars would cost   A. $17.64   B. $4N$ C. $\frac{\$17.64}{N}$

9. $\frac{5}{6} \div \frac{3}{20} =$ A. $\frac{50}{9}$ B. $\frac{1}{8}$ C. $\frac{9}{50}$

10. $\frac{21 + 56}{7} = 11$ A. 59   B. 11   C. 29

STOP! This is the end of Workout A.

1	2	3	4	5	6	7	8	9	10
✓	✓	✓	✓	B	✓	B	C	✓	✓

$\left[\dfrac{\frac{5}{6}}{\frac{3}{20}}\right] = \dfrac{(5)(20)}{(6)(3)}$

$\dfrac{5(10)}{(3)(3)} = \dfrac{50}{9}$

$\frac{1}{3} + \frac{1}{6} = \frac{2+1}{6} = \frac{3}{6}$

Solutions A

#	A	B	C
1	Don't add the numerators and denominators separately. To combine fractions, first get a common denominator.	✓	When expressing the given fractions as equivalent fractions, be sure to adjust the numerators accordingly. $$\frac{1}{2}+\frac{1}{3}=\frac{3}{6}+\frac{2}{6}=\frac{5}{6}$$
2	✓	Be careful not to first subtract 5 from 35. Following the order of operations: $(7)(5) - 5(5 - 8)$ $= (7)(5) - 5(-3)$ $= 35 + 15 = 50.$	Watch the signs! You should be adding 15, not subtracting it.
3	In general, $\sqrt{a}+\sqrt{b}$ does *not* equal $\sqrt{a+b}$. $\sqrt{16}+\sqrt{9}=4+3=7$	You neglected the radical signs.	✓
4	✓	Be careful not to add exponents when the bases are different. $2^3 \cdot 3^3 = 2 \cdot 2 \cdot 2 \cdot 3 \cdot 3 \cdot 3$ $= 6 \cdot 6 \cdot 6 = 6^3.$	Don't be tempted to multiply the exponents in this situation.
5	$387 \times 100{,}000 = 3.87 \times 10{,}000{,}000 = 3.87 \times 10^7.$ **TIP:** You can always rely on an easy example to help you to remember a procedure. For example, 456 is 4.56×10^2. This reminds you of how to move the decimal point.	✓	This expression is not in scientific notation. **FACT:** A number expressed in scientific notation must be written in the form $A \times 10^B$, where $1 \le A < 10$, and B is an integer.
6	✓	You probably divided -12 by -3 AND -6 by -3, and then multiplied.	The -6 should be multiplied by -12 first.
7	Convert the repeated decimals to equivalent fractions first. $\left(\frac{1}{3}\right)\left(\frac{2}{3}\right)=\frac{2}{9}=.222\ldots$ **TIP:** $.111\ldots=\frac{1}{9}$, $.222\ldots=\frac{2}{9}$, $.333\ldots=\frac{3}{9}$ $=\frac{1}{3}$, etc. Yes, .999 . . . *does* equal 1.	✓	Did you *add* by mistake?

#	A	B	C
8	First find the cost of *one* item. It is 84/*N* (total cost divided by the number of items). Thus 21 bars would cost 21 × (84/*N*) = $17.64/*N*.	There is no logical reason to divide 84 by 21.	✓
9	✓	You forgot to "invert" before multiplying.	You inverted the wrong fraction before multiplying. $\left(\frac{5}{6}\right) \div \left(\frac{3}{20}\right) = \left(\frac{5}{6}\right) \times \left(\frac{20}{3}\right) = \frac{50}{9}$ after reducing.
10	When the numerator is a sum, you must either first combine the terms, or divide *each* term of the numerator by the denominator. You have only divided 21 by 7. **TIP:** $\frac{a+b}{c} = \frac{a}{c} + \frac{b}{c}$	✓	See Column A. You only divided the 56 by 7.

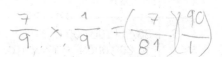

Follow-Up A

Answers are on page 154.

1. $\frac{1}{3} - \frac{1}{4} =$ $\frac{4-3}{12} = \frac{1}{12}$

2. Compute: $(5-3)(8) - 2$ $2 \times 8 = 16 - 2 = 14$

3. Compute: $\sqrt{5^2} - \sqrt{4^2} = 1$

4. Express in scientific notation: 5,430,000,000,000 5.43^{12}

5. $\frac{9}{50} \div \frac{3}{20} =$

6. Compute the value of x if $12^5 = (2)^x (3)^5$. $x = 10$

7. Compute: $(14)(-8) \div (-2)$ $112 \div 2 = 56$

8. Compute: $(.\overline{7})(.\overline{1})(90)$ $.9$

9. $\frac{50-40}{-10} = -1$

10. The total cost of G granola bars is 90 cents. Express the total cost of 3 granola bars in terms of G. $\frac{270}{G}$

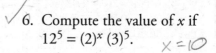

Arithmetic II

Directions for Workout B: 10 Questions   15-Minute Time Limit
Place your answer (A, B, or C) in the answer space provided.

1. The sum of two odd numbers is

   A. always odd   B. always even
   C. sometimes even, sometimes odd

2. The number of primes less than 12 is

   A. 4   B. 5   C. 6

3. Which of the following is divisible
   by 6 but not by 9?

   A. $2^8 \cdot 3^3 \cdot 5^2$ B. $2 \cdot 3 \cdot 5^4$ C. $3^4 \cdot 5^4$

4. How many integers are there from
   17 to 111, including 17 and 111?

   A. 94   B. 95   C. 96

5. What is the greatest common factor
   of $2^3 \times 3^2 \times 5^4$ and $2^2 \times 5^3 \times 7^5$?

   A. $2^3 \times 3^2 \times 5^4$ B. $2 \times 3 \times 5$ C. $2^2 \times 5^3$

6. If 25**Q**781 is divisible by 3, then the
   number of different possible values
   for the digit **Q** is

   A. 1   B. 2   C. 3

7. The least common multiple of
   2, 3, 4, 5, and 6 is

   A. 720   B. 120   C. 60

8. How many integers between 1 and
   400 are multiples of 7?

   A. 56   B. 57   C. 58

9. If $\frac{5}{7} > \frac{8}{N}$ then *N could* be

   A. 10   B. 11   C. 12

10. If the number *N* is a 5-digit prime
    number, which one of the following
    might be a prime number?

    A. $N - 2$ B. $N + 31$ C. $3N + 18$

STOP! This is the end of Workout B.

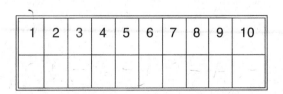

Solutions B

#	A	B	C
1	**TIP:** When checking to determine whether some combination of integers produces an even or odd result, try using some simple numbers. For example, $3 + 5 = 8$ (even).	✓	See Column A and apply the TIP... **TIP:** The sum of two odd numbers is always even. The product of two odd numbers is always odd. **FACT:** 0 is an even number.
2	You neglected to include 2 in your count. **FACT:** The number 2 is the first prime number.	✓	The primes less than 12 are 2, 3, 5, 7, and 11. You may have inadvertently included 1 or 9.
3	$6 (= 2 \cdot 3)$ is a factor of the given expression, but so is $9 (= 3^2)$.	✓	The expression *is not* divisible by 6, and *is* divisible by 9.
4	Compute $111 - 17 = 94$. THEN add back 1 (because subtracting doesn't count the starting number) to get 95. **TIP:** Check your ideas using smaller numbers. For example, if you try to count the number of integers from 7 to 11 inclusive, it's easy to see that $11 - 7$ produces one number too few.	✓	You added back one too many numbers. Check using a smaller set of numbers. (See Column A.)
5	The number 3 is not *common* to both of the given numbers. It cannot be part of the greatest common factor.	The number 3 is not a common factor. Furthermore, there are greater powers of 2 and 5 that are common factors. **FACT:** When integers are expressed as powers of their prime factors, the greatest common factor can be found by multiplying together the *lowest-appearing powers of their common primes.*	✓

#	A	B	C
6	One possible value for Q is 1. However, the question calls for the *number* of possible values.	**FACT:** An integer is divisible by 3 if the *sum of its digits is divisible by 3.* The sum of the digits is 23 + **Q**. Thus if **Q** = 1, 4, or 7, the sum of the digits (24, 27, or 30) is divisible by 3. There are three possibilities. You left out one of them.	✓
7	The LCM is not always found by multiplying the given numbers together. This works only when the individual numbers have no common factor other than 1.	120 is a common multiple since all of the given numbers go into 120. But there is a smaller common multiple.	✓
8	You undercounted.	✓	**TIP:** To count the number of multiples of 7 from 1 to 400, simply divide 400 by 7: *retain the quotient and discard the remainder.* The quotient is the answer.
9	One method is to convert $\frac{5}{7}$ and $\frac{8}{10}$ to equivalent fractions having the same denominator. Clearly $\frac{50}{70}$ is not greater than $\frac{56}{70}$.	You could change $\frac{5}{7}$ and $\frac{8}{11}$ to fractions having 77 as their common denominator, or you could use the powerful method indicated in the following tip. **TIP:** For positive numbers $a, b, c,$ and $d, \frac{a}{b}$ is greater than $\frac{c}{d}$ only if ad is greater than bc. For $\frac{5}{7}$ to be greater than $\frac{8}{N}$, 5 times N must be larger than 7 times 8. For which of the given values of N is $5N > 56$? Choices A and B are thus incorrect.	✓
10	✓ All primes greater than 2 are odd. An unknown odd number, therefore, has the potential to be prime.	Odd + odd = even. But 2 is the only even prime and $N + 31$ is clearly bigger than 2. (See Example 1.)	The number $3N + 18$ is divisible by 3. It can be written as $3(N + 6)$, or it may be thought of as the sum of two multiples of 3, namely $3N$ and 18. The sum of multiples of 3 is a multiple of 3. The only multiple of 3 that is a prime is 3×1.

Follow-Up B

Answers are on page 154.

1. How many odd integers are there from 17 to 59 inclusive?

2. Find the smallest positive integer N such that $\frac{7}{16} < \frac{N}{9}$.

3. What is the smallest positive integer that is a multiple of both $(2^2)(3)$ and $(2)(3^2)$?

4. If 25**Q**781 is a multiple of 9, what is the value of the digit **Q**?

5. How many prime numbers are there whose squares are less than 250?

6. The sum of an odd number of odd numbers is

   (A) always odd
   (B) always even
   (C) sometimes odd, sometimes even

7. What is the greatest common factor of $2^3 \cdot 5^2 \cdot 7^5$ and $5^3 \cdot 7^3 \cdot 11^8$?

8. How many integers between 1 and 40 are multiples of 3 or 7?

9. If p, q, and r are all odd primes, which of the following *might* also be a prime?

   (A) $p^2 - q^2 + 1$
   (B) $pqr + 3$
   (C) $(p + 2)(r + 2) + 1$

10. How many distinct positive integer factors does the number 125 have? (Include 1 and 125.)

Algebra

Directions for Workout C: 10 Questions   15-Minute Time Limit
Place your answer (A, B, or C) in the answer space provided.

1. $7x - x =$ $7x - 1x$ **(A.)** $6x$ **B.** 7 **C.** 6

2. $(y^3)(y^5) =$ $X = +$ **(A.)** y^8 **B.** $2y^8$ **C.** y^{15}

3. If $x = 3$, then $-x^2 =$ $-3^2 -$ **A.** -6 **B.** 9 **C.** -9

   $-x^2$
   $-(3)^2$
   -9

4. If n represents a number, then "5 less than twice a number" may be written as   **(A.)** $5 < 2n$ **B.** $5 - 2n$ **(C.)** $2n - 5$

5. $(2x)^3 =$ **A.** $2x^3$ **B.** $6x^3$ **(C.)** $8x^3$

6. If $3 - x > 10$, then   **A.** $x < -7$ **B.** $x > -7$ **(C.)** $x < 7$

7. $(5 + 4x) - (3 - 3x) =$ **(A.)** $2 + 7x$ **B.** $8 + 7x$ **C.** $2 + x$

8. $(x + 2)(x + 5) =$ **A.** $x^2 + 10$ **(B.)** $x^2 + 7x + 10$ **C.** $2x + 10$

9. $\dfrac{8x + 4}{2} =$ $8x \div 2 = 4x$ $4 \div 2 = 2$ **(A.)** $4x + 2$ **B.** $4x + 4$ **C.** $6x$

   $4x + 2$

10. Let $0 < x < 1$. Which of the following has the largest value?   **A.** x^2 **(B.)** $2x$ **C.** x

    $x = 0.4$

STOP! This is the end of Workout C.

$2 \cdot 0.4 = .8$
$.4 < .8$

$3 - x > 10$
$-x > 10 - 3$
$-x > 7$
$x < -7$

1	2	3	4	5	6	7	8	9	10

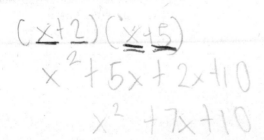

$(x + 2)(x + 5)$
$x^2 + 5x + 2x + 10$
$x^2 + 7x + 10$

Solutions C

#	A	B	C
1	✓	$7x - x = 7x - 1x = 6x$. Don't "take away" the x.	Combining like terms produces terms of the same type.
2	✓	$(y^3)(y^5) =$ $(y \cdot y \cdot y)(y \cdot y \cdot y \cdot y \cdot y) =$ $y^{3+5} = y^8$ **FACT:** When multiplying expressions having the same base, *add* the exponents: $(y^a)(y^b) = y^{a+b}$	Be careful! $(y^a)(y^b)$ *does not* equal y^{ab}. **TIP:** When in doubt, try replacing the variable with a number. For example, $(2^3)(2^5) =$ $(2 \cdot 2 \cdot 2)(2 \cdot 2 \cdot 2 \cdot 2 \cdot 2) =$ 2^8, not 2^{15}.
3	x^2 means "x times x," not "2 times x".	This is a very common error! To evaluate $-x^2$, *first square x, then negate.* Thus, -3^2 is the negative of 3^2. Do not square -3 in this case. Consider, for example, $15 - 3^2 = 15 - 9$, not $15 + 9$. -3^2 is not the same as $(-3)^2$.	✓
4	$5 < 2n$ means 5 *is less* than $2n$.	Consider the phrase "4 less than 10" (which equals 6). This means $10 - 4$. Similarly $5 - 2n$ means $2n$ less than 5 or 5 decreased by $2n$.	✓
5	$(2x)^3$ means $(2x)(2x)(2x)$, which produces $8x^3$. Be careful not to limit the exponentiation to only one of the factors. **FACT:** $(ab)^t = a^t \times b^t$	2^3 is 8, not 6.	✓
6	✓	If you divide both sides of the inequality by a negative number, be sure to reverse the sense of the inequality. If $-x > 7$, then $x < -7$.	Pay proper attention to the signs when dividing.
7	✓	$-(3 - 3x)$ is $-3 + 3x$.	When removing parentheses preceded by a negative sign, be sure to change the signs of *all* the terms contained within the parentheses. $-(3 - 3x) = -3 + 3x$.

#	A	B	C
8	The most common error when multiplying binomials is to neglect the middle terms. Don't forget to include 2 times x and 5 times x.	✓	x times x is x^2 (not $2x$), and you neglected the middle terms. (See Column A.)
9	✓	Be sure to divide *every* term in the numerator by the denominator.	$8x + 4$ is not $12x$.
10	If $0 < x < 1$, then x^2 will be less than x. **TIP:** Try several well-chosen numbers to reveal what actually happens. Using $x = .5$, for example, it is easy to see that x^2 is less than x.	✓	If x represents any positive number, then $2x > x$.

(handwritten: $8x^2 - 1x^2 = 7x^2$)

Follow-Up C

Answers are on page 154.

1. Simplify: $8x^2 - x^2$ *(handwritten: $7x^2$)*

2. Multiply: $(x^4)(x^{12})$ *(handwritten: x^{16})*

3. If $x = -5$, compute the value of $-x^2 - 2x$.   *(handwritten: $-5^2 - 2x = -15$)*

4. Simplify: $(3x^2)^3$ *(handwritten: $= 3x^6$)*

5. $(y - 3)(y - 4) =$ *(handwritten: $y^2 - 7y + 12$)*

6. Simplify: $\dfrac{7x + 14}{7}$

(handwritten: $7x \div 7 = 1x$ $14 \div 7 = 2$ $1x + 2$)

7. Translate into algebraic symbols: *11 less than the square of a number.* Use x to represent the number.   *(handwritten: $x^2 - 11$)*

8. Simplify: $(3x + 5) - (3 - 5x)$ *(handwritten: $3x + 5 - 3 + 5x$ $8x + 2$)*

9. Solve for x if $-3x < -6$.

10. If $-1 < x < 0$, which of the following has the smallest value?

    (A) x^2
    (B) x^3
    (C) x^4

(handwritten: $x = -0.5$ $-0.5^2 = +0.25$ $-0.5^3 = -.125$ $-0.5^4 = +.625$)

(handwritten for 9: $\dfrac{-3x}{-3} < \dfrac{-6}{-3}$ $x < +2$)

(handwritten for 3: $-(-5)^2 - 2(-5) = -25 - 10 = -15$)

(handwritten: $(y-3)(y-4)$ $y^2 + 4y + 3y + 12$ $y^2 + 7y + 12$)

Geometry

Directions for Workout D: 10 Questions   15-Minute Time Limit
Place your answer (A, B, or C) in the answer space provided.

1. Two sides of an isosceles triangle are 7 and 3. The perimeter of this triangle is

   $P = 7 + 7 + 3 = 17$

   A. 17   **B.** 13
   C. There is more than one possible answer.

2. If each side of a square is doubled, then its area is multiplied by

   A. 2   **B.** 4   **C.** 16

3. Which of the following could NOT be the length of a leg of a right triangle whose hypotenuse is 5?

   A. 1   **B.** $\sqrt{26}$ **C.** 4.1

4. The ratio of the circumference of a circle to its diameter is

   A. π   **B.** twice its radius   **C.** 2

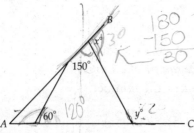

5. The value of $x + y$ is

   A. 210   **B.** 150   **C.** 180

$$\begin{array}{r} 180 \\ -150 \\ \hline 30 \end{array}$$

$$\begin{array}{r} 180 \\ -60 \\ \hline 30 \end{array}$$

6. Line p is parallel to line q as shown in the figure. What is the value of z?

   A. cannot be determined from the given information
   B. 45°   **C.** 65°

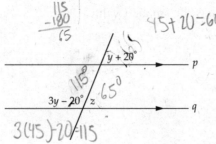

$45 + 20 = 65$

$\begin{array}{r} 115 \\ -180 \\ \hline 65 \end{array}$

$3(45) - 20 = 115$

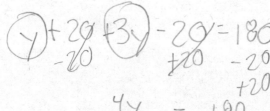

$y + 20 + 3y - 20 = 180$

$4y = 180$

$y = 45$

7. In the figure, angle *AOB* and angle *XOY* are right angles. Which angles must be equal?

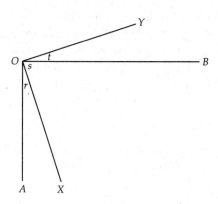

A. *r* and *t*   **B.** *r, s,* and *t*
C. None of the angles *r, s,* and *t* must necessarily be equal.

8. Triangle *ABC* contains an angle of 60° and a side whose length is 8. Which of the following additional pieces of information would allow you to uniquely determine the perimeter of the triangle? Triangle *ABC* is

A. scalene   **B.** isosceles
C. a right triangle

9. $\overline{AOB}$, $\overline{COD}$, and $\overline{EO}$ are line segments. Which of the following must be true?

A. $d = b$ **B.** $a = d$ **C.** $c = b + d$

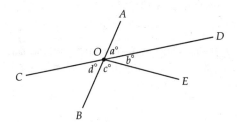

10. The area of triangle *ABC* is 20. The area of triangle *BDC* is

A. 8   **B.** 5   **C.** 4

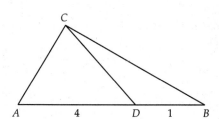

STOP! This is the end of Workout D.

1	2	3	4	5	6	7	8	9	10

Solutions D

#	A	B	C
1	✓	**FACT:** The sum of any two sides of a triangle must be greater than the third side. The sides cannot be 3, 3, and 7 since $3 + 3 < 7$.	The only possible cases are 3, 3, and 7—which is impossible—and 7, 7, and 3. The perimeter is 17.
2	The area is NOT doubled. It is multiplied by 4. Try several numerical values to convince yourself.	✓	Watch your arithmetic.
3	The only restriction is that any leg must be less than the hypotenuse.	✓ $\sqrt{26} > 5$, so it may *not* be a leg of the given right triangle.	4.1 is less than 5, and therefore permissible. The question *did not* imply that the sides had to be integers! Also, the fact that the hypotenuse is 5 does not mean that the legs must be 3 and 4.
4	✓	The circumference of a circle is $C = \pi d = 2\pi r$. Therefore $\dfrac{C}{d} = \dfrac{\pi d}{d} = \pi$.	You probably used an incorrect formula for the circumference of a circle.
5	✓	**FACT:** The sum of the interior angles of a quadrilateral is 360°. Therefore, the *sum* of the measures of the two angles adjacent to x and y is 150°. That is *not* the sum of x and y. The angles adjacent to x and y, together with x and y, form two straight angles. That total is 360°, so, $x + y$ must be 210°.	The sum of x and y would be 180° only if $\overline{AB}$ and $\overline{BC}$ were parallel.
6	**FACT:** When two parallel lines are cut by a transversal, the "corresponding angles" (angles that are in the same relative positions) are equal. So $z = y + 20$. Then $z + (3y - 20) = (y + 20) + (3y - 20) = 180$. Then, $y = 45$. But that is not the final answer. $z = y + 20 = 65°$.	Although 45° looks reasonable from the diagram, there is no logical support for this guess. Also, diagrams may not always be drawn to scale.	✓

#	A	B	C
7	✓	The information given does not lock the two right angles in position. Picture angle *XOY* pivoting around point *O*. Notice, for example, how the sizes of *s* and *t* change. They need not be equal.	$r + s = 90$, so $r = 90 - s$. Also, $t + s = 90$, so $t = 90 - s$. Thus, *r* and *t* are equal.
8	If the triangle is scalene, then the sides may assume an infinite number of lengths, regardless of the relative position of the 60° angle and the side whose length is 8.	✓ An isosceles triangle, one of whose angles is 60°, must be an equiangular triangle and therefore equilateral. The three sides are therefore equal and the perimeter is determined.	The fact that the triangle is a right triangle does not fix the position of the side whose length is 8. Being opposite the 60° angle produces a different perimeter from being opposite the 30° angle.
9	There is no reason for *d* and *b* to be equal.	✓ **FACT:** When two straight lines intersect, the "vertical angles" formed are equal.	Although $b + c + d = 180°$, the relative sizes of these angles are undetermined.
10	You most probably forgot to divide by 2.	Since the area of triangle *ABC* is 20, the altitude to side $\overline{AB}$ is 8. $[\frac{1}{2}(8)(5) = 20.]$ Triangle *BDC* shares that altitude, using $\overline{DB}$ as a base. Therefore its area is $\frac{1}{2}(8)(1) = 4$. You may have gotten 5 by thinking that triangle *BDC* was one quarter of triangle *ABC*, improperly using the lengths 1 and 4.	✓

Follow-Up D

Answers are on page 154.

1. All three sides of an isoceles triangle are integers. What is the smallest possible perimeter this triangle can have if one side has a length of 4?

2. What is the value of $a + b + c$?

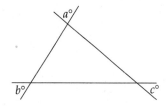

3. Compute the value of $x + y$.

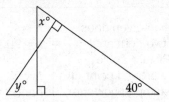

4. Find the value of w.

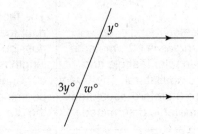

5. A circle of radius 3 passes through the center of and a point on the larger circle as shown. What is the ratio of the area of the shaded region to that of the unshaded region?

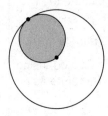

6. The area of triangle I is 36. What is the area of triangle II?

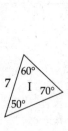 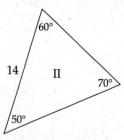

7. In the figure, $AB = BD$. Find the measure of angle x.

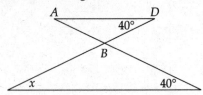

8. The area of triangle ACB is 28. What is the area of triangle XCY?

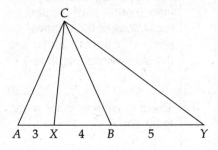

9. Compute x.

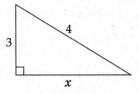

10. Triangle ABC and triangle XYC are both equilateral. Which pair of angles do not necessarily have the same measures?

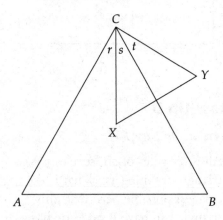

(A) A and Y
(B) r and t
(C) s and t

Graphs and Charts

Directions for Workout E: 10 Questions   15-Minute Time Limit
Place your answer (A, B, or C) in the answer space provided.

1. A point *T* on the line is not shown. The length
   of $\overline{RT}$ is 3 times the length of $\overline{RS}$. *How many*
   such points T are possible?   **A.** 1   **B.** 2   **C.** more
   than 2

Questions 2, 3, and 4 refer to the following chart,
which shows the number of students achieving
a score of 0, 1, 2, 3, or 4 on a four-question quiz.

Number of Students	Score
5	4
3	3
4	2
7	1
1	0

2. The mean score is   **A.** 2   **B.** 2.2   **C.** 4

3. The median score is   **A.** 2   **B.** 2.2   **C.** 2.5

4. The mode is   **A.** 1   **B.** 2   **C.** 7

5. The straight line graph shows the total wages earned versus the number of days worked. What is the total amount earned for 7 days worked?

A. $300   **B.** $315   **C.** $1,575

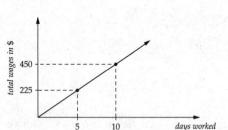

6. The pie chart displays each type of fruit sold at the GARDEN FRESH FARM during one week, as a percentage of the weight of all fruits sold during that week.

If 200 pounds of cherries were sold, how many pounds of melons were sold?

A. 30   **B.** 120   **C.** 800

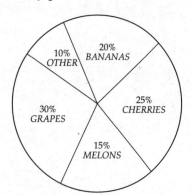

7. The grid shown is composed of 1 by 1 squares. What is the area, in square units, of the shaded figure?

A. 6   **B.** 7   **C.** 8

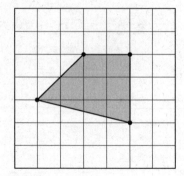

8. If M is the midpoint of $\overline{RT}$, then the value of a is

A. 6   **B.** 8   **C.** 13

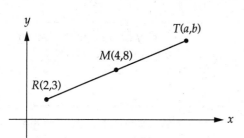

9. What is the distance between the points (–1, 7) and (5, 7)?

A. 0   **B.** 4   **C.** 6

10. The graph shows the number of students who selected each choice on a difficult question on the SHSAT. The correct choice was the one least frequently chosen. The percentage of students who selected that correct choice was

A. 40%   **B.** 20%   **C.** 10%

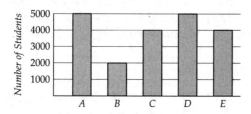

STOP! This is the end of Workout E.

1	2	3	4	5	6	7	8	9	10

Solutions E

#	A	B	C
1	You must consider points both to the right and to the left of *R*. There are two possible positions for point *T*.	✓	*T* may only be to the left of *S* or to the right of *S*.
2	The mean is the sum of all of the scores, counting all occurrences, divided by the total number of scores. In this case we have $\frac{44}{20}$ = 2.2. Do not simply add $0 + 1 + 2 + 3 + 4 = 10$, then divide by 5 to get 2.	✓	You may have chosen the "middle" number of students.
3	✓	The median score is the score in the middle when all the data is arranged in order. It is not necessarily the mean.	You may have computed the mean of 2 and 3 to arrive at 2.5.
4	✓	The mode is the score that occurs most frequently. Don't confuse it with the median.	The mode is the actual score, not the number of students achieving that score.
5	The daily wage is $\frac{\$225}{5}$ = $45. In 7 days the total amount earned is $45 \times 7 = \$315$. Don't rely upon visual estimation.	✓	Be careful to interpret the graph. First compute the daily wage. It is not $225.
6	Cherries are 25% of the total weight. Therefore the total weight is 800 pounds. Be careful not to take 15% of 200.	✓	The cherries represent 25% of the total weight sold. Therefore the total weight of all fruits sold is 800 pounds. This is not the weight of the melons alone.
7	You probably made an error in arithmetic. A quick visual estimation points to an area more than 6.	Don't try to simply count boxes. This could lead to an error. One way to compute the shaded area is to view it as a rectangle minus two triangles. This produces $(4 \times 3) - \left(\frac{1}{2}\right)(4)(1) - \left(\frac{1}{2}\right)(2)(2)$ $= 12 - 2 - 2 = 8$.	✓

#	A	B	C
8	✓	**FACT:** The coordinates of the midpoint of a line segment are the averages of the coordinates of the endpoints of that line segment. You may have tried to find *a* by doubling the 4.	13 is the value of *b*.
9	Since the *y*-coordinates are the same, the distance is found by subtracting the *x*-coordinates. $5 - (-1) = 6$.	Be careful when subtracting the negative value.	✓
10	The correct choice was B. The total number of students involved was 20,000. Therefore the percentage is $\frac{2000}{20000} \times 100 = 10\%$. Be careful not to use 5,000 as the total number of students.	Be careful not to simply associate 2,000 with 20%. You must do the necessary computations.	✓

Follow-Up E

Answers are on page 154.

1. If $AB = 4(BC)$, what is the coordinate of point C?

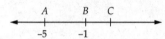

2. The grid shown is composed of 1×1 squares. What is the area of the shaded figure?

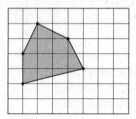

3. The midpoint of line segment $\overline{AB}$ is $(5, -3)$. The coordinates of point A are (m, n) and those of point B are (r, s). What is the value of $m + n + r + s$?

4. The straight line graph shows the water level in an open container over time as the water evaporates. What is the water level in cm. when the time is 300 hours?

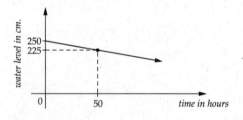

Questions 5, 6, and 7 all refer to the following list:

3, 4, 7, 4, 5, 2, 2, 5, 12, 5

5. What is the mean?

6. What is the median?

7. What is the mode?

8. In 1999, 18% of the Martinez family budget went to clothing, and 22% more than that went to food. The total budget for the year was $20,000. How much was spent on food?

9. What is the distance between the points $(7, -1)$ and $(7, -9)$?

10. The bar graph shows the number of students who selected each choice (A, B, C, D, or E) on a particular question of a multiple choice test. The correct answer was the one chosen by 25% of the total number of students. What choice was the correct choice?

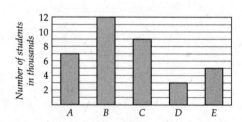

Miscellaneous 9th-Year Topics

Topics covered on the 9th-year test may vary as curricula change. Problems marked with an asterisk (*) represent topics that have not appeared recently.

Directions for Workout F: 10 Questions   15-Minute Time Limit
Place your answer (A, B, or C) in the answer space provided.

1. The inequality having the shaded region
   as its graph is

   A. $y > -3x + 12$
   B. $y \geq -3x + 12$
   C. $y < -3x + 12$

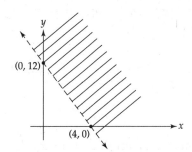

2. The area of an equilateral triangle whose
   side has a length of $4z$ is

   A. $z^2 \sqrt{3}$ **B.** $4z^2 \sqrt{3}$ **C.** $16z^2 \sqrt{3}$

3. The value of $6!/3!$ is

   A. $2!$ **B.** $3!$ **C.** 120

*4. In right triangle ABC, angle C is the right
   angle, $AC = 3$, and $BC = 4$. The value of
   $\sin A + \cos B$ is

   A. $\dfrac{7}{5}$ **B.** $\dfrac{8}{5}$ **C.** $\dfrac{6}{5}$

5. The figure is a cube whose edge is 4. What
   is the volume of the solid $ADCF$?

   A. $\dfrac{16\sqrt{3}}{3}$ **B.** $\dfrac{32}{3}$ **C.** 16

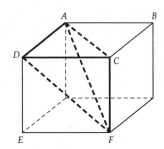

6. If $(10)(9)(8)(7)(6)(5)(4)(3)(2)(1) = (2^a)(y)$, where y is an odd integer, then $a =$

 A. 8 **B.** 6 **C.** 5

7. From an ordinary deck of 52 cards, a single card is selected at random. What is the probability that it is a 10 or is a red card?

 A. $\dfrac{7}{13}$ **B.** $\dfrac{15}{26}$ **C.** $\dfrac{1}{26}$

8. A group of 30 people are in a room. Which of the following *must* be true?

 A. At least 5 of these people must have been born on the same day of the week.

 B. At least 7 of these people must have been born on the same day of the week.

 C. At least 24 of these people must have been born on the same day of the week.

9. The ratio of a to b is 2:3, and the ratio of b to c is 4:5. The ratio of a to c is

 A. 8:15 **B.** 2:5 **C.** 5:6

10. If $|x - 3| + |y + 2| = 0$, then $(x + y)$

 A. is 5
 B. is 1
 C. cannot be determined from the given information

STOP! This is the end of Workout F.

1	2	3	4	5	6	7	8	9	10

Solutions F

#	A	B	C
1	✓	The dashed line indicates that points on the line are not included as part of the shaded region. Thus, the type of inequality is strictly less than ($<$) or strictly greater than ($>$).	**TIP:** To check which inequality symbol is correct, first pick a convenient "test point" such as $(0, 0)$. Determine whether the test point is or is not part of the shaded region. Choose the correct inequality accordingly. Since $0 < -3(0) + 12$, the point $(0,0)$ lies in the "less than" region. Since $(0,0)$ is not in the shaded region, the correct inequality is $y > -3x + 12$ (the "greater than" region).
2	**FACT:** The area of an equilateral triangle having side s is $\frac{s^2}{4}\sqrt{3}$. The area of the given triangle is $\frac{(4z)^2}{4}\sqrt{3} = \frac{16z^2}{4}\sqrt{3} = 4z^2\sqrt{3}$. In squaring $4z$, be sure to square the 4 as well as the z.	✓	You may have neglected to divide by 4.
3	$a!/b!$ is not necessarily equal to $\left(\frac{a}{b}\right)!$ $6! = 720$, while $3! = 6$. Thus, $\frac{6!}{3!} = \frac{720}{6} = 120$.	You cannot simply subtract the 3 from the 6.	✓
4	Sin $A = \frac{4}{5}$ and cos $B = \frac{4}{5}$. Don't confuse cos B with cos A $\left(= \frac{3}{5}\right)$. This leads to the given incorrect answer.	✓	Remember the definitions of sine and cosine.
5	Figure $ADCF$ is a tetrahedron. **FACT:** The volume of a tetrahedron (or any pyramid) is one-third the area of a base times the height to that base. Use triangle ADC as a base and use $CF = 4$ as the height.	✓	Did you divide by 2 instead of 3?

#	A	B	C
	Note that triangle *ADC* is a right triangle with the right angle at *D*. Its area is 8, half the area of square *ABCD*. Mistaking it for an equilateral triangle produces this incorrect answer.		
6	✓	The desired exponent is the number of times 2 occurs as a factor in the given product. The numbers 10, 6, and 2 each contribute a single 2. The 8 contributes three 2s and the 4 contributes two 2s. That is a total of eight 2s.	Your count was inaccurate.
7	✓	There are four 10s and 26 red cards. However, two of the 10s are red. Be careful not to count them twice. Therefore, there are only 28 (= 26 + 4 − 2) favorable outcomes. The probability is $\frac{28}{52}$ or $\frac{7}{13}$.	Did you confuse the meaning of "or" with "and"? There are only two cards that are red and 10.
8	✓	It is possible for the 30 people to distribute themselves into 7 groups of 4, each group corresponding to one day of the week. Then fill in two more days with the remaining two people. Thus, no more than 5 people need share birthdays on any one day of the week.	If 30 objects are distributed among 7 boxes, it is relatively easy to see that at least one box must contain at least 5 of the original objects. By distributing as "evenly as possible" we manage to place no more than 5 objects in any one box.
9	✓	Try to make the numbers representing *b* equal. 2:3 becomes 8:12, while 4:5 becomes 12:15. Thus, *a:b:c* = 8:12:15. So *a:c* = 8:15. Failure to convert the ratios correctly could lead to the incorrect answer 2:5.	Several arithmetical errors can lead to this result.
10	**FACT:** The absolute value of a number cannot be negative. The sum of two absolute values can therefore be 0 only if *both* absolute values are 0. Thus $x = 3$ and $y = -2$, so $x + y = 1$. Letting *x* and *y* both be zero could lead to the incorrect answer 5.	✓	The information *is* sufficient.

Follow-Up F

Answers are on page 154.

1. What is the value of $5!/4!$?

2. If $|3x + y| + |y - z| = 0$, and $x = -7$, what is the value of z?

3. At the Ice Cream Store, ice cream cones are available in 9 different flavors. Sam buys one cone every day. What is the greatest number of days that Sam can buy cones without buying any one flavor three times?

4. The side of an equilateral triangle has length $6x$. What is the area of this equilateral triangle in terms of x?

5. The ratio of a to b is 2:3, and the ratio of a to c is 3:10. What is the ratio of b to c?

6. From an ordinary deck of 52 cards, a single card is selected at random. What is the probability that the chosen card is a 9 or a club?

7. The length of the edge of a cube is 6. A solid is formed whose vertices consist of the four vertices of one face of the cube together with the center of the opposite face. What is the volume of this solid?

8. If $(9)(8)(7)(6)(5)(4)(3)(2)(1) = 3^a(y)$, where y is not divisible by 3, compute the value of a.

*9. In right triangle ABC, with right angle at C, $AC = 5$ and $BC = 12$. Find the value of $(\sin A)^2 + (\sin B)^2$.

10. In right triangle ABC, angle C is the right angle, $AC = 3$, and $AB = 5$. Point D is on hypotenuse AB, such that $DB = 1$. Find the area of triangle DBC.

Answers to Follow-Ups

	Follow-Up A	Follow-Up B	Follow-Up C	Follow-Up D	Follow-Up E	Follow-Up F
1.	$\dfrac{1}{12}$	22	$7x^2$	9	0	5
2.	14	$N = 4$	x^{16}	180	10	21
3.	1	36	-15	100	4	18
4.	5.43×10^{12}	$Q = 4$	$27x^6$	45	100	$9x^2\sqrt{3}$
5.	$\dfrac{6}{5}$	6	$y^2 - 7y + 12$	$\dfrac{1}{3}$ or 1:3	4.9	9:20
6.	10	A	$x + 2$	144	4.5	$\dfrac{4}{13}$
7.	56	$5^2 \times 7^3$	$x^2 - 11$	$x = 40°$	5	72
8.	$\dfrac{70}{9}$	17	$8x + 2$	36	$8,000	4
9.	-1	A	$x > 2$	$\sqrt{7}$	8	1
10.	$\dfrac{270}{G}$	4	B	C	C	$\dfrac{6}{5}$

The SHSAT does not provide formulas or reference material for use during the test. You must know the formulas and be familiar with technical mathematical terms.

This section provides you with a brief reference guide. It is not intended to be a complete list. These, as well as many other terms and concepts, are found among the detailed solutions to the sample exam problems and in the "Diagnosers."

Arithmetic

Integers   Positive and negative whole numbers together with zero.

. . . , −3, −2, −1, 0, 1, 2, 3, 4, 5, . . .

$\sqrt{9}$, 0, $-\frac{12}{2}$ and 2.0 are integers.

$\sqrt{7}$, $\frac{4}{3}$ and 13.3 are not integers.

Even Integers   . . . , −6, −4, −2, 0, 2, 4, 6, 8, . . .
All even integers are multiples of 2.
Note that 0 is an even integer.

Odd Integers   . . . , −5, −3, −1, 1, 3, 5, 7, . . .
All odd integers are 1 more (or 1 less) than even integers.

Consecutive Integers   −1, 0, 1, 2, 3 are five consecutive integers.
−9, −8, −7 are three consecutive integers.
−2, 0, 2, 4, 6 are five *consecutive even integers*.
3, 5, 7 are three *consecutive odd integers*.

Operations on Even and Odd Integers

Odd ± Odd = Even	Odd × Odd − Odd
Odd ± Even = Odd	Odd × Even = Even
Even ± Even = Even	Even × Even = Even

TIP: When checking for evenness or oddness you can use 0 and 1 to represent "typical" even or odd numbers. Example: even + odd = 0 + 1 = 1 = odd.

Factors   A factor of a number is any positive integer that may be divided evenly into the number—that is, leaving a remainder of zero.
(Factors are considered to be positive integers unless otherwise noted.)
3 is a factor of 12.
Both 1 and 2001 are factors of 2001.
5 is *not* a factor of 19.
8 is a factor of both 24 and 80.
8 is called a *common factor* of 24 and 80.

Multiples   If a is a factor of b, then b is called a multiple of a.

15 is a multiple of 3.

15 is also a multiple of 5.

4, 8, 12, 16, 20, are five consecutive multiples of 4.

Prime Numbers   A prime (or prime number) is any positive integer having exactly two different integer factors. For example, the factors of 7 are 1 and 7 only. Thus, 7 is a prime.

The first ten primes are 2, 3, 5, 7, 11, 13, 17, 19, 23, and 29

- The number 1 is *not* a prime number.
- The only even prime number is 2.
- There is an infinite number of prime numbers.

Every positive integer can be factored into primes.

$144 = 2 \times 2 \times 2 \times 2 \times 3 \times 3$

Often it is convenient to write the factorization in terms of powers of primes.

$144 = 2^4 \times 3^2$

$100,080 = 2^4 \times 3^2 \times 5 \times 139$

Composite Numbers   A composite is any positive integer with more than two different factors.

6 is composite. It has 1, 2, 3, and 6 as factors.

25 is composite. It has 1, 5, and 25 as factors.

1 is neither prime nor composite. It is called a *unit*.

Greatest Common Factor   The greatest common factor (also known as the greatest common divisor or highest common factor) of two numbers is the *largest* positive integer that is a *factor of both* numbers. Standard abbreviations are GCF, or GCD, or HCF.

The GCF of 24 and 30 is 6.

The GCF of 27 and 32 is 1.

The GCF of $2 \times 3 \times 3 \times 5 \times 7 \times 7 \times 7$ and $2 \times 2 \times 3 \times 5 \times 5 \times 7 \times 7 \times 11$ is $2 \times 3 \times 5 \times 7 \times 7$.

Least Common Multiple   The least common multiple (LCM) of two positive integers is the *smallest* positive integer having *both* of these integers as factors.

The LCM of two positive integers must be

(1) a positive multiple of both integers **and**

(2) the smallest of all of those positive multiples.

The LCM of 4 and 6 is 12.

The LCM of 9 and 18 is 18.

The LCM of 11 and 13 is 143 ($= 11 \times 13$).

The LCM of $2 \times 3 \times 3 \times 5 \times 7 \times 7 \times 7$ and $2 \times 2 \times 3 \times 5 \times 5 \times 7 \times 7 \times 11$ is $2 \times 2 \times 3 \times 3 \times 5 \times 5 \times 7 \times 7 \times 7 \times 11$.

Division   When 42 is divided by 8, the *quotient* is 5 and the *remainder* is 2. The number 42 is called the *dividend* and 8 is called the *divisor*.

This can be written as

42   = 5×8 $+ 2$

dividend = quotient $\times$ divisor + remainder

73 divided by 10 is 7 with a remainder of 3

73 = 7 × 10 + 3

Exponents 3 × 3 is written as 3^2.

The *base* is 3 and the *exponent* is 2.

$5^7 = 5 \times 5 \times 5 \times 5 \times 5 \times 5 \times 5$

$13^1 = 13$

$6^0 = 1$.

In general, if *n* is any nonzero number, then $n^0 = 1$.

Square Roots Since $6^2 = 36$, 6 is the square root of 36.

The square root of 64 is 8.

The square root of 61 lies between 7 and 8.

Inequality Symbols > means "is greater than." (5 > 3)

< means "is less than." (3 < 5)

≥ means "is greater than or equal to." (10 ≥ 6 is a true statement)

≤ means "is less than or equal to."

The age of every person in the room "is less than or equal to" 38 means that everyone in the room is 38 years of age or younger.

Order of Operations When several types of operations are present, there is a designated order in which they should be performed.

Parentheses

Exponents

Multiplication   In Order from Left to Right

Division   In Order from Left to Right

Addition   In Order from Left to Right

Subtraction   In Order from Left to Right

$37 + (2 \times 4 - 3)^2 \div 5 =$ In the parentheses, do the multiplication before the subtraction.

$37 + (8 - 3)^2 \div 5 =$

$37 + (5)^2 \div 5 =$ Now do exponents.

$37 + 25 \div 5 =$ Next do division.

$37 + 5 =$

42

Averages The mean (average, or arithmetic mean) is

the *sum* of the values

divided by

the *number* of values.

The mean age of four people whose ages are 13, 23, 17, and 27 is

$\frac{13 + 23 + 17 + 27}{4}$ or $\frac{80}{4}$, which equals 20.

Often in solving problems involving averages, it is convenient to express the formula in an alternate but equivalent form:

The *sum* of the values = (the number of values) × (the *average* of these values).

Thus, if the average of 4 values is 20, their sum is 80.

Median	The median is the *middle value* of a set of values.
	To find the median, first place the values in order.
	CASE 1
	When there is an odd number of values: 2, 4, 7, 9, 12, 38, 39
	The median is 9.
	CASE 2
	When there is an even number of values: 1, 4, 9, 20
	The median is the mean (average) of the two middle values.

$$\frac{4+9}{2}=6.5$$

Mode	The mode of a set of values is the value that occurs most frequently.
	2, 4, 5, 7, 7, 8, 9, 9, 9, 12, 23, 23 The mode is 9.
	2, 4, 7, 9, 12, 38, 39 There is *no* mode.
	2, 4, 4, 4, 5, 5, 5, 9, 9, 13 There are two modes, 4 and 5.

Absolute Value	The absolute value of a number expresses the undirected distance from that number to zero.
	The absolute value of any number is always positive or zero.

$$|5| = 5$$
$$|-7| = 7$$
$$\left|\frac{1}{3}\right| = \frac{1}{3}$$
$$|0| = 0$$

Algebra

Exponents	When multiplying expressions involving the *same base:* add the exponents

$$t^3 \cdot t^7 = (t \cdot t \cdot t)(t \cdot t \cdot t \cdot t \cdot t \cdot t \cdot t) = t^{10}$$

When dividing expressions involving the *same base:* subtract the exponents

$$\frac{y^6}{y^2} = \frac{y \cdot y \cdot y \cdot y \cdot y \cdot y}{y \cdot y} = y^{6-2} = y^4$$

Be sure to subtract the denominator's exponent from the numerator's exponent.

When an expression involving an exponent is raised to a power, multiply the exponents.

$$(x^2)^3 = (x^2)(x^2)(x^2) = x^{2 \cdot 3} = x^6$$

Like Terms	Like terms are terms that differ, at most, in their numerical coefficients.
	Like terms $6x^5$ and $13x^5$
	Unlike terms $6x^5$ and $13x^4$

Like terms may be combined (added or subtracted) by simply combining their coefficients.

$6x^5 + 13x^5 = 19x^5$ Caution: Retain the same exponent.

$x^2 + x^2 = 2x^2$

$6x^5 + 13x^4$ cannot be combined into a single term.

Translating Words into Symbols
Examples:

5 more than a number or a number increased by 5:	$x + 5$
5 less than a number or a number decreased by 5:	$x - 5$
x less than 5 or 5 decreased by x:	$5 - x$

   Be careful! $x - 5$ and $5 - x$ have different meanings.

4 more than twice a number:	$2x + 4$
Five times the quantity $(4y - 7)$:	$5(4y - 7)$
Half of a number:	$\left(\dfrac{1}{2}\right)x$ or $\dfrac{x}{2}$
75% of a number:	$.75x$ or $\dfrac{75}{100}x$

When attempting a direct translation of words into symbols, it is sometimes helpful to replace the "number" with some number of your choice. Using this chosen number, work through the expression and pay careful attention to what you did.

For example,   for "five less than a number"
             use "5 less than 17"; ["a number" is replaced by 17]
             the result, of course, is 12.
             Ask yourself, how did I get 12?
             You translated "5 less than 17" into $17 - 5$
             So "5 less than a number" is $x - 5$

Words	Indicated Operation	Symbols
sum, increased by, more than, total,	+	
The sum of twice a number and 7		$2a + 7$
Fifty-two more than three times a number		$3a + 52$
Milton is three years older than Irving		$M = I + 3$
difference, decreased by, less than, fewer	−	
The difference between x and y		$x - y$
Seven less than twice a number		$2x - 7$
Be careful not to confuse $2x - 7$ with $7 - 2x$		
Matt is three years younger than Louisa		$M = L - 3$
product, times, of	×	
The product of two consecutive integers		$x(x + 1)$
One-third of a number		$\left(\dfrac{1}{3}\right)x$
85% of the sum of Tim's age and Minna's age		$.85(T + M)$
quotient, divided by, ratio, over	/ or ÷	
12 divided by x		$\dfrac{12}{x}$
The ratio of 19 to y		$\dfrac{19}{y}$

Geometry

Triangles

The sum of the measures of the interior angles of a triangle is 180°.

$a + b + c = 180$

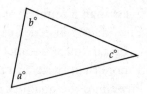

The measure of an exterior angle of a triangle is the sum of the measures of the two nonadjacent interior angles.

$e = a + b$

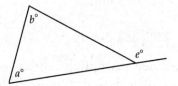

The sum of the lengths of any two sides of a triangle must be greater than the length of the third side.

$AB + BC > AC$

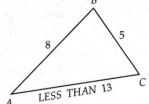

The length of any side of a triangle must be greater than the difference of the lengths of the other two sides.

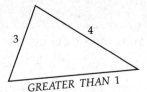

Pythagorean Theorem

In a right triangle, the square of the hypotenuse is equal to the sum of the squares of the legs.

$c^2 = a^2 + b^2$

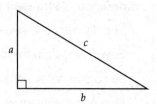

It is not necessary for the lengths of the sides of a right triangle to be integers.

Angle Sum for Quadrilaterals

The sum of the interior angles of a quadrilateral is 360°.

$a + b + c + d = 360$

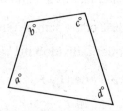

Lines and Angles

The sum of the measures of all of the angles about a point is 360°.

$a + b + c + d + e = 360$

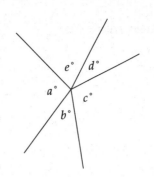

The sum of the measures of all of the angles about a point on one side of a straight line is 180°.

$a + b + c + d = 180$

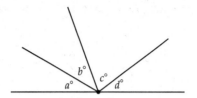

Parallel Lines

When two parallel lines are crossed by a third line, called a *transversal*, certain angles formed will have equal measures. (See the figure.)

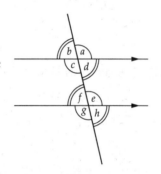

Perimeter, Area, and Volume

Circumference $C = 2\pi r$ or $C = \pi d$
Area $A = \pi r^2$

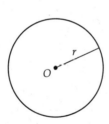

Perimeter $P = 2l + 2w$
Area $A = lw$

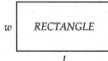

Perimeter $P = 4s$
Area $A = s^2$

Area $A = \dfrac{1}{2}bh$

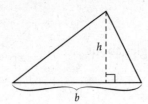

You may choose any vertex and draw a perpendicular line segment to the opposite side. The opposite side becomes a base (b) and the perpendicular becomes the height (h), or altitude, to that base.

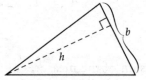

An altitude may fall outside of the triangle.

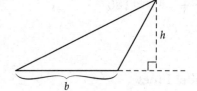

Area of a trapezoid $A = \dfrac{1}{2}h(b_1 + b_2)$

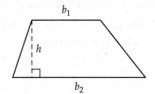

The volume of a rectangular solid is length × width × height.
$V = lwh$

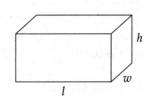

Practice Tests

ANSWER SHEET
Minitest 2

Part I English Language Arts

Revising/Editing Part A

1. Ⓐ Ⓑ Ⓒ Ⓓ
2. Ⓔ Ⓕ Ⓖ Ⓗ
3. Ⓐ Ⓑ Ⓒ Ⓓ
4. Ⓔ Ⓕ Ⓖ Ⓗ
5. Ⓐ Ⓑ Ⓒ Ⓓ
6. Ⓔ Ⓕ Ⓖ Ⓗ

Revising/Editing Part B

7. Ⓐ Ⓑ Ⓒ Ⓓ
8. Ⓔ Ⓕ Ⓖ Ⓗ
9. Ⓐ Ⓑ Ⓒ Ⓓ
10. Ⓔ Ⓕ Ⓖ Ⓗ
11. Ⓐ Ⓑ Ⓒ Ⓓ
12. Ⓔ Ⓕ Ⓖ Ⓗ
13. Ⓐ Ⓑ Ⓒ Ⓓ

Reading

14. Ⓐ Ⓑ Ⓒ Ⓓ
15. Ⓔ Ⓕ Ⓖ Ⓗ
16. Ⓐ Ⓑ Ⓒ Ⓓ
17. Ⓔ Ⓕ Ⓖ Ⓗ
18. Ⓐ Ⓑ Ⓒ Ⓓ
19. Ⓔ Ⓕ Ⓖ Ⓗ

20. Ⓐ Ⓑ Ⓒ Ⓓ
21. Ⓔ Ⓕ Ⓖ Ⓗ
22. Ⓐ Ⓑ Ⓒ Ⓓ
23. Ⓔ Ⓕ Ⓖ Ⓗ
24. Ⓐ Ⓑ Ⓒ Ⓓ
25. Ⓔ Ⓕ Ⓖ Ⓗ

Part II Mathematics

26.

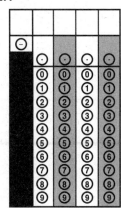

27.

28. Ⓐ Ⓑ Ⓒ Ⓓ
29. Ⓔ Ⓕ Ⓖ Ⓗ
30. Ⓐ Ⓑ Ⓒ Ⓓ
31. Ⓔ Ⓕ Ⓖ Ⓗ
32. Ⓐ Ⓑ Ⓒ Ⓓ
33. Ⓔ Ⓕ Ⓖ Ⓗ
34. Ⓐ Ⓑ Ⓒ Ⓓ
35. Ⓔ Ⓕ Ⓖ Ⓗ
36. Ⓐ Ⓑ Ⓒ Ⓓ

37. Ⓔ Ⓕ Ⓖ Ⓗ
38. Ⓐ Ⓑ Ⓒ Ⓓ
39 Ⓔ Ⓕ Ⓖ Ⓗ
40. Ⓐ Ⓑ Ⓒ Ⓓ
41. Ⓔ Ⓕ Ⓖ Ⓗ
42. Ⓐ Ⓑ Ⓒ Ⓓ
43. Ⓔ Ⓕ Ⓖ Ⓗ
44. Ⓐ Ⓑ Ⓒ Ⓓ
45. Ⓔ Ⓕ Ⓖ Ⓗ

46. Ⓐ Ⓑ Ⓒ Ⓓ
47. Ⓔ Ⓕ Ⓖ Ⓗ
48. Ⓐ Ⓑ Ⓒ Ⓓ
49. Ⓔ Ⓕ Ⓖ Ⓗ
50. Ⓐ Ⓑ Ⓒ Ⓓ
51. Ⓔ Ⓕ Ⓖ Ⓗ
52. Ⓐ Ⓑ Ⓒ Ⓓ

Minitest 2

PART 1—ENGLISH LANGUAGE ARTS

25 QUESTIONS

SUGGESTED TIME: 30 MINUTES

Revising/Editing

QUESTIONS 1–13

Revising/Editing Part A

Directions: Read and answer each of the following questions. You will be asked to recognize and correct errors in sentences or short paragraphs. Mark the **best** answer for each question.

1. Read this paragraph.

(1) If you've ever driven past Jones Beach, you might have noticed the signs for Robert Moses State Park. (2) Who exactly is this man, whose park sits majestically at the end of Jones Beach? (3) Known as the "master builder," Robert Moses's plans helped develop the streets and highways of New York City. (4) While his public works project was undoubtedly influential, the impact of his policies remains controversial today.

Which sentence should be revised to correct a misplaced modifier?

A. sentence 1
B. sentence 2
C. sentence 3
D. sentence 4

2. Read this sentence.

> Although most people are indifferent to the drab, gray New York pigeon paleontologists are fascinated by its ancestor, one of the fiercest predators of its time.

Which edit should be made to correct this sentence?

E. delete the comma after *drab*

F. insert a comma after *pigeon*

G. delete the comma after *ancestor*

H. insert a comma after *predators*

3. Read this paragraph.

> (1) Before the invention of the Internet, people in New York City used to do a lot of different things to keep themselves entertained. (2) One of them was playing sports, games like stickball and handball were summer favorites. (3) If physical activity wasn't your thing, you could go to an underground arcade, where kids would insert quarters into a giant machine to play video games. (4) Whatever you did, you can be sure that you were with real human beings.

Which sentence should be revised to correct a run-on?

A. sentence 1

B. sentence 2

C. sentence 3

D. sentence 4

4. Read this paragraph.

> (1) The British Empire is noted for its powerful influence all over the globe. (2) This power was maintained by a formidable navy, which kept a rule to maintain a number of ships that were equal to the combined ships of their two largest rivals. (3) This rule became untenable once the United States matured because its industrial capacity outpaced that of Britain. (4) Nonetheless, the British Empire continued to thrive due largely to its successful economic strength.

Which sentence should be revised to correct an inappropriate shift in pronoun?

E. sentence 1

F. sentence 2

G. sentence 3

H. sentence 4

5. Read this paragraph.

(1) Several members of the committee believe that the school made a mistake. (2) In a recent meeting, parents of sixth, seventh, and eighth graders plan to speak about the problem. (3) One of the biggest issues are nutrition, homework, and the graduation venue. (4) Parents believe that addressing all these issues is critical to running a successful year.

Which edit should be made to correct these sentences?

A. change *believe* to *believes* in sentence 1
B. change *plan* to *plans* in sentence 2
C. change *one* to *some* in sentence 3
D. change *is* to *are* in sentence 4

6. Read this paragraph.

(1) Coffee beans are not really beans in the truest sense. (2) They are, in fact, seeds from the fruit of a coffee tree, which may produce coffee beans for as long as 50 to 60 years. (3) The oldest and most popular method of processing coffee beans is called the "dry process." (4) In this process, the drying operation is the most important stage that affected the final quality of the coffee.

Which sentence should be revised to correct an inappropriate shift in verb tense?

E. sentence 1
F. sentence 2
G. sentence 3
H. sentence 4

Revising/Editing Part B

Directions: Read the passage below and answer the questions following it. You will be asked to improve the writing quality of the passage and to correct errors so that the passage follows the conventions of standard written English. You may reread the passage if you need to. Mark the best answer for each question.

Errors in Our Food Economy

(1) Scientific research need not confine itself to the laboratory, especially when we need to diagnose a problem in our relationship to food. (2) By interpreting the observations of practical life, science has found that several errors are common in the use of food. (3) We must work hard to eliminate food waste so that we can make the world a better place.

(4) First, many people purchase needlessly expensive kinds of food. (5) Mutton costs $12 per pound, whereas chicken costs only $2. (6) Unfortunately, those who spend the most are often the ones who can least afford it, but they do so under this mistaken assumption.

(7) Secondly, the food which we eat does not always contain the proper proportions of the different kinds of nutritive ingredients. (8) We consume relatively too much of the fuel ingredients of food. (9) These ingredients consist primarily of the fats of meat, butter, and the starch which makes up the larger part of the nutritive material of flour. (10) These make muscle and sinew, serving as the basis of blood, bone and brain. (11) Conversely, we consume relatively too little of the protein of flesh-forming substances, like the lean of meat and fish and the gluten of wheat.

(12) Thirdly, many people, not only the well-to-do, but those in moderate circumstances, waste tons of food. (13) Part of the excess is simply thrown away with the wastes of the table and the kitchen; so that the injury to health, great as it may be, is doubtless much less than if all were eaten. (14) Probably the worst sufferers from this evil are well-to-do people of sedentary occupations—brain workers as distinguished from hand workers.

(15) We are guilty of serious errors in our cooking. (16) We waste a great deal of fuel in the preparation of our food, and even then a great deal of the food is very badly cooked. (17) Can we afford to spend such a large part of our budget on food? (18) A reform in these methods of cooking is one of the economic demands of our time.

7. Which sentence should replace sentence 3 to best introduce the main claim of the passage?

   A. These errors are all around us, and it need not take a particularly onerous effort to identify the problems.
   B. Science can help mankind become a better, more responsible steward of the world it has received.
   C. Food waste must be discouraged as the population trend reveals no indication of slowing down.
   D. Mankind has looked upon all its creatures and imperiously decided to domesticate four primary food groups.

8. Which sentence can best follow and support sentence 4?

   E. Much of the food they purchase can easily be bought at a butcher rather than a supermarket.
   F. They do this under the impression that there is a benefit in the costlier materials, when there really isn't.
   G. A vegetarian diet, for example, doesn't necessarily mean that one eats only plants.
   H. The most nutritious foods often do not have the labeling to differentiate themselves from others.

9. Which transition word or phrase should be added to the beginning of sentence 8?

    A. Therefore,
    B. Nonetheless,
    C. In fact,
    D. Nevertheless,

10. Where should sentence 11 be moved to improve the organization of the third paragraph (sentences 7–11)?

    E. to the beginning of the paragraph
    F. between sentences 7 and 8
    G. between sentences 8 and 9
    H. between sentences 9 and 10

11. Which revision of sentence 12 best maintains the formal style of the passage?

    A. Thirdly, many people, not only the well-to-do, but those in moderate circumstances, waste tons of food.
    B. Thirdly, many people, not only the well-to-do, but those in moderate circumstances, blow all their dough on food.
    C. Thirdly, many people, not only the well-to-do, but those in moderate circumstances, waste needless quantities of food.
    D. Thirdly, many people, not only the well-to-do, but those in moderate circumstances, eat like a savage.

12. Which sentence is irrelevant and should be removed?

    E. sentence 8
    F. sentence 13
    G. sentence 16
    H. sentence 17

13. Which concluding sentence should be added after sentence 18 to support the main claim presented in the passage?

    A. Another economic demand is the pollution, resulting from corporate agriculture.
    B. With the aid of science, we simply cannot fail to rise up and meet that demand.
    C. In the end, we must find a way to encourage the conservation of resources or suffer the consequences.
    D. After all, the American public is notorious for waste and cannot be expected to change its behavior.

Directions: Read each passage and answer the questions that follow it. Base your answers **only on the material contained in the passage.** Select the one **best** answer for each question. Bubble in the letter corresponding to that answer on the answer sheet.

I. Irish Travellers are an interesting ethnic group with a mysterious past. Called "Irish Tinkers" until recently, these people have
Line their own distinct beliefs and customs and
(5) even their own secret language, Shelta. Traditionally they have followed an itinerant lifestyle separate from their Irish compatriots, moving about in horse caravans or, more recently, motor-drawn trailers.

(10) There are several theories about the origins of the Travellers. It is possible that they are descended from ancient Celtic rivetmakers. Or they may be the vestiges of a class of vassals or servants who lost their
(15) homes when English conquerors confiscated the estates of their overlords. Some historians think it more likely that the group had its beginnings in the seventeenth-century invasion by the English
(20) general Cromwell, when many Irish were driven from their homes. The nineteenth-century potato famines, according to this theory, increased the numbers of those dispossessed and itinerant.

(25) The secret language Shelta, however, indicates a more romantic past. Greek, Hebrew, and ancient Gaelic elements in the language seem to be of scholarly origin. They suggest that Shelta probably arose several centuries
(30) ago among bands of wandering poets. If this is the case, it seems likely that in times of upheaval the original wanderers would accept uprooted families, who eventually adopted Shelta as their own tongue. The
(35) blended group, according to this theory, became the Irish Tinkers.

The traditional occupation of the Tinkers was metalworking. In fact, the name "Tinker" comes from the Celtic *tinceard,* or

(40) *tinsmith.* Tinkers could manage to support their families by mending spoons and pots and by crafting metal wares. With the introduction of plastics and of machine-made metal goods, however, they lost their
(45) chief means of livelihood along with the name "Tinker." Many turned to scrap-dealing to earn a living in the accustomed nomadic lifestyle, whereas others have continued to travel but subsist on odd jobs and
(50) begging. Some have left the road, settling into a mainstream job or "going on the dole," relying on the government for support instead of working.

Irish Travellers are not as distinct an ethnic
(55) group as they once were. In addition to lifestyle changes, intermarriage and emigration have blurred the identifying markers. Some have migrated to European countries and even Australia; others have moved to
(60) the southern United States. Typical Irish Traveller families in Georgia and South Carolina live in permanent homes, but the menfolk support their families as itinerant workers, frequently in roofing or other
(65) aspects of home repair. And although there is some intermarriage, the tendency of these communities is to maintain a degree of separation from their neighbors.

14. Which of the following best states the author's purpose?

A. To explain the origins of a mysterious language

B. To describe an extinct Irish class

C. To trace the history of uprooted Irish families

D. To explain the distinct features and evolution of an ethnic group

15. Which of the following is **not** given as a possible origin of the Irish Travellers?

   E. Great Irish lords who were driven from their lands
   F. People made homeless in a time of starvation
   G. Irish poets of long ago
   H. Celtic metal workers

16. Which of the following features of American Irish Traveller culture is according to ancient tradition?

   A. The family's nomadic lifestyle
   B. The occupation of the men
   C. The tendency of the Travellers to keep to themselves
   D. The stress placed on education

17. What is meant by "going on the dole"?

   E. Changing one's occupation
   F. Receiving public financial assistance
   G. Depending on one's neighbors for emotional support
   H. Advertising for work

18. What does the passage suggest about Shelta?

   A. It has a literary origin.
   B. It is known by all Irish people.
   C. It is several thousand years old.
   D. It is no longer known to the younger Irish Travellers.

19. All of the following are factors in the loss of distinctive "Irish Traveller" identity **except**

   E. separation from the homeland.
   F. intermarriage with other groups.
   G. changes in occupation.
   H. loss of the secret language.

II. Those who are unfamiliar with the teachings of Muhammad, the founder of Islam, might be surprised to learn about his
Line attitudes toward women and their rights.
(5) His teachings are particularly striking in view of some of the rigid and even harsh restrictions placed on women in some Islamic cultures.

Muhammad's life was enriched by close
(10) relationships with the female members of his family. His wife Khadija, a competent, successful businesswoman fifteen years older than her husband, was his adviser as well as his spouse and the mother of his
(15) children. He seems to have been devoted also to his second wife, Aysha, and to have dearly loved his four daughters.

In the seventh-century Arabian city of Mecca, before Muhammad had the visions
(20) that gave birth to Islam, the legal position of women was precarious. An unmarried woman whose father had died could only hope a brother would take her in. She had no legal right to protection and economic
(25) support, as a man usually left his property to his male children. A married woman lived with her husband and his family and had little or no freedom or security. She was kept closely under their eye and could be
(30) arbitrarily cast out by her husband.

Law and custom favored males in other ways as well. Unwanted female children could be killed, and women accused of adultery were customarily stoned to death,
(35) a fate males similarly accused were likely to escape.

Islamic law as proclaimed by Muhammad made significant changes in the status of women. In the important area of economic
(40) rights, Muhammad gave crucial guarantees to women. Not only did a bride receive a dowry from her bridegroom, but this dowry belonged to her to do with as she chose. She was also assured of a partial

(45) inheritance from her husband and from her father, as well as support by her sons after their father's death. Furthermore, a woman was allowed to choose her own husband, and in the case of divorce he was *(50)* responsible for her support.

The position of females improved in other ways as well. Education was opened to girls, and as a result the writers and scholars of early Islam included women as well *(55)* as men. Muhammad expected women to participate fully in religion, and in some cases women even served as congregational leaders. Female infanticide was outlawed. The penalty for adultery was changed from *(60)* stoning to public whipping and applied to men as well as women.

Although not all of these rights survived Muhammad, laws concerning marriage and financial security remained in place for *(65)* centuries. These laws gave women not only more security but also more status than they had known before the establishment of Islam.

20. Which of the following best expresses the author's purpose?

   A. To show how Muhammad bettered the position of women
   B. To explain the dominant position of women in early Islam
   C. To explain current restrictions on women in some Islamic cultures
   D. To reveal the earlier injustices against women

21. Which of the following was **not** true of women in early Islam?

   E. They had a certain degree of economic security.
   F. They could enjoy the advantages of education.
   G. Their position in the practice of religion was fully equal to men's.
   H. They retained some financial protection in the case of divorce.

22. Why might some people be surprised to learn about the position of women in early Islam?

   A. They know nothing of Islam as it is today.
   B. All of the laws passed by Muhammad were changed within a few decades.
   C. They are more familiar with the history of pre-Islamic cultures.
   D. They are aware of current repression of Moslem women in some places.

23. What does the passage suggest about Muhammad?

   E. He is the founder of a minor religious cult.
   F. He believed that religion was the exclusive function of men.
   G. He made divorce easier for both men and women.
   H. He was influenced by his regard for the women in his life.

24. Which of the following best states the position of women in pre-Islamic Mecca as described in the passage?

    A. They had financial security but no family security.

    B. They usually had to depend on men to take care of them.

    C. They had no rights under the law.

    D. According to law, they could not inherit property.

25. What does the passage indicate about the origins of Islam?

    E. It began with laws proclaimed by Muhammad.

    F. It developed through mystic experiences of Muhammad.

    G. It was based on the religion of seventh-century Mecca.

    H. It was inspired by his love for his daughters.

PART 2—MATHEMATICS

QUESTIONS 26–52

SUGGESTED TIME: 45 MINUTES

Grid-In Problems

Directions: Solve each problem. On the answer sheet, write your answer in the boxes at the top of the grid. Start on the left side of each grid. Print only one number or symbol in each box. **DO NOT LEAVE A BOX BLANK IN THE MIDDLE OF AN ANSWER.** Under each box, fill in the circle that matches the number or symbol you wrote above. **DO NOT FILL IN A CIRCLE UNDER AN UNUSED BOX.**

26. It takes 3 hours to completely fill Demarco's empty tank. Water is pumped at a constant rate. During the first 40 minutes, 800 gallons of water was pumped into the tank. How many gallons does it take to completely fill his tank?

27. The square root of 1,000 lies between the two consecutive integers N and $N + 1$. Compute the value of N.

Multiple-Choice Problems

Directions: For each of the following questions, select the **best** answer from the given choices. Bubble in the letter corresponding to your answer on the answer sheet. **DO NOT PUT ANY OTHER WORK ON THE ANSWER SHEET.** All necessary work can be done in your test booklet or on scrap paper that is provided.

NOTE: Diagrams other than graphs might not be drawn to scale. Do not assume any relationships that are not specifically stated unless they are implied by the given information.

28. $\dfrac{60 \times 30}{60 + 30} =$

A. 2
B. 20
C. 200
D. none of these

29. Which of the following is closest in value to .213?

E. $\dfrac{1}{2}$

F. $\dfrac{1}{3}$

G. $\dfrac{1}{4}$

H. $\dfrac{1}{5}$

30. In triangle ABC, $\overline{CD}$ bisects angle ACB. Compute the value of $x + y$, in degrees.

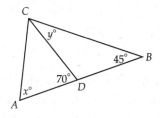

A. 45
B. 70
C. 80
D. 110

31. Two consecutive odd primes, such as 11 and 13, are called a pair of "twin primes." How many *pairs* of twin primes are there between 15 and 45?

E. 2
F. 3
G. 4
H. 5

32. For any number x, the symbol $\lceil x \rceil$ means the smallest integer that is greater than or equal to x. For example, $\lceil 3.2 \rceil$ is 4. What is $\lceil \sqrt{156.3} \rceil$?

A. 11
B. 12
C. 13
D. 156

33. Eight years from now, Oana will be twice as old as her brother is now. Oana is now 12 years old. How old is her brother now?

E. 2
F. 4
G. 6
H. 10

34. Suppose a snail crawls $\dfrac{2}{5}$ inch per second. At this rate, what is the total number of inches the snail crawls in 2 minutes?

A. 48
B. 30
C. 24
D. $\dfrac{4}{5}$

35. The straight line graph shows the relationship between the number of tickets sold and the amount of money in the cash register if the register contained $150 before any tickets were sold. What is the price of 1 ticket?

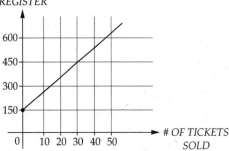

E. $100
F. $22.50
G. $15
H. $10

36. If $15 - 2x < 7$, then for all possible values of x that make the inequality true,

A. $x < 8$
B. $x > 8$
C. $x > 4$
D. $x < 4$

37. Four congruent circles are enclosed in a square as shown. The perimeter of the square is 64. What is the circumference of *one* of the circles (in terms of π)?

- **E.** 4π
- **F.** 8π
- **G.** 16π
- **H.** 32π

38. If $3x + 2y = 19$ and $2x + 3y = 91$, what is the value of $x + y$?

- **A.** 8
- **B.** 9
- **C.** 21
- **D.** 22

39. Kenny buys candy bars at 9 for $1 and sells them at 3 for $1. How many candy bars must he sell in order for him to make a profit of exactly $10?

- **E.** 27
- **F.** 30
- **G.** 45
- **H.** 60

40. Juan travels at the rate of 30 miles per hour for 4 hours. He then returns over the same route in 3 hours. What was his average rate for the return trip, in miles per hour?

- **A.** $22\frac{1}{2}$
- **B.** $34\frac{2}{7}$
- **C.** 35
- **D.** 40

41. The value of $3^5 + 3^5 + 3^5$ is

- **E.** 3^6
- **F.** 3^{15}
- **G.** 9^5
- **H.** 9^{125}

42. Lindsay has P dollars and Mark has $9 less than Lindsay. If Mark receives an additional $11, how many dollars will Mark now have, in terms of P?

- **A.** $P - 20$
- **B.** $20 - P$
- **C.** $P + 2$
- **D.** $2 - P$

43. $R = 2 \cdot 3 \cdot 3 \cdot 5 \cdot 7 \cdot 11 \cdot 11$ and $S = 3 \cdot 7 \cdot 13 \cdot 17$. What is the greatest common factor of R and S?

- **E.** $2 \cdot 3 \cdot 3 \cdot 3 \cdot 5 \cdot 7 \cdot 7 \cdot 11 \cdot 11 \cdot 13 \cdot 17$
- **F.** $2 \cdot 3 \cdot 3 \cdot 5 \cdot 7 \cdot 11 \cdot 13 \cdot 17$
- **G.** $3 \cdot 7$
- **H.** $3 \cdot 3 \cdot 7 \cdot 7$

44. The counting numbers are placed in order in the chart, as shown. Assuming the pattern continues, in which column will the number 200 appear?

p	q	r	s	t	u	v
		1	2	3	4	5
6	7	8	9	10	11	12
13	14	15	16	17	18	19
20	21	...				

- **A.** q
- **B.** s
- **C.** t
- **D.** u

45. The equation $2(3x + 6) = 3(2x + 4)$ is satisfied by

- **E.** no value of x
- **F.** only negative values of x
- **G.** only $x = 0$
- **H.** all values of x

46. Wai Ling averaged 84 on her first three exams, and 82 on her next 2 exams. What grade must she obtain on her sixth test in order to average 85 for all six exams?

A. 96
B. 94
C. 90
D. 89

47. How many prime numbers between 8 and 60 leave a remainder of 2 when divided by 6?

E. 0
F. 1
G. 4
H. 6

48. In the diagram, each small box is a square whose side is 3. What is the area of the shaded figure?

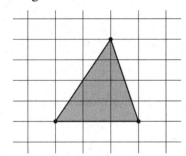

A. 108
B. 54
C. 36
D. 18

49. When expressed in scientific notation, the number 1,230,000,000 is 1.23×10^B. The value of B is

E. 2
F. 7
G. 8
H. 9

50. In the diagram, lines m and n are parallel. What is the value of x?

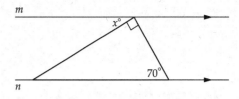

A. 20
B. 40
C. 45
D. 60

51. If $P = \sqrt{2+\sqrt{10}}$, $Q = \sqrt{10+\sqrt{2}}$, and $R = \sqrt{5+\sqrt{5}}$, then

E. $P < Q < R$
F. $P < R < Q$
G. $Q < R < P$
H. $P = Q$

52. The sides of a triangle *all* have integer lengths. Two sides have lengths 7 and 10. If the largest and smallest possible *perimeters* for the triangle are L and S, the value of $L + S$

A. is 20
B. is 51
C. is 54
D. cannot be determined from the information given

Revising/Editing Part A

1. C	3. B	5. C
2. F	4. F	6. H

Revising/Editing Part B

7. A	9. C	11. C	13. B
8. F	10. H	12. H	

Reading

14. D	18. A	22. D
15. E	19. H	23. H
16. A	20. A	24. B
17. F	21. G	25. F

Mathematics

26. **3,600**	33. H	40. D	47. E
27. **31**	34. A	41. E	48. B
28. B	35. H	42. C	49. H
29. H	36. C	43. G	50. A
30. D	37. F	44. D	51. F
31. F	38. D	45. H	52. C
32. C	39. G	46. B	

ANSWER EXPLANATIONS
MINITEST 2

Revising/Editing Part A

1. **(C)** Examine the pairings of <u>modifiers</u> and *modified objects* below.

   Incorrect: <u>Known as the "master builder,"</u> *Robert Moses's plans* helped develop the streets and highways of New York City.

   Correct: <u>Known as the "master builder,"</u> *Robert Moses* created plans that helped develop the streets and highways of New York City.

   **Notice the difference between *Robert Moses's plans* and *Robert Moses*. A master builder is a person, not the person's plans.

2. **(F)** Rule number 4. *Although most people are indifferent to the drab, gray New York pigeon* is a subordinate clause. Therefore, a comma is necessary to split it from the following independent clause.

3. **(B)**

   Sentence 1 contains a modifier and an independent clause. This is not a run-on.

Before the invention of the Internet,	people in New York City used to do a lot of different things to keep themselves entertained.
Modifier	Independent Clause

   Sentence 2 contains two independent clauses. This is a run-on.

One of them was playing sports,	games like stickball and handball were summer favorites.
Independent Clause	Independent Clause

   Correction: One of them was playing sports, **and** games like stickball and handball were summer favorites.

   Sentence 3 contains a dependent clause, an independent clause, and a dependent clause.

If physical activity wasn't your thing,	you could go to an underground arcade,	where kids would insert quarters into a giant machine to play video games.
Dependent Clause	Independent Clause	Dependent Clause

   Sentence 4 contains a dependent clause, independent clause, and a dependent clause.

Whatever you did,	you can be sure	that you were with real human beings.
Dependent Clause	Independent Clause	Dependent Clause

4. **(F)** Examine the pairings of <u>antecedents</u> and **pronouns** below.

   (1) <u>The British Empire</u> is noted for **its** powerful influence all over the globe. (2) This power was maintained by a formidable <u>navy</u>, which kept a rule to maintain a number of ships that were equal to the combined ships of **their** two largest naval rivals. (3) The rule became untenable once the <u>United States</u> matured because **its** industrial capacity outpaced that of Britain. (4) Nonetheless, <u>the British Empire</u> continued to thrive due largely to **its** successful economic strength.

   Sentence 1: The correct antecedent to the singular pronoun **its** is <u>The British Empire</u>.
   Sentence 2: The plural pronoun **their** is an inappropriate replacement for the singular antecedent <u>navy</u>. **Their** should be revised to **its**.

   Sentence 3: The correct antecedent to the singular pronoun **its** is <u>United States</u>.

   Sentence 4: The correct antecedent to the singular pronoun **its** is <u>the British Empire</u>.

5. **(C)** Examine the subject noun and predicate verb pairings for each sentence. The incorrect pairing is *italicized*. Sentence 4 contains two subject noun/predicate verb pairings that are separated by the word "that."

(1) Several <u>members</u> ~~of the committee~~ <u>believe</u> that the school made a mistake. (2) In a recent meeting, <u>parents</u> ~~of sixth, seventh, and eighth graders~~ <u>plan</u> to speak about the problem. (3) *One* ~~of the biggest issues~~ *are* nutrition, homework, and the graduation venue. (4) <u>Parents believe</u> that <u>addressing</u> all these issues <u>is</u> critical to running a successful year.

6. **(H)** Examine all the predicate verbs underlined below.

(1) Coffee beans <u>are</u> not really beans in the truest sense. (2) They <u>are</u>, in fact, seeds from the fruit of a coffee tree, which <u>may</u> produce coffee beans for as long as 50 to 60 years. (3) The oldest and most popular method of processing coffee beans <u>is</u> called the "dry process." (4) In this process, the drying operation <u>is</u> the most important stage that <u>affected</u> the final quality of the coffee.

The paragraph is written in the present tense and the predicate verb that doesn't agree is the past tense verb *affected*.

Revising/Editing Part B

7. **(A)** The purpose of this essay is to inform the audience of the errors we make with food. The phrase *These errors* in choice A connects the phrase *several errors* in sentence 1 and introduces the three ways in which science has identified our errors in food economy.

Choice B introduces the idea that mankind can become more responsible stewards, which is not supported by the passage.

Choice C is implied, but it is not the main claim.

Choice D deals with food, but man's powers over food sources are not discussed anywhere in the passage.

8. **(F)** Choice F explains why people purchase food needlessly, and it connects with the phrase *this mistaken assumption* in sentence 5.

Choice E discusses access to food, not necessarily price.

Choice G is an example of a particular diet. Sentence 4 does not introduce any particular types of diets.

Choice H focuses on the labeling of foods and makes no connection to sentence 4 or 5.

9. **(C)** Sentence 8 adds more information to the claim in sentence 7.

10. **(H)** Sentence 8 discusses the tendency to consume too much of a food. In Sentence 9 are examples of the food mentioned in sentence 8. Therefore, sentence 11 would best fit in after sentence 9 to show the contrast. The phrase *These* in sentence 10 connects with the phrase *meat and fish and gluten of wheat* in sentence 11.

11. **(C)** The phrase *waste needless quantities of food* aligns with the style and vocabulary. The other answer choices are too informal.

12. **(H)** Sentence 17 introduces the problem of a person's overall budget.

13. **(B)** Overall, it addresses the main claim, which is identifying the errors in food economy. Secondly, the phrase *that demand* best connects with the phrase *economic demands* in sentence 18.

Choice A introduces another problem rather than concluding the main idea.

Choice C is too general as it advocates the conservation of resources rather than food.

Choice D proposes a skeptical attitude about American behavior, which is not discussed at all in the passage.

Reading

Passage I

14. **(D)** Main Idea   A is too narrow. B is inaccurate, as the Travellers are not extinct. C limits the subject to uprooted families, wheras the passage suggests a core of wandering poets. Since the passage gives both history and description, and the Travellers can be considered an ethnic group, D is correct.

15. **(E)** Detail   All of the other choices can be found in the passage. E is not given. The passage states as a possible origin people who *served* lords, not the lords themselves (line 14).

16. **(A)** Detail   The itinerant lifestyle as a tradition is specifically mentioned in lines 6–9. The other choices are either wrong or refer to the group as it exists today.

17. **(F)** Detail   Usually definition questions require inference, but in some cases the definition is provided. In this case, it is given immediately following the phrase (lines 52–53).

18. **(A)** Inference   The idea that Shelta arose among poets suggests that its origin may be in literature. All of the other choices contradict statements in the passage.

19. **(H)** E, F, and G are given as factors in the last paragraph. H, however, contradicts the second sentence in the passage, which says that the people have (present tense) their own language (line 5).

Passage II

20. **(A)** Main Idea   A is the only answer both broad enough and also accurate. B is broad, but not accurate. The passage indicates that women achieved equality in some areas, but does not state or suggest a superior position for women. C and D are too narrow. D is both narrow and inaccurate, as the passage is not about how Islam began but rather certain early developments in Islam.

21. **(G)** Detail   The word "fully" makes this choice inaccurate because it is too extreme.

The passage states (lines 56–57) that women *sometimes* led congregations, which indicates that a position of leadership for women was not the usual thing. Thus, women's position was not fully equal. The other choices are all stated.

22. **(D)** Inference   D is suggested in the first paragraph (lines 3–4). B contradicts the information given in the last paragraph. Nothing in the passage supports C as a choice.

23. **(H)** Inference   The fact that an entire paragraph is devoted to the important females in Muhammad's life suggests that he may have been influenced by his feelings about them. None of the other choices can be inferred. The words "minor" and "cult" make E incorrect because nothing in the passage suggests that Islam is either a cult or minor. F contradicts information given in the next-to-last paragraph (lines 55–58). Divorce is mentioned only once (line 49), and the information given does not suggest that divorce was made easier, so G is incorrect.

24. **(B)** Main Idea   The answer is found in the third paragraph. A contradicts the statement that a woman had no "legal right to . . . economic support" (lines 24–25). C is too extreme; the third and fourth paragraphs indicate a weak legal position but do not suggest that women had no rights at all. D is incorrect because of the word "usually" (line 25), which indicates that men could and sometimes did leave property to women.

25. **(F)** Detail   The answer is directly stated in the third paragraph (lines 19–20).

Mathematics

26. **(3,600)** 3 hours = 3 × 60 minutes = 180 minutes. Every 40 minutes, 800 gallons is pumped into the tank. Compute how many times 40 minutes goes into 3 hours, then multiply that by 800. Our final answer will be $\left(\frac{180}{40}\right) \cdot 800$, which is 3,600 gallons.

27. **(31)** The problem indicates that N^2 would be less than 1,000, but $(N + 1)^2$ would be more than 1,000. Testing well-chosen numbers, $30^2 = 900$, $31^2 = 961$, and $32^2 = 1,024$, so $N = 31$.

28. **(B)** This is $\frac{1800}{90} = 20$.

29. **(H)** We must check each of the choices. Changing each to a decimal, they become .5, .333 . . . , .25, .2, and .1666 . . . . The closest to .213 is .2, which is H.

30. **(D)** Since $\overline{CD}$ bisects angle *ACB,* it must be true that angle *ACD* is also equal to $y°$. In triangle *ACD,* one angle measures 70°. Therefore the sum of the other two angles, $x + y$, must be 110°.

31. **(F)** The primes between 15 and 45 are 17, 19, 23, 29, 31, 37, 41, and 43. There are three pairs of twin primes (namely 17 and 19, 29 and 31, and 41 and 43).

32. **(C)** Since $12^2 = 144$ and $13^2 = 169$, $\sqrt{156.3}$ is a number between 12 and 13. The smallest integer that is greater than or equal to that number is 13.

33. **(H)** Oana is now 12 years old, so in eight years she will be 20. Since she will then be twice as old as her brother is now, her brother must now be 10.

34. **(A)** Two minutes is equal to 120 seconds. In that time, the snail crawls $120\left(\frac{2}{5}\right) = 48$ inches.

35. **(H)** Eliminating the initial $150 that was in the cash register, we see that 30 tickets sold for $300. Therefore each ticket sells for $\frac{300}{30} = \$10$.

36. **(C)** One method of solution is to subtract 15 from both sides of the inequality, getting $-2x < -8$. Then we divide both sides of the new inequality by -2, getting $x > 4$.

> **FACT:** When both sides of an inequality are multiplied or divided by a negative number, the sense of the inequality must be reversed.

37. **(F)** Each side of the square is 16. Therefore, each circle has a diameter of 8. The circumference of each circle is given by $C = \pi d = 8\pi$.

38. **(D)** Adding the two equations produces $5x + 5y = 110$. When we divide both sides of this equation by 5, we get $x + y = 22$.

> **TIP:** It is not always necessary to obtain x and y individually (and the problem may not call for that).

39. **(G)** Kenny is selling 9 bars for $3, but those 9 bars cost him only $1. Therefore he makes $2 for every 9 bars he sells. In order to make a profit of exactly $10, he must sell $(5)(9) = 45$ candy bars.

40. **(D)**

> **FACT:** *Distance = rate × time*

Juan's first trip covered $(30)(4) = 120$ miles. This formula can be rewritten in the form $rate = \frac{distance}{time}$. Therefore his return trip was done at the average rate of $\frac{120}{3} = 40$ miles per hour.

41. **(E)** Combining terms, this is 3×3^5, which is 3^6.

42. **(C)** Mark started with $P - 9$ dollars. Adding $11 gives him $P - 9 + 11 = P + 2$ dollars.

43. **(G)**

> **FACT:** The greatest common factor (also called the greatest common divisor) of R and S consists of the primes common to both R and S, with each such prime raised to the smaller of the exponents it had in R or S.

Since $R = 2 \cdot 3^2 \cdot 5 \cdot 7 \cdot 11^2$ and $S = 3 \cdot 7 \cdot 13 \cdot 17$, the greatest common factor is $3 \cdot 7$.

44. **(D)** Column q contains the multiples of 7. If we divide 7 into 200, we get a quotient of 28 and a remainder of 4. That means $200 = (7)(28) + 4$. The number $(7)(28)$, being a multiple of 7, will be in column q.

The number 200 will appear 4 columns later, in column *u*.

45. **(H)** Carrying out the multiplications, we get $6x + 12 = 6x + 12$. Since both sides are identical, any value for *x* will satisfy the equation.

46. **(B)**

> **TIP:** If the mean of *n* numbers is *A*, then the numbers add up to $n \times A$.

Wai Ling's first three exam grades added up to $3 \times 84 = 252$. Her next two grades added up to $2 \times 82 = 164$. So far all her grades add up to 416. In order for six grades to average 85, they must add up to $6 \times 85 = 510$. Her sixth grade will have to be $510 - 416 = 94$.

47. **(E)** Any multiple of 6 is even. If a number is 2 more than a multiple of 6, that number is also even. There are no even primes between 8 and 60.

> **FACT:** The only even prime is the number 2.

48. **(B)** The base of this triangle is 9, and its height is 12. The area of the triangle is $\frac{1}{2}bh = \frac{1}{2}(9)(12) = 54$. If you chose 6 as your answer, you forgot that the side of each small box was 3, not 1. Even then, you could have found the correct area by using the fact

> **FACT:** If two figures are "similar" (same shape), then the ratio of their areas is the *square* of the ratio of their corresponding sides.

For example, if the corresponding sides are in the ratio 3:1, their areas are in the ratio 9:1. Thus, if the side of a square is tripled, its area is multiplied by 9.

49. **(H)**

> **FACT:** For a number to be in scientific notation, it must be of the form $A \times 10^B$, where $1 \leq A < 10$ and *B* is an integer.

We start by placing the decimal point after the 1, getting 1.23. Now we count how many

positions to the right the decimal point would have to be moved to produce the original number. It would have to move 9 places (the decimal point for the original number is actually after its final 0). That means the exponent *B* must be a 9.

> **TIP:** If you have difficulty remembering how to adjust the exponent of 10 when you move a decimal point, try using smaller numbers. For example, 25×10 (or 250) is equal to 2.5×100 (that is 2.5×10^2).

50. **(A)** The third angle of the right triangle is equal to 20°. Because of the parallel lines, that angle must also equal *x*.

> **FACT:** If two parallel lines are crossed by a transversal, the "alternate-interior" angles formed must be equal.

51. **(F)** $\sqrt{10}$ is a little more than 3, $\sqrt{2}$ is a little more than 1, and $\sqrt{5}$ is a little more than 2. Then *P* is a little more than $\sqrt{2+3}$ or $\sqrt{5}$, *Q* is a little more than $\sqrt{10+1}$ or $\sqrt{11}$, and *R* is a little more than $\sqrt{5+2}$ or $\sqrt{7}$. Therefore *P* is the smallest, *R* is next, and *Q* is the largest.

52. **(C)**

> **FACT:** The sum of the lengths of two sides of a triangle is greater than the length of the third side.

Since two sides are 7 and 10, the third side must be less than 17. Therefore the longest that the third side could be is 16, and $L = 7 + 10 + 16 = 33$. The shortest the third side could be is 4, because a side of 3 plus a side of 7 is not greater than a side of 10. Therefore $S = 7 + 4 + 10 = 21$. Then $L + S = 33 + 21 = 54$.

ANSWER SHEET
Minitest 3

Part I English Language Arts

Revising/Editing Part A

1. Ⓐ Ⓑ Ⓒ Ⓓ
2. Ⓔ Ⓕ Ⓖ Ⓗ
3. Ⓐ Ⓑ Ⓒ Ⓓ
4. Ⓔ Ⓕ Ⓖ Ⓗ
5. Ⓐ Ⓑ Ⓒ Ⓓ
6. Ⓔ Ⓕ Ⓖ Ⓗ

Revising/Editing Part B

7. Ⓐ Ⓑ Ⓒ Ⓓ
8. Ⓔ Ⓕ Ⓖ Ⓗ
9. Ⓐ Ⓑ Ⓒ Ⓓ
10. Ⓔ Ⓕ Ⓖ Ⓗ
11. Ⓐ Ⓑ Ⓒ Ⓓ
12. Ⓔ Ⓕ Ⓖ Ⓗ
13. Ⓐ Ⓑ Ⓒ Ⓓ

Reading

14. Ⓐ Ⓑ Ⓒ Ⓓ
15. Ⓔ Ⓕ Ⓖ Ⓗ
16. Ⓐ Ⓑ Ⓒ Ⓓ
17. Ⓔ Ⓕ Ⓖ Ⓗ
18. Ⓐ Ⓑ Ⓒ Ⓓ
19. Ⓔ Ⓕ Ⓖ Ⓗ

20. Ⓐ Ⓑ Ⓒ Ⓓ
21. Ⓔ Ⓕ Ⓖ Ⓗ
22. Ⓐ Ⓑ Ⓒ Ⓓ
23. Ⓔ Ⓕ Ⓖ Ⓗ
24. Ⓐ Ⓑ Ⓒ Ⓓ
25. Ⓔ Ⓕ Ⓖ Ⓗ

Part II Mathematics

26.

27.

28. Ⓐ Ⓑ Ⓒ Ⓓ
29. Ⓔ Ⓕ Ⓖ Ⓗ
30. Ⓐ Ⓑ Ⓒ Ⓓ
31. Ⓔ Ⓕ Ⓖ Ⓗ
32. Ⓐ Ⓑ Ⓒ Ⓓ
33. Ⓔ Ⓕ Ⓖ Ⓗ
34. Ⓐ Ⓑ Ⓒ Ⓓ
35. Ⓔ Ⓕ Ⓖ Ⓗ
36. Ⓐ Ⓑ Ⓒ Ⓓ

37. Ⓔ Ⓕ Ⓖ Ⓗ
38. Ⓐ Ⓑ Ⓒ Ⓓ
39. Ⓔ Ⓕ Ⓖ Ⓗ
40. Ⓐ Ⓑ Ⓒ Ⓓ
41. Ⓔ Ⓕ Ⓖ Ⓗ
42. Ⓐ Ⓑ Ⓒ Ⓓ
43. Ⓔ Ⓕ Ⓖ Ⓗ
44. Ⓐ Ⓑ Ⓒ Ⓓ
45. Ⓔ Ⓕ Ⓖ Ⓗ

46. Ⓐ Ⓑ Ⓒ Ⓓ
47. Ⓔ Ⓕ Ⓖ Ⓗ
48. Ⓐ Ⓑ Ⓒ Ⓓ
49. Ⓔ Ⓕ Ⓖ Ⓗ
50. Ⓐ Ⓑ Ⓒ Ⓓ
51. Ⓔ Ⓕ Ⓖ Ⓗ
52. Ⓐ Ⓑ Ⓒ Ⓓ

Minitest 3

PART 1—ENGLISH LANGUAGE ARTS

25 QUESTIONS

SUGGESTED TIME: 30 MINUTES

Revising/Editing

QUESTIONS 1–13

Revising/Editing Part A

Directions: Read and answer each of the following questions. You will be asked to recognize and correct errors in sentences or short paragraphs. Mark the **best** answer for each question.

1. Read this paragraph.

> (1) The public, enamored of the rising popularity of intellectuals, often views scientists as logical and infallible beings. (2) While logic and precision are important, a strong intuition, as well as perseverance, are just as important. (3) A scientist's work, either in the lab or out in the field, requires more than just brains. (4) There are many other things that contribute to a successful scientific intellectual.

Which sentence in this paragraph contains an error in subject-verb agreement?

A. sentence 1
B. sentence 2
C. sentence 3
D. sentence 4

2. Read this sentence.

> Streaking across the sky the Bobo meteor is one of the most amazing cosmic objects to grace the majestic night sky.

Which edit should be made to correct this sentence?

E. add a comma after *across*
F. add a comma after *sky*
G. add a comma after *amazing*
H. add a comma after *majestic*

3. Read this sentence.

> In the 17th and 18th century, Americans encouraged a relatively, lax immigration policy into the "land of the free," but the economic decline of the 1880s resulted in the passage of the Chinese Exclusion Act, which placed restrictions on immigration from China.

Which edit should be made to correct this sentence?

A. delete the comma after *relatively*
B. delete the comma after *free*
C. delete the comma after *century*
D. delete the comma after *Act*

4. Read this paragraph.

> (1) Prior to the rise of the cell phone, people kept in touch through a gadget called the beeper. (2) Invariably rectangular in shape, black in color, and plastic in cover, the beeper would beep and vibrate as a phone number blinked on a tiny gray screen illuminated by a green light. (3) Soon enough, cell phones gain popularity and the prices drop, so that people began to abandon beepers for phones. (4) One of the leading manufacturers of beepers decided to ride the wave of the cell phone and reshaped itself as a cell phone manufacturer.

Which sentence should be revised to correct an inappropriate shift in verb tense?

E. sentence 1
F. sentence 2
G. sentence 3
H. sentence 4

5. Read this paragraph.

> (1) It is difficult to attribute one defining factor that contributed to China's rise for analysts. (2) However, China's entrance into the WTO (World Trade Organization) in 2000 coincided with an exponential increase in the country's economic output. (3) Each year, China's economy grew by more than 10%. (4) Today, the growth has subsided to 6%, but that number is still higher than America's, which currently stands at about 2%.

Which sentence should be revised to correct a misplaced modifier?

A. sentence 1
B. sentence 2
C. sentence 3
D. sentence 4

6. Read these sentences.

> (1) The colonization of Mars is a daunting task that presents numerous challenges. (2) Many people are enthused by the idea of the one-way trip.

What is the best way to combine these sentences to clarify the relationship between the ideas?

E. The colonization of Mars is a daunting task that presents numerous challenges for many people, enthused by the idea of the one-way trip.
F. The colonization of Mars is a daunting task that presents numerous challenges because many people are enthused by the idea of the one-way trip.
G. When many people are enthused by the idea of the one-way trip, the colonization of Mars is a daunting task that presents numerous challenges.
H. Although the colonization of Mars is a daunting task that presents numerous challenges, many people are enthused by the idea of the one-way trip.

Revising/Editing Part B

Directions: Read the passage below and answer the questions following it. You will be asked to improve the writing quality of the passage and to correct errors so that the passage follows the conventions of standard written English. You may reread the passage if you need to. Mark the best answer for each question.

The Harmful Effects of Acid Rain

(1) An ecosystem is a society of plants, animals, and other organisms, along with the environment. (2) Everything in an ecosystem is connected.

(3) The profound effects of acid rain are most clearly seen in aquatic environs, such as lakes, streams, and marshes where it can be detrimental to wildlife. (4) As it flows

through the soil, acidic rainwater can be harmful to the environment. (5) The more acid that is introduced to the wild, the more aluminum is released.

(6) Some types of flora and fauna are able to withstand acidic waters and moderate amounts of aluminum. (7) Others are highly sensitive and will be lost as the acidity declines. (8) Generally, the young offspring of most organisms are more sensitive to surrounding conditions than adults. (9) For instance, most fish eggs cannot hatch at a pH level of 5, while at lower pH levels, some adult fish die. (10) Even if a fish or animal can endure moderately acidic water, the animals or plants it eats might not. (11) For example, frogs can survive in an environmental pH of 4, but the mayflies they eat may not survive pH below 5.

(12) Decaying trees are a common sight in areas affected by acid pollution. (13) Acid rain leaches aluminum from the soil. (14) That aluminum can be used in the manufacturing process through new techniques that have made the United States a leader in aluminum production. (15) Acid rain also removes important nutrients from the soil. (16) Without the chlorophyll-rich covering, the trees are then less able to absorb sunlight, which makes them weak and less able to withstand freezing temperatures. (17) At high elevations, acidic fog and clouds might strip nutrients from trees' foliage, leaving them with a cover of brown or dead leaves and needles.

(18) For humans, exposure to acid rain or even swimming in a lake affected by acid rain is no more dangerous than walking in normal rain or swimming in non-acidic lakes. (19) However, when the acid rain evaporates into the atmosphere, the particles can be harmful to humans.

7. Which sentence can best follow and support sentence 2?

   A. If something harms one part of an ecosystem—one species of plant or animal, the soil, or the water—it can have an impact on everything else.
   B. Likewise, humans create connections primarily through technology, such as telephones and the Internet.
   C. The government currently manages 58 national parks around the country, each with its unique needs.
   D. The consequences of overdevelopment and pollution are apparently manageable precisely because of the redundancies built into these interconnections.

8. Which revision of sentence 4 uses the most precise language?

   E. As it flows through the soil, acidic rainwater can absorb harmful stuff from the soil and then flow into other bodies of water.
   F. As it flows through the soil, acidic rainwater can absorb harmful elements from the earth and then flow into streams and lakes.
   G. As it flows through the soil, acidic rainwater can absorb contaminants from soil clay particles and then flow into other bodies of water.
   H. As it flows through the soil, acidic rainwater can absorb contaminants from soil clay particles and then flow into streams and lakes.

9. Which transition word or phrase should be added to the beginning of sentence 6?

    A. As a result,
    B. However,
    C. Unfortunately,
    D. In other words,

10. What is the best way to combine sentences 12 and 13 to clarify the relationship between ideas?

    E. Dead or dying trees are a common sight in areas affected by acid rain, and acid rain leaches aluminum from the soil.
    F. Dead or dying trees are a common sight in areas affected by acid rain, which leaches aluminum from the soil.
    G. Although dead or dying trees are a common sight in areas affected by acid rain, it leaches aluminum from the soil.
    H. Whereas dead or dying trees are a common sight in areas affected by acid rain, acid rain leaches aluminum from the soil.

11. Which sentence is irrelevant to the argument presented in the passage and should be deleted?

    A. sentence 2
    B. sentence 6
    C. sentence 10
    D. sentence 14

12. Where should sentence 17 be moved to improve the organization of the fourth paragraph (sentences 12–17)?

    E. to the beginning of the paragraph (before sentence 12)
    F. between sentences 13 and 14
    G. between sentences 14 and 15
    H. between sentences 15 and 16

13. Which sentence could best follow sentence 19 and support the main point of the fourth paragraph?

    A. This air pollution affects our enjoyment of national parks, such as Shenandoah and the Great Smoky Mountains, which we visit for clean, healthy air as well as for scenic views.
    B. Acid rain also contains nitrogen, and this element can have an impact on some ecosystems.
    C. Many scientific studies have shown a causal relationship between these particles and negative effects on heart function, including heart attacks, and lung function, such as increased breathing difficulties for people with asthma.
    D. In areas such as the mountainous parts of the northeastern United States, the soil is thin and lacks the ability to adequately neutralize the acid in the rainwater.

> **Directions:** Read each passage and answer the questions that follow it. Base your answers **only on the material contained in the passage.** Select the one **best** answer for each question. Bubble in the letter corresponding to that answer on the answer sheet.

I. The samurai were the warrior class of Japan during that country's feudal period, which lasted from the twelfth to the mid-nineteenth century. Their position was
(5) much like that of the knights of medieval Europe: They were warriors dedicated to the service of a nobleman, and they followed a strict code of honor. Bushido—"the way of the warrior"—enjoined loyalty to lord and
(10) country, upright behavior, endurance, courage, courtesy, and truthfulness.

A unique feature of samurai culture was the practice of hara-kiri, or seppuku, a form of ritual suicide by disembowelment. Performed
(15) as a way of preserving honor, its earliest use was by warriors who faced the disgrace of capture by the enemy. Later it served as a way of acknowledging and being purged of guilt. In this context it could be practiced voluntarily,
(20) the more admired way, or involuntarily by order of the ruler, a death considered honorable if not wholly admirable.

Sometimes samurai lost their noble masters, in which case they became *ronin*, or
(25) unattached samurai. The most common reasons for such loss were punishment for some improper behavior, defeat in battle, or the master's death or deposition. Some ronin, apparently unable to lay aside their weapons,
(30) turned to a life of highway robbery. Others were able to successfully adopt a peaceful existence.

The most celebrated ronin were those who carried out the famous Ako vendetta in
(35) 1703. A nobleman named Lord Asano had assaulted an official named Lord Kira. Lord Kira's conduct had provoked the assault, but because he was an official of the shogun, or military dictator, he was under the protec-
(40) tion of the ruler. As punishment Lord Asano was ordered to commit hara-kiri. After he carried out the fatal sentence, his 47 ronin acted according to their code of honor. They swore vengeance on Lord Kira, the official
(45) whose provocation had led to their master's violent act and subsequent downfall.

Lord Kira knew of their vow and exercised extreme caution. The ronin were forced to bide their time for two years, pretending that
(50) they had abandoned their oath. When they judged that their enemy had finally relaxed his guard, the band of 47 attacked and killed him. Their courageous deed of honor made them overnight heroes. Condemned to die
(55) for the murder, the faithful followers of Lord Asano were nevertheless deemed worthy to commit hara-kiri. Thus they preserved their honor even in death.

14. Which of the following is the best title for the passage?

   A. "The Shogun's Official"
   B. "Daily Life of a Samurai"
   C. "The Role of Hara-Kiri in Feudal Japan"
   D. "Samurai Honor"

15. What is the most likely reason why the author included the story of the ronins' vengeance?

   E. It is a good illustration of Bushido.
   F. It shows the injustice of involuntary hara-kiri.
   G. It explains how a samurai could become masterless through no fault of his own.
   H. It provides an example of patience.

16. How did the practice of hara-kiri originate?

A. As a way to atone for cowardice in battle

B. As a way for a person guilty of some crime to preserve honor

C. As a way for a ronin to remain with his master in death

D. As a way to avoid becoming a prisoner of war

17. Why did Lord Asano's ronin desire to kill Lord Kira?

E. He had ordered their master to commit hara-kiri.

F. He was an official of the shogun who had ordered their master to commit hara-kiri.

G. He had assaulted their master.

H. His behavior had indirectly led to their master's death.

18. With which of the following statements would the author most likely agree?

A. The ronin in the story were ideals of samurai virtue.

B. Although they were courageous, the ronin should have followed legal means.

C. The shogun overreacted in ordering such a severe penalty against Lord Asano.

D. People of today should follow the example of the 47 ronin.

19. Which of the following is **not** a similarity between European knights and samurai?

E. Ritual suicide

F. A military career

G. Attachment to a lord

H. Binding rules of behavior

II. Emeralds, scarcer than diamonds, are a sort of geological miracle because they contain elements that combine only under
Line extraordinary conditions. They are classi-
(5) fied as beryls, which are composed of the elements beryllium, aluminum, silicon, and oxygen. However, emeralds differ from other beryls in that they also contain traces of chromium or vanadium, which give
(10) them their distinctive green color.

A "miracle" is required to bring the heavier chromium or vanadium together with the lighter beryllium because they naturally occur in different layers of rock. But when
(15) the movement of the earth's crust shoves an oceanic layer onto a continental layer, the heavier elements and the lighter ones are brought together. With this mixture in place, emeralds are a possibility, but
(20) not until another dramatic geologic event occurs. If the shifting plates of the crust create sufficient pressure, some rock may be forced downward until it melts. This process produces jets of superheated liquid
(25) which rise, leaching out elements in the rock layer above. When these elements are the essential ingredients of emeralds, and the ingredients combine, the miracle is complete.

(30) Emeralds occur in several regions of the world, including South Africa, Egypt, Pakistan, Brazil, and Colombia. Because of their color, clarity, and size, those of Colombia are the most prized. Their magnificent difference is
(35) due to a difference in their creation.

The basic processes—a combination of usually separated minerals and a bath of hot liquid—are the same as those that produced all other emeralds. But there are some dif-
(40) ferences. In the first place, in Colombia the heavier and lighter elements were originally mixed by the shifting of the earth's crust but then were washed off and superimposed on the floor of an inland sea, where they formed

(45) potentially emerald-bearing shales. With the elements in place, plate tectonics—the movement of the earth's crust—began to play its crucial part. Tremendous pressure built up as the South American continent was pushed *(50)* westward. Undersea rock layers folded and split, and hot water flowed upward through layers of salt and shale, leaching out the emerald components. Over a period of time, the solution collected in a pocket in the *(55)* earth's crust, where pressure built to the exploding point. When the pocket burst, the sudden eruption produced instant emerald crystals, created so quickly that they had no time to mix with other minerals. The purity *(60)* of the crystals lends Colombian emeralds their superior color and clarity.

An intriguing feature of emeralds is that each one encloses a minute droplet of fluid, fancifully dubbed a "garden." In Colom- *(65)* bian gems the garden is a salt crystal, a reminder of their unique origin.

20. Which of the following best states what this passage is about?

- **A.** The superiority of Colombian emeralds
- **B.** Some unusual effects of plate tectonics
- **C.** The production of a rare mineral
- **D.** The function of chromium and vanadium

21. What is the meaning of "superimposed" as it is used in the passage (line 43)?

- **E.** Absorbed throughout
- **F.** Deposited from above
- **G.** Melted because of geologic factors
- **H.** Applied as an effect of extreme heat

22. Which of the following best explains why Colombian emeralds are so clear?

- **A.** Each one contains a salt crystal.
- **B.** They don't contain adulterating elements.
- **C.** They were produced in a purifying explosion.
- **D.** They have not mixed with vanadium or chromium.

23. Which of the following is **not** true of emeralds?

- **E.** They are beryls.
- **F.** Plate tectonics is involved in their creation.
- **G.** They occur only when shales form on a sea bed.
- **H.** Part of the production process always involves the action of fluid.

24. What does the passage suggest about emeralds from places other than Colombia?

- **A.** They are greener than Colombia's emeralds.
- **B.** They are more abundant than Colombian emeralds.
- **C.** They are considered more desirable than Colombian emeralds.
- **D.** Their "gardens" do not consist of salt crystals.

25. What is the most likely reason why chromium and vanadium do not occur in the same rock layer as beryllium?

- **E.** They were produced on different parts of the earth's surface.
- **F.** They have been leached out of their original layer.
- **G.** The layers have been separated by plate tectonics.
- **H.** Their heavier weight caused them to settle in a lower layer.

PART 2—MATHEMATICS

QUESTIONS 26–52

SUGGESTED TIME: 45 MINUTES

Grid-In Problems

Directions: Solve each problem. On the answer sheet, write your answer in the boxes at the top of the grid. Start on the left side of each grid. Print only one number or symbol in each box. **DO NOT LEAVE A BOX BLANK IN THE MIDDLE OF AN ANSWER.** Under each box, fill in the circle that matches the number or symbol you wrote above. **DO NOT FILL IN A CIRCLE UNDER AN UNUSED BOX.**

26. Solve for x if $\dfrac{2.8}{0.14} = \dfrac{x}{0.09}$.

27. How many even, two-digit numbers do not contain the digit 6? (Reminder: The tens digits of a two-digit number cannot be zero (0).)

Multiple-Choice Problems

Directions: For each of the following questions, select the **best** answer from the given choices. Bubble in the letter corresponding to your answer on the answer sheet. **DO NOT PUT ANY OTHER WORK ON THE ANSWER SHEET.** All necessary work can be done in your test booklet or on scrap paper that is provided.

NOTE: Diagrams other than graphs might not be drawn to scale. Do not assume any relationships that are not specifically stated unless they are implied by the given information.

28. How many multiples of 3 between 1 and 22 are even?
  - **A.** 7
  - **B.** 5
  - **C.** 3
  - **D.** None

29. $2x(3y) =$
  - **E.** $12xy$
  - **F.** $6xy$
  - **G.** $5xy$
  - **H.** $6x + 6y$

30. In triangle ABC, $AB = AC$ and the measure of angle C is 70°. What is the measure of angle A, in degrees?

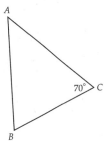

  - **A.** 40
  - **B.** 55
  - **C.** 60
  - **D.** 70

31. $\sqrt{36} \times \sqrt{9} + \sqrt{16} =$

    E. $\sqrt{340}$
    F. 22
    G. 30
    H. 42

32. At 9 A.M. it was 12 degrees *below zero.*
By noon the temperature had dropped
7 degrees. Over the next two hours, the
temperature rose 5 degrees. What was the
temperature at 2 P.M.?

    A. 10° below zero
    B. 14° below zero
    C. 24° below zero
    D. none of these

33. Bob's age is now 3 times Tom's age. Twelve
years from now, Tom will be 15 years old.
How many years old is Bob now?

    E. 3
    F. 5
    G. 9
    H. 27

34. In rectangle *ABCD,* point *E* is on side $\overline{AB}$.
What is the measure of angle *DEC*?

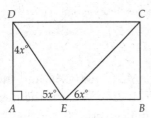

    A. 10°
    B. 48°
    C. 60°
    D. 70°

35. If $1 < 4n < 50$, and *n* is a positive integer,
what is the largest possible value for *n?*

    E. 199
    F. 49
    G. 13
    H. 12

36. Which of the following is equal to $\dfrac{8x - 8}{2}$?

    A. $8x - 4$
    B. $4x - 4$
    C. $4x - 8$
    D. $4x$

37. If $7x - 14 = 14 - 7x$, then $x =$

    E. −4
    F. −2
    G. 0
    H. 2

38. If *N* granola bars cost 3 dollars, then the
cost of 3 granola bars is

    A. $\dfrac{9}{N}$ dollars
    B. *N* dollars
    C. 3*N* dollars
    D. 1 dollar

39. In Mr. Romano's class, the ratio of the
number of girls to the number of boys is
3:2. A student is selected at random from
the class. The probability that the selected
student is a boy is

    E. $\dfrac{1}{6}$
    F. $\dfrac{1}{3}$
    G. $\dfrac{2}{5}$
    H. $\dfrac{3}{5}$

40. Each of the integers from –3 to 5 inclusive is placed in the diagram, with one number going into each box. If the sum of the numbers in each row is the same, what is that sum?

- **A.** 0
- **B.** 3
- **C.** 5
- **D.** 6

41. What is the median of the set of numbers {4, 16, 12, 10, 6, 8, 12, 12}?

- **E.** 9
- **F.** 10
- **G.** 11
- **H.** 12

42. If $\underline{X}$ means $\dfrac{X+3}{X}$ then the value of $(\underline{3})(\underline{6})$ is

- **A.** $\dfrac{7}{6}$
- **B.** $\dfrac{4}{3}$
- **C.** 3
- **D.** 16

43. What is the least common multiple of P and Q if $P = 3 \cdot 3 \cdot 11 \cdot 11 \cdot 13$ and $Q = 3 \cdot 5 \cdot 11 \cdot 11 \cdot 11$?

- **E.** $3 \cdot 11$
- **F.** $3 \cdot 5 \cdot 11 \cdot 13$
- **G.** $3 \cdot 11 \cdot 11$
- **H.** $3 \cdot 3 \cdot 5 \cdot 11 \cdot 11 \cdot 11 \cdot 13$

44. What is the perimeter of figure *ABCDEF*?

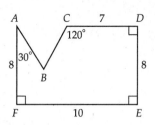

- **A.** 33
- **B.** 34
- **C.** 35
- **D.** none of these

45. The value of $\dfrac{808080}{80}$ is

- **E.** 111
- **F.** 10101
- **G.** 101010
- **H.** 640

46. From 7:00 P.M. to 8:00 P.M., José completed one-third of his homework. From 8:00 P.M. to 9:00 P.M., he completed $\dfrac{1}{4}$ of the *remaining* part of his homework. What fraction of his homework still remained to be completed after 9:00 P.M.?

- **A.** $\dfrac{1}{2}$
- **B.** $\dfrac{1}{3}$
- **C.** $\dfrac{1}{4}$
- **D.** $\dfrac{1}{5}$

47. Which of the following represents the phrase "5 less than 8 times *n*"?

- **E.** $5 < 8n$
- **F.** $5 - 8n$
- **G.** $8n + 5$
- **H.** $8n - 5$

48. If $p = -3$ and $q = 2$, what is the value of $p^2 - (q - p)$?

A. -14
B. 14
C. -4
D. 4

49. What is the area of triangle ABC?

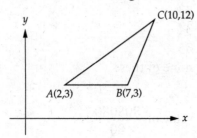

E. 15
F. 18
G. $22\frac{1}{2}$
H. 25

50. If $\dfrac{64}{x-8} + 7 = 11$, what is the value of $\dfrac{64}{x+8}$?

A. 2
B. 4
C. 16
D. 24

51. If the diameter of a circle is 6.4×10^8, then the radius of the circle is

E. 3.2×10^8
F. 3.2×10^4
G. 3.2×5^8
H. 6.4×10^4

52. When $\dfrac{1}{11}$ is expressed as a decimal, what digit appears in the 16th place to the right of the decimal point?

A. 0
B. 1
C. 2
D. 9

ANSWER KEY
Minitest 3

Revising/Editing Part A

1. **B**   3. **A**   5. **A**
2. **F**   4. **G**   6. **H**

Revising/Editing Part B

7. **A**   9. **B**   11. **D**   13. **C**
8. **H**   10. **F**   12. **H**

Reading

14. **D**   18. **A**   22. **B**
15. **E**   19. **E**   23. **G**
16. **D**   20. **C**   24. **D**
17. **H**   21. **F**   25. **H**

Mathematics

26. **1.8**   33. **G**   40. **B**   47. **H**
27. **32**   34. **D**   41. **G**   48. **D**
28. **C**   35. **H**   42. **C**   49. **G**
29. **F**   36. **B**   43. **H**   50. **A**
30. **A**   37. **H**   44. **D**   51. **E**
31. **F**   38. **A**   45. **F**   52. **D**
32. **B**   39. **G**   46. **A**

ANSWER EXPLANATIONS
MINITEST 3

Revising/Editing Part A

1. **(B)** Examine the subject noun and predicate verb pairings for each sentence. The incorrect pairing is *italicized*.

   (1) The <u>public</u>, enamored of the rising popularity of intellectuals, often <u>views</u> scientists as logical and infallible beings. (2) While <u>logic and precision are</u> important, a strong *intuition*, as well as perseverance, *are* just as important. (3) A scientist's <u>work</u>, either in the lab or out in the field, <u>requires</u> more than just brains. (4) There <u>are</u> many other <u>things</u> that contribute to a successful scientific intellectual.

2. **(F)** *Streaking across the sky* modifies the sky, so a comma is appropriate. Choice E is wrong because it creates an odd subject, *the sky the Bobo*. Choices G and H are wrong because the adjective modifying the noun *object* and the adjective modifying the noun *sky* are not coordinate adjectives.

3. **(A)** A comma is unnecessary between an adverb (a word that adds information to adjectives or verbs) and the adjective. Choice B is wrong because a comma is necessary between two clauses. Choice C is incorrect because the beginning of the sentence, *In the 17th and 18th century*, is a prepositional phrase which requires a comma. Choice D is wrong because *which placed restrictions on immigration from China* modifies *the Chinese Exclusion Act*.

4. **(G)** Examine all the predicate verbs underlined below.

   (1) Prior to the rise of the cell phone, people <u>kept</u> in touch through a gadget called the beeper. (2) Invariably rectangular in shape, black in color, and plastic in cover, the beeper <u>would</u> beep and vibrate as a phone number <u>blinked</u> on a tiny grey screen illuminated by a green light. (3) Soon enough, cell phones <u>gain</u> popularity and the prices <u>drop</u>, so that people <u>began</u> to abandon beepers for phones. (4) One of the leading manufacturers of beepers <u>decided</u> to ride the wave of the cell phone and <u>reshaped</u> itself as a cell phone manufacturer.

5. **(A)** Examine the pairings of <u>modifiers</u> and *modified object*s below.

   Incorrect: It is *difficult* to attribute one defining factor that contributed to China's rise <u>for</u> <u>analysts</u>.

   Correct: It is *difficult* <u>for analysts</u> to attribute one defining factor that contributed to China's rise.

6. **(H)**

   E. The colonization of Mars is a daunting task that presents numerous challenges for many people, enthused by the idea of the one-way trip.

   This sentence creates an illogical relationship between *colonization of Mars* and *many people*. The colonization presents numerous challenges in the general sense, but the sentence suggests that it presents challenges for people who are excited about the idea.

   F. The colonization of Mars is a daunting task that presents numerous challenges because many people are enthused by the idea of the one-way trip.

   This sentence creates an illogical causal relationship between the clauses. The enthusiasm of many people should not cause the colonization to be a daunting task.

   G. When many people are enthused by the idea of the one-way trip, the colonization of Mars is a daunting task that presents numerous challenges.

   This sentence creates an illogical causal relationship between the clauses. The enthusiasm of many people should not occur when the colonization is a daunting task.

   H. Although the colonization of Mars is a daunting task that presents numerous challenges, many people are enthused by the idea of the one-way trip.

   This sentence creates a proper contrast through the word *Although*.

Revising/Editing Part B

7. **(A)** The answer choice more fully explains what it means for an ecosystem to be connected. Choice B makes a comparison with humans, which is not addressed further anywhere in the passage. Choice C provides irrelevant details. Choice D introduces an idea that is not discussed in the passage.

8. **(H)**

Least Precise (cross out)	Most Precise
harmful stuff	contaminants
soil	soil clay particles
other bodies of water	streams and lakes

9. **(B)** Sentence 5 presents one scenario. Sentence 6 presents a contrasting scenario.

10. **(F)** Choice E is grammatically correct, but Choice F is shorter. Choices G and H use transition words unnecessarily to create a contrast.

11. **(D)** The information about the United States leading the aluminum manufacturing industry is irrelevant.

12. **(H)** The key phrase in sentence 16 is *Without the chlorophyll-rich covering.* This phrase connects with the ending phrase *a cover of brown or dead leaves* in sentence 17.

13. **(C)** Choice C provides more information on the ways in which acid rain can be harmful for humans.

Reading

Passage I

14. **(D)** Main Idea   D is the only choice broad enough. Every paragraph except the third discusses some aspect of honor, and that paragraph is necessary for understanding the story. A and C are too narrow. B is inaccurate, as the passage does not relate a daily routine.

15. **(E)** Main Idea   The emphasis in the story is on the idea that the ronin acted according to their code of honor, Bushido. The other choices all miss the emphasis on honor.

16. **(D)** Detail   The correct answer is stated in the second paragraph (lines 14–17).

17. **(H)** Inference   The passage indicates that the ronin blamed Lord Kira for their master's death. E contradicts the information given in the fourth paragraph, which says that Lord Kira was under the protection of the ruler and thus Lord Asano was ordered to commit hara-kiri (lines 40–41). This suggests that the ruler gave the order. F and G contradict the details of the story.

18. **(A)** Inference   Since the story of the ronin is used as an example of honor, it can be inferred that the main characters of the story exemplify this quality.

> **NOTE:** Individual readers may agree with one or more of these incorrect choices, but no details in the story state or suggest them.

19. **(E)** Detail   All of the other choices are stated in the first paragraph.

Passage II

20. **(C)** Main Idea   The entire passage focuses on the geologic processes that produce emeralds, which are described as scarce. A, B, and D are too narrow. Only two sentences in the passage concern A. The production of emeralds involves other factors in addition to plate tectonics, so B is incorrect. D is wrong for the same kind of reason—the chemicals named are only a part of the production process.

21. **(F)** Inference   E is not a correct answer because the passage says that the elements were "superimposed *on.*" The word *on* contradicts the word *throughout* in E. No mention of melting, heat, or salt water is made in the context, so G and H are incorrect. F is the only possible choice according to the context. The fact that the elements were superimposed on the *floor* of the ocean suggests that they came from above.

22. **(B)** Detail The passage says that the Colombian emerald crystals did not mix with other elements (line 60); thus they are not adulterated. The following sentence says that this lack of adulteration is the reason for their clarity (line 63).

23. **(G)** Detail   G contradicts the explanation given in the second paragraph. Shales are involved only in the production of Colombian emeralds. All the other choices are true and stated in the passage.

24. **(D)** Inference The last sentence in the passage makes a connection between the salt crystal in Colombian emeralds and the uniqueness of these stones, suggesting that the salt crystal is unique to Colombian emeralds. A is nowhere suggested or stated in the passage. B is not stated or suggested, and also is contra-indicated by the statement that the reasons Colombian emeralds are especially prized involve their color, clarity, and size (lines 32–33). Rarity is not mentioned.

25. **(H)** Inference The first sentence of the second paragraph says that chromium and vanadium are heavier than beryllium (lines 11–12) and that they "naturally" occur in different layers of rock (lines 13–14). The inference can be made that weight caused them to sink. Leaching is mentioned as part of the process that brings the elements together, so F is incorrect. The same is true of plate tectonics (line 46), so G is also incorrect.

Mathematics

26. **(1.8)** Multiplying both the numerator and the denominator of the fraction on the left side of the equation by 100 produces $\frac{280}{14}$, which is equal to 20. Multiplying both the numerator and the denominator of the fraction on the right side of the equation by 100 produces $\frac{100x}{9}$. Therefore, $2 = \frac{100x}{9}$. Multiplying both sides of this last equation by 9 produces $180 = 100x$, which means that $x = 1.8$.

27. **(32)** There are eight possibilities for the tens digit (1, 2, 3, 4, 5, 7, 8, 9) and four possibilities for the units digit (0, 2, 4, 8; these are the even digits, excluding 6), so the answer is $8 \times 4 = 32$. Another method of solving this problem is making an organized list, which is not very difficult and will lead to the correct answer rather quickly.

28. **(C)** Even numbers are multiples of 2. In order to also be a multiple of 3, the numbers must actually be multiples of $(2)(3) = 6$. Between 1 and 22 there are three multiples of 6.

29. **(F)** Rearranging terms, we have $2 \cdot 3 \cdot x \cdot y = 6xy$.

30. **(A)**

> **FACT:** The base angles (those are the angles opposite the equal sides) of an isosceles triangle are equal.

Angle B also measures 70°, so the third angle of the triangle is 40°.

31. **(F)** This is $6 \times 3 + 4$. The order of operations indicates that we do the multiplication first, so we have $18 + 4 = 22$.

32. **(B)** Numerically, the given changes are equivalent to $(-12) - (7) + (5) = -14$.

33. **(G)** Tom will be 15 years old in 12 years, so he is now 3. Bob is now 3 times Tom's present age, so Bob is 9.

34. **(D)** From right triangle ADE, $4x + 5x = 90$, so $x = 10$. Then $6x = 60$. Finally, $5x + 6x = 50 + 60 = 110$. That leaves 70° for angle DEC.

35. **(H)** Dividing *each* of the three parts of the inequality by 4, we get $\frac{1}{4} < n < \frac{50}{4}$. The largest integer that is less than $\frac{50}{4} \left(= 12\frac{1}{2} \right)$ is 12.

36. **(B)** Dividing each term of the numerator by 2 produces $4x - 4$.

37. **(H)** Adding $7x$ to both sides produces $14x - 14 = 14$, so $14x = 28$. Then $x = 2$.

38. **(A)** If N granola bars cost 3 dollars, then 1 granola bar costs $\dfrac{3}{N}$ dollars. Therefore, 3 granola bars will cost $3 \times \dfrac{3}{N} = \dfrac{9}{N}$ dollars. If that first concept seems difficult, try using simple numbers: If 2 granola bars cost \$3, then 1 granola bar costs \$1.50. You had to divide the total cost by the number of bars.

39. **(G)** If we use $2x$ to represent the number of boys in the class, and $3x$ to represent the number of girls, then the total number of students is $5x$. Since there are $2x$ ways to pick a boy, the probability that the selected student is a boy is $\dfrac{2x}{5x} = \dfrac{2}{5}$. If it helps, try using simple numbers such as 20 for the number of boys and 30 for the number of girls.

40. **(B)** The sum of the numbers in the nine boxes is the sum of the integers from -3 to 5. That is 9. Since the sum of the numbers in each row is the same, that sum must be $\dfrac{1}{3}$ of 9, which is 3.

41. **(G)** Arranging the elements of the set in increasing order produces {4, 6, 8, 10, 12, 12, 12, 16}. The median is the middle number if there are an odd number of elements. When there are an even number of elements, we use the mean of the two central numbers. That is $\dfrac{10 + 12}{2} = 11$. Do not confuse this with the mean of all the numbers, which is $\dfrac{4 + 6 + 8 + 10 + 12 + 12 + 12 + 16}{8} = 10$.

Also do not confuse it with the mode of all the numbers, which is 12.

42. **(C)** The value of $(\underline{3})(\underline{6})$ is

$$(\frac{3+3}{3})(\frac{6+3}{6}) = (\frac{6}{3})(\frac{9}{6}) = 3.$$

43. **(H)**

> **TIP:** The least common multiple of P and Q must contain every prime that is in *either P or Q*, and must contain each of those primes the greater number of times it appears in either P or Q.

In this case, the least common multiple will be $3 \cdot 3 \cdot 5 \cdot 11 \cdot 11 \cdot 11 \cdot 13$.

44. **(D)** Since AD must equal EF (=10), the missing segment $\overline{AC}$ must equal 3. The missing angles of triangle ABC must be 60° and 60°, so that triangle is equilateral. That means $AB = BC = 3$. We now see that the perimeter of figure $ABCDEF$ is $3 + 3 + 7 + 8 + 10 + 8 = 39$.

45. **(F)** When dividing, be careful not to omit needed zeros. The answer is 10101.

46. **(A)** When José completed one-third of his homework, there was still $\dfrac{2}{3}$ to be done. He then completed $\dfrac{1}{4}$ of that, which means he completed $\dfrac{1}{4} \times \dfrac{2}{3} = \dfrac{1}{6}$ more. So far, he has done $\dfrac{1}{3} + \dfrac{1}{6} = \dfrac{1}{2}$ of his homework. That means there is still $\dfrac{1}{2}$ of his homework to go.

47. **(H)** "8 times n" is represented by $8n$. "Five less than n" is $8n - 5$. [For example, "Five less than 100" is $100 - 5$, or 95.] That is choice H.

   Actually, the phrase "5 less than 8 times n" can really be interpreted in two different ways, producing two different representations. This can best be seen by putting parentheses into the text phrase! Thus the expression "5 less than (8 times n)" is clearly $8n - 5$. But the expression "(5 less than 8) times n" is $(8 - 5) \times n$, which is $3n$. This shows how mathematical language is usually clearer than plain words!

IMPORTANT: Since a phrase like "5 less than 8 times *n*" comes up so frequently, it is generally agreed that it will be interpreted as $8n - 5$.

48. **(D)** Substituting the numbers, the expression becomes $(-3)^2 - [(2) - (-3)] = 9 - [5] = 4$.

49. **(G)** Using $\overline{AB}$ as the base of the triangle, we have $AB = 7 - 2 = 5$. The length of the altitude from C to that base is $12 - 3 = 9$. The area of a triangle equals

$$\frac{1}{2}(\text{base})(\text{height}) = \frac{1}{2}(5)(9) = \frac{45}{2} = 22\frac{1}{2}.$$

50. **(A)** Subtracting 7 from both sides, we get $\frac{64}{x-8} = 4$. Clearly $x - 8$ must be 16. Then $x = 24$, so $x + 8 = 32$. The final answer is 2.

51. **(E)** The radius is half the diameter, which is $\frac{1}{2} \times 6.4 \times 10^8 = 3.2 \times 10^8$. Be careful not to take half of *both* terms of the product.

52. **(D)** $\frac{1}{11}$ is equal to .090909. . . . The digit in the 16th decimal place will be a 9.

ANSWER SHEET
Minitest 4

Part I   English Language Arts

Revising/Editing Part A

1. Ⓐ Ⓑ Ⓒ Ⓓ
2. Ⓔ Ⓕ Ⓖ Ⓗ
3. Ⓐ Ⓑ Ⓒ Ⓓ
4. Ⓔ Ⓕ Ⓖ Ⓗ
5. Ⓐ Ⓑ Ⓒ Ⓓ
6. Ⓔ Ⓕ Ⓖ Ⓗ

Revising/Editing Part B

7. Ⓐ Ⓑ Ⓒ Ⓓ
8. Ⓔ Ⓕ Ⓖ Ⓗ
9. Ⓐ Ⓑ Ⓒ Ⓓ
10. Ⓔ Ⓕ Ⓖ Ⓗ
11. Ⓐ Ⓑ Ⓒ Ⓓ
12. Ⓔ Ⓕ Ⓖ Ⓗ
13. Ⓐ Ⓑ Ⓒ Ⓓ

Reading

14. Ⓐ Ⓑ Ⓒ Ⓓ
15. Ⓔ Ⓕ Ⓖ Ⓗ
16. Ⓐ Ⓑ Ⓒ Ⓓ
17. Ⓔ Ⓕ Ⓖ Ⓗ
18. Ⓐ Ⓑ Ⓒ Ⓓ
19. Ⓔ Ⓕ Ⓖ Ⓗ

20. Ⓐ Ⓑ Ⓒ Ⓓ
21. Ⓔ Ⓕ Ⓖ Ⓗ
22. Ⓐ Ⓑ Ⓒ Ⓓ
23. Ⓔ Ⓕ Ⓖ Ⓗ
24. Ⓐ Ⓑ Ⓒ Ⓓ
25. Ⓔ Ⓕ Ⓖ Ⓗ

Part II   Mathematics

26.

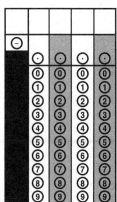

27.

28. Ⓐ Ⓑ Ⓒ Ⓓ
29. Ⓔ Ⓕ Ⓖ Ⓗ
30. Ⓐ Ⓑ Ⓒ Ⓓ
31. Ⓔ Ⓕ Ⓖ Ⓗ
32. Ⓐ Ⓑ Ⓒ Ⓓ
33. Ⓔ Ⓕ Ⓖ Ⓗ
34. Ⓐ Ⓑ Ⓒ Ⓓ
35. Ⓔ Ⓕ Ⓖ Ⓗ
36. Ⓐ Ⓑ Ⓒ Ⓓ

37. Ⓔ Ⓕ Ⓖ Ⓗ
38. Ⓐ Ⓑ Ⓒ Ⓓ
39 Ⓔ Ⓕ Ⓖ Ⓗ
40. Ⓐ Ⓑ Ⓒ Ⓓ
41. Ⓔ Ⓕ Ⓖ Ⓗ
42. Ⓐ Ⓑ Ⓒ Ⓓ
43. Ⓔ Ⓕ Ⓖ Ⓗ
44. Ⓐ Ⓑ Ⓒ Ⓓ
45. Ⓔ Ⓕ Ⓖ Ⓗ

46. Ⓐ Ⓑ Ⓒ Ⓓ
47. Ⓔ Ⓕ Ⓖ Ⓗ
48. Ⓐ Ⓑ Ⓒ Ⓓ
49. Ⓔ Ⓕ Ⓖ Ⓗ
50. Ⓐ Ⓑ Ⓒ Ⓓ
51. Ⓔ Ⓕ Ⓖ Ⓗ
52. Ⓐ Ⓑ Ⓒ Ⓓ

Minitest 4

PART 1—ENGLISH LANGUAGE ARTS

25 QUESTIONS

SUGGESTED TIME: 30 MINUTES

Revising/Editing

QUESTIONS 1–13

Revising/Editing Part A

Directions: Read and answer each of the following questions. You will be asked to recognize and correct errors in sentences or short paragraphs. Mark the **best** answer for each question.

1. Read this paragraph.

(1) Mercury is a naturally occurring chemical element found in the earth's crust. (2) On the periodic table, it has the symbol Hg and the atomic number of 80. (3) Methylmercury, along with organic mercury compounds, are formed when mercury combines with carbon. (4) Microscopic organisms all around the world convert mercury into methylmercury, the most common organic mercury compound.

Which sentence in this paragraph contains an error in subject-verb agreement?

A. sentence 1
B. sentence 2
C. sentence 3
D. sentence 4

2. Read this sentence.

> Serving over a million students the New York City school system has a budget that is bigger than that of entire countries.

Which edit should be made to correct this sentence?

    E. insert a comma after *students*
    F. insert a comma after *City*
    G. insert a comma after *budget*
    H. insert a comma after *bigger*

3. Read this paragraph.

> (1) NASA's first Chief of Astronomy in the Office of Space Science, Nancy Grace Roman, became a research astronomer at a time when women were discouraged from pursuing math and science. (2) In addition, she was the first woman in an executive position. (3) As the executive, she was the key figure who helped develop the Cosmic Background Explorer and the Hubble Space Telescope. (4) She has taken them from ideas to reality, establishing NASA's program of space-based astronomical observatories.

Which sentence should be revised to correct an inappropriate shift in verb tense?

    A. sentence 1
    B. sentence 2
    C. sentence 3
    D. sentence 4

4. Read these sentences.

> (1) John was replaced by Harry.
> (2) Harry thanked John for his services.
> (3) These services were invaluable for the community.

What is the best way to combine these sentences?

    E. John was replaced by Harry, who thanked John for his services, and these services were invaluable for the community.
    F. Providing services that were invaluable for the community, Harry replaced John, who was thanked for his services.
    G. John was replaced by Harry, who thanked John for his invaluable services to the community.
    H. The services were invaluable for the community, and for this reason, Harry was thanked by John, who replaced him.

5. Read this sentence.

> Hippotherapy uses horses to treat people for many things.

Which of these is the most precise revision for the words **people for many things**?

A. people for a wide variety of ailments.
B. people for a wide range of cognitive, physical, and emotional ailments.
C. patients for a wide variety of ailments.
D. patients for a wide range of cognitive, physical, and emotional ailments.

6. Read this paragraph.

> (1) A century ago, a bird called the passenger pigeon lived in North America. (2) It was a common thing to see this pigeon everywhere. (3) Today, there is not a single passenger pigeon left. (4) They have gone extinct.

Which sentence should be revised to correct an inappropriate shift in pronoun?

E. sentence 1
F. sentence 2
G. sentence 3
H. sentence 4

Revising/Editing Part B

Directions: Read the passage below and answer the questions following it. You will be asked to improve the writing quality of the passage and to correct errors so that the passage follows the conventions of standard written English. You may reread the passage if you need to. Mark the best answer for each question.

Managing Bedbugs

(1) Bothering their human hosts, the common bedbug has long been around a long time. (2) Today, health agencies all consider bedbugs a public health nuisance and a growing problem. (3) Unlike most public health pests, bedbugs are not known to transmit or spread disease. (4) They can cause other public health issues.

(5) Recently the cases of bedbugs have increased dramatically in the United States. (6) First, lower airfares and greater accessibility has led to more travel, where these critters get a free ride from their unsuspecting hosts. (7) There is also a severe lack of knowledge about preventing infestations. (8) Many fail to recognize the steps necessary to decontaminate if ever exposed to bedbugs. (9) Increased resistance of bedbugs to pesticides and ineffective pest control practices have made Mother Nature an accomplice in strengthening these pests.

(10) Getting solid information is the first step in both prevention and control. (11) While there is no chemical quick fix, there are a wide range of options to treat an infestation. (12) Bedbugs can be hard to find and identify, given their small size and their habit of staying hidden. (13) It helps to know what they look like, since the various life stages have different forms. (14) Once you've confirmed the presence of bedbugs, then it's time for control. (15) Some of these include pyrethrin compounds, desiccants like diatomaceous earth or boric acid, and insect growth regulators.

(16) If these options fail, don't hesitate to contact professionals. (17) Hiring a pest management professional is a good option in many cases. (18) You need to be careful in how you select a company.

7. Which revision of sentence 1 uses the most precise language?

   A. A big bother to its human host, the common bedbug has long been around for a long time.
   B. A significant bother to its human host, the common bedbug has long been a pest.
   C. Feeding on blood, causing itchy bites, and generally irritating their human hosts, the common bedbug has been a pest for a long time.
   D. Feeding on blood, causing itchy bites, and generally irritating their human hosts, the common bedbug has been around a long time.

8. Which transition word or phrase should be added to the beginning of sentence 4?

   E. Moreover,
   F. However,
   G. In particular,
   H. As a matter of fact,

9. Which sentence can best follow sentence 5 to help develop the ideas in the second paragraph (sentences 5–9)?

   A. Baltimore, Chicago, and New York top the list of the cities with the worst bedbug problems.
   B. Experts believe the recent increase in bedbugs in the United States may be due to several factors.
   C. Bedbugs are very hard to manage, so it's best to ignore the problem.
   D. An individual bug can lay 200 to 250 bugs in its lifetime.

10. Which of the following sentences can best introduce the topic in paragraph 3 (sentences 10–15)?

   E. The good news is that there are ways to control and contain bedbug problems.
   F. Bedbugs can be an international problem as well.
   G. Bedbugs generally come out at night to feed, sensing the exhalation of carbon dioxide from their sleeping victims.
   H. Before managing the bedbug problem on your own, it might be useful to consult professionals.

11. Where should sentence 11 be moved to improve the organization of the third paragraph (sentences 10–15)?

    A. between sentences 9 and 10
    B. between sentences 12 and 13
    C. between sentences 13 and 14
    D. between sentences 14 and 15

12. What is the best way to combine sentences 17 and 18 to clarify the relationship between ideas?

    E. Because hiring a pest management professional is a good option in many cases, you need to be careful in how you select a company.
    F. Hiring a pest management professional is a good option in many cases, while you need to be careful in how you select a company.
    G. Hiring a pest management professional is a good option in many cases, but you need to be careful in how you select a company.
    H. Due to the fact that hiring a pest management professional is a good option in many cases, you need to be careful in how you select a company.

13. Which concluding sentence would best follow sentence 18 to support the ideas in the fourth paragraph?

    A. Make sure that they are licensed and meet the regulations outlined by your local municipality.
    B. Government agencies simply do not have the ability to develop a unified approach to bedbug epidemics.
    C. Bedbugs are a problem, but they don't always have to be.
    D. Cockroaches have the potential to be a larger problem if left unmanaged.

Directions: Read each passage and answer the questions that follow it. Base your answers **only on the material contained in the passage.** Select the one **best** answer for each question. Bubble in the letter corresponding to that answer on the answer sheet.

I. Folk epics—long narratives that relate the exploits of national heroes—are typically a mixture of history and fiction.
Line The *Iliad*, for example, tells the story of a
(5) war between the Trojans and Greeks that began when a Trojan prince abducted the most beautiful woman in the world from her Greek husband. The romantic story and probably most of the details of the
(10) subsequent siege of Troy are fictitious, but archeology has proved that there was indeed a war and a besieged city exactly where the epic places them.

The Anglo-Saxon folk epic *Beowulf* relates
(15) the deeds of the hero Beowulf, who comes to Denmark to save the followers of King Hrothgar from a monster named Grendel. The monster, who makes nightly raids on Hrothgar's communal hall, is never seen
(20) by the Danes. He attacks in the dark, wreaking bloody havoc upon the sleeping Danes and leaving only grisly remains for the daylight. In the daytime the Danes can sense his presence nearby, lurking in
(25) the shadows of the forest, but they never see him. The heroic visitor Beowulf battles the monster and mortally wounds him, but there is no dead body to be viewed, for Grendel flees to his underwater home
(30) to die, leaving behind only the clawed arm that Beowulf has ripped off.

Readers often speculate about the factual basis for the story. Did Hrothgar's tribe really suffer a long and bloody siege of
(35) unknown origin? Was there really a "monster," perhaps a marauding bear or other animal? Was Grendel a primitive humanoid, a Scandinavian Bigfoot who had some-

how been provoked by Hrothgar's men?
(40) In his novel *Eaters of the Dead,* writer Michael Crichton speculates that Grendel was a band of invaders who came at night, carrying torches, which in the dark produced a monstrous, serpentine effect.

(45) Another explanation, possibly the most likely, has its basis in the blood-feud culture of that time and place. An injury to a tribe member by an outsider demanded vengeance in kind. The violent revenge
(50) required a similar response, so a bloody feud between neighboring tribes could go on for years, with murder after murder decimating both groups. It may be that Hrothgar's people were locked in a blood
(55) feud with a particularly vicious and cowardly enemy who attacked only in darkness, when all were asleep. There are lines in *Beowulf* that support the interpretation that the monster "[kept] the bloody feud/alive,
(60) seeking no peace, offering/no truce . . ." The hero Beowulf, who owed Hrothgar a debt of honor, may have come to help settle the disastrous vendetta that was crushing the old king's people.

14. Which of the following is the most likely purpose of the author of the passage?

   A. To explain how epics originate
   B. To offer an explanation for a legend
   C. To examine the blood-feud culture of an earlier time
   D. To prove that all epics are based in truth

15. What is a blood feud?

    E. A war between tribes in which there is no possibility of a truce

    F. An especially bloody battle between individuals

    G. An intertribal war based on revenge

    H. A series of violent raids by an outsider

16. In this passage, what is the function of the reference to the *Iliad*?

    A. It illustrates the statement that many epics have some basis in fact.

    B. It reveals the romantic aspect of epics.

    C. It demonstrates the influence of archeology.

    D. It explains why the *Iliad* cannot properly be called a "folk epic."

17. Which of the following most precisely explains why Grendel's nature is a mystery?

    E. Hrothgar's people never see him.

    F. He can cause inhuman destruction.

    G. He is able to carry on a feud for years.

    H. A monster would not be expected to carry a torch.

18. According to the passage, which of the following is the best definition of an epic?

    A. Mostly fact and a little fiction

    B. The story of a fictitious hero whose actions take place in a historical context

    C. The story of a country and its heroes

    D. A long story about the adventures of a heroic figure

19. According to the passage, which of the following statements about the hero Beowulf is the most accurate?

    E. He is a national hero of Denmark.

    F. He is the only one who gets a clear look at Grendel.

    G. After killing Grendel, he rips the monster's arm from his body.

    H. He is under obligation to Hrothgar.

II. The fishing industry is in worldwide trouble. Some fisheries, while cutting back on operations, and others are closing down
Line entirely. Large numbers of men and women
(5) who once earned their living from the sea are unemployed. Once-abundant fishing grounds are so barren that they are being put off-limits. The ocean, once considered an inexhaustible resource, is yielding
(10) smaller and smaller catches. In response, both environmentalists and industry leaders struggle to find ways to restore the former abundance. And many worry out loud that restoration efforts may be too feeble and
(15) too late.

Seafood has always been important to the human diet wherever people have had access to it, but in recent decades demand has soared as the earth's population has
(20) burgeoned, transportation and refrigeration have broadened availability of seafood, and nutritionists have touted its benefits. To supply the demand, commercial fisheries have improved their efficiency and enlarged
(25) their operations. The result was by no means foreseen by every observer, although it was certainly inevitable. Overfishing, induced by demand, has reduced stocks so drastically that many formerly plentiful fish
(30) and shellfish are disappearing from the nets they used to fill. Some species that were once staple are so endangered that they can no longer be legally harvested.

In addition to taking too much from
(35) the earth's oceans, fishers have also been unknowingly wreaking such havoc on the bottom that the remaining populations are deprived of the means to rebuild their numbers. The most efficient way to gather
(40) large numbers of fish is to drag enormous nets across the bottom. Unfortunately this is an extremely destructive method. A drag-net carries weights and rigid side-planks to keep it open, and as it moves it scrapes
(45) away the upper layers of the bottom. Only a few inches are removed, but those inches

are crucial to the ecology of the ocean, for important invertebrate species live, feed, and hide there.

(50) The scraped area does not quickly rebuild, either. Sometimes recovery takes years—years in which surviving fish populations lack the food and the hiding places necessary to bounce back from overfishing. The
(55) area affected by dragging is so enormous—two to three million square miles a year—that it is easy to conceptualize oceans with few or no fishing areas left undamaged.

One reason why this destruction has gone on
(60) for so long may be that people cannot readily see it. Anyone can view the devastation that remains when a once-beautiful mountain area has been strip-mined or a once-beautiful forest clear-cut. But not even the experts can
(65) look out over the ocean and see a ravaged bottom. Human beings have been inflicting large-scale harm on the oceans for more than a hundred years without knowing what they were doing. Only in recent years have marine
(70) biologists begun to understand the complex impact of industries, especially commercial fishing, on the oceans. And much remains to be learned. We can only hope that the knowledge comes in time to save the oceans
(75) and their bounty.

20. What is an apparent purpose of this passage?

   A. To educate people about how the oceans can be saved
   B. To explain the necessity for banning commercial fishing
   C. To explain the mechanics of drag fishing
   D. To explain how the success of commercial fishing has led to its decline

21. Which of the following best states the reason why overfished species cannot quickly rebuild?

   E. They are too small in number.
   F. It naturally takes many years for a fish population to rebound.
   G. Only a few inches of ocean bottom remain.
   H. Their habitat has been altered.

22. What difference between damage to land and damage to ocean is pointed out in the passage?

   A. Damage to land is more quickly healed.
   B. Human beings can see the land but not the ocean bottom.
   C. Marine biologists have been less aggressive than other environmental scientists.
   D. Damage to the ocean is impossible to detect.

23. What best states the effect of a net's being dragged across the ocean bottom?

   E. It destroys everything in its path.
   F. It damages the habitat and the food chain.
   G. It removes large quantities of fish.
   H. It scrapes away several feet of protective mud and sand.

24. All of the following are mentioned as causative factors in the fishing boom described in the second paragraph **except**

   A. more people to feed.

   B. ability to deliver goods to distant areas more quickly.

   C. promotion by nutritionists.

   D. discovery of the nutritive quality of seafood.

25. Which of the following is suggested by the passage?

   E. Commercial fishing should be banned.

   F. Much is still unknown about the impact of technology on the ocean.

   G. People should eat more meat and less seafood.

   H. Drag fishing causes irreparable damage to the ocean bottom.

Grid-In Problems

Directions: Solve each problem. On the answer sheet, write your answer in the boxes at the top of the grid. Start on the left side of each grid. Print only one number or symbol in each box. **DO NOT LEAVE A BOX BLANK IN THE MIDDLE OF AN ANSWER.** Under each box, fill in the circle that matches the number or symbol you wrote above. **DO NOT FILL IN A CIRCLE UNDER AN UNUSED BOX.**

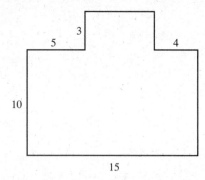

26. The diagram above shows a scale drawing of a room as part of a floor plan. The lengths are indicated in centimeters (cm). In this drawing, 5 cm represents 8 feet. What is the perimeter, *in feet*, of the actual room that is represented in this scale drawing? Note that all "corners" meet at right angles.

27. The mean of five consecutive integers is M. The number 18 is one of the five integers. When 18 is removed, the mean of the remaining four integers is 16.75. What is the smallest of the original five numbers?

Multiple-Choice Problems

Directions: For each of the following questions, select the **best** answer from the given choices. Bubble in the letter corresponding to your answer on the answer sheet. **DO NOT PUT ANY OTHER WORK ON THE ANSWER SHEET.** All necessary work can be done in your test booklet or on scrap paper that is provided.

NOTE: Diagrams other than graphs might not be drawn to scale. Do not assume any relationships that are not specifically stated unless they are implied by the given information.

28. $(7)(6) - 6 =$

   A. 0
   B. 1
   C. 7
   D. 36

29. Fred and Michael collected money for the school trip. Fred collected 50% more than Michael. If Michael collected $150, how much did Fred and Michael collect all together?

   E. $150
   F. $225
   G. $375
   H. $450

30. 5.835×10^4 is equal to

   A. .0005835
   B. .005835
   C. 58,350
   D. 583,500

31. What is the value of $|x - y| + |y - x|$ if $x = 9$ and $y = 2x$?

   E. 18
   F. 9
   G. 4.5
   H. 0

32. When 54 is divided by the positive integer N, the quotient is 13 and the remainder is R. The value of R is

   A. 0
   B. 1
   C. 2
   D. 3

33. If $N = \sqrt{36 + 49}$, then N is

   E. a number between 9 and 10
   F. a number between 10 and 11
   G. a number between 11 and 12
   H. 13

34. Susan is 5 years older than Phen is now. In N years, Susan will be twice as old as Phen is now. If Susan is now 22 years old, what is the value of N?

   A. 5
   B. 12
   C. 17
   D. 22

35. The number of integer values of n for which $1 \le \sqrt{n} \le 3$ is

   E. 3
   F. 9
   G. 7
   H. 1

36. In right triangle *ABC*, angle *ACB* is 90°. The number of degrees in angle *BEC* is

A. 70
B. 60
C. 50
D. 40

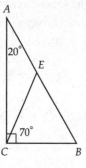

37. If it is now 12:00 noon, what time was it 40 hours ago?

E. 6 A.M.
F. 8 A.M.
G. 4 P.M.
H. 8 P.M.

38. The mean of all the odd integers between 6 and 24 is

A. 12
B. 13
C. 14
D. 15

39. Let *x* be an element of the set {.2, 1.2, 2.2, 3.2, 4.2}. For *how many* values of *x* is $\frac{10x}{3}$ an integer?

E. 0
F. 1
G. 2
H. 3

40. George has just enough money to buy 3 chocolate bars and 2 ice cream cones. For the same amount of money, he could buy exactly 9 chocolate bars. For the same amount of money, how many ice cream cones could George buy?

A. 3
B. 5
C. 6
D. 7

41. The length of $\overline{AB}$ is twice the length of $\overline{RS}$, where *S* is a point (not shown) to the right of *R*. The coordinate of the midpoint of $\overline{RS}$ is

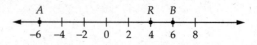

E. 4
F. 5
G. 6
H. 7

42. *ABCD* and *PQRS* are squares, as shown. The area of *PQRS* is

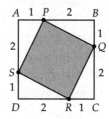

A. 3
B. 4
C. 5
D. 6

43. If *x* = 10 and *y* = 8, what is the value of *y*(3*x* − 2*y*)?

E. 112
F. 224
G. 1792
H. −144

44. One-third the product of two numbers is 24. One-half the product of these same two numbers is

A. 72
B. 54
C. 48
D. 36

45. The area of rectangle *ABCD* is 72. Point *F* is on $\overline{AB}$ such that *BF* = 4. What is the *sum* of the areas of triangles *CBF* and *DAF*?

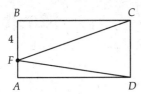

- **E.** 18
- **F.** 24
- **G.** 36
- **H.** cannot be determined from the given information

46. Ms. Brady has 28 students in her class. The ratio of boys to girls in the class is 2 to 5. How many new boys must be added to the class to make the ratio of boys to girls 1:2?

- **A.** 1
- **B.** 2
- **C.** 4
- **D.** 12

47. The vertices of rectangle *ABCD* all lie on the same circle as shown. The circumference of the circle is 64π. What is the length of $\overline{AC}$?

- **E.** 8
- **F.** 16
- **G.** 32
- **H.** 64

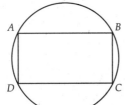

48. Ten cards are numbered 10, 11, 12, . . . , 19, one number per card. Brian removes three cards whose numbers are primes, and puts the remaining cards in a hat. If one card is then drawn at random from the hat, what is the probability that its number is a prime?

- **A.** $\dfrac{1}{10}$
- **B.** $\dfrac{1}{9}$
- **C.** $\dfrac{1}{5}$
- **D.** none of these

49. For any number *N*, we define ■ *N* ■ to mean $\dfrac{N}{2}$ if *N* is even and (5*N* – 1) if *N* is odd. The value of ■ 9 ■ + ■ 10 ■ is

- **E.** $9\dfrac{1}{2}$
- **F.** 19
- **G.** 29
- **H.** 49

50. In the figure, all line segments meet at right angles. What is the area enclosed by the figure?

- **A.** 84
- **B.** 72
- **C.** 70
- **D.** 68

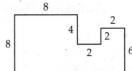

51. Apu has some nickels and some pennies. If the pennies were nickels and the nickels were pennies, he would have 80¢ less than he has now. The difference between the number of nickels and the number of pennies that he has

- **E.** is 12
- **F.** is 20
- **G.** is 24
- **H.** cannot be determined

52. Wei Jing has between 70 and 150 baseball cards in his collection. When he arranges them in groups of 10, he has 3 left over. When he arranges them in groups of 9, he has 5 left over. If he arranges them in groups of 8, how many will he have left over?

- **A.** 1
- **B.** 3
- **C.** 5
- **D.** 7

Revising/Editing Part A

1. C	3. D	5. D
2. E	4. G	6. H

Revising/Editing Part B

7. C	9. B	11. D	13. A
8. F	10. E	12. G	

Reading

14. B	18. D	22. B
15. G	19. H	23. F
16. A	20. D	24. D
17. E	21. H	25. F

Mathematics

26. **89.6**	33. E	40. A	47. H
27. **15**	34. B	41. H	48. D
28. D	35. F	42. C	49. H
29. G	36. D	43. E	50. A
30. C	37. H	44. D	51. F
31. E	38. D	45. G	52. A
32. C	39. G	46. B	

ANSWER EXPLANATIONS
MINITEST 4

Revising/Editing Part A

1. **(C)** Examine the subject-noun and predicate verb pairings for each sentence. The incorrect pairing is *italicized*.

   (1) <u>Mercury</u> <u>is</u> a naturally occurring chemical element found in the earth's crust. (2) On the periodic table, <u>it</u> <u>has</u> the symbol Hg and the atomic number of 80. (3) *Methylmercury*, along with organic mercury compounds, *are* formed when mercury combines with carbon. (4) Microscopic <u>organisms</u> of all around the world <u>convert</u> mercury into methylmercury, the most common organic mercury compound.

2. **(E)** The phrase *Serving over a million students* is a modifier that needs a comma to modify *the New York City school system*.

   Choice F is wrong because *New York City school system* refers to one specific entity and does not need a comma.

   Choice G is wrong because the pronoun *that* does not need a comma before it.

   Choice H is wrong because commas are not typically placed between a comparative word and the word *than*. For example, *bigger, than*; *stronger, than*; *happier, than* are not acceptable.

3. **(D)** Examine all the predicate verbs below.

   (1) NASA's first Chief of Astronomy in the Office of Space Science, Nancy Grace Roman, <u>became</u> a research astronomer at a time when women were discouraged from pursuing math and science. (2) In addition, she <u>was</u> the first woman in an executive position. (3) As the executive, she <u>was</u> the key figure who <u>helped</u> develop the Cosmic Background Explorer and the Hubble Space Telescope. (4) She <u>has</u> taken them from ideas to reality, establishing NASA's program of space-based astronomical observatories.

4. **(G)** It contains the fewest number of clauses.

5. **(D)**

Least Precise (cross out)	Most Precise
people	patients
ailments	cognitive, physical, and emotional ailments

6. **(H)** The pronoun *They* does not agree with its antecedent *the passenger pigeon*.

Revising/Editing Part B

7. **(C)**

Least Precise (cross out)	Most Precise
A big bother A significant bother	Feeding on blood, causing itchy bites, and generally irritating
has been around for a long time	has long been a pest

8. **(F)** Sentence 3 claims that bedbugs are unrelated with disease. Sentence 4 claims that they can cause other problems. The best transition is the contrast transition word *However*.

9. **(B)** Choice B best introduces the reasons for increasing bedbug problems, which are discussed in sentences 6 through 9.

10. **(E)** Paragraph 2 discusses the growing bedbug problem, while paragraph 3 discusses possible solutions. Sentence E best links those two ideas.

11. **(D)** Sentence 15 contains the pronoun *these*. The pronoun links with the antecedent *options* in sentence 11.

12. **(G)** The transition word *but* best sets up the contrast between *good option* and *careful in how you select a company*.

13. **(A)** Sentence 18 claims that one needs to be careful in selecting a company, and choice A explains how.

Choice B is wrong because it discusses the government.

Choice C is tempting because it restates the idea of the entire passage, but it is too general and does not conform to the main idea of the fourth paragraph.

Choice D is wrong because the paragraph is not about cockroaches.

Reading

Passage I

14. **(B)** Main Idea Since most of the passage discusses *Beowulf,* with only one other epic mentioned, the main idea must be related to the Beowulf legend. A places the emphasis on epics in general and thus is incorrect. C is too narrow, as only the last paragraph discusses the blood-feud culture. D is too extreme, as the passage does not attempt either to *prove* a point or to cover *all* epics.

15. **(G)** The explanation is found in the last paragraph, in its second and third sentences (lines 47–54).

16. **(A)** Inference and Main Idea The reference to the *Iliad* follows the statement that epics are a mixture of fact and fiction. Furthermore, it contains the phrase "for example" and states a factual basis for the *Iliad.* Therefore A is the correct answer. B and C contain some truth concerning the reference but do not relate to the main idea of the paragraph and therefore are incorrect choices. D contradicts the language of the first paragraph.

17. **(E)** Inference F is incorrect because "inhuman" destruction might suggest an animal of some kind, but not necessarily a mystery. G is incorrect because the last paragraph indicates that a reign of terror lasting for years was a familiar feature of the culture.

H is incorrect because the Grendel of the epic is not known to carry a torch.

18. **(D)** Detail *Epic* is defined in the first sentence of the passage.

19. **(H)** Detail The information is stated in the last sentence of the passage.

E is inaccurate because Beowulf is identified as an Anglo-Saxon hero; it is not suggested that he is also a hero of Denmark. F is incorrect because there is no evidence to support the idea that Beowulf gets a *clear* look, or even that he sees Grendel—they may have battled in the dark. G is inaccurate because Grendel dies *after* his arm is ripped off.

Passage II

20. **(D)** Main Idea A misses the emphasis of the passage, which is damage and not salvation. B is too extreme, as there is no such suggestion. C is too narrow; the passage contains other topics. Only D is both broad enough and accurate.

21. **(H)** Inference The third paragraph explains that the top layers of the bottom that are scraped away are important to the ecology (lines 46–47), and the next paragraph says that the remaining population cannot quickly rebound because it loses (its usual) food and hiding places (lines 48–49). Thus H is the correct response. E and F are not stated or suggested, and G contradicts the information given in lines 45–46.

22. **(B)** Detail The correct answer is stated in the first three sentences of the last paragraph.

23. **(F)** Detail The effect is given in the last sentence of the third paragraph (lines 45–49) and the first two sentences of the fourth paragraph (lines 50–54).

24. **(D)** Detail A, B, and C are directly stated in the second paragraph. D is inaccurate and is therefore the correct choice as not stated. The paragraph says that nutritionists pro-

moted the benefits of seafood but not that the benefits were newly discovered.

25. **(F)** Inference   E is too extreme. Overfishing is blamed, but banning is not suggested. G is incorrect because meat is not mentioned in the passage. H is inaccurate because it contradicts the detail given in lines 50–51. F is suggested in the last paragraph, which says that scientists are *beginning* to understand the impact (lines 70–71).

Mathematics

26. **(89.6)** The sum of the lengths of the horizontal segments is $15 + 15 = 30$. The sum of the lengths of the vertical line segments is $10 + 3 + 3 + 10 = 26$. Thus, the perimeter, P, as represented on the scale drawing, is 56 cm. The scaling factor is $\frac{8}{5}$. Using the proportion $\frac{8}{5} = \frac{P}{56}$ produces $P = 89.6$ feet.

27. **(15)** Let the original set of numbers be x, $x + 1$, $x + 2$, $x + 3$, and $x + 4$. Their mean is their sum divided by 5, which is $\frac{5x + 10}{5}$, which is $x + 2 = M$. If we remove 18, the mean of the remaining four numbers is their sum divided by 4, which is $\frac{(5x + 10 - 18)}{4}$, or $\frac{(5x - 8)}{4}$. Setting this equation to 16.75 and multiplying both sides by 4, we get $5x - 8 = 67$. Solving for x, we get $x = 15$.

28. **(D)** According to the order of operations, we must multiply first. This produces $42 - 6 = 36$.

29. **(G)** Michael collected $150. 50% or $\left(\frac{1}{2}\right)$ of that is $75. Therefore Fred collected $150 + 75 = \$225$. Fred and Michael together collected $225 + 150 = \$375$.

30. **(C)** Multiplying by 10^4 moves the decimal point 4 places to the right (or just multiply 5.835 by 10,000).

31. **(E)** If $x = 9$, $y = 18$. Substitute these values in the expression, getting $|9 - 18| + |18 - 9|$.

> **TIP:** Combine the terms inside the absolute value signs before you compute the absolute value.

We have $|-9| + |9| = 9 + 9 = 18$.

32. **(C)** 54 must equal $13 \times N + R$. Since N is the divisor, R must be less than N. Trying $N = 4$, we get $R = 2$. Larger values of N don't work, and smaller values make R too big.

33. **(E)**

> **TIP:** $\sqrt{a + b}$ is generally not the same as $\sqrt{a} + \sqrt{b}$

First we must combine the numbers that are under the square root symbol. This results in $N = \sqrt{85}$, which is more than $9\,(= \sqrt{81})$ but less than $10\,(= \sqrt{100})$.

34. **(B)** Susan is 5 years older than Phen is now, so Phen is now $22 - 5 = 17$. In N years, Susan will be twice as old as Phen is now, so Susan will be 34. Since Susan is now 22, she will be 34 in 12 years.

35. **(F)** $\sqrt{1} = 1$ and $\sqrt{9} = 3$, so n can be any integer from 1 through 9 inclusive. That is 9 possible values for n.

36. **(D)** Angle ABC is also 70°, so angle $BEC = 180° - 70° - 70° = 40°$.

37. **(H)** Every 24 hours is a full day. The simplest solution is to go back 48 hours (to 12:00 noon, once again) and then go forward 8 hours. The time will then be 8:00 P.M.

38. **(D)** Those odd integers are 7, 9, 11, 13, 15, 17, 19, 21, and 23. One way to find the mean is to add those nine numbers (getting 135), then divide by 9. The answer is 15. Another way to add those numbers is to notice that they are "equally spaced," so we can add them more easily in pairs as follows: $7 + 23 = 30$, $9 + 21 = 30$, $11 + 19 = 30$, and $13 + 17 = 30$. The total is therefore $4 \times 30 + 15 = 120 + 15 = 135$.

39. **(G)** For $\dfrac{10x}{3}$ to be an integer, the number $10x$ must be divisible by 3. We quickly find that only two values of x satisfy this requirement, namely 1.2 and 4.2.

40. **(A)** Using single letters to represent chocolate bars and ice cream cones, we see that George can just buy $3c + 2i$. He can also just buy $9c$. Therefore, $3c + 2i = 9c$. Solving this for i, we get $2i = 6c$, so $i = 3c$. George can just buy $9c$, which is equivalent to $3i$. He can buy exactly 3 ice cream cones.

41. **(H)** $AB = 12$, so $RS = 6$. Since S is to the right of R, the coordinate of S must be $4 + 6 = 10$. The midpoint of $\overline{RS}$ is halfway between 4 and 10. That coordinate is the average of 4 and 10, which is $\dfrac{4+10}{2} = 7$.

42. **(C)** The side of the big square is 3, so its area is 9.

> **FACT:** The area of a right triangle is $\dfrac{1}{2}$ the product of its legs.

The area of each small triangle is $\left(\dfrac{1}{2}\right)(2)(1)$ $= 1$. Subtracting the areas of the four small triangles from the area of the big square, we get the area of the small square. That is $9 - 4(1) = 5$. Do not go on to find the side of the small square, as that is not what is called for.

43. **(E)** We must evaluate $8(30 - 16)$. That is $8(14) = 112$.

44. **(D)** If one-third the product is 24, then the entire product is $3(24) = 72$. Now one-half that product is 36.

45. **(G)** Let $CB = DA = h$. The sum of the areas of triangles CBF and DAF is $\left(\dfrac{1}{2}\right)(h)(BF) +$ $\left(\dfrac{1}{2}\right)(h)(FA) = \left(\dfrac{h}{2}\right)(BF) + \left(\dfrac{h}{2}\right)(FA)$. We can factor $\dfrac{h}{2}$ out of both terms, getting the total area to be $\left(\dfrac{h}{2}\right)(BF + FA)$. That is $\left(\dfrac{1}{2}\right)(BA)$. Finally, notice that this is equal to $\left(\dfrac{1}{2}\right)(h)(BA)$, which is $\dfrac{1}{2}$ the area of the rectangle. The answer is $\left(\dfrac{1}{2}\right)(72) = 36$. The fact that $BF = 4$ is irrelevant.

Point F can be anywhere on side $\overline{AB}$, and the answer would be the same. Another approach is to realize that the area of triangle CFD is half the area of the rectangle. Therefore the required sum is the other half.

46. **(B)** If the number of boys is $2x$ and the number of girls is $5x$, then $2x + 5x = 28$. This produces $x = 4$, so there are 8 boys and 20 girls in the class. To make the ratio of boys to girls equal to 1:2, we need 10 boys total. Therefore we must add 2 boys.

47. **(H)**

> **FACT:** If a rectangle is "inscribed" in a circle, the diagonal of the rectangle will be the diameter of the circle.

The circumference of a circle equals πd, where d is the diameter of the circle. Therefore $\pi d = 64\pi$, so $d = 64$. Thus $AC = 64$.

48. **(D)** First realize that there are 10 cards to start with. Thinking that there are only nine is a common counting error. The numbers from 10 through 19 contain four primes (namely 11, 13, 17, and 19). Brian removes three of these, so only one is left. Therefore there is only one prime number among the 7 cards that go into the hat. The probability that the prime number will be drawn is $\dfrac{1}{7}$. None of the first three choices is correct.

49. **(H)** This is $(5 \cdot 9 - 1) + \dfrac{10}{2} = 44 + 5 = 49$.

50. **(A)** If we extend both inner vertical segments down to the base, the figure will be broken into three rectangles. The dimensions of those rectangles are 8×8, 4×2, and 6×2. The total of their areas is $64 + 8 + 12 = 84$.

51. **(F)** If there were n nickels and p pennies to start, their value in cents would be $5n + p$. When the coins are interchanged, their new value is $5p + n$. The difference between these is $(5n + p) - (5p + n) = 5n + p - 5p - n = 4n - 4p$. We know that this difference is 80¢, so $4n - 4p = 80$. Dividing both sides by 4, we get $n - p = 20$.

52. **(A)** In order to have 3 cards left over when they are arranged in groups of 10, the number of cards could be 73, 83, 93, 103, 113, 123, 133, or 143 (notice how these numbers differ by 10). To have 5 left over when they are arranged in groups of 9, the number of cards could be 77, 86, 95, 104, 113, 122, ·131, 140, or 149 (notice how these numbers differ by 9). The only number common to both of these arrangements is 113. If these 113 cards are arranged in groups of 8, the number left over is the same as the remainder when 113 is divided by 8. That is 1.

ANSWER SHEET
Practice Test 1

Part I English Language Arts

Revising/Editing Part A

1. Ⓐ Ⓑ Ⓒ Ⓓ
2. Ⓔ Ⓕ Ⓖ Ⓗ
3. Ⓐ Ⓑ Ⓒ Ⓓ
4. Ⓔ Ⓕ Ⓖ Ⓗ
5. Ⓐ Ⓑ Ⓒ Ⓓ
6. Ⓔ Ⓕ Ⓖ Ⓗ

Revising/Editing Part B

7. Ⓐ Ⓑ Ⓒ Ⓓ
8. Ⓔ Ⓕ Ⓖ Ⓗ
9. Ⓐ Ⓑ Ⓒ Ⓓ
10. Ⓔ Ⓕ Ⓖ Ⓗ
11. Ⓐ Ⓑ Ⓒ Ⓓ
12. Ⓔ Ⓕ Ⓖ Ⓗ
13. Ⓐ Ⓑ Ⓒ Ⓓ
14. Ⓔ Ⓕ Ⓖ Ⓗ
15. Ⓐ Ⓑ Ⓒ Ⓓ
16. Ⓔ Ⓕ Ⓖ Ⓗ
17. Ⓐ Ⓑ Ⓒ Ⓓ
18. Ⓔ Ⓕ Ⓖ Ⓗ
19. Ⓐ Ⓑ Ⓒ Ⓓ
20. Ⓔ Ⓕ Ⓖ Ⓗ

Reading

21. Ⓐ Ⓑ Ⓒ Ⓓ
22. Ⓔ Ⓕ Ⓖ Ⓗ
23. Ⓐ Ⓑ Ⓒ Ⓓ
24. Ⓔ Ⓕ Ⓖ Ⓗ
25. Ⓐ Ⓑ Ⓒ Ⓓ
26. Ⓔ Ⓕ Ⓖ Ⓗ
27. Ⓐ Ⓑ Ⓒ Ⓓ
28. Ⓔ Ⓕ Ⓖ Ⓗ
29. Ⓐ Ⓑ Ⓒ Ⓓ
30. Ⓔ Ⓕ Ⓖ Ⓗ
31. Ⓐ Ⓑ Ⓒ Ⓓ
32. Ⓔ Ⓕ Ⓖ Ⓗ
33. Ⓐ Ⓑ Ⓒ Ⓓ
34. Ⓔ Ⓕ Ⓖ Ⓗ
35. Ⓐ Ⓑ Ⓒ Ⓓ
36. Ⓔ Ⓕ Ⓖ Ⓗ
37. Ⓐ Ⓑ Ⓒ Ⓓ
38. Ⓔ Ⓕ Ⓖ Ⓗ
39. Ⓐ Ⓑ Ⓒ Ⓓ

40. Ⓔ Ⓕ Ⓖ Ⓗ
41. Ⓐ Ⓑ Ⓒ Ⓓ
42. Ⓔ Ⓕ Ⓖ Ⓗ
43. Ⓐ Ⓑ Ⓒ Ⓓ
44. Ⓔ Ⓕ Ⓖ Ⓗ
45. Ⓐ Ⓑ Ⓒ Ⓓ
46. Ⓔ Ⓕ Ⓖ Ⓗ
47. Ⓐ Ⓑ Ⓒ Ⓓ
48. Ⓔ Ⓕ Ⓖ Ⓗ
49. Ⓐ Ⓑ Ⓒ Ⓓ
50. Ⓔ Ⓕ Ⓖ Ⓗ
51. Ⓐ Ⓑ Ⓒ Ⓓ
52. Ⓔ Ⓕ Ⓖ Ⓗ
53. Ⓐ Ⓑ Ⓒ Ⓓ
54. Ⓔ Ⓕ Ⓖ Ⓗ
55. Ⓐ Ⓑ Ⓒ Ⓓ
56. Ⓔ Ⓕ Ⓖ Ⓗ
57. Ⓐ Ⓑ Ⓒ Ⓓ

ANSWER SHEET
Practice Test 1

Part II   Mathematics

58.

59.

60.

61.

62.

63. Ⓐ Ⓑ Ⓒ Ⓓ
64. Ⓔ Ⓕ Ⓖ Ⓗ
65. Ⓐ Ⓑ Ⓒ Ⓓ
66. Ⓔ Ⓕ Ⓖ Ⓗ
67. Ⓐ Ⓑ Ⓒ Ⓓ
68. Ⓔ Ⓕ Ⓖ Ⓗ
69. Ⓐ Ⓑ Ⓒ Ⓓ
70. Ⓔ Ⓕ Ⓖ Ⓗ
71. Ⓐ Ⓑ Ⓒ Ⓓ
72. Ⓔ Ⓕ Ⓖ Ⓗ
73. Ⓐ Ⓑ Ⓒ Ⓓ
74. Ⓔ Ⓕ Ⓖ Ⓗ
75. Ⓐ Ⓑ Ⓒ Ⓓ
76. Ⓔ Ⓕ Ⓖ Ⓗ
77. Ⓐ Ⓑ Ⓒ Ⓓ
78. Ⓔ Ⓕ Ⓖ Ⓗ
79. Ⓐ Ⓑ Ⓒ Ⓓ
80. Ⓔ Ⓕ Ⓖ Ⓗ
81. Ⓐ Ⓑ Ⓒ Ⓓ
82. Ⓔ Ⓕ Ⓖ Ⓗ
83. Ⓐ Ⓑ Ⓒ Ⓓ
84. Ⓔ Ⓕ Ⓖ Ⓗ
85. Ⓐ Ⓑ Ⓒ Ⓓ
86. Ⓔ Ⓕ Ⓖ Ⓗ
87. Ⓐ Ⓑ Ⓒ Ⓓ
88. Ⓔ Ⓕ Ⓖ Ⓗ

89. Ⓐ Ⓑ Ⓒ Ⓓ
90. Ⓔ Ⓕ Ⓖ Ⓗ
91. Ⓐ Ⓑ Ⓒ Ⓓ
92. Ⓔ Ⓕ Ⓖ Ⓗ
93. Ⓐ Ⓑ Ⓒ Ⓓ
94. Ⓔ Ⓕ Ⓖ Ⓗ
95. Ⓐ Ⓑ Ⓒ Ⓓ
96. Ⓔ Ⓕ Ⓖ Ⓗ
97. Ⓐ Ⓑ Ⓒ Ⓓ
98. Ⓔ Ⓕ Ⓖ Ⓗ
99. Ⓐ Ⓑ Ⓒ Ⓓ
100. Ⓔ Ⓕ Ⓖ Ⓗ
101. Ⓐ Ⓑ Ⓒ Ⓓ
102. Ⓔ Ⓕ Ⓖ Ⓗ
103. Ⓐ Ⓑ Ⓒ Ⓓ
104. Ⓔ Ⓕ Ⓖ Ⓗ
105. Ⓐ Ⓑ Ⓒ Ⓓ
106. Ⓔ Ⓕ Ⓖ Ⓗ
107. Ⓐ Ⓑ Ⓒ Ⓓ
108. Ⓔ Ⓕ Ⓖ Ⓗ
109. Ⓐ Ⓑ Ⓒ Ⓓ
110. Ⓔ Ⓕ Ⓖ Ⓗ
111. Ⓐ Ⓑ Ⓒ Ⓓ
112. Ⓔ Ⓕ Ⓖ Ⓗ
113. Ⓐ Ⓑ Ⓒ Ⓓ
114. Ⓔ Ⓕ Ⓖ Ⓗ

Practice Test 1

PART 1—ENGLISH LANGUAGE ARTS

57 QUESTIONS

SUGGESTED TIME: 90 MINUTES

Revising/Editing

QUESTIONS 1–20

IMPORTANT NOTE: The Revising/Editing section (Questions 1–20) is in two parts: Part A and Part B.

Revising/Editing Part A

Directions: Read and answer each of the following questions. You will be asked to recognize and correct errors in sentences or short paragraphs. Mark the **best** answer for each question.

1. Read this paragraph.

(1) People often associate monosodium glutamate, better known as MSG, with headaches and nausea, but there was no evidence to substantiate that link. (2) In fact, the compounds associated with MSG are commonly found in beef, pork, and chicken. (3) Scientists believe the sicknesses might be the result of a "nocebo effect." (4) The nocebo effect, like the placebo effect, isn't caused by an actual substance but merely by suggestion.

Which sentence in this paragraph contains an error in verb tense?

A. sentence 1
B. sentence 2
C. sentence 3
D. sentence 4

2. Read this sentence.

> Typically occurring in the spring, a nor'easter, a gigantic cyclone, gets its name from the direction of the winds, that tend to blow northeast to southwest.

Which edit should be made to correct this sentence?

E. delete the comma after *spring*
F. delete the comma after *nor'easter*
G. delete the comma after *cyclone*
H. delete the comma after *winds*

3. Read this paragraph.

> (1) Molasses syrup, a product made from sugar and beets, are primarily used for sweetening foods. (2) Molasses syrup is rich with glucose and fructose, compounds rich with energy. (3) Because of its taste, sugar molasses syrup is used for human consumption, while beet molasses syrup is used for animal consumption. (4) Because of its adhesive properties, molasses syrup is also used as an additive component in mortar for brickwork.

Which sentence should be revised to correct a subject-verb agreement?

A. sentence 1
B. sentence 2
C. sentence 3
D. sentence 4

4. Read these sentences.

> (1) In ancient Greece, there were two major philosophical schools.
> (2) Stoicism advocated a quiet contemplation.
> (3) Epicureanism pursued worldly pleasures.

What is the best way to combine these sentences?

E. In ancient Greece, there were two major philosophical schools, and one was Stoicism, which advocated a quiet contemplation, and the other was Epicureanism, which pursued worldly pleasures.
F. In the two major philosophical schools of ancient Greece, Stoicism advocated a quiet contemplation, while Epicureanism pursued worldly pleasures.
G. While Stoicism advocated a quiet contemplation, Epicureanism pursued worldly pleasure, and these were the two major philosophical schools of ancient Greece.
H. The two major philosophical schools, one being Stoicism that advocated quiet contemplation and the other being Epicureanism that pursued worldly pleasures, were in ancient Greece.

5. Read this sentence.

> Bombogenesis occurs when a storm rapidly intensifies, quickly dropping in pressure.

Which of these is the most precise revision for the words *a storm rapidly intensifies, quickly dropping in pressure*?

A. a storm intensifies rapidly quickly dropping in pressure
B. a cyclone intensifies and the atmospheric pressure drops in a matter of hours
C. a storm intensifies rapidly and quickly drops in pressure
D. a cyclone intensifies and the atmospheric pressure drops 30 percent within 24 hours

6. Read this paragraph.

> (1) People often use the terms democracy and a republic interchangeably, as if it means the same thing. (2) While both forms of government provide powers to their respective citizens, they differ in the way they provide that power. (3) A democracy is simply a rule by the majority, which plays a very large role in the affairs of government policies. (4) In contrast, republics are run by a constitution, which enables the people to elect their leaders.

Which sentence should be revised to correct an inappropriate shift in pronoun?

E. sentence 1
F. sentence 2
G. sentence 3
H. sentence 4

Directions: Read the passage below and answer the questions following it. You will be asked to improve the writing quality of the passage and to correct errors so that the passage follows the conventions of standard written English. You may reread the passage if you need to. Mark the best answer for each question.

The Importance of Sleep

(1) People will often reduce their sleep for careers, family schedules, or even a movie. (2) If insufficient sleep is a routine in your life, you may be at an increased risk for diabetes, obesity, heart disease, poor mental health, and even death. (3) Even one night of insufficient sleep can have a strong impact on you the next day.

(4) How much sleep you need fluctuates as you get older. (5) Scientists recommend that you get a certain amount of sleep as you age. (6) To prevent dementia in old age, some scientists recommend keeping your brain active by playing games.

(7) There are some important practices that can help your sleep health. (8) Be consistent, and head to bed at the same time every night and wake up at the same time in the morning, including on the weekends. (9) Make sure your bedroom is silent, dim, calming, and at a comfortable temperature. (10) Avoid large meals, coffee, and alcoholic drinks before bedtime.

(11) Better sleep practices can improve the quality of your sleep. (12) Getting sufficient sleep is important, but good sleep quality is also necessary. (13) Good sleep is difficult to define, but indicators of bad sleep are unmistakable. (14) These include feeling sleepy or tired even after getting enough sleep, constantly waking up during the night, and having symptoms of sleep disorders (such as snoring or gasping for air). (15) It's important to identify these indicators because they can lead to better habits.

7. Which transition word or phrase should be added to the beginning of sentence 2?

   A. As a result,
   B. However,
   C. Therefore,
   D. Regardless,

8. Which sentence could best follow sentence 3 and support the main point of the first paragraph?

   E. A third of U.S. adults report that they usually get less than the recommended amount of sleep.

   F. Sleeping aids, such as melatonin and CPAP machines, can help solve for the lack of sleep.

   G. You're more likely to feel sleepy, be in a bad mood, be less productive at work, and be involved in a motor vehicle crash.

   H. It is unlikely that most people will do something about this neglected issue.

9. Which revision of sentence 5 uses the most precise language?

   A. Scientists recommend that a person get more sleep as they grow older.

   B. The American Academy of Sleep Medicine and the Sleep Research Society recommend more sleep as people age.

   C. The American Academy of Sleep Medicine and the Sleep Research Society recommend 9 to 12 hours for school-age children, 8 to 10 for teens, and 7 or more for adults.

   D. The American Academy of Sleep Medicine and the Sleep Research Society recommend more sleep for more people of different ages, shapes, and sizes.

10. Which sentence best follows the structure and style of the sentences in paragraph 3 (sentences 7–10)?

    E. Get some exercise because being physically active during the day can help you fall asleep more easily at night.

    F. If you get some exercise, then being physically active during the day can help you fall asleep more easily at night.

    G. Physical activity during the day can help you fall asleep with exercise.

    H. Being physically active by getting some exercise can help you fall asleep more easily at night.

11. Where should sentence 11 be moved to improve the organization of the fourth paragraph (sentences 11–15)?

    A. between sentences 12 and 13
    B. between sentences 13 and 14
    C. between sentences 14 and 15
    D. after sentence 15

12. Which sentence is irrelevant in the passage and should be deleted?

    E. sentence 1
    F. sentence 6
    G. sentence 9
    H. sentence 12

The Bay of Pigs Invasion

(1) In the 1950s, a young, charismatic Cuban nationalist named Fidel Castro led a guerrilla army against the forces of General Fulgencio Batista from a base camp deep within the largest mountain range in Cuba. (2) Castro's goal was to overthrow Batista, the US-backed leader of Cuba. (3) After three years of guerrilla warfare, Castro and his ragtag army descended from the mountains and entered Havana on January 1, 1959. (4) He forced Batista to flee the country. (5) Castro took control of the Cuban military and declared himself the leader.

(6) Castro established diplomatic relations with America's Cold War rival, the Soviet Union. (7) Castro and Soviet Premier Nikita Khrushchev signed a series of pacts that resulted in large deliveries of economic and military aid in 1960. (8) Castro proclaimed himself a communist, formally allied his country with the Soviet Union, and seized remaining American and foreign-owned assets.

(9) The establishment of a communist state 90 miles off the coast of Florida raised obvious security concerns in Washington and did not sit well with President Eisenhower. (10) The CIA formulated a plan to recruit Cuban exiles living in the Miami area. (11) It would train and equip the exiles to infiltrate Cuba. (12) Military exercises can greatly enhance a soldier's abilities only if they provide the right types of equipment. (13) Once inside, they would start a revolution to ignite an uprising across the island and overthrow Castro.

(14) Top U.S. Government officials watched as their decisions led to an entirely different outcome. (15) General incompetence left the covert operation exposed and ultimately led to utter failure. (16) The Kennedy administration suffered a blow to its credibility. (17) American allies were equally embarrassed. (18) Most importantly, the plan completed exactly the opposite of its intent.

13. What is the best way to combine sentences 3 and 4 to clarify the relationship between ideas?

   A. After three years of guerrilla warfare, Castro and his ragtag army descended from the mountains and entered Havana on January 1, 1959, but he forced Batista to flee the country.
   B. After three years of guerrilla warfare, Castro and his ragtag army descended from the mountains and forced Batista to flee the country, doing this when he entered Havana on January 1, 1959.
   C. After three years of guerrilla warfare, Castro and his ragtag army descended from the mountains and entered Havana on January 1, 1959, forcing Batista to flee the country.
   D. Three years of guerrilla warfare passed for Castro and his ragtag army to descend from the mountains, which is when he entered Havana on January 1, 1959, forcing Batista to flee the country.

14. Which revision of sentence 5 uses the most precise language?

    E. Castro took control of the Cuban military and declared himself prime minister.

    F. Castro took control of the Cuban government's army and declared himself prime minister.

    G. Castro took control of the Cuban government's 30,000-man army and declared himself leader.

    H. Castro took control of the Cuban government's 30,000-man army and declared himself prime minister.

15. Which transition word or phrase should be added to the beginning of sentence 8?

    A. In addition,

    B. However,

    C. Soon,

    D. Nevertheless,

16. Which sentence should follow 9 to more clearly introduce the topic of this passage?

    E. The American people wanted a true democracy to take place in Cuba.

    F. Eisenhower authorized the CIA to conduct a covert operation to rid the island of its self-appointed leader.

    G. Cubans, however, were not of all the same opinion when it came to the new regime.

    H. Florida decided to enhance the possibility of losing tourism by advertising its attractions on national television.

17. Which sentence is irrelevant to the ideas presented in the third paragraph (sentences 9–13) and should be deleted?

    A. sentence 10

    B. sentence 11

    C. sentence 12

    D. sentence 13

18. Which sentence should be added before sentence 14 to improve the organization of the fourth paragraph (sentences 14–18)?

    E. The American counterespionage program was one of the most secretive and successful programs in the world.

    F. At least that was the intended outcome.

    G. The plan would be a complete success.

    H. The biggest part of the plan was in the element of surprise.

19. Read this sentence.

> It embarrassed the new Kennedy administration and ended the career of the longest-serving Director of Central Intelligence Allen Dulles.

Where should this sentence be added to best support the ideas in the fourth paragraph (sentences 14–18)?

A. between sentences 14 and 15
B. between sentences 15 and 16
C. between sentences 16 and 17
D. between sentences 17 and 18

20. Which concluding sentence should follow sentence 18 to best support the information in the paragraph?

E. Fidel Castro was able to remain in power for decades to come.
F. American democracy, nonetheless, would persevere throughout the world.
G. Fidel Castro finally died in 2016, the year Donald Trump was elected president of the United States.
H. The United States placed a heavily restrictive embargo, but Cuba continued to thrive.

Directions: Read each passage and answer the questions that follow it. Base your answers **only on the material contained in the passage**. Select the one **best** answer for each question. Bubble in the letter corresponding to that answer on the answer sheet.

Read each of the following passages and answer the questions that follow it. Base your answers only on the material contained in the passages. Do not rely on memory alone: verify each answer by checking the passage. Select the one best response for each question.

I. One of the most remarkable creatures ever to live on Earth is the despised cockroach. When people see cockroaches in their homes, they stomp them, spray them (5) with poison, set traps for them—anything to get rid of the hated brown insects. But the battle is often a losing one, and for good reason. Cockroaches have a superb ability to survive, an ability that has made them (10) thrive on Earth for millions and millions of years.

Living fossils, cockroaches were crawling around on Earth 320 million years ago, about 150 million years before dinosaurs (15) appeared. They even have an era named after them, the Age of Cockroaches, otherwise known as the Carboniferous period. Because of their adaptability, including their willingness to eat almost anything (20) available, they have seen many species come and go.

The easygoing food habits of cockroaches are due to the variety of organisms dwelling in their digestive tract. These bacteria (25) and protozoans enable the insects to eat a wide range of matter, including flower buds, leaf litter, feces, paper, glue, paint, soap, and wood. They will eat their own shed skin, cockroach eggs, and even other (30) cockroaches.

Unusual survival skills have promoted the success of this order of insects. Cockroaches have adapted to most of Earth's environments. They live in the desert, in the forest, (35) in underground burrows, in electrical equipment, and in almost any kind of human habitation—including space capsules. They can live without food and water for a month and can survive on only water for (40) two months. If they have dry food, they can go without water for five months. And they have good defenses against enemies. Their eyes are extremely sensitive and their bodies are equipped with extra warning devices— (45) sense organs that detect the tiniest motion in the air. A fetid odor keeps some potential predators away and hard, compressible bodies make them amazingly tough.

Although most human beings shudder at (50) them, cockroaches play an important role in both natural and artificial settings. Most species prefer to live outdoors where they aid in decomposition of vegetable matter and animal feces. Furthermore, in spite of (55) their built-in protection devices, they are significant in the food chain, being eaten by many animals, including (in some circumstances) human beings. In the laboratory they are docile and easy to handle, and they (60) are cooperative research subjects in areas such as disease and nutrition studies.

21. Which of the following is the best title for this passage?

    A. "The Amazing Eating Machine"
    B. "Survivor and Contributor"
    C. "The Pest and the Dinosaur"
    D. "The Living Fossil"

22. According to the passage, which of the following is **not** true of the cockroach?

    E. Most of them are outdoor insects.
    F. They lived on Earth at the same time as dinosaurs.
    G. They are used in scientific research.
    H. They can eat anything.

23. What does the passage suggest about cockroaches?

    A. Humans may find them bad-smelling.
    B. It would be good if they could be eradicated.
    C. They live everywhere on Earth.
    D. They are important in space research.

24. What is meant by the expression "they have seen many species come and go" (lines 20–21)?

    E. They have lived on Earth before and after some extinct species.
    F. They have acute eyesight.
    G. They lived on Earth long before the dinosaurs and are still living on Earth.
    H. They can perceive approaching enemies and escape them.

25. Which of the following best explains why cockroaches are such a successful insect?

    A. Most insects are amazingly successful creatures.
    B. They have excellent defense mechanisms.
    C. They are adaptable and well protected.
    D. They are significant factors in the ecology.

26. Why can cockroaches eat so many different kinds of foods?

    E. Their taste buds are adaptable.
    F. They live in a wide variety of habitats.
    G. They are basically easygoing, docile creatures.
    H. Their bodies contain organisms that help them process a variety of matter.

II. In the centuries just before Rome converted to Christianity, two philosophies were very influential there. One was Epicur-
Line eanism, founded in Greece early in the
(5) fourth century B.C.E. by the philosopher Epicurus. The other was Stoicism, which originated in Cyprus around the same time. Both taught that the highest good in life is a state of inner tranquility that one can achieve
(10) by conquering anxieties and passions.

Both schools of thought were materialistic. That is, they taught that everything that exists is composed of matter. They did not recognize a spiritual world. The Epicurean
(15) universe contained empty space and matter composed of atoms and compounds. Not only the human body, but also the human soul was thought to be material. Epicurus taught that death brings an end to both. The
(20) Stoics also considered both body and soul to be composed of matter. However, they believed that there is a dynamic force they called the Logos. It also consists of matter, according to them, but it is the source of the
(25) human soul's ability to reason.

Epicureanism taught that pleasure is the ultimate goal of life. Some versions of this philosophy emphasized bodily pleasure and self-indulgence. But Epicurus argued that
(30) intellectual pleasure is a greater good than physical pleasure. According to Epicurus, true pleasure depends on inner serenity. People can achieve the serene state by controlling impulses and desires, behaving in
(35) moderation, and freeing themselves from

attachments and fears. It is especially important, he maintained, to conquer fear of death
and of the gods. Epicurus explained that
since death is merely the end of existence,
(40) it should not be frightening. He also taught
that the gods are too far removed from
human life to affect it in any way.

Stoicism taught that one should strive for
a "tranquil soul" free of all anxiety and
(45) fear. The major key to the tranquil soul,
according to the Stoics, is to be moderate
in all things. Wisdom, courage, and justice, however, were also considered crucial.
The Stoics saw a divine order in the uni-
(50) verse. They taught that people can live in
harmony with the divine order by letting
reason—that is, Logos—guide their lives.

Since Logos, the dynamic source of reason,
was thought to be a part of all human beings,
(55) all human souls are related. Each people
should feel equal to all other people and
connected to all others. A sense of equality
and relatedness should lead a person to act
according to the rule of brotherly love.

27. Which of the following best states the
author's purpose?

A. To show contrasts between
Epicureanism and Stoicism
B. To explain the origin of the doctrine of
brotherly love
C. To demonstrate how philosophical
teachings can be misunderstood
D. To explain the basic teachings of two
ancient philosophies

28. Which of the following is **not** a principle of
Epicureanism?

E. Materialism
F. The existence of Logos
G. The importance of pleasure
H. The need to achieve serenity

29. According to Stoicism, why should people
treat others with brotherly love?

A. Because there is a divine order in the
universe
B. Because wisdom and justice are
important virtues
C. Because love leads to intellectual
pleasure
D. Because all people are related and equal

30. According to Epicurus, why should people
not fear the gods?

E. Because they are kind gods of brotherly
love
F. Because there is no afterlife and
therefore no punishment for sin
G. Because the gods have nothing to do
with human life
H. Because Logos joins humankind to the
gods

31. Which of the following is a similarity
between Epicureanism and Stoicism?

A. Belief in a universal order ordained by
the gods
B. Rejection of the idea of a spiritual
world
C. Belief in Logos
D. Belief that pleasure is the proper goal of
life

32. Which of the following is an example of
Stoic behavior?

E. Avoiding excessive eating and drinking
F. Striving for pleasures of the mind
G. Developing the spiritual aspect of one's
nature
H. Giving away one's worldly goods

III. For several decades the novels of Louisa May Alcott were a favorite among young readers, especially girls. Her most famous
Line book, *Little Women,* is still popular in print
(5) as well as in its three or four film versions. Most of her works tell of the trials and joys of young people in nineteenth-century New England. *Little Women,* for example, a novel based on her own early life and the
(10) early lives of her three sisters, tells of the struggles of a close-knit family during and after the Civil War. To some modern readers Alcott's stories seem sentimental and moralistic, for she sometimes exaggerates
(15) emotion, and she sprinkles her narratives with little sermons. But her emotional scenes can still make readers cry, and her heartwarming vignettes of domestic happiness can still bring smiles to their faces.

(20) The author was born in Germantown, Pennsylvania, but grew up in Boston. Her father, Bronson Alcott, was a well-known philosopher and educator with radical ideas. Dissatisfied with contemporary educational
(25) practices, he developed an innovative teaching method and put it into practice in his own school, which he opened in 1834. His method used conversation instead of drill and memorization in the teaching of young
(30) children. In spite of much negative criticism of his system, he managed to keep the school open for five years.

Although Bronson Alcott went on to become well known as a philosopher, lec-
(35) turer, and leader in the movement for the abolition of slavery, he was a poor provider for his family. The family seldom had more than the basic necessities, and the female members of the family had to work hard to
(40) provide those. In fact it is said that during one particularly hard winter they would have starved if friends had not given them food.

Their poverty motivated Louisa to venture
(45) into a field that would startle some of her fans. Pulp magazines were good markets for thrillers—stories with plenty of action and suspense and, often, violence. Although the magazines were cheap and of inferior
(50) quality, they paid well, and Louisa needed the money to help her family. She became a frequent contributor to this market, but always under assumed names. In *Little Women,* Jo, the main character, helps her
(55) family financially by selling stories to the pulp magazines. She stops after a friend, not knowing who the author is, harshly criticizes one of her thrillers. Motivated to write something better, she produces a
(60) warm and highly moral narrative based on her own family!

33. Which of the following best tells what this passage is about?

   A. The poor family of a famous man
   B. The motives of a famous author
   C. The background and work of Louisa May Alcott
   D. How *Little Women* came to be written

34. What are pulp magazines?

   E. Nineteenth-century magazines using paper made from pulpwood
   F. A magazine of the kind that first published *Little Women*
   G. An inexpensive magazine produced for a young but well-educated audience
   H. A magazine of poor quality that published sensational fiction

35. What does the passage suggest about the novels of Louisa May Alcott?

   A. They are not as popular today as they used to be.
   B. They are sensational but enjoyable.
   C. In their own day they were considered too sentimental.
   D. She wrote them because she could not make money any other way.

36. Which of the following is **not** stated about Bronson Alcott?

    E. He operated his own school for a time.
    F. He struggled unsuccessfully to support his family.
    G. He was a philosopher.
    H. He provided leadership for a social cause.

37. Why did Louisa May Alcott begin writing sensational fiction?

    A. She wanted to start out in a highly lucrative market.
    B. She needed the money it could provide.
    C. Such fiction had a large readership.
    D. She wanted to train for the writing of her first novel.

38. Which of the following is true about most of the main characters in the novels of Alcott?

    E. They are young.
    F. They are all based on her own family.
    G. They are sensationalized.
    H. They are immoral.

IV. The land of Mesopotamia, centered around the valley of the Tigris and Euphrates rivers, has been called "the cradle
Line of civilization." Western civilization had its
(5) beginnings there and in the surrounding areas, which produced the great cultures of Phoenicia, India, Persia, and Egypt. Even in earlier prehistoric times, Mesopotamia saw important beginnings, for it is thought
(10) that the people of this land were the first to develop agriculture. And ages ago a Mesopotamian people called the Sumerians gave the Western world its first system of writing.

(15) The Sumerians moved into the Tigris-Euphrates region six or seven thousand years ago and settled in the delta at the confluence of the two rivers. It was a muddy area, and over the centuries the Sumerians
(20) made the most of mud as a resource. They drained land to build on and channeled water into irrigation ditches. They turned the mud into bricks with which they built protective walls, dwellings and temples, and
(25) they also used it to create superior pottery and terra-cotta sculpture. The Sumerians even wrote on mud, shaping it into soft tablets on which they carved the first letters of Western civilization, wedge-shaped char-
(30) acters called *cuneiform*.

Each prosperous Sumerian city-state was built around an elevated temple dedicated to a god whose representative ruled the city. Sumerian gods were distant from the people
(35) and sometimes cruel, reflecting perhaps the harsh conditions in which their subjects lived. The floods, storms, and wild beasts that threatened the people and sometimes overwhelmed them must have seemed like
(40) manifestations of supernatural power. Nor did the Sumerians have the comfort of an afterlife to look forward to, for in their religion death brought only gloomy darkness.

A story in the Sumerian epic *Gilgamesh*
(45) reflects this people's beliefs about life and death. The hero Gilgamesh's beloved friend Enkidu has just died, and Gilgamesh is so inconsolable at his loss that for seven days and nights he refuses to give up his friend's
(50) body for burial. After he finally relents, he goes on a long journey to the underworld, seeking the goddess who he thinks can grant him immortality. But the answer given him by all those he meets on his journey is "You
(55) will never find that life that you seek." He is told to go home and to make the best of his life. He is to love those close to him and to make them happy. When he returns home, he is reminded of his great achievements;
(60) and when he dies, he is cherished in the memory of his people.

39. Which of the following best tells what the passage is about?

   A. The invention of writing

   B. The history of "the cradle of civilization"

   C. A civilization that flourished in Mesopotamia

   D. The quest of the hero Gilgamesh

40. What is the most likely reason why Gilgamesh goes to the underworld?

   E. The death of Enkidu has made him afraid of dying.

   F. He thinks that as a hero he deserves special consideration.

   G. He wants one more achievement to add to his heroic deeds.

   H. He is a hero and wishes to go where no one has gone before.

41. Why did the Sumerians make so many things out of mud?

   A. It was easier to work with than stone.

   B. They wanted to use it up.

   C. It was easy to write on.

   D. It was their most abundant material.

42. Which of the following best describes the Sumerians' attitude toward their gods?

   E. Mystical devotion and adoration

   F. Respect and fear

   G. Personal love

   H. Confident dependence

43. In addition to writing, what other Mesopotamian invention does the passage mention?

   A. Temples

   B. Pottery

   C. Terra-cotta sculpture

   D. Agriculture

44. According to the passage, what kind of lives did the Sumerians live?

   E. Adventurous and bold

   F. Helpless and terrified

   G. Happy and optimistic

   H. Prosperous but often difficult

V. French Impressionism was one of the most controversial artistic movements of modern times. The Impressionists were nineteenth-century painters who rebelled against the strict rules of classical art laid down by the French Academy. According to eighteenth-century standards, acceptable paintings had to be executed in smooth, precise lines. Except for formal portraits, art had to depict subjects above the level of common life—for example, mythology and history. The Impressionists cast off these restrictions, using experimental techniques to produce spontaneous-looking representations of outdoor scenes and everyday life.

The aim of these rebels was to reproduce what the eye actually sees rather than to give an exact rendering of form. For this reason they studied light and its effects on colors and shapes and strove to represent these effects on canvas. Some Impressionists would paint several pictures of a scene at different times of the day to catch the varying influences of the light. One of their discoveries was that shadows are not always tones of black or brown but tend to contain reflections of the colors in nearby objects. Another discovery was that light can soften the outlines of objects, making shapes appear less precise to the eye than they actually are, and causing the eye to overlook some detail.

The resulting paintings embody techniques drastically different from those used in classical art. Brushstrokes do not carefully outline a shape; rather they suggest it, often with short, side-by-side touches of different colors. These tints look separate only upon close examination, blending when viewed from farther away. Colors are especially radiant because the artists would lay two contrasting primary colors next to each other on the canvas instead of blending them beforehand on a pallette.

The Impressionists organized their first joint exhibition in 1874. Although some of the public were enthusiastic about this new kind of painting, the establishment (50) was scornful of such radical work. In fact, the term "Impressionist" comes from an excoriating review of Claude Monet's painting *Impression: Sunrise,* in which the critic condemned the work as being not a work (55) of art, but rather an art-less impression, and dubbed the painters not arists, but "impressionists." Rather than denouncing this label for their work, the new school adopted it. In 1877, for the third exhibition of their paint- (60) ings, the artists themselves described their work as Impressionist. Appreciated at first by other artists and by a small segment of the public, Impressionism gradually gained ground, finally earning acceptance among (65) both the general public and the critics.

45. Which of the following is the best title for the passage?

    A. "Light Effects in Art"
    B. "A Classical Style"
    C. "Success at Last"
    D. "A New Movement in Art"

46. Which of the following is **not** a feature of Impressionist art?

    E. Short strokes
    F. Contrasting colors side-by-side
    G. Precise outlines
    H. Brilliant color effects

47. Why did the public and the critics not like Impressionism at first?

    A. They thought it was too classical.
    B. It did not follow the established standards.
    C. They felt that there was too much study behind it.
    D. They felt it was too colorful.

48. Which of the following best expresses what the Impressionists were trying to accomplish?

    E. To shake up the establishment
    F. To paint more realistic portraits
    G. To achieve unusual color effects
    H. To depict what the eye really sees

49. What is the meaning of "excoriating" (line 52)?

    A. Harshly critical
    B. Puzzling
    C. Humorous
    D. Reluctant

50. Why did some Impressionists paint the same scene at different times of the day?

    E. They were trying to achieve perfection.
    F. They were trying to duplicate the blacks and browns of shadows.
    G. They liked painting outdoor scenes.
    H. They were trying to learn more about the effects of light.

VI. In this serious hour in our nation's history, when we are confronted with grave crises in Berlin and Southeast Asia, when *Line* we are devoting our energies to economic (5) recovery and stability, when we are asking Reservists to leave their homes and families for months on end, and servicemen to risk their lives—and four were killed in the last two days in Vietnam—and asking union (10) members to hold down their wage requests, at a time when restraint and sacrifice are being asked of every citizen, the American people will find it hard, as I do, to accept a situation in which a tiny handful of steel (15) executives whose pursuit of private power and profit exceeds their sense of public responsibility can show such utter contempt for the interests of 185 million Americans.

If this rise in the cost of steel is imitated by
(20) the rest of the industry, instead of rescinded,
it would increase the cost of homes, autos,
appliances, and most other items for every
American family. It would increase the cost
of machinery and tools to every American
(25) businessman and farmer. It would seriously
handicap our efforts to prevent an infla-
tionary spiral from eating up the pensions
of our older citizens, and our new gains in
purchasing power. It would add, Secretary
(30) McNamara informed me this morning, an
estimated one billion dollars to the cost of
our defenses, at a time when every dollar
is needed for national security and other
purposes. It would make it more difficult
(35) for American goods to compete in foreign markets, more difficult to withstand
competition from foreign imports, and
thus more difficult to improve our balance
of payments position, and stem the flow
(40) of gold. And it is necessary to stem it for
our national security, if we are going to
pay for our security commitments abroad.
And it would surely handicap our efforts
to induce other industries and unions to
(45) adopt responsible price and wage policies.

The facts of the matter are that there is
no justification for an increase in the
steel prices. The recent settlement between
the industry and the union, which does
(50) not even take place until July 1st, was
widely acknowledged to be non-inflation-
ary, and the whole purpose and effect
of this Administration's role, which both
parties understood, was to achieve an agree-
(55) ment which would make unnecessary any
increase in prices.

Price and wage decisions in this country,
except for very limited restrictions in the
case of monopolies and national emergency
(60) strikes, are and ought to be freely and privately made, but the American people have
a right to expect in return for that freedom,
a higher sense of business responsibility for

the welfare of their country than has been
(65) shown in the last two days.

Some time ago I asked each American to
consider what he would do for his country
and I asked the steel companies. In the last
24 hours we had their answer.

51. Which statement best reflects the central
    idea of this passage?

    A. America needs to produce more steel.
    B. Business profits are being hurt by high
       costs.
    C. Steel companies should not raise their
       prices.
    D. Americans must govern themselves
       wisely.

52. Which of the following is most likely the
    attitude of the speaker on the "rise in the
    cost of steel" (line 19)?

    E. He finds it an evil necessity.
    F. He is unconcerned about its impact on
       American values.
    G. He finds that it is unwarranted.
    H. He is optimistic that it will never come
       to pass.

53. The information from Secretary McNamara
    is significant because it

    A. identifies the problem necessary to
       reduce steel prices.
    B. proposes a solution to the rising prices.
    C. predicts a probable harm from rising
       prices.
    D. praises the efforts of American
       businessmen.

54. In the second paragraph, the author includes details about the rising costs in order to

  E. highlight the importance of steel.
  F. emphasize the widespread impact of higher costs.
  G. highlight that Americans prefer domestic to foreign steel.
  H. emphasize the importance of steel to the military.

55. Why does the author mention "Price and wage decisions" in the fourth paragraph?

  A. To anticipate a criticism before addressing it
  B. To reveal his realization of dissatisfaction with his proposal
  C. To concede that he has made an error
  D. To acknowledge that change is difficult

56. Based on the third paragraph, what can be concluded about the "recent settlement" (line 48)?

  E. It was intended to increase prices.
  F. It did not involve the government.
  G. It was not put into effect immediately.
  H. It did not prefer the union to the industry.

57. How does the final paragraph contribute to the passage?

  A. It presents the most probable reason for the rise in steel prices.
  B. It criticizes the steel companies.
  C. It offers a plan to fix the problem.
  D. It predicts what the steel companies will do in the future.

Grid-In Problems

Directions: Solve each problem. On the answer sheet, write your answer in the boxes at the top of the grid. Start on the left side of each grid. Print only one number or symbol in each box. **DO NOT LEAVE A BOX BLANK IN THE MIDDLE OF AN ANSWER.** Under each box, fill in the circle that matches the number or symbol you wrote above. **DO NOT FILL IN A CIRCLE UNDER AN UNUSED BOX.**

58. In a bakery that sells cookies, there are 4 oatmeal cookies for every 11 chocolate cookies. If there are 285 cookies altogether, how many oatmeal cookies are there?

59. Solve for x: $|10 - 14| + |4.5 - 5.9| = 10 + x$

60. A survey asked students about what classes they were taking. Based on the results, the following statements are all true:

32 students are taking math
38 students are taking English
18 students are taking both math and English
5 students are taking neither math nor English

How many students were surveyed?

61.

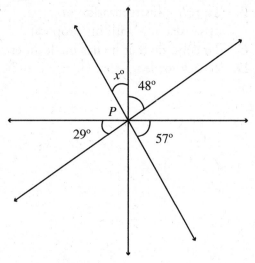

Four straight lines intersect at point P, as shown above. What is the value of x?

62. How many ways can the letters of the word SNOW be arranged horizontally so that the letters N and O are always immediately next to each other (either NO or ON)?

Multiple-Choice Problems

Directions: For each of the following questions, select the **best** answer from the given choices. Bubble in the letter corresponding to your answer on the answer sheet. **DO NOT PUT ANY OTHER WORK ON THE ANSWER SHEET.** All necessary work can be done in your test booklet or on scrap paper that is provided.

NOTE: Diagrams other than graphs might not be drawn to scale. Do not assume any relationships that are not specifically stated unless they are implied by the given information.

63. $(3 + 4)^2 =$

    A. 13
    B. 14
    C. 19
    D. 49

64. The exact value of $\sqrt{49} - \sqrt{24}$ is

    E. 2
    F. between 2 and 5
    G. 5
    H. more than 5

65. 200% of 7 is

    A. .14
    B. 7
    C. 14
    D. 21

66. (All line segments are either horizontal or vertical, as shown.) The perimeter of the figure is

    E. 5
    F. 6
    G. 7
    H. 14

67. What is the value of N if $\frac{1}{5} - \frac{1}{6} = \frac{1}{N}$?

    A. 7
    B. 30

    C. $\frac{1}{30}$

    D. −30

68. Find the value of $(2^4 - 4^2) + (2^3 - 3^2)$.

    E. −11
    F. −8
    G. −1
    H. 0

69. On the number line shown, Q (not shown) is the midpoint of $\overline{PR}$. What is the midpoint of $\overline{QS}$?

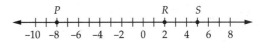

    A. −5
    B. −4
    C. 0
    D. 1

70. The ratio of boys to girls at a dance was 2 to 3. If 45 girls attended, what is the number of boys who attended?

    E. 9
    F. 18
    G. 27
    H. 30

71. If the measure of angle A is 40°, then $x + y =$

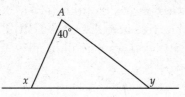

A. 80°
B. 120°
C. 180°
D. 220°

72. If $6x$ is increased by $4y$, and the sum is divided by 2, the result is equivalent to

E. $3x + 4y$
F. $6x + 2y$
G. $3x + 2y$
H. $\dfrac{10x + y}{2}$

73. If $a*b$ means a^b, then $2*(3*2)$ is

A. 512
B. 256
C. 81
D. 64

74. Let n be an integer from 9 to 38. For *how many* values of n will $\dfrac{n}{5}$ be a prime?

E. 3
F. 4
G. 6
H. 8

75. $|2 - 8| - |7 - 3| =$

A. −10
B. −2
C. 2
D. none of these

76. Mary is m years old now. Joe is 3 years younger than Mary. Express Joe's age 10 years from now in terms of m.

E. $13 - m$
F. $m - 3$
G. $m + 7$
H. $m + 10$

77. The smaller angle between the hands of a clock at 10:00 is

A. 15°
B. 30°
C. 45°
D. 60°

78. Find the smallest positive integer that is a multiple of both 21 and 77.

E. 7
F. 33
G. 98
H. 231

79. Over which interval was the growth in the value of the stock of the ABC Company *most* rapid?

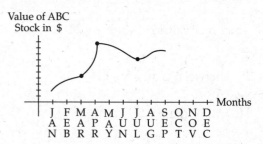

A. March to April
B. April to May
C. May to June
D. June to July

80. Express the *sum* of 1.2×10^2 and 1.2×10^3 in scientific notation.

E. 0.144×10^6
F. 1.32×10^3
G. 1.44×10^5
H. 2.4×10^5

81. Today is Saturday. What day of the week will it be 65 days from today?

A. Sunday
B. Monday
C. Tuesday
D. Wednesday

82. The circles are "tangent" to the rectangle and to each other, as shown. If the area of each circle is 16π, then the area of the rectangle is

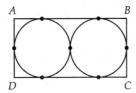

E. 32
F. 48
G. 96
H. 128

83. Thirty of the fifty students who took an exam received a grade of 90% or greater. What percentage of those fifty students received a grade of less than 90%?

A. 70
B. 35
C. 40
D. 30

84. Let n be a number from -3 to 4 inclusive. What is the range of values of n^2?

E. $-9 \leq n^2 \leq 16$
F. $9 \leq n^2 \leq 16$
G. $3 \leq n^2 \leq 4$
H. $0 \leq n^2 \leq 16$

85. A is 3 times C. B is 8 less than C. For what value of C does $A = B$?

A. -4
B. 0
C. 1
D. 2

86. In a class of 28 students, everyone likes math, English, or both. If 17 like math and 19 like English, how many like both?

E. 2
F. 8
G. 16
H. 20

87. Let $x = 3^2 \cdot 5^3 \cdot 7^4$ and $y = 2^3 \cdot 3 \cdot 5^2$. What is the greatest common factor of x and y?

A. $2 \cdot 3 \cdot 5 \cdot 7$
B. $2^3 \cdot 3^2 \cdot 5^3 \cdot 7^4$
C. $3 \cdot 5$
D. $3 \cdot 5^2$

88. The equation $2(3x + 8) = 3(2x + 4)$ is satisfied by

E. no value of x
F. only negative values of x
G. only positive values of x
H. all values of x

89. In the formula $V = s^2 h$, if s is doubled and h is tripled, then V is multiplied by

A. 5
B. 6
C. 12
D. 18

90. You have 10 large boxes that can each hold 8 soccer balls, and 10 small boxes that can each hold 5 of the same soccer balls. If you have 99 soccer balls, what is the greatest number of boxes you can completely fill?

E. 13
F. 14
G. 15
H. 16

91. The straight line graph shows the relationship between number of hours worked and amount earned. How much would be earned for 50 hours of work?

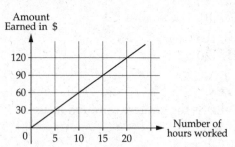

A. $50
B. $83
C. $120
D. $300

92. The perimeter of a triangle, all of whose sides have integer length, is 19. A possible length for the largest side is

E. 6
F. 8
G. 10
H. 15

93. A value of x that satisfies the inequality $2x - 10 > 3x$ is

A. −11
B. −10
C. −1
D. 0

94. The midpoints of the four sides of square *ABCD* are joined to form square *WXYZ* as shown. The area of square *WXYZ* is 16. The area of triangle *YCX* is

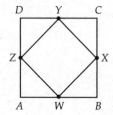

E. 4
F. 2
G. 1.5
H. none of these

95. The mean of 3 numbers is 7. The mean of 4 other numbers is 8. The mean of 5 other numbers is 11. What is the mean of all 12 numbers?

A. 4
B. $4\frac{2}{13}$
C. $8\frac{2}{3}$
D. 9

96. There were 20 socks in a drawer. Of these, 8 were blue, 10 were black, and 2 were white. Someone then removed 4 blue socks. If one sock is now drawn at random, what is the probability that it is *not* white?

E. $\frac{1}{10}$
F. $\frac{9}{10}$
G. $\frac{7}{8}$
H. none of these

97. Two sides of a right triangle are 3 and 4. The third side is

A. 1
B. 3
C. 5
D. not uniquely determined

98. A cube 3 by 3 by 3 is painted red on all six faces and then cut into 27 smaller 1 by 1 by 1 cubes. How many of these new smaller cubes have exactly two faces that are painted red?

E. 6
F. 8
G. 12
H. 21

99. If 2 blobs = 3 glops and 3 blobs = 2 chunks, then 1 chunk =

A. 1 glop

B. $\frac{2}{3}$ glop

C. $\frac{3}{2}$ glops

D. $\frac{9}{4}$ glop

100 and 101 The two pie charts show the ice cream flavor preferences of the students at two high schools.

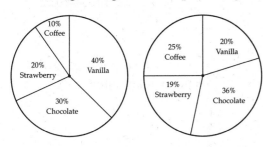

Montague High   Capulet High

100. The ratio of Montague students who prefer vanilla to Montague students who prefer chocolate is

E. 10:9

F. 4:3

G. 3:10

H. 3:4

101. If the *number* of Montague students who prefer vanilla is M and the *number* of Capulet students who prefer vanilla is C, then

A. $M = 2C$

B. $M = C$

C. $M < C$

D. cannot be determined from the given information

102. If x is an integer, which one of the following *must* be odd?

E. $3x + 1$

F. $3x + 2$

G. $4x - 1$

H. $4x - 2$

103. In the sequence of numbers 1, 2, 2, 3, 3, 3, . . . [assume the pattern of one 1, two 2s, three 3s, four 4s, and so on continues], the number in the 40th position will be

A. 8

B. 9

C. 10

D. 11

104. Each side of a square is an integral number of inches, and its area is 576 square inches. If each side of the square is increased by 1 *foot*, forming a new square, the area of the new square, in square *inches*, is

E. 577

F. 720

G. 1,296

H. not determined

105. Let $P = \frac{18}{25}$, $Q = \frac{5}{7}$, and $R = \frac{3}{4}$. Then

A. $P < Q < R$

B. $P < R < Q$

C. $Q < P < R$

D. $Q < R < P$

106. A water container is $\frac{3}{4}$ full. After 20 ounces of water is removed, the container is $\frac{1}{4}$ full. How many ounces of water does a full container hold?

E. 20

F. 40

G. 60

H. 80

107. For *how many* integer values of n will the expression $\dfrac{n-10}{14-n}$ have a positive value?

A. 0
B. 1
C. 3
D. 4

108. A square of side 4 is topped by a semicircle, as shown. Point P is the center of the arc at the top. Then the shaded area is equal to

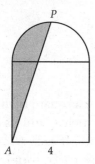

E. $\pi + 2$
F. $\dfrac{\pi}{2} + 2$
G. $2\pi + 2$
H. $2\pi - 4$

109. $\dfrac{4^6 \times 3^4 \times 2^2}{4^2 \times 3^4 \times 2^6} =$

A. 1
B. 2
C. 8
D. 16

110. Which one of the following numbers is *less* than $\dfrac{1}{3}$?

E. $\dfrac{1111}{3333}$

F. $\dfrac{299}{895}$

G. $.1 \times 4$

H. $\dfrac{5!}{6!}$

111. The ratio of a to b is 3 to 4. The ratio of b to c is 5 to 6. The ratio of a to c is

A. 9:10
B. 5:8
C. 1:2
D. none of these

112. (All lines shown are either vertical or horizontal.) If x and y are integers, and the shaded area is 52, then the perimeter of the figure is

E. 20
F. 24
G. 52
H. 56

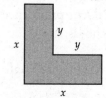

113. If $x < x^3 < x^2$, which of the following could be a possible value for x?

A. $-\dfrac{1}{2}$

B. 0.1

C. 0.5

D. $\dfrac{2}{3}$

114. On the number line below, point A is located at -4 and point B is located at 20. AQ is $\dfrac{3}{8}$ of the distance from A to B, while BR is $\dfrac{3}{8}$ of the distance from B to A. Find the length of QR.

E. 6
F. 9
G. 12
H. 15

ANSWER KEY
Practice Test 1

Revising/Editing Part A

1. A	3. A	5. D
2. H	4. F	6. E

Revising/Editing Part B

7. B	10. E	13. C	16. F	19. B
8. G	11. D	14. H	17. C	20. E
9. C	12. F	15. C	18. F	

Reading

21. B	29. D	37. B	45. D	53. C
22. H	30. G	38. E	46. G	54. F
23. A	31. B	39. C	47. B	55. A
24. E	32. E	40. E	48. H	56. G
25. C	33. C	41. D	49. A	57. B
26. H	34. H	42. F	50. H	
27. D	35. A	43. D	51. C	
28. F	36. F	44. H	52. G	

Mathematics

58. **76**	70. H	82. H	94. E	106. F
59. **–4.6**	71. D	83. C	95. D	107. C
60. **57**	72. G	84. H	96. G	108. E
61. **46**	73. A	85. A	97. D	109. D
62. **12**	74. F	86. F	98. G	110. H
63. D	75. C	87. D	99. D	111. B
64. F	76. G	88. E	100. F	112. H
65. C	77. D	89. C	101. D	113. A
66. H	78. H	90. H	102. G	114. E
67. B	79. A	91. D	103. B	
68. G	80. F	92. F	104. G	
69. D	81. B	93. A	105. C	

Revising/Editing Part A

1. **(A)** Examine all the predicate verbs underlined below.

   (1) People often <u>associate</u> monosodium glutamate, or better known as MSG, with headaches and nausea, but there <u>was</u> no evidence to substantiate that link. (2) In fact, the compounds associated with MSG <u>are</u> commonly found in beef, pork, or chicken. (3) Scientists <u>believe</u> the sicknesses might be the result of a "nocebo effect." (4) The nocebo effect, like the placebo effect, <u>isn't</u> caused by an actual substance, but merely by suggestion.

2. **(H)** Commas should not be placed before the relative pronoun *that*. Choice E is wrong because it separates the modifier *Typically occurring in the spring* and the modified object *a nor'easter*. Choices F and G are wrong because *a gigantic cyclone* is also another modifier that needs the commas.

3. **(A)** In sentence (1) the subject noun is *syrup* and the connecting predicate noun is *are*.

   (1) Molasses *syrup, ~~a product made from sugar and beets,~~ are* primarily used for sweetening foods. (2) Molasses syrup is rich with glucose and fructose, compounds rich with energy. (3) Because of its taste, sugar molasses syrup is used for human consumption, while beet molasses syrup is used for animal consumption. (4) Because of its adhesive properties, molasses syrup is also used as an additive component in mortar for brickwork.

4. **(F)** It expresses the idea with the fewest number of clauses.

5. **(D)**

Least Precise (cross out)	Most Precise
storm	cyclone
dropping in pressure drops in pressure drops in a matter of hours	drops 30 percent within 24 hours

6. **(E)** Examine the pairings of <u>antecedents</u> and **pronouns** below.

   (1) People often use the <u>terms</u> democracy and republic interchangeably, as if **it** means the same thing. (2) While both <u>forms</u> of government provide powers to their respective citizens, **they** differ in the way **they** provide that power. (3) A democracy is simply a rule by the <u>majority</u>, **which** plays a very large role in the affairs of government policies. (4) In contrast, republics are run by a constitution, which enables the <u>people</u> to elect **their** leaders.

   Sentence 1: The singular pronoun **it** incorrectly replaces the plural antecedent <u>terms</u>. The pronoun **it** should be revised to **they**. The correct antecedent to plural pronoun **they** is democracy and republic.

   Sentence 2: The correct antecedent to the plural pronoun **they** is <u>forms</u>.

   Sentence 3: The correct antecedent to the relative pronoun **which** is <u>majority</u>.

   Sentence 4: The correct antecedent to the plural pronoun **their** is <u>people</u>.

Revising/Editing Part B

7. **(B)** Sentence 1 discusses a situation in which people cut back on sleep for perceived benefits. Sentence 2 provides a contrasting image in which cutting back on sleep produces harmful impacts.

8. **(G)** Choice G provides more information in the phrase *affect you next day* of sentence 1. Choice E is related to sleep, but the statistic is irrelevant. Choice F provides a solution, but a discussion of the solution is not discussed until later in the paragraph. Choice H introduces a new idea, which is irrelevant.

9. (C)

Least Precise (cross out)	Most Precise
more sleep	9 to 12 hours
people age / people of ages, shapes, and sizes	school-age children, 8 to 10 for teens, and 7 or more for adults.

10. (E) The previous sentences begin with a verb (*Be, Make, Avoid*). Choice E follows that style.

11. (D) The phrase *Better sleep habits* connects best with the ending phrase *better habits* in sentence 15.

Choice A is wrong because it interrupts the discussion of good sleep and definition of good sleep. Choice B is wrong because it would interrupt the link between the antecedent *signs* and its pronoun *These*. Choice C is wrong because it interrupts the link between the symptoms of poor sleep and the phrase *these indicators*.

12. (F) Although choice F discusses the importance of sleep, it unnecessarily emphasizes dementia, which is irrelevant in that paragraph.

13. (C) It expresses the idea most clearly with the fewest number of clauses. Choice A is wrong because it uses an unnecessary contrast word *but* to join two ideas. Choices B and D are wrong because they are unnecessarily wordy.

14. (H)

Least Precise (cross out)	Most Precise
Cuban military / Cuban government's army	Cuban government's 30,000-man army
leader	prime minister

15. (C) Sentence 7 describes what happened in 1960. Sentence 8 describes what happened after. The transition word *Soon* best connects the two sequence of events.

16. (F) Sentence 9 introduces President Eisenhower's displeasure. Choice F follows up on that information.

17. (C) Sentence 10 cannot be removed because doing so would eliminate the link between the *CIA formulated plan* and *It would train* of sentence 11. Sentence 13 cannot be removed because it links with the phrase *infiltrate Cuba* in sentence 11. Sentence 12 makes a generalized descriptive sentence about military training.

18. (F) It introduces the series of events that contrasts with the intended outcome. Choice E is wrong because a description of the American counterespionage program has nothing to do with the failings of the covert CIA mission. Choice G is wrong because the passage suggests otherwise. Choice H is wrong because it has no relevance to the failure of the mission.

19. (B) The key here is to identify the word *it* in the sentence. The thing that embarrassed the administration would have to be the *failure* mentioned in sentence 15.

20. (E) Sentence E provides the impact of the mission's failure.

Reading

Passage I

21. (B) Main Idea A and C are too narrow: A relates only to one sentence in the second paragraph and to the third paragraph; C relates only to the first paragraph. D could be correct except that it does not cover the last paragraph. B is correct because every paragraph discusses either the survival or the contributions of the cockroach.

> **TIP:** Be sure the main-idea choice you select involves the entire passage.

22. (H) Detail For a question that asks what is not true or not stated, you should work by a process of elimination. E can be eliminated because it is mentioned in the last paragraph (line 52). The second paragraph says that cockroaches were on Earth before dinosaurs (line 14), and since they are still here they must have been on Earth when the dinosaurs were, so F is an incorrect choice. The last sentence states their use in research, making G incorrect. H is the right answer because it is too extreme. The passage says they will eat "almost anything available"; it does **not** say that they will eat anything.

> **FACT:** Answers that are more extreme than the stated information are inaccurate.

23. **(A)** Inference   A is correct because the fourth paragraph says that cockroaches have a fetid odor that keeps some predators away (lines 46–47). It can be inferred that humans also might find them bad-smelling. B is wrong because although they are seen as pests, the passage says that they are important in more ways than one (lines 51–52). C is too extreme. According to the fourth paragraph, they have adapted to "most" of Earth's environments, not all (lines 33–34). D is wrong because although it is mentioned that they can live in space capsules, no mention is made of their being used in space research.

24. **(E)** Inference

> **TIP:** Always determine a definition answer by examining the context in which a word or phrase occurs.

The expression "they have seen many species come and go" occurs in the context of their long survival on Earth and their outlasting the dinosaurs, so E is the correct choice.

25. **(C)** Main Idea   This item requires you to summarize information. "Adaptable" and "well protected" cover every reason given in the paragraphs that discuss why they have survived for so long, paragraphs 2, 3, and 4. A may be true but is not given or suggested in the passage.

> **FACT:** An answer may be true but a wrong choice because it is not given or suggested in the passage.

B is true but too narrow, as it involves only one reason for survival, and more than one is given. D is true but not mentioned or suggested as being a reason for survival.

26. **(H)** Detail   The correct answer is clearly stated in the first sentence of the third paragraph (lines 23–24).

Passage II

27. **(D)** Main Idea   A is incorrect because the passage doesn't focus on contrasts, and it also points out some similarities. B and C are both too narrow. Brotherly love (B) is mentioned only in the last paragraph, and misunderstanding (C) only in one sentence. The first sentence says that they were influential just before Rome converted to Christianity but not that they influenced the religion. D is both broad enough and accurate.

28. **(F)** Detail   E is stated in the second paragraph (line 11). G and H are both stated in the third paragraph (lines 26–27 and line 32). F is correct because Logos is a concept of Stoicism, not Epicureanism.

29. **(D)** Detail   The correct answer is stated in the last sentence of the passage.

30. **(G)** Detail   Paragraph three states Epicurus' teaching that people should not fear the gods (lines 37–38). The last sentence in the paragraph gives the reason stated in G.

31. **(B)** Detail   The correct answer is stated in the third sentence of the second paragraph (lines 13–14). A and C are given as concepts of Stoicism only, and D as a concept of Epicureanism only.

32. **(E)** Inference   Although eating and drinking are not specifically mentioned, the fourth paragraph does say the Stoics taught moderation in "all things" (line 47). "All things" includes eating and drinking, so it can be inferred that one should not be immoderate, or excessive, in these activities. F is an Epicurean concept. G is incorrect since Stoics do not believe in a spiritual world. H is not mentioned or suggested.

Passage III

33. **(C) Main Idea** All of the other choices are too narrow. A does not include Louisa May Alcott's writing. B is mentioned only in the fourth paragraph, and the same is true of D. It is also inaccurate because contrast is not stressed in the passage. C covers ideas in all paragraphs of the passage, so C is correct.

34. **(H) Detail** The correct answer is stated in the second and third sentences of the last paragraph (lines 46–52).

35. **(A) Inference** The first two sentences make the suggestion stated in A. The first sentence states the novels' popularity "For several decades" and uses the past tense verb "were." The second sentence indicates indirectly that only *Little Women* is still popular. B contradicts the information about the novels that is stated in the first paragraph, and also contradicts the suggestion of "something better" made in the last sentence of the passage. C is incorrect because the first paragraph says only that "some modern readers" find the stories too sentimental; no such suggestion is made for readers of the nineteenth century. D contradicts the fact that Alcott made money by writing stories for pulp magazines.

36. **(F) Detail** All of the other answers are stated in the second and third paragraphs. The third paragraph says that he was a poor provider and that the females in the family worked hard, but no suggestion is made that Alcott actually struggled or even cared about his family's poverty.

37. **(B) Detail** The correct answer is stated in the first three sentences of the last paragraph.

38. **(E) Detail** The correct answer is stated in the first paragraph (line 7). F is inaccurate because only the *Little Women* characters are stated as being based on her family. Neither G or H is stated or suggested.

Passage IV

39. **(C) Main Idea** Only C is both accurate and broad enough. A is too narrow, as writ-ing is mentioned in only two sentences. B is inaccurate because the passage discusses only one civilization of the "cradle" and doesn't attempt to give its history. D is too narrow because Gilgamesh is mentioned only in the last paragraph.

40. **(E) Inference** Several sentences make this suggestion. The third paragraph says that the Sumerian afterlife brought no comfort (line 43). The last paragraph says that after his friend's death Gilgamesh goes to the under-world looking for a goddess who can grant him immortality. The suggestion is that his friend's death made Gilgamesh fear death.

FACT: Sometimes it is necessary to read several sentences to draw a correct inference.

None of the other choices are stated or sug-gested.

41. **(D) Inference** A is incorrect because the passage doesn't mention stone. Although the second paragraph says that mud was abun-dant, no suggestion is made that the people tried to "use it up," so B is incorrect. C is true but an incorrect choice, as it does not involve most of the things that were made of mud.

FACT: A choice may be true but incorrect as an answer.

42. **(F) Inference** The fact that every city was centered around a temple dedicated to a god indicates respect. The gods are called "sometimes cruel," suggesting that they were to be feared for what they sometimes did. E is wrong as mysticism and devotion are not stated or suggested. The gods are called "distant from the people," contradicting the devotion mentioned in E and the love men-tioned in G. Confident dependence contra-dicts the idea that the gods were cruel and distant.

43. **(D) Detail** The answer is stated in the first paragraph (line 11).

44. **(H) Detail** Two sentences in the third paragraph give the correct answer. The cities

are described as "prosperous," suggesting that the citizens were also prosperous. Hardships and disasters are mentioned in this same paragraph (line 37). Adventure is mentioned only in connection with Gilgamesh, so E is wrong. F is wrong because although fear is suggested in the third paragraph, helplessness is not stated or suggested. G is incorrect because it contradicts the suggestions of fear and discomfort in the third paragraph.

Passage V

45. **(D)** Main Idea   A and C are too narrow, as they each involve information given in only one paragraph. B is inaccurate because Impressionism violates "classical" rules.

46. **(G)** Detail   G is the correct choice because it contradicts the fact that Impressionist "brushstrokes do not carefully outline a shape" (lines 36–37) E, F, and H are all stated in the third paragraph.

47. **(B)** Inference   The passage says that the "establishment" rejected the Impressionist style because it was "radical" (lines 49–50), suggesting that this departure from the norm was why it was not popular at first. A contradicts the information given above and also in the first paragraph. C and D are not stated or suggested in the passage.

48. **(H)** Detail   The correct answer is stated in the first sentence of the second paragraph.

49. **(A)** Inference   The context in which the word is used concerns condemnation and negative criticism (lines 53–55); thus "harshly critical" is the correct interpretation of the word. None of the other choices fits the tone indicated by criticism and condemnation.

50. **(H)** Detail   The correct answer is stated in the second paragraph (line 20).

Passage VI

51. **(C)** Main Idea   Choices A and B are too narrow, as they make unnecessary inferences. Choice D is out of scope.

52. **(G)** Detail   Lines 47–48 make it clear that there is no justification for price increases.

53. **(C)** Inference   Line 19 starts with the word "If" and the sentences following suggest a hypothetical "would." Therefore choice C is the best choice.

54. **(F)** Detail   The second paragraph deals with the impact of rise in steel prices by starting with cost of homes, autos, appliances . . . machinery . . . tools . . . pensions . . . national security . . . and security commitments abroad.

55. **(A)** Inference   The key word is *but*. The first part of the sentence suggests that companies have the right to set their own prices, but only under the condition that they demonstrate a "higher sense of business responsibility." Therefore, he is anticipating anyone who might suggest that companies have a right to set their own prices.

56. **(G)** Inference   Lines 49–50 state that it "does not take place until July 1st," meaning that it was not put into effect immediately.

57. **(B)** Inference   Since the companies decided to raise wages, their answers in the last 24 hours was unjustifiable. Therefore, the author is indirectly attacking the companies.

Mathematics

58. **(76)** Let x be the total number of oatmeal cookies. Since 4 out of every 15 cookies are oatmeal cookies, we can solve the proportion $\frac{x}{285} = \frac{4}{15}$ for x:

$$x = (285)\frac{4}{15} = \left(\frac{285}{15}\right)4 = 19 \times 4 = 76$$

59. **(–4.6)** Begin by simplifying the absolute value expressions, working from the inside out: $|10 - 14| + |4.5 - 5.9| = |-4| + |-1.4| = 4 + 1.4 = 5.4$. Now $5.4 = 10 + x$, so $x = 5.4 - 10 = -4.6$.

60. **(57)** Since 32 students are taking math and 18 are taking both math and English, that means $32 - 18 = 14$ are taking only math.

Similarly, 38 − 18 = 20 students are taking only English. Every one of the students must fall into exactly one of the following categories: taking only math; taking only English; taking both math and English; and taking neither math nor English. Thus the total number of students is 14 + 20 + 18 + 5 = 57.

61. **(46)** Since vertical angles are congruent, the angle vertical to the 57° angle also measures 57°. Since the angle of a straight line is 180°, we know that 29 + x + 48 + 57 = 180. Thus, x = 46.

62. **(12)** There are two kinds of arrangements: those that include "NO" and those that include "ON." Let's count each kind separately. For those that contain an "NO," we imagine "NO" as a single unit. So we need to count the arrangements of "S," "W," and "NO." There are 3! = 3 × 2 × 1 = 6 such arrangements. Similarly, there are 6 such arrangements of "S," "W," and "ON," for a total of 12 arrangements.

63. **(D)** $7^2 = 49$.

64. **(F)** $\sqrt{24}$ is a little less than 5, so $\sqrt{49} - \sqrt{24}$ is a little more than 7 − 5. The result is actually between 2 and 3, so the best choice is F.

> **TIP:** $\sqrt{a} - \sqrt{b}$ is generally not the same as $\sqrt{a-b}$.

Also note that $\sqrt{24}$ is an exact number, even though its decimal form never ends. The same is true of $\frac{1}{3}$, for example, which is an exact number even though its decimal form never ends.

65. **(C)** $\frac{200}{100} \cdot 7 = 14$. This is quite logical, since 100% of 7 is 7.

66. **(H)** The two unmarked vertical sides must add up to 3, and the two unmarked horizontal sides must add up to 4. Therefore the perimeter is 3 + 4 + 3 + 4 = 14.

67. **(B)** The difference between the fractions on the left is $\frac{6}{30} - \frac{5}{30} = \frac{1}{30}$. Since this equals $\frac{1}{N}$, N must be 30.

68. **(G)** This is (16 − 16) + (8 − 9) = 0 − 1 = −1.

69. **(D)** The coordinate of Q is $\frac{(-8)+(2)}{2} = -3$. Then the midpoint of $\overline{QS}$ is $\frac{(-3)+(5)}{2} = 1$.

70. **(H)** Let 2x and 3x represent the number of boys and girls at the dance. Then 3x = 45, so x = 15. Therefore, 2x = 30 boys attended. Do not misread the problem to think that 45 people attended, or that the value of x is the answer to the problem.

71. **(D)** If we call the other interior angles of the triangle p and q, then x + p + q + y = 180 + 180 = 360. Since p + q = 140, then x + y must equal 220°.

72. **(G)** The answer is $\frac{6x+4y}{2} = 3x + 2y$.

73. **(A)** First compute 3 * 2 = 3^2 = 9. Then 2 * 9 = 2^9 = 512.

74. **(F)** The smallest integer value of $\frac{n}{5}$ occurs when n = 10, and is $\frac{10}{5} = 2$. The largest integer value occurs when n = 35, and is $\frac{35}{5} = 7$.

The only primes from 2 to 7 are 2, 3, 5, and 7. Thus, there are 4 values of n that produce primes. Don't forget that 2 is a prime number.

75. **(C)**

> **TIP:** Combine the terms inside the absolute value signs before you compute the absolute value.

This is |−6| − |4| = 6 − 4 = 2.

76. **(G)** Joe's age is now m − 3. Ten years from now Joe's age will be (m − 3) + 10 = m + 7.

77. **(D)** At 9:00, the hands obviously form a 90° angle. At 10:00 the angle is $\frac{2}{3}$ as large, or 60°.

78. **(H)** The integer must be a multiple of both $3 \cdot 7$ and $7 \cdot 11$. The least common multiple of these is $3 \cdot 7 \cdot 11 = 231$.

79. **(A)** We must find the one-month interval where the graph rises most quickly. This is between March and April.

80. **(F)** We have $1.2 \times 10^2 = 120$ and $1.2 \times 10^3 = 1200$. Their sum is 1,320. In scientific notation, that is 1.32×10^3.

> **FACT:** For a number to be in scientific notation, it must be of the form $A \times 10^B$, where $1 \le A < 10$ and B is an integer.

> **FACT:** If you have difficulty remembering how to adjust the exponent of 10 when you move a decimal point, try using smaller numbers. For example, 25×10 is equal to 2.5×100 (that is 2.5×10^2).

81. **(B)** Every 7th day after Saturday is also a Saturday. Dividing 65 by 7 gives a remainder of 2, so it will be 2 days after Saturday, which is Monday.

82. **(H)** Using the fact that the area of a circle is πr^2, the radius of each circle is 4. That makes each diameter 8. Then the height and width of the rectangle must be 8 and 16, and the area of the rectangle is $(8)(16) = 128$.

83. **(C)** Twenty of the fifty students got less than 90%. That is $\frac{20}{50} \cdot 100 = 40\%$.

84. **(H)** The square of the given numbers can never be negative, and they cannot be more than 16.

85. **(A)** We have $A = 3C$ and $B = C - 8$. When $A = B$, we have $3C = C - 8$, so $C = -4$.

86. **(F)** Method 1. Make a Venn diagram showing two overlapping circles. Let one circle represent the students who like math and the other circle represent the students who like English. The overlapping section would represent students who like both. If x students like both, we can put an x in that center section. Then the other sections of the circles would be represented by $17 - x$ and $19 - x$. Since there are 28 students altogether, we can now add all three sections and get $(17 - x) + (19 - x) + x = 28$. This produces $x = 8$.

Method 2. Another method would be to add 17 and 19 to get 36. This is 8 more than the number of students in the class because the overlapping section ($= 8$) is counted twice.

87. **(D)**

> **FACT:** The greatest common factor (also called the greatest common divisor) of x and y consists of the primes common to both x and y, with each such prime raised to the smaller of the exponents it had in x or y.

In this case the answer is $3 \cdot 5^2$.

88. **(E)** When simplified, the equation becomes $6x + 16 = 6x + 12$, or $4 = 0$. This is impossible, so no value of x can satisfy this. Compare this with the equation $2(4x + 6) = 4(2x + 3)$, which leads to $8x + 12 = 8x + 12$. This equation is true for all values of x. Finally, compare these with an equation like $3x + 7 = 22$, which is only satisfied by one value of x.

89. **(C)** Replacing s by $2s$ and h by $3h$ produces $V = (2s)^2(3h) = 12s^2h$. The original V has been multiplied by 12.

90. **(H)** To maximize the number of boxes filled, start by filling the smaller boxes. The 10 small boxes hold 50 balls all together. We can use the remaining 49 balls to fill 6 large boxes, leaving one ball out. Thus, we can completely fill 16 boxes at most.

91. **(D)** Every 5 hours earns us $30, so 50 hours would earn us $10 \times \$30 = \$300$.

92. **(F)**

> **FACT:** The sum of the lengths of two sides of a triangle is greater than the length of the third side.

The sum of the three lengths is given as 19. If the longest side is 10, the sum of the other two sides would be 9, which is impossible. Therefore the longest side must be less than 10. On the other hand, if the longest side is only 6, then the perimeter cannot be more than 18. The only valid choice is F. As an example, the three sides could be 8, 7, 4.

93. **(A)** If we subtract $2x$ from each side of the inequality, we get $-10 > x$. The only choice for x that is less than -10 is A.

94. **(E)** Each side of square $WXYZ$ must be 4. If we let CY and CX each equal x, then in right triangle YCX we have $x^2 + x^2 = 4^2 = 16$. Thus $2x^2 = 16$, so $x^2 = 8$. But the area of triangle YCX is $\left(\frac{1}{2}\right)(\text{base})(\text{height}) = \left(\frac{1}{2}\right)(x)(x) = \left(\frac{1}{2}\right)x^2 = \left(\frac{1}{2}\right)(8) = 4$.

95. **(D)**

> **TIP:** If the mean of n numbers is A, then the numbers add up to $n \times A$.

The sum of all 12 numbers is

$$3 \cdot 7 + 4 \cdot 8 + 5 \cdot 11 = 108.$$

The mean of those numbers is $\frac{108}{12} = 9$.

96. **(G)** After the 4 blue socks are removed, the drawer still contains 4 blue socks, 10 black socks, and 2 white socks. Of these 16 socks, 14 are *not* white. Therefore the probability of drawing a sock that is not white is $\frac{14}{16} = \frac{7}{8}$.

97. **(D)** If the 3 and 4 are the lengths of the legs of the triangle, the hypotenuse would be 5. But the 3 could be a leg and the 4 could be the hypotenuse. That would produce a different length for the missing leg. Thus, the third side is not uniquely determined.

98. **(G)** Only the small center cube on each *edge* of the original cube would be painted on exactly 2 faces. The original cube has 12 edges, so there are 12 such small cubes. The answer is G. Try figuring out how many of the small cubes have exactly 1 painted face. Finally, try for 3 (then 0) painted faces.

99. **(D)** Using single letters for the "nonsense words," we have $2b = 3g$ and $3b = 2c$. We can relate g and c if we can eliminate the bs. One easy way to do this is to change each equation to an equivalent one. Multiplying each side of the first equation by 3, and each side of the second equation by 2, we get $6b = 9g$ and $6b = 4c$. Therefore $4c = 9g$, so $c = \frac{9}{4}g$.

100. **(F)** If Montague High has N students, the ratio of vanilla preference to chocolate preference is $\frac{40}{100}N : \frac{30}{100}N$, which equals 4:3.

101. **(D)** We cannot compare 40% of one population with 20% of another because we do not know how large the populations are. For example, if Capulet High is very large, 20% of its population may be much larger than 40% of Montague's population.

102. **(G)** If x is an integer, $4x$ must be even. Then $4x - 1$ must be odd. Notice that $3x$ could be odd or even.

103. **(B)** Counting numbers, we have 1 one + 2 of the twos + 3 of the threes + 4 of the fours + etc. Adding through the eights gives us a total of $1 + 2 + 3 + \ldots + 8 = 36$ numbers. The next set of numbers (nines) will include the 40th position.

104. **(G)** We first find the side of the original square. Since $20^2 = 400$ and $25^2 = 625$ the side of that square is between 20 and 25. Of those integers, only 24^2 could end in a 6. (You can check that 24^2 does equal 576.) Increasing each side of that square by 12 inches (= 1 foot) produces a new square with each side being $24 + 12 = 36$ inches long. Its area would be $36^2 = 1,296$ square inches.

105. **(C)** We could get a common denominator for each fraction, then compare them. However, it is easier to change each to a decimal and then compare. The decimal equivalents are

$$P = \frac{18}{25} = \frac{72}{100} = .72, \quad Q = \frac{5}{7} = .714\ldots,$$

and $R = .75$. Clearly, $Q < P < R$.

106. **(F)** To reduce the contents of the container from $\frac{3}{4}$ full to $\frac{1}{4}$ full, we must have removed $\frac{3}{4} - \frac{1}{4} = \frac{1}{2}$ of what the container could hold. Since that was 20 ounces, the full container can hold 40 ounces.

107. **(C)** Method 1. If n is less than 10, the numerator will be negative and the denominator will be positive. That would give the fraction a negative value. If n is more than 14, the numerator will be positive but the denominator will be negative. That also gives the fraction a negative value. But when the numerator is between 10 and 14, the numerator and the denominator (and the fraction) will be positive. That means n can be 11, 12, or 13. We must check $n = 10$ and $n = 14$ separately. The former makes the fraction equal to 0, which is not positive. The latter is not a permitted value of n because it would make the denominator equal to 0. Therefore there are 3 values of n that are acceptable.

Method 2. This problem can also be done using inequalities as follows: The fraction will be positive if the numerator and denominator are either both positive or both negative. That produces either $n - 10 > 0$ and $14 - n > 0$ (these lead to $14 > n > 10$), or else $n - 10 < 0$ and $14 - n < 0$ (these lead to $14 < n < 10$, which is impossible). We get the possibilities 11, 12, and 13 this way also.

108. **(E)** Drop a perpendicular from P to the base of the square, and let it hit that base at a point B. It will also go through the "center of the semicircle." Looking to the left of altitude PB, we can see that the shaded area consists of one-fourth the area of a circle, plus one-half the area of a square, minus the area of right triangle PBA. Notice that each side of the square is 4, and the radius of the circle is 2. Then the shaded area is

$$\left(\frac{1}{4}\right)(4\pi) + \left(\frac{1}{2}\right)(16) - \left(\frac{1}{2}\right)(2+4)(2) =$$

$$\pi + 8 - 6 = \pi + 2$$

109. **(D)** Using the laws of exponents for division, the fraction is equal to

$$\frac{4^4}{2^4} = \frac{4^4}{16} = \frac{4^4}{4^2} = 4^2 = 16$$

110. **(H)** If you quickly glance over the choices, you may see that H is the obvious answer, since it is equal to $\frac{1}{6}$. You would then save time by not bothering with the other choices. Otherwise, you must check out each of the choices. The first choice is equal to $\frac{1111}{3(1111)} = \frac{1}{3}$. In the second choice, 3 times the numerator is 897 (that is $900 - 3$); since the denominator is smaller, the fraction is larger than $\frac{1}{3}$. The third choice equals .4, which is more than $\frac{1}{3}$ ($= .333\ldots$).

111. **(B)** We have $a{:}b = 3{:}4 = 15{:}20$. We also have $b{:}c = 5{:}6 = 20{:}24$. We have purposely gotten the same value into the "b" position, so we can now say that $a{:}b{:}c = 15{:}20{:}24$. Therefore, $a{:}c = 15{:}24$, which is also equal to 5:8.

112. **(H)** Method 1. Extend both "y" segments across the shaded region until they meet the "x" segments. Call each of the four unmarked segments "r" (they must all be equal). Then the shaded area will be $r^2 + ry + ry = r^2 + 2ry = 52$. Pick values for r, starting with $r = 1$, and see if there is a corresponding integer value for y. We quickly get

a value at $r = 2$ ($y = 12$). Then, $x = r + y =$ 14, and the perimeter is $2x + 2r + 2y = 56$.

Method 2. If we complete the square whose sides are of length x, we see that the shaded area is $x^2 - y^2$. Then we have $x^2 - y^2 = 52 = (x - y)(x + y)$.

> **FACT:** If the product of two integers is even, at least one of them must be even.

Since x and y are integers, at least one of these factors must be even.

> **FACT:** If the sum of two integers is even, the integers are either both even or both odd.

Therefore x and y are either both even or both odd. That further means that *both* factors will be even. The only way to factor 52 so that both factors are even is $(2)(26)$.

Then $x - y = 2$ and $x + y = 26$. It is not hard to find that $x = 14$ and $y = 12$. Finally, we see that the two smaller horizontal segments of the figure must add up to x, and the two smaller vertical segments must also add up to x. Therefore the perimeter of the figure will be $4x$, which equals 56.

113. **(A)** $-\frac{1}{2} < -\frac{1}{8} < \frac{1}{4}$ (choice A is right);

$0.1 > (0.1)^3 = 0.001$ (choice B is wrong); $0.5 > (0.5)^2 = 0.25$ (choice C is wrong);

$\frac{2}{3} > \left(\frac{2}{3}\right)^2 = \frac{4}{9}$ (choice D is wrong).

114. **(E)** $AB = 20 - (-4) = 24$, so $AQ = \left(\frac{3}{8}\right)(24)$ $= 9$. Similarly, $BR = \left(\frac{3}{8}\right)(24) = 9$. Finally,

$QR = AB - AQ - BR = 24 - 9 - 9 = 6$.

ANSWER SHEET
Practice Test 2

Part I English Language Arts

Revising/Editing Part A

1. Ⓐ Ⓑ Ⓒ Ⓓ
2. Ⓔ Ⓕ Ⓖ Ⓗ
3. Ⓐ Ⓑ Ⓒ Ⓓ
4. Ⓔ Ⓕ Ⓖ Ⓗ
5. Ⓐ Ⓑ Ⓒ Ⓓ
6. Ⓔ Ⓕ Ⓖ Ⓗ

Revising/Editing Part B

7. Ⓐ Ⓑ Ⓒ Ⓓ
8. Ⓔ Ⓕ Ⓖ Ⓗ
9. Ⓐ Ⓑ Ⓒ Ⓓ
10. Ⓔ Ⓕ Ⓖ Ⓗ
11. Ⓐ Ⓑ Ⓒ Ⓓ
12. Ⓔ Ⓕ Ⓖ Ⓗ
13. Ⓐ Ⓑ Ⓒ Ⓓ
14. Ⓔ Ⓕ Ⓖ Ⓗ
15. Ⓐ Ⓑ Ⓒ Ⓓ
16. Ⓔ Ⓕ Ⓖ Ⓗ
17. Ⓐ Ⓑ Ⓒ Ⓓ
18. Ⓔ Ⓕ Ⓖ Ⓗ
19. Ⓐ Ⓑ Ⓒ Ⓓ
20. Ⓔ Ⓕ Ⓖ Ⓗ

Reading

21. Ⓐ Ⓑ Ⓒ Ⓓ
22. Ⓔ Ⓕ Ⓖ Ⓗ
23. Ⓐ Ⓑ Ⓒ Ⓓ
24. Ⓔ Ⓕ Ⓖ Ⓗ
25. Ⓐ Ⓑ Ⓒ Ⓓ
26. Ⓔ Ⓕ Ⓖ Ⓗ
27. Ⓐ Ⓑ Ⓒ Ⓓ
28. Ⓔ Ⓕ Ⓖ Ⓗ
29. Ⓐ Ⓑ Ⓒ Ⓓ
30. Ⓔ Ⓕ Ⓖ Ⓗ
31. Ⓐ Ⓑ Ⓒ Ⓓ
32. Ⓔ Ⓕ Ⓖ Ⓗ
33. Ⓐ Ⓑ Ⓒ Ⓓ
34. Ⓔ Ⓕ Ⓖ Ⓗ
35. Ⓐ Ⓑ Ⓒ Ⓓ
36. Ⓔ Ⓕ Ⓖ Ⓗ
37. Ⓐ Ⓑ Ⓒ Ⓓ
38. Ⓔ Ⓕ Ⓖ Ⓗ
39. Ⓐ Ⓑ Ⓒ Ⓓ

40. Ⓔ Ⓕ Ⓖ Ⓗ
41. Ⓐ Ⓑ Ⓒ Ⓓ
42. Ⓔ Ⓕ Ⓖ Ⓗ
43. Ⓐ Ⓑ Ⓒ Ⓓ
44. Ⓔ Ⓕ Ⓖ Ⓗ
45. Ⓐ Ⓑ Ⓒ Ⓓ
46. Ⓔ Ⓕ Ⓖ Ⓗ
47. Ⓐ Ⓑ Ⓒ Ⓓ
48. Ⓔ Ⓕ Ⓖ Ⓗ
49. Ⓐ Ⓑ Ⓒ Ⓓ
50. Ⓔ Ⓕ Ⓖ Ⓗ
51. Ⓐ Ⓑ Ⓒ Ⓓ
52. Ⓔ Ⓕ Ⓖ Ⓗ
53. Ⓐ Ⓑ Ⓒ Ⓓ
54. Ⓔ Ⓕ Ⓖ Ⓗ
55. Ⓐ Ⓑ Ⓒ Ⓓ
56. Ⓔ Ⓕ Ⓖ Ⓗ
57. Ⓐ Ⓑ Ⓒ Ⓓ

ANSWER SHEET
Practice Test 2

Part II   Mathematics

58.

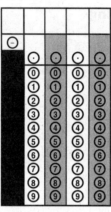

59.

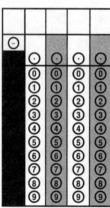

60.

61.

62.

63	Ⓐ Ⓑ Ⓒ Ⓓ
64.	Ⓔ Ⓕ Ⓖ Ⓗ
65.	Ⓐ Ⓑ Ⓒ Ⓓ
66.	Ⓔ Ⓕ Ⓖ Ⓗ
67.	Ⓐ Ⓑ Ⓒ Ⓓ
68.	Ⓔ Ⓕ Ⓖ Ⓗ
69.	Ⓐ Ⓑ Ⓒ Ⓓ
70.	Ⓔ Ⓕ Ⓖ Ⓗ
71.	Ⓐ Ⓑ Ⓒ Ⓓ
72.	Ⓔ Ⓕ Ⓖ Ⓗ
73.	Ⓐ Ⓑ Ⓒ Ⓓ
74.	Ⓔ Ⓕ Ⓖ Ⓗ
75.	Ⓐ Ⓑ Ⓒ Ⓓ
76.	Ⓔ Ⓕ Ⓖ Ⓗ
77.	Ⓐ Ⓑ Ⓒ Ⓓ
78.	Ⓔ Ⓕ Ⓖ Ⓗ
79.	Ⓐ Ⓑ Ⓒ Ⓓ
80.	Ⓔ Ⓕ Ⓖ Ⓗ
81.	Ⓐ Ⓑ Ⓒ Ⓓ
82.	Ⓔ Ⓕ Ⓖ Ⓗ
83.	Ⓐ Ⓑ Ⓒ Ⓓ
84.	Ⓔ Ⓕ Ⓖ Ⓗ
85.	Ⓐ Ⓑ Ⓒ Ⓓ
86.	Ⓔ Ⓕ Ⓖ Ⓗ
87.	Ⓐ Ⓑ Ⓒ Ⓓ
88.	Ⓔ Ⓕ Ⓖ Ⓗ

89.	Ⓐ Ⓑ Ⓒ Ⓓ
90.	Ⓔ Ⓕ Ⓖ Ⓗ
91.	Ⓐ Ⓑ Ⓒ Ⓓ
92.	Ⓔ Ⓕ Ⓖ Ⓗ
93.	Ⓐ Ⓑ Ⓒ Ⓓ
94.	Ⓔ Ⓕ Ⓖ Ⓗ
95.	Ⓐ Ⓑ Ⓒ Ⓓ
96.	Ⓔ Ⓕ Ⓖ Ⓗ
97.	Ⓐ Ⓑ Ⓒ Ⓓ
98.	Ⓔ Ⓕ Ⓖ Ⓗ
99.	Ⓐ Ⓑ Ⓒ Ⓓ
100.	Ⓔ Ⓕ Ⓖ Ⓗ
101.	Ⓐ Ⓑ Ⓒ Ⓓ
102.	Ⓔ Ⓕ Ⓖ Ⓗ
103.	Ⓐ Ⓑ Ⓒ Ⓓ
104.	Ⓔ Ⓕ Ⓖ Ⓗ
105.	Ⓐ Ⓑ Ⓒ Ⓓ
106.	Ⓔ Ⓕ Ⓖ Ⓗ
107.	Ⓐ Ⓑ Ⓒ Ⓓ
108.	Ⓔ Ⓕ Ⓖ Ⓗ
109.	Ⓐ Ⓑ Ⓒ Ⓓ
110.	Ⓔ Ⓕ Ⓖ Ⓗ
111.	Ⓐ Ⓑ Ⓒ Ⓓ
112.	Ⓔ Ⓕ Ⓖ Ⓗ
113.	Ⓐ Ⓑ Ⓒ Ⓓ
114.	Ⓔ Ⓕ Ⓖ Ⓗ

Practice Test 2

PART 1—ENGLISH LANGUAGE ARTS

57 QUESTIONS

SUGGESTED TIME: 90 MINUTES

Revising/Editing

QUESTIONS 1–20

IMPORTANT NOTE: The Revising/Editing section (Questions 1–20) is in two parts: Part A and Part B.

Revising/Editing Part A

Directions: Read and answer each of the following questions. You will be asked to recognize and correct errors in sentences or short paragraphs. Mark the **best** answer for each question.

1. Read this paragraph.

> (1) Many holidays today can be traced to pagan holidays, which were often celebrated to welcome seasonal changes. (2) Christmas, for example, was celebrated as Saturnalia by the Romans, which feasted on the surplus from their harvests. (3) Valentine's Day replaced Lupercalia, which was celebrated in the spring to welcome the start of a new year. (4) Finally, Halloween took over Lemuria, which took place in the fall.

Which sentence should be revised to correct an inappropriate shift in pronoun?

A. sentence 1
B. sentence 2
C. sentence 3
D. sentence 4

2. Read this paragraph.

> (1) Times Square today isn't what it used to be, in the past, it was a very dark, lawless place. (2) In the 1990s, crime rates dropped drastically, and tourist-friendly establishments sprouted all along the streets. (3) Many credit Mayor Rudy Giuliani, who decided to make the area more friendly by passing harsh laws and by increasing the number of police officers patrolling the area. (4) Critics, however, point to an overall decline in crime rates all across the United States and suggest that Giuliani's policies were insignificant.

Which sentence should be revised to correct a run-on?

E. sentence 1
F. sentence 2
G. sentence 3
H. sentence 4

3. Read this sentence.

> Anyone who is serious about losing weight should consider both physical activities and eating right.

Which of these is the most precise revision for the words *physical activities and eating right*?

A. physical activities and limiting caloric intake
B. cardio exercises and eating right
C. physical activities and dieting
D. cardio exercises and limiting caloric intake

4. Read these sentences.

> (1) The killer whale feeds on most marine animals.
> (2) Many of these animals are seabirds, cephalopods, turtles, sharks, and fish.
> (3) The killer whale avoids eating dolphins and manatees.

What is the best way to combine these sentences?

E. The killer whale feeds on most marine animals, and some of these are seabirds, cephalopods, turtles, sharks, and fish, but it avoids dolphins and manatees.
F. The killer whale feeds on most marine animals, of the types to be included being seabirds, cephalopods, turtles, sharks, and fish, with some avoidance of dolphins and manatees.
G. The killer whale feeds on most marine animals, such as seabirds, cephalopods, turtles, sharks, and fish, but avoids dolphins and manatees.
H. The killer whale feeds on most marine animals, seabirds, cephalopods, turtles, sharks, and fish, and avoids dolphins and manatees.

5. Read this sentence.

> Eaten at both breakfast and dinner, Koreans all over the world love kimchee.

How should this sentence be revised?

A. Eaten at both breakfast and dinner, all over the world are Koreans who love kimchee.

B. All over the world, kimchee is loved by Koreans eaten at both breakfast and dinner.

C. Eaten at both breakfast and dinner, kimchee is loved by Koreans all over the world.

D. Koreans, eaten at both breakfast and dinner, love kimchee all over the world.

6. Read this paragraph.

> (1) The fall of the Roman Empire is commonly associated with the rise of the Germanic leader Odoacer in 476 C.E. (2) However, the Roman Empire didn't completely crumble. (3) In fact, the eastern half of the empire, called the Byzantine Empire, thrived well into the fifteenth century. (4) The Ottoman army storms into its capital city Constantinople and took over to create a new Ottoman Empire.

Which sentence should be revised to correct an inappropriate shift in verb tense?

E. sentence 1

F. sentence 2

G. sentence 3

H. sentence 4

Directions: Read the passage below and answer the questions following it. You will be asked to improve the writing quality of the passage and to correct errors so that the passage follows the conventions of standard written English. You may reread the passage if you need to. Mark the best answer for each question.

The Importance of Eating Healthy

(1) Evidence shows that healthy eating patterns are connected to healthy outcomes. (2) The evidence database for the relationship between eating patterns and specific health outcomes continues to grow. (3) Americans are defined not by what they eat, but how they eat from a variety of cultural cuisines. (4) These categories are strong, moderate, and emerging. (5) Strong evidence shows that healthy eating patterns are associated with a reduced risk of cardiovascular disease (CVD). (6) Moderate evidence indicates that healthy eating patterns also are associated with a reduced risk of certain types of cancers, such as colorectal and postmenopausal breast cancers, type 2 diabetes, and obesity.

(7) Within this body of evidence, higher consumption of vegetables and fruits has been identified as a characteristic of healthy eating patterns. (8) Whole grains contain healthy amounts of fiber, which makes a person feel more full for a longer period of time. (9) Other characteristics of healthy eating patterns have been identified with less consistency and include fat-free or low-fat dairy, seafood, legumes, and nuts. (10) Lower intakes of meat, including processed meats, processed poultry, sugar-sweetened foods, and refined grains have often been identified as characteristics of healthy eating patterns.

(11) Making these shifts can help support a healthy body weight, meet nutrient needs, and lessen the risk for chronic disease. (12) Without a doubt, the change toward healthy eating patterns can be overwhelming. (13) That's why it's important to emphasize that every food choice is an opportunity to move toward a healthy eating pattern. (14) Food choices can make a big difference. (15) Current eating patterns can be moved toward healthier eating patterns by making shifts in food choices over time.

7. Which sentence should replace sentence 3 to better introduce the information presented in the passage?

   A. Americans, however, fail to examine their diets and neglect the importance of healthy eating.
   B. Schools must routinely teach students the importance of a healthy diet.
   C. An exercise regimen is also, if not more, important to ensure a healthy outcome.
   D. The evidence can be divided into three categories.

8. Which of the following would best follow sentence 6 in paragraph 1 (sentences 1–6)?

   E. There is emerging evidence also, which suggests that relationships may exist between eating patterns and some neurocognitive disorders.

   F. Relationships may exist between eating patterns and neurocognitive disorders, which is shown by emerging evidence.

   G. Emerging evidence also suggests that relationships may exist between eating patterns and some neurocognitive disorders.

   H. Between eating patterns and neurocognitive disorders, emerging evidence suggests that a relationship exists.

9. Which sentence is irrelevant in paragraph 2 and should be deleted?

   A. sentence 7
   B. sentence 8
   C. sentence 9
   D. sentence 10

10. Where should sentence 15 be moved to improve the organization of the third paragraph (sentences 11–15)?

   E. at the beginning of the paragraph
   F. between sentences 11 and 12
   G. between sentences 12 and 13
   H. between sentences 13 and 14

11. Which revision of sentence 14 uses the most precise language?

   A. Shifts in food choices can be significant.
   B. Small shifts in food choices can make a lasting difference.
   C. Small shifts in food choices—over the course of a week, a day, or even a meal—can make a lasting difference.
   D. Over the course of a week, a day, or even a meal, food choices can make a difference.

12. Which transition word or phrase should be added to the beginning of sentence 14?

   E. Therefore,
   F. In other words,
   G. On the other hand,
   H. For example,

Gut Check!

(1) Your digestive system is always at work. (2) When you scarf down a pizza, it takes a twisty trip that starts with being chewed up and ends with you going to the bathroom. (3) Pizza can upset your stomach if you are not too careful with the grease.

(4) The most extensive component of the digestive system is the gastrointestinal (GI) tract. (5) The gastrointestinal tract is a long, muscular tube that runs from your mouth to your rectum. (6) It's over 25 feet long and works with other parts of the digestive system to break that pizza and soda down into smaller particles of nutrients. (7) Blood absorbs these nutrients and carries them throughout the body to be used for energy, growth, and repair.

(8) With such a long GI road, it's common to run into bumps or potholes. (9) About 50 to 70 million Americans are affected by diseases in the digestive tract, like gastroesophageal reflux disease (GERD) or irritable bowel syndrome (IBS). (10) GERD occurs when your stomach acid come back up into your throat. (11) This causes unpleasant symptoms like heartburn and indigestion. (12) IBS constitutes a variety of symptoms like pain in the abdomen, constipation, diarrhea, and changes in bowel habits. (13) People with IBS often live with shame. (14) Many more people have other digestive problems, like bloating and stomach pain.

(15) There are many factors that can impact gut health. (16) How your body's built, your family and genetic history, how you manage stress, and what you eat can all affect your gut. (17) There are a lot of lifestyle-related GI issues, and there are often no quick fixes for that. (18) In general, people do well when they practice healthy habits.

(19) Research has found that people who have early life stress are more likely to develop IBS. (20) This increased risk for IBS went down when people confided in someone they trust about the stress they experienced.

13. Which sentence should replace sentence 3 to more clearly introduce the topic of this passage?

   A. Sometimes this can lead to an embarrassing situation, which most people would rather not talk about.
   B. There are numerous over-the-counter drugs that can relieve an upset stomach or indigestion, but these medicines should be taken with care.
   C. The digestive system is known to possess a particular type of intelligence, so trusting your gut isn't too far off the mark.
   D. A lot happens in between, and the health of your gut plays a key role in your overall health and well-being.

14. What is the best way to combine sentences 4 and 5 to clarify the relationship between the ideas?

    E. The most extensive component of the digestive system is the gastrointestinal (GI) tract because the gastrointestinal tract is a long, muscular tube that runs from your mouth to your rectum.

    F. The most extensive component of the digestive system is the gastrointestinal (GI) tract, a long, muscular tube that runs from your mouth to your rectum.

    G. Whereas the most extensive component of the digestive system is the gastrointestinal (GI) tract, the gastrointestinal tract is a long, muscular tube that runs from your mouth to your rectum.

    H. Since the most extensive component of the digestive system is the gastrointestinal (GI) tract, the gastrointestinal tract is a long, muscular tube that runs from your mouth to your rectum.

15. Which sentence is irrelevant to the ideas presented in the third paragraph (sentences 8–14) and should be deleted?

    A. sentence 9
    B. sentence 11
    C. sentence 13
    D. sentence 14

16. Which transition word or phrase should be added to the beginning of sentence 15?

    E. In addition,
    F. For instance,
    G. As a result,
    H. Consequently,

17. Which revision of sentence 18 uses the most precise language?

    A. In general, people do well when they create a more routine schedule, eat a healthy diet and smaller, more frequent meals, add in some exercise, and get a good amount of sleep.

    B. In general, people do well when they decide to create a life that focuses on habits that ensure a good balance of restful and exciting activities.

    C. In general, people do well when they focus on many habits that will enable them to get both rest and exercise.

    D. In general, people do well when they decide to live a healthy life.

18. Read this sentence.

> Doctors, dieticians, or even a perceptive friend may help you identify some of those issues and address poor habits to improve your GI health.

Where should this sentence be added to best support the ideas in the fourth paragraph (sentences 15–18)?

- **E.** at the top of the paragraph
- **F.** between sentences 15 and 16
- **G.** between sentences 16 and 17
- **H.** between sentences 17 and 18

19. Which sentence should be added before sentence 19 to most clearly introduce the topic of the paragraph?

- **A.** Technological advances have made early detection of GI diseases easier, but they are still difficult to identify without the diagnosis of a learned physician.
- **B.** Exercise and meditation is a useful way to reduce stress.
- **C.** Strangely, GI diseases affect women more than men.
- **D.** One of the biggest factors associated with GI disease is stress.

20. Which concluding sentence should follow sentence 20 to best support the topic presented in the passage?

- **E.** When Americans decide to take care of their GI health, their GI health physicians may lose their jobs.
- **F.** Finding healthy ways to manage stress is important for GI health, and your health overall.
- **G.** Another problem that can be helped by managing stress is insomnia.
- **H.** Without good GI health, other systems cannot function properly and may be at risk.

Directions: Read each passage and answer the questions that follow it. Base your answers **only on the material contained in the passage.** Select the one **best** answer for each question. Bubble in the letter corresponding to that answer on the answer sheet.

I. The movie, *Shakespeare in Love,* tells the intimate story of the romantic relationship of young William Shakespeare and a
Line beautiful woman. The film is entertaining
(5) but not factual, for little is actually known about the young manhood of Shakespeare. The bare facts of his early life are available. He was born in Stratford-on-Avon in April of 1564 into a well-respected family. At the
(10) age of eighteen he married Anne Hathaway, who bore him three children in the next three years. However, there are few details to flesh out the story of his beginnings. Even the extent of his formal education is
(15) uncertain. He probably attended school in Stratford, but no official record confirms this assumption.

Literary historians know even less about his life from age twenty-one to age twenty-
(20) eight. No one knows exactly when he moved from Stratford to London or exactly how he became involved in the theater. In 1592 he was important enough to attract the public attention of a professional rival,
(25) whose jealous attack on Shakespeare reveals that the latter was at the time active as both actor and playwright.

Scholars have more information about his later career if not his private life. His the-
(30) ater career endured a two-year interruption caused by a shutdown of theaters during a time of plague. However, after this brief setback he achieved remarkable artistic and financial success as actor, playwright, and
(35) shareholder in the company that was the

favorite of two monarchs, Elizabeth and James I. It is also known that he made considerable money in Stratford real estate and retired a wealthy man.

(40) Many gaps in his history remain. Most mysterious, perhaps, is the question of how he acquired some of the knowledge his plays display. For example, how did this middle-class man gain familiarity with aristocratic and
(45) even royal lifestyle? How did this product of the Stratford school acquire a complex understanding of the law? Questions such as these have led some scholars to believe that William Shakespeare is not the author of the
(50) works bearing his name. The scholar Francis Bacon, the playwright Christopher Marlowe, and the 17th Earl of Oxford, Edward de Vere, are three of the often-mentioned possible real authors.

(55) Most critics and literary historians, however, feel that the puzzle of authorship is likely to remain unresolved. Most think that it is less important to know with finality who wrote Shakespeare's works than it is to know and
(60) appreciate the author's wondrous genius.

21. Which of the following best tells what this passage is about?

   A. History versus legend
   B. The scarcity of biographical information about Shakespeare
   C. The mystery surrounding authorship of the works of William Shakespeare
   D. The question of how the writers of *Shakespeare in Love* knew so much about his private life

22. What does the passage suggest about the film *Shakespeare in Love?*

   E. It required painstaking research.
   F. It gives private details of a real love affair.
   G. It has won many awards.
   H. It is pure fiction.

23. What is the most likely reason for the written attack by Shakespeare's rival?

   A. He was envious of Shakespeare's success.
   B. Shakespeare had insulted or otherwise offended him personally.
   C. They were romantic rivals.
   D. He was the real author of plays produced under Shakespeare's name.

24. Which of the following is **not** given as a detail of Shakespeare's life?

   E. His birthplace
   F. His monetary success in his chosen career
   G. His poverty during a two-year period of plague
   H. A secondary source of income

25. Which of the following means about the same as "flesh out" (line 13)?

   A. Add information to
   B. Give a visual image of
   C. Contradict
   D. Detect

26. Why are literary researchers intrigued by Shakespeare's depictions of royalty and court life?

   E. They provide historical detail that would otherwise be unknown.
   F. They suggest the plays could not have been written by a member of the middle class.
   G. They suggest that William Shakespeare had important social contacts with the aristocracy.
   H. They explain the attack by the rival playwright.

II. Just a few decades ago mushrooms were infrequently seen on the dinner tables of most American households, and those that
Line did find their way into home-cooked food
(5) were almost always the cultivated white "button" mushrooms. In recent years, however, mushroom popularity in America has burgeoned. This tasty vegetable is now a highly favored ingredient in numerous
(10) everyday recipes, and readily available to the consumer are several varieties of mushrooms ranging from common commercially grown types to the more expensive wild varieties favored by gourmets.

(15) Not everyone who enjoys mushrooms knows much about what they are or where they come from. They are members of a family of fungi that grow mainly underground. The part of the organism that appears above
(20) ground and is harvested is the fruiting body that sprouts from the underground part, the mycelium. In commercial cultivation they are grown in carefully controlled environments, often in cellars or caves. In the
(25) wild they flourish in fields, forests, lawns and backyards, some sprouting from the ground and others growing on decaying or decayed trees. At least one important type grows entirely underground: Rare and costly
(30) truffles are harvested with the help of pigs and other animals trained to sniff them out.

Because some varieties are highly toxic, it is unwise for an untrained person to gather wild mushrooms. Even experienced "mush-
(35) roomers" can get in trouble because poisonous varieties in one region may resemble edible varieties in another area. In a case widely reported a few years ago, several people in California became gravely ill
(40) when an experienced gatherer from the Far East mistook the deadly amanita for an edible Asian type.

This element of danger has until recent years made the harvesting of the highly favored
(45) wild varieties—chanterelles, shaggy manes, morels, and others—a specialized calling of the few. Nowadays, however, high demand has encouraged so many entrepreneurs in the field that competition among them
(50) is fierce. Encounters of rival gatherers are almost always unpleasant and sometimes actually violent. Moreover, environmentalists as well as marketers worry about serious overharvesting, which could result
(55) in scarcity or even complete elimination of the most desirable kinds of this delectable fungus.

27. Which of the following best tells what this passage is about?

   A. The recent demand for mushrooms
   B. Edible and poisonous mushrooms
   C. Description and popularity of mushrooms
   D. Little-known facts about mushrooms

28. Which of the following means about the same as "burgeoned" (line 8)?

   E. Grown
   F. Become more available
   G. Declined
   H. Become more varied

29. According to the information given, which of the following statements about mushrooms is the most accurate?

   A. They need dark places like caves and cellars to grow.
   B. They achieved worldwide popularity only in the last few decades.
   C. Their fruiting bodies grow underground.
   D. It is sometimes hard to distinguish between toxic and nontoxic varieties.

30. What is the most likely reason that truffles are costly?

   E. They are scarce.
   F. They must be grown by professionals under the most exacting conditions.
   G. They are difficult to find.
   H. Both E and G

31. What does the passage suggest about mushroom gathering?

   A. It requires extensive classroom training.
   B. It is lucrative.
   C. It is a relatively new activity.
   D. Until recent years it involved only white "button" mushrooms.

32. Why did the mushroom gatherer mentioned in the passage make such a deadly mistake?

   E. She did not know what *amanita* means.
   F. She lacked professional training.
   G. She was unfamiliar with local mushroom varieties.
   H. She was careless.

III. In recent years the word *Cajun* has become familiar to most Americans. Cajun food appears on restaurant menus across
Line the country, Cajun music entertains radio
(5) listeners, and Cajun festivals pop up in places remote from their more likely venues. However, relatively few people outside Louisiana and other Gulf states fully understand what a Cajun is.

(10) The word *Cajun* is a corruption of *Acadian*, the Acadians being a people of French ancestry who once lived in Acadia in eastern Canada. After the former French colony fell under British rule, its Catholic
(15) inhabitants were required to swear allegiance to Great Britain. In 1755, those who refused to take the required oath were expelled. After a period of wandering, the Acadians eventually found homes in scat-
(20) tered locations in Canada and what is now the United States. Several thousand settled in the bayou country of south Louisiana, and these are the people who came to be called Cajuns.

(25) Bayous, which would be called creeks in other parts of the country, are often associated with marshy or swampy areas. But bayou country includes rich, productive farmland as well. The Acadian settlers of
(30) this area became farmers, hunters, and fishermen. Because of their relatively isolated situation, they developed the distinctive culture that now charms so many Americans.

(35) The cuisine of these descendants of the Acadians features local seafood such as shrimp and oysters as well as the popular freshwater crawfish and such meats as tasso, a highly seasoned ham, and boudin, a kind
(40) of pork sausage. *Cajun* cooks have created the soup called gumbo and the rice-based mixture called jambalaya, which are favorites on tables across the country. And the Cajuns continue to be adventurous cooks.
(45) They were pioneers in the art of turkey frying, originally cooking the big birds in galvanized tubs filled with used vegetable oil from local fast-food restaurants.

Cajun music often has the feel of bluegrass,
(50) but it has its own characteristic sound. The accordion, not featured in most contemporary music, is an integral part of this Cajun sound. Cajun songs are still frequently sung in French, another unique feature. And the
(55) music has its modern offshoots, including Zydeco, which is considered to be based on a combination of African-American and Cajun rhythms and instrumentation.

Today, these people may live in San
(60) Francisco or Manhattan, and may be electrical engineers, psychologists, carpenters, or clerks. Irish names like Terrence O'Brien and English names like Mary Elizabeth Carter belong to people claiming Cajun
(65) descent. But in Louisiana there are still enclaves of Acadians who make their living off the land, speak the old language, and cling to an old way of life.

33. Which of the following best states the author's purpose?

   A. To explain the popularity of Cajun music and food
   B. To explain the derivation of the word *Cajun*
   C. To give a history of south Louisiana
   D. To describe a distinct culture

34. What is the most likely reason for the expulsion of the Acadians?

   E. The British saw them as a threat.
   F. The British were carrying out "ethnic cleansing."
   G. The British wished to punish them.
   H. The British wished to make room for English settlers.

PRACTICE TEST 2

35. According to the passage, which of the following is **not** true of the Cajuns?

   A. Some of them have intermarried with other ethnic groups.

   B. They remained a distinct group for so long because they were somewhat separated from people of other cultures.

   C. Some of them still speak a form of French.

   D. Their cooks stick to traditional recipes.

36. Which of the following means the same as *venues* as it is used in the passage (lines 6–7)?

   E. Sites

   F. Locations of courtroom trials

   G. Musicians

   H. Restaurants

37. What is a bayou?

   A. An elevated piece of land in a swamp

   B. A lake

   C. A tidal creek

   D. A swamp

38. Which of the following is most essential to the Cajun style of music?

   E. Zydeco

   F. French lyrics

   G. The African-American influence

   H. The sound of an accordion

IV. A relatively recent discovery has given support to the theory that the dinosaurs became extinct because of a collision between
Line Earth and a giant asteroid. Scientists have
(5) discovered the element iridium and granules of shocked quartz in the late Cretaceous rock layer. The presence of the two substances indicates that a large asteroid or comet did indeed strike the earth during the geologic
(10) era in which the dinosaurs became extinct. Such a collision could have drastic environmental consequences.

Such collisions are considered "common" in terms of geologic time—time in the context
(15) of the earth's billions-year-old existence. Asteroids, after all, are our close neighbors. At one time they were considered the last remaining fragments of a destroyed planet. Now, however, they are currently thought to
(20) be ancient matter that might have coalesced into a single planet if the gravity of the nearby planet Jupiter had not interfered. Classed as small planets, they behave like their larger sisters in orbiting the sun. In one
(25) form or another they have been with us since the beginning of the solar system.

For most of our solar system's history, visitation between asteroids and Earth were one-way. Particles of these bodies constantly
(30) shower the earth in the form of meteorites, and the much rarer big collisions do occur. In recent years, however, earthlings have turned the tables. In 1991 the *Galileo* space probe passed near the asteroid 951
(35) Gaspara and successfully photographed its surface. The NEAR (Near Earth Asteroid Rendezvous) project carried out a flyby of 253 Mathilde in 1997. NEAR is also planning a year-long orbit of Eros in the
(40) year 2000. A privately funded NEAP (Near Earth Asteroid Prospector) group is planning to send a vehicle to a nearby asteroid for the purpose of studying the composition of its surface. NEAP intends to complete its
(45) mission at a cost minuscule in comparison with the costly ventures of NASA.

Scientific curiosity aside, the inhabitants of Earth continue to be intrigued and sometimes frightened by the prospect of (50) a catastrophic asteroid strike. In 1999 NASA announced that on August 7, 2027, asteroid 1999AN10 will pass by Earth. According to NASA, it could come as close as 19,000 miles, or it could pass by at a dis- (55) tance of 600,000 miles. In either case, say astronomers, it will not hit Earth. Most earthlings have seemed to take NASA's word for it. Some, however, fret over a possible error in calculation or a shift in the (60) asteroid's path. There is even an Internet website that flaunts a day-by-day Asteroid Doomsday Countdown Clock. But according to astronomers the chance of a cata- strophic collision occurring within the next (65) several thousand years is remote.

39. What is the best title for the passage?

   A. "Dinosaurs and Asteroids"
   B. "Disaster from the Stars"
   C. "Earth's Planetary Neighbors"
   D. "The Origins of Asteroids"

40. Which of the following means the same as "minuscule" (line 45)?

   E. Terrifying
   F. Reasonable
   G. Tiny
   H. Privately funded

41. Which of the following is the most likely result of the collision of a large asteroid with the earth?

   A. The extinction of human life
   B. The destruction of all life on Earth
   C. Fragmentation similar to that which produced the asteroids
   D. Ecological damage

42. Why is the word "common" (line 13) enclosed in quotation marks?

   E. It is being used in a special context.
   F. It is a direct quotation.
   G. It is an attempt at humor.
   H. It is a synonym of "close neighbors" in line 16.

43. Which of the following is **not** true about asteroids?

   A. They have collided with Earth many times in the past.
   B. They are responsible for most of the environmental changes on Earth.
   C. In other evolutionary circumstances, they would have been a single planet.
   D. They are considered planets.

44. Which of the following most accurately states why some people are worried about the approach of 1999AN10?

   E. They think NASA is lying to calm people's fears.
   F. They feel that such events are not entirely predictable.
   G. They detect a conflict between the interests of the International Astronomical Union and those of NASA.
   H. A distance of 600,000 miles is no protection from an asteroid.

   V. The shorelines of Earth's continents have shifted and changed shape as long as there have been oceans to wash them. Offshore *Line* currents carry sand along the coast, moving (5) it from one beach to another. As one beach accretes, another erodes. Storms also play their part as they push huge waves against the dunes, carrying tons of sand out to sea. This continual movement and reshaping (10) is a natural phenomenon that is environ- mentally benign. Only when human beings invade the beach does trouble begin.

People are attracted to the beach. Beachfront property is highly desirable, valuable real
(15) estate. But when a shore is lined with houses, the inevitable sooner or later occurs. Natural erosion, often hastened by the removal of protective dunes, begins to eat away at the beach. Homeowners and local author-
(20) ities scramble to put up protective devices. Either the devices don't work, or they work to protect one beach while increasing the erosion on others.

Even the best modern technology does not
(25) control the sea. In 1998 a storm attacked Long Island and dumped a $750,000 house into the sea. In Galveston, Texas, an entire subdivision is in danger of being washed away. In a Virginia beach community a
(30) huge steel bulkhead erected in 1989 as a shield against ocean currents is now a use-less wreck.

Historically, the battle against the sea has been a losing one. In the past jetties and
(35) groins—structures built out from the shore or offshore—were favorite remedies. Unfor-tunately, the engineers who built them did not understand what the long-range conse-quences of such hard devices could be. Not
(40) understanding the natural action of offshore currents, they failed to take into consid eration the effects of blocking the sand flow to other areas. Disastrous erosion has resulted from these ill-conceived projects.
(45) Today a favored approach is beach renour-ishment. Typically this process involves dredging sand from the ocean floor and pumping it onto the beach. It is expensive, and although does build up the beach, it
(50) is at best a temporary solution. The same currents that have washed it away once will wash it away again.

Some environmentalists, although acknow-ledging that beach renourishment does
(55) provide at least a stopgap solution, vigor-ously oppose it on several grounds. One is

the huge cost to taxpayers, most of whom get no benefit from such projects. Another objection is based on its appearance of
(60) success. This, they say, will only encour-age more beachfront building and more shoreline destruction. By the same logic they oppose federal subsidies for beachfront construction and federally subsidized flood
(65) insurance for such properties.

45. Which of the following best states the author's purpose?

A. To explain why beachfront property is expensive

B. To describe the intricate balance between ocean currents and shoreline

C. To explain the detrimental effects of human meddling in a delicate ecosystem

D. To present the best methods for beach protection

46. Which of the following is the most likely reason why some states now ban hard erosion-control devices?

E. They have no effect on erosion.

F. They encourage more beachfront building.

G. They increase erosion in other areas.

H. They require federal subsidies.

47. For what purpose is the bulkhead in Virginia (line 30) mentioned?

A. It provides an example of the futility of trying to control the ocean.

B. It implies that the builder of the bulkhead was incompetent.

C. It proves that stronger materials must be used in such projects.

D. It suggests that a jetty would have been a better device.

48. Why was beach erosion in former times seldom a serious problem?

    E. Communities would work together on a continual basis to combat erosion.

    F. Ocean currents were more stable without human interference.

    G. Dunes and forests prevented erosion from occurring.

    H. Erosion did not usually directly affect human beings.

49. With which of the following statements would the author probably agree?

    A. Many useful erosion-control devices have been invented.

    B. Beachfront building should be avoided.

    C. Federal subsidies for beachfront construction are to be encouraged as a way of controlling development.

    D. In previous centuries people did not live near the coast.

50. Which of the following does the passage not present as possibly detrimental to the stability of beach areas?

    E. Groins

    F. Jetties

    G. Beach renourishment

    H. Dunes

VI. Researchers found a key antibody that protected rodents from infection with the most lethal malaria parasite, *Plasmodium falciparum*. The researchers' findings pro-
(5) vide the foundation for future testing in humans to find out if the antibody can provide temporary protection against malaria. Ultimately, the efforts may lead to breakthroughs in malaria vaccine design.

(10) Scientists at the National Institute of Allergy and Infectious Diseases (NIAID), part of the National Institutes of Health, coordinated the research with colleagues at the Fred Hutchinson Cancer Research
(15) Center in Seattle. Currently, no highly effective, long-lasting vaccine exists to prevent malaria, a mosquito-spread disease that claims more than 400,000 lives each year, primarily among young children in
(20) sub-Saharan Africa.

The research focused on an antibody, called CIS43, from the blood of a volunteer who had received an experimental vaccine. This experimental vaccine was made
(25) from whole, weakened malaria parasites. The volunteer was later exposed to infectious malaria-carrying mosquitoes under carefully controlled laboratory conditions. Amazingly, he remained immune from
(30) malaria infections, regardless of the number of times he was bitten by malaria carriers.

In two different studies of malaria infection in mice, CIS43 was highly effective at preventing malaria infection. If
(35) confirmed through additional studies in people, CIS43 could be developed as a preventive measure to halt infection for several months after administration. Such a powerful antibody could be useful for military
(40) personnel, healthcare professionals, tourists, government officials, and others who travel to areas where malaria is common. Moreover, if the antibody is successful in fighting malaria infection, it might be

(45) combined with antimalarial drugs and be implemented as part of global vaccination efforts. This would virtually eliminate the disease in malaria-endemic regions.

Detailed examination of CIS43 revealed *(50)* that it works by binding to a specific portion, called an epitope, of a key parasite surface protein. This epitope occurs only once along the side of the protein of a cell. It was therefore remarkable when the scientists *(55)* conserved the CIS43-binding epitope from 99.8% of all known strains of *P. falciparum*. This high yield makes CIS43 an attractive target for next-generation experimental malaria vaccines.

(60) The next step for the researchers is to assess the safety and protective effectiveness of the CIS43 antibody in more robust controlled human trials. Because of the scope of this project, additional collaborators on the *(65)* study will include scientists from various universities, government agencies, and professional laboratories.

51. Which of the following best tells what this passage is about?

   A. the extent of the problem of malaria
   B. an innovative breakthrough in research
   C. the importance of preventing disease
   D. the effectiveness of collaboration amongst scientists

52. What is most likely the reason scientists were interested in *P. falciparum*?

   E. It was the most readily available parasite.
   F. It was the most unique parasite.
   G. It was the most deadly parasite.
   H. It was found accidentally.

53. As of today, malaria vaccine design most likely

   A. can wipe out malaria.
   B. is not completely adequate.
   C. is created from rodents.
   D. came from one human being.

54. The author includes the details about the experiment in lines 21–31 in order to

   E. emphasize that more tests are necessary.
   F. highlight the fact that exposure to malaria can lead to resistance.
   G. provide information about a key study.
   H. suggest that malaria can easily be cured.

55. Which of the following could be concluded from the two different studies of malaria in mice?

   A. CIS43 is highly effective in humans.
   B. CIS43 alone would not be a permanent solution.
   C. CIS43 will be used only for a select group of people.
   D. CIS43 can eliminate malaria around the world.

56. What is the most likely reason that the author mentions the epitopes in the fifth paragraph?

   E. to point out that epitopes and CIS43 are similar in composition
   F. to cast doubt on the studies in mice
   G. to explain how CIS43 derives its effectiveness
   H. to open up the possibility for a new line of research

57. What evidence best supports the idea that the malaria vaccine is not completely ready for use on humans?

   A. the details about the most deadly parasite
   B. the details about the studies on mice
   C. the details about epitope
   D. the details about the additional collaborators

Grid-In Problems

Directions: Solve each problem. On the answer sheet, write your answer in the boxes at the top of the grid. Start on the left side of each grid. Print only one number or symbol in each box. **DO NOT LEAVE A BOX BLANK IN THE MIDDLE OF AN ANSWER.** Under each box, fill in the circle that matches the number or symbol you wrote above. **DO NOT FILL IN A CIRCLE UNDER AN UNUSED BOX.**

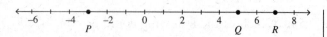

58. On the number line above, S (not shown) is the midpoint of $\overline{PR}$. What is number will be at the midpoint of $\overline{SQ}$?

59. $\dfrac{3.6}{0.2} \times 0.32 =$

60. The sum of two consecutive integers is –17. If 2 is added to the smaller integer and 1 is subtracted from the larger integer, what is the product of the two resulting numbers?

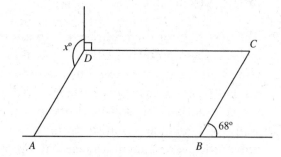

61. In the diagram above, *ABCD* is a parallelogram. What is the value of *x*?

62. How many five-digit numbers can be created using only even digits and without repeating any digit within that five-digit number? (Note: a five-digit number cannot begin with the digit 0.)

Multiple-Choice Problems

NOTE: Diagrams other than graphs might not be drawn to scale. Do not assume any relationships that are not specifically stated unless they are implied by the given information.

63. One-half of one-sixth is equal to

   A. one-third of one-fourth
   B. one-third
   C. one
   D. two

64. The areas of triangles ABC and XYZ are each 10. The area of the shaded region is 14. Then the area of triangle XWC is

   E. 12
   F. 8
   G. 6
   H. 3

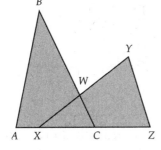

65. $1\dfrac{1}{10} + 2\dfrac{11}{100} + 3\dfrac{111}{1000} =$

   A. 6.111
   B. 6.123
   C. 6.111111
   D. 6.321

66. If x is positive and $x^2 + x = 50$, then x is a number between

   E. 6 and 7
   F. 7 and 8
   G. 8 and 9
   H. 9 and 10

67. In the figure, C is a point on line segment $\overline{AE}$. If $AB = BC$, what is the measure of angle DCE?

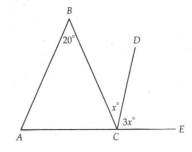

   A. 80°
   B. 75°
   C. 60°
   D. 25°

68. Barbara is 7 years older than Carole is now. Katie is half as old as Carole is now. If Katie is now 16 years old, how many years old is Barbara now?

   E. 15
   F. 23
   G. 32
   H. 39

69. $3.4 \times 10^2 + 3.4 \times 10^2$ is equal to

   A. 6.8×10^2
   B. 6.8×10^4
   C. 3.4×10^4
   D. 3,400

70. The points S, P, Q, and R are on the sides of rectangle $ABCD$ such that $\overline{SQ}$ is perpendicular to $\overline{PR}$. $APXS$ is a square whose side is 3. The area of $SXRD$ is 12 and the area of $PBQX$ is 27. What is the perimeter of rectangle $ABCD$?

   E. 84
   F. 72
   G. 38
   H. 36

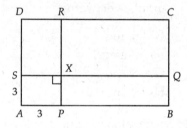

71. Kobi has $9.83, made up of nickels and pennies only. Which of the following *could not* be a possible value for the number of pennies?

   A. 208
   B. 113
   C. 93
   D. 85

72. If $\dfrac{2x-3}{4} = 8$, then $2x + 3 =$

   E. 41
   F. 38
   G. 35
   H. 29

73. Five apples and 6 bananas together cost as much as 8 bananas and 9 pears. One apple costs as much as 2 pears. For the same price as 1 pear, how many bananas could be bought?

   A. 1
   B. 2
   C. 3
   D. 4

74. Let $R = 8 \cdot 9 \cdot 7 \cdot 13$ and $S = 4 \cdot 6 \cdot 11 \cdot 49$. The greatest common factor of R and S is

   E. 12
   F. 24
   G. 56
   H. 168

75. What is the value of $4|x - y| - 3|xy|$ if $x = -5$ and $y = 2$?

   A. -42
   B. -18
   C. -2
   D. 42

76. In the following sequence of eight numbers, each number has one more "1" than the number before it:

2, 12, 112, 1112, . . . , 11111112

What is the hundreds digit in the sum of all eight of these numbers?

   E. 0
   F. 6
   G. 7
   H. 8

77. In Ms. Hsiao's class there are twice as many boys as there are girls. Half of the boys are in the math club and all of the girls are in the math club. What percent of Ms. Hsiao's class is in the math club?

   A. 25%
   B. $33\dfrac{1}{3}\%$
   C. 50%
   D. $66\dfrac{2}{3}\%$

78. $(16 + 5x) - (8 - 2x) =$

   E. $8 + 3x$
   F. $8 - 3x$
   G. $8 - 7x$
   H. $8 + 7x$

79. The three lines shown intersect in a point. The value of x

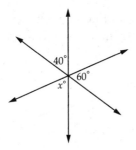

   A. is 100
   B. is 80
   C. is 50
   D. cannot be determined from the given information

80. The straight line graph shows how many people are in a large cafeteria eating lunch at different times. If the people leave at a steady rate, at what time will only 150 people remain?

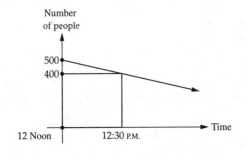

   E. 1:15 P.M.
   F. 1:30 P.M.
   G. 1:45 P.M.
   H. 2:15 P.M.

81. Two congruent circles have centers P and Q as shown. What is the measure of angle PXQ?

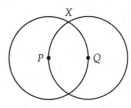

   A. 30°
   B. 45°
   C. 55°
   D. 60°

82. Andrew has d dollars. He has one-third as many dollars as Bruce has. Carlos has $80 less than half the total of Andrew's and Bruce's dollars. In terms of d, how many dollars does Carlos have?

   E. $4d - 40$
   F. $2d - 40$
   G. $2d + 40$
   H. $2d - 80$

83. The sum of 7 unequal positive integers is 61. What is the largest possible value that any of those integers can have?

   A. 55
   B. 40
   C. 39
   D. 13

84. In the set $\{1, 5, x, 10, 15\}$, the integer x is the median. The mean of the five numbers is one less than x. The value of x is

   E. 7
   F. 8
   G. 9
   H. none of these

85. If $\dfrac{7}{50} < \dfrac{1}{x} < \dfrac{8}{51}$ where x is an integer, then $x =$

A. 8
B. 7
C. 6
D. 5

86. Half of 2^8 is

E. 2^7
F. 2^6
G. 2^4
H. 1^8

87. If x is greater than $\dfrac{1}{2}$ but less than 1, which of the following has the largest value?

A. $2x - 1$
B. x^2
C. $\dfrac{1}{x}$
D. $1 - x$

88. Maria, Anoki, and Boris are teenagers, and the sum of their ages now is 49. The sum of their ages 8 years from now will be F, and the sum of their ages 10 years ago was P. The value of $F - P$ is

E. 54
F. 18
G. 17
H. 6

89. If $\dfrac{1}{4} + \dfrac{1}{x} = 1$, then $x =$

A. $\dfrac{1}{8}$
B. $\dfrac{2}{3}$
C. $\dfrac{4}{3}$
D. 2

90. When the integer N is divided by 7, the quotient is Q and the remainder is 5. When $N + 24$ is divided by 7, the remainder is

E. 4
F. 3
G. 2
H. 1

91. Point B is on line segment $\overline{AD}$, and point E is on line segment $\overline{BC}$. The value of x is

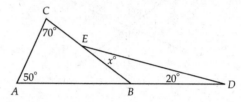

A. 20
B. 40
C. 50
D. 60

92. Three-fourths of a number is equal to L. What is three-halves of that original number, in terms of L?

E. $\dfrac{4}{3}L$
F. $\dfrac{3}{2}L$
G. $2L$
H. $3L$

93. For *how many* positive integer values of N will the expression $\dfrac{18}{N + 2}$ be an integer?

A. 1
B. 2
C. 3
D. 4

94. In the figure, numbers are to be placed in each of the nine small squares such that the sum of the numbers in any row, column, or diagonal must be the same. The number x

	13	
		x
10	9	14

   E. will be 1.
   F. will be 7.
   G. will be 9.
   H. cannot be determined from the given information

95. The two straight line graphs indicate the change in the price per pound of coffee and the change in the price per pound of sugar during part of a year. The initials on the horizontal axis represent January, February, March, and so on, and the vertical lines indicate the start of each month. During which month did it occur that the price per pound of coffee was twice the price per pound of sugar?

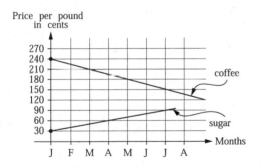

   A. March
   B. April
   C. May
   D. June

96. The pie chart shows the yearly expenses of the Jones family. Each expense is indicated as a percent of the total money they spent. Which one of the following bar charts, which indicate actual money spent in each area, best represents the data in the pie chart?

E.

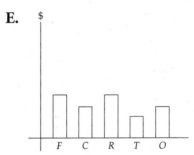

F.

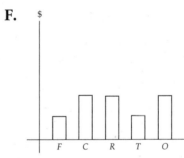

G.

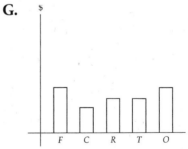

H.

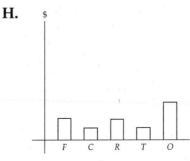

97. A fence encloses a triangular field. There is a vertical wooden fence post at each corner (vertex) of the field, and vertical posts all along the fence, placed 5 feet apart. If the sides of the field measure 20 feet by 35 feet by 25 feet, how many posts are there altogether?

    A. 13
    B. 14
    C. 15
    D. 16

98. The longest side in the figure (which need not be drawn to scale) must be

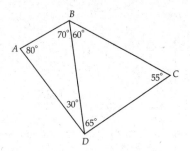

    E. $\overline{BC}$
    F. $\overline{BD}$
    G. $\overline{CD}$
    H. $\overline{AB}$

99. $(x^2y^3)(xy^2) =$

    A. x^2y^6
    B. x^3y^6
    C. $2x^3y^6$
    D. x^3y^5

100. The smallest positive integer value of n that will make $12n$ exactly divisible by 56 is

    E. 7
    F. 12
    G. 14
    H. 21

101. If $2x + 2y + 2z = 110$ and $x + y = 11$, then $z =$

    A. 99
    B. 50
    C. $49\frac{1}{2}$
    D. 44

102. Suppose $a \oplus b$ means $a^2 - ab$. (For example, $3 \oplus 2 = 9 - 6 = 3$ and $5 \oplus 3 = 10$.) Which of the following has the smallest value?

    E. $19 \oplus 18$
    F. $15 \oplus 14$
    G. $17 \oplus 15$
    H. $14 \oplus 11$

103. Box A contains exactly four cards, numbered 3, 5, 6, and 9. Box B contains exactly three cards, numbered 1, 4, and 7. One card is selected at random from Box A, and one card is selected at random from Box B. What is the probability that the *sum* of the numbers on the two selected cards is even?

    A. $\dfrac{1}{4}$
    B. $\dfrac{1}{3}$
    C. $\dfrac{5}{12}$
    D. $\dfrac{7}{12}$

104. Gil is now 80 miles ahead of Larry. Gil is traveling at a constant rate. Larry is traveling in the same direction, at a rate 5 miles per hour faster than Gil. In how many hours will Larry catch up to Gil?

    E. 16
    F. 15
    G. 12
    H. Larry cannot catch up to Gil.

105. If $\dfrac{3x+3}{3} = 2.5$, then $x =$

    A. −.5
    B. .5
    C. .75
    D. 1.5

106. On Thursday, the ABC Company stock lost 60% of its value. On Friday it lost another 10% of its remaining value. The total loss for the two days would have been the same if the stock had lost x% of its value the first day and x% of its remaining value the second day. Then $x =$

    E. 30
    F. 35
    G. 38
    H. 40

107. The area of triangle AOE

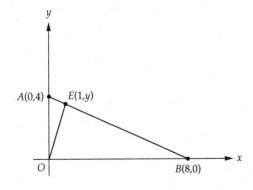

    A. is 1
    B. is 2
    C. is 2.5
    D. cannot be determined from the given information

108. Given triangles ABC and DEB as shown, the value of y in terms of x is

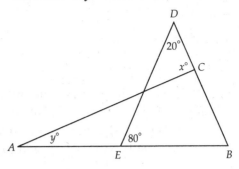

    E. $y = x + 120$
    F. $y = x - 120$
    G. $y = 100 - x$
    H. $y = x - 80$

109. Here are two sequences:

Sequence F: 2, 7, 12, 17, 22, . . .
Sequence S: 3, 10, 17, 24, 31, . . .

The numbers in sequence F increase by fives. The numbers in sequence S increase by sevens. The first number that occurs in both sequences is 17. What is the next number that occurs in both sequences?

    A. 87
    B. 85
    C. 72
    D. 52

110. A certain type of drinking glass holds exactly $\dfrac{5}{8}$ liter of water. How many of those glasses can be filled if you have 40 liters of water?

    E. 72
    F. 64
    G. 30
    H. 25

111. $5^4 + 5^4 + 5^4 + 5^4 + 5^4 =$

   A. 5^5
   B. 5^{20}
   C. 25^{20}
   D. 25^4

112. Points C, D, E, and H lie on the sides of rectangle $ABFG$ as shown. $AB = 8$ and $AG = 15$. What is the mean of the areas of the three triangles ACG, ADH, and HEG?

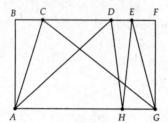

   E. 120
   F. 60
   G. 40
   H. There is more than one possible answer.

113. In the diagram below, three of the four straight lines intersect in a single point. Certain angles have their degree measures indicated. The value of x is

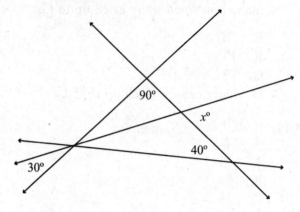

   A. 50
   B. 60
   C. 70
   D. 80

114. The sum of five consecutive positive integers is 40. At least one of them must be greater than

   E. 9
   F. 10
   G. 11
   H. 12

Revising/Editing Part A

1. **B**	3. **D**	5. **C**
2. **E**	4. **G**	6. **H**

Revising/Editing Part B

7. **D**	10. **E**	13. **D**	16. **F**	19. **D**
8. **G**	11. **C**	14. **F**	17. **A**	20. **F**
9. **B**	12. **F**	15. **C**	18. **H**	

Reading

21. **B**	29. **D**	37. **C**	45. **C**	53. **B**
22. **H**	30. **H**	38. **H**	46. **G**	54. **F**
23. **A**	31. **B**	39. **C**	47. **A**	55. **B**
24. **G**	32. **G**	40. **G**	48. **H**	56. **G**
25. **A**	33. **D**	41. **D**	49. **B**	57. **D**
26. **F**	34. **E**	42. **E**	50. **H**	
27. **C**	35. **D**	43. **B**	51. **B**	
28. **E**	36. **E**	44. **F**	52. **G**	

Mathematics

58. **3.5**	70. **G**	82. **H**	94. **F**	106. **H**
59. **5.76**	71. **D**	83. **B**	95. **D**	107. **B**
60. **63**	72. **F**	84. **G**	96. **E**	108. **H**
61. **158**	73. **B**	85. **B**	97. **D**	109. **D**
62. **96**	74. **H**	86. **E**	98. **E**	110. **F**
63. **A**	75. **C**	87. **C**	99. **D**	111. **A**
64. **G**	76. **F**	88. **E**	100. **G**	112. **G**
65. **D**	77. **D**	89. **C**	101. **D**	113. **B**
66. **E**	78. **H**	90. **H**	102. **F**	114. **E**
67. **B**	79. **B**	91. **B**	103. **D**	
68. **H**	80. **G**	92. **G**	104. **E**	
69. **A**	81. **D**	93. **D**	105. **D**	

Revising/Editing Part A

1. **(B)** Examine the pairings of <u>antecedents</u> and **pronouns** below.

(1) Many holidays today can be traced to pagan <u>holidays</u>, **which** were often celebrated to welcome seasonal changes. (2) Christmas, for example, was celebrated as Saturnalia by the <u>Romans</u>, **which** feasted on the surplus from their harvests. (3) Valentine's Day replaced <u>Lupercalia</u>, **which** was celebrated in the spring to welcome the start of a new year. (4) Finally, Halloween took over <u>Lemuria</u>, **which** took place in the fall.

Sentence 1: The correct antecedent to the relative pronoun **which** is <u>holidays</u>.

Sentence 2: The relative pronoun **which** inappropriately replaces the word <u>Romans</u>. Romans refers to people, so the pronoun should be revised to **who**.

Sentence 3: The correct antecedent to the relative pronoun **which** is <u>Lupercalia</u>.

Sentence 4: The correct antecedent to the relative pronoun **which** is <u>Lemuria</u>.

2. **(E)** Sentence 1 contains an independent clause, a modifier, and an independent clause. This is a run-on.

Times Square today isn't what it used to be,	in the past,	it was a very dark, lawless place.
Independent Clause	Modifier	Independent Clause

Correction: Times Square today isn't what it used to be. **In** the past, it was a very dark, lawless place.

Sentence 2 contains a modifier, an independent clause, and a dependent clause. This is not a run-on.

In the 1990s	crime rates dropped drastically,	and tourist-friendly establishments sprouted all along the streets.
Modifier	Independent Clause	Dependent Clause

Sentence 3 contains an independent clause and a dependent clause. This is not a run-on.

Many credit Mayor Rudy Giuliani,	who decided to make the area more friendly by passing harsh laws and by increasing the number of police officers patrolling the area.
Independent Clause	Dependent Clause

Sentence 4 contains an independent clause and a dependent clause. This is not a run-on.

Critics, however, point to an overall decline in crime rates all across the United States and suggest	that Giuliani's policies were insignificant.
Independent Clause	Dependent Clause

3. **(D)**

Least Precise (cross out)	Most Precise
physical activities	cardio exercises
eating right	limiting caloric intake
dieting	

4. **(G)**

    E. The killer whale feeds on most marine animals, and some of these are seabirds, cephalopods, turtles, sharks, and fish, but it avoids dolphins and manatees.

    Grammatically, the sentence is sound. However, the sentence combines three clauses. Since there is an option with a shorter alternative, this choice should be eliminated.

    F. The killer whale feeds on most marine animals, *of the types to be included being* seabirds, cephalopods, turtles, sharks, and fish, with some avoidance of dolphins and manatees.

    The italicized portion of the sentence above is considered an awkward construction.

    G. The killer whale feeds on most marine animals, such as seabirds, cephalopods, turtles, sharks, and fish, but avoids dolphins and manatees.

    This sentence best combines the information in one clause.

    H. The killer whale feeds on most marine animals, seabirds, cephalopods, turtles, sharks, and fish, and avoids dolphins and manatees.

    This sentence is a run-on.

5. **(C)** The modifier is *Eaten at both breakfast and dinner*, so the word that follows should be *kimchee*.

6. **(H)** Examine the predicate verbs below. Sentence 4 uses the present tense to describe a situation that occurred in the fifteenth century. Sentence 1 correctly uses the present tense to state the current understanding.

    (1) The fall of the Roman Empire <u>is</u> commonly associated with the rise of the Germanic leader Odoacer in 476 C.E. (2) However, the Roman Empire <u>didn't</u> completely crumble. (3) In fact, the eastern half of the empire, called the Byzantine Empire, <u>thrived</u> well into the fifteenth century. (4) The Ottoman army <u>storms</u> into its capital city Constantinople and took over to create a new Ottoman Empire.

Revising/Editing Part B

7. **(D)** Choice D introduces the *three categories*, which links with the phrase *These categories* in sentence 4.

8. **(G)** Sentence 5 begins with *Strong evidence*, and sentence 6 begins with *Moderate evidence*. To complete the paragraph as outlined by sentence 4, the sentence that follows 6 should begin with *Emerging evidence*.

9. **(B)** The purpose of this paragraph is to identify characteristics of healthy eating patterns. Sentence 8 discusses the impact of fiber on a person's appetite.

10. **(E)** Sentence 11 contains the phrase *these shifts*, which needs to connect to the phrase *making shifts* in sentence 15.

11. **(C)**

Least Precise (cross out)	Most Precise
Shifts	Small shifts
significant	lasting difference
different	

12. **(F)** Sentence 14 summarizes and highlights the importance of the idea in sentence 13.

13. **(D)** The purpose of this paragraph is to introduce the importance of the gastrointestinal tract. Choice D best serves that purpose.

14. **(F)** Sentence 5 provides more information about the gastrointestinal tract. Choice F combines the additional detail most concisely.

    Choices E and H are wrong because both of them use a causal connection.

    Choice G is wrong because the transition word *Whereas* is used for comparisons.

15. **(C)** The purpose of this paragraph is to discuss problems in the GI tract. Sentence 13 makes a claim about how people feel about IBS and is therefore not important to this paragraph.

16. **(F)** Sentence 16 provides concrete examples of the *factors* mentioned in sentence 15, so a transition word to introduce examples is most appropriate.

17. **(A)**

Least Precise (cross out)	Most Precise
decide to live a healthy life	create a more routine schedule, eat a healthy diet and smaller, more frequent meals, add in some exercise, and get a good amount of sleep
focus on many habits	
decide to create a life	

18. **(H)** Connect the phrase *those issues* to *lifestyle-related GI issues* in sentence 17.

19. **(D)** The paragraph discusses the impact of stress on the development of IBS. Sentence D introduces that idea.

20. **(F)** The main purpose of this passage is to highlight the importance of the GI tract and to recommend healthy habits. Choice F captures that idea.

Reading

Passage I

21. **(B)** Main Idea   A is incorrect because while history is given in the passage, no reference is made to legend. B is correct because it is broad enough to cover all the information in the passage, and it is also accurate as every paragraph mentions the scarcity of information. C is too narrow. D contradicts the statement (line 5) that the movie is not factual.

22. **(H)** Inference   H is correct because while the passage does not state that the movie is pure fiction, it states (line 5) that it is not factual. E and F contradict the statement that the film is not factual. G is not stated or suggested in the passage.

23. **(A)** Inference   A is correct because the rival is described as "jealous," and his attack reveals Shakespeare's activity in the theater, suggesting that his jealousy was professional. C might be correct if there were any suggestion that his attack mentions an affair, but there is no such suggestion. B and D are incorrect because there is no information in the passage that would support them.

24. **(G)** Detail   G is the correct answer because the passage does not say that Shakespeare endured poverty during the plague, only that his theater career was interrupted. E and F are directly stated, and H is incorrect because it is stated (line 38) that he made money in real estate—a secondary source of income.

25. **(A)** Inference   The context (line 13) involves a lack of information, leading to the definition given in A. None of the other choices is consistent with the topic of this part of the passage.

26. **(F)** Detail   The passage asks how a middle-class man could have been familiar with aristocratic and court life and calls this knowledge "mysterious." None of the other choices are mentioned or suggested by any detail in the passage.

Passage II

27. **(C)** Main Idea   Only C is broad enough to cover all the information in the passage. A is incorrect because only the first and last paragraphs mention recent demand. B is also too narrow. D is both too narrow and also inaccurate. There is no suggestion made that the information given is "little-known."

28. **(E)** Inference   The sentence using the word (line 6) is followed by details that exemplify how mushroom popularity has grown; thus *grown* is the correct choice. G contradicts the context. The other choices are unsuitable because *burgeoned* modifies *popularity,* and the other choices do not refer to popularity.

29. **(D)** Detail   A contradicts the information given in (lines 25–27). The word *worldwide* makes B incorrect since the passage refers only to mushroom popularity in America.

C contradicts the statement that the fruiting body appears above ground (lines 19–20). D is stated in lines 34–37.

30. **(H)** Inference   It is stated that truffles are "rare and costly" (line 29) and that animals are trained to find them; it can be inferred that both the scarcity and the difficulty in finding them contribute to their cost. F contradicts the statements (lines 24–28) about where they grow and how they are harvested.

31. **(B)** Inference   A is incorrect because although training is stated as important (line 33), there is no suggestion of a classroom setting. The statement that "high demand" encourages "enterpreneurs" suggests that mushroom gathering must be profitable; therefore B is correct. C and D contradict the statement in the last paragraph that mushroom gathering took place before recent years (lines 43–47).

32. **(G)** Detail   It is stated that the Asian gatherer mistook a local variety for an Asian type; therefore she was not familiar with the local deadly amanita. E and H are not stated or suggested in the passage. F contradicts the fact that she was experienced (line 40).

Passage III

33. **(D)** Main Idea   A and B are too narrow, and C is too broad, as the passage focuses only on Cajuns, not other people and cultures of south Louisiana. Although the second paragraph does give history, that history is related to the description of culture since it explains the French influence as well as the early separation of the group, so D is correct.

34. **(E)** Inference   The reason stated for expulsion is refusal to sign a loyalty oath. One can infer that a person who made such a refusal might be rebellious and thus a threat. G might be correct if E were not given, but E is clearly the more logical answer of the two. F and G are neither stated nor suggested.

35. **(D)** Detail   A, B, and C are all stated in the passage. D is correct because it not only is not stated, but contradicts the statement that Cajun cooks are adventurous.

36. **(E)** Inference   The context compares remote places with "more likely venues," indicating that a venue is a place. F is one definition of the word venue but does not fit the context in which the word is used.

> **TIP:** Don't rely on a known definition of a word; rely on context.

37. **(C)** Detail   The third paragraph says that another name for a bayou is a creek (line 25).

38. **(H)** Detail   French rhythms are not mentioned, so E is incorrect. Choices F and G are mentioned as "frequent" (line 53) in the music or related to the music as an "offshoot" (line 55). Only the accordion is stated to be "integral" (line 52) or essential.

Passage IV

39. **(C)** Main Idea   A is mentioned only in the first paragraph. Most of the passage does not involve collisions, choice B. Only one paragraph discusses origins. A, B, and D are all too narrow. Only C is broad enough to incorporate all the content of the passage.

40. **(G)** Inference   The "minuscule" cost of the NEAP project is compared with the "costly" projects of NASA; therefore the cost of the NEAP project must be small, making G the correct choice. None of the other choices are words that compare or contrast with "costly," so they cannot be correct definitions.

41. **(D)** Detail   The first paragraph says that the collision of a large asteroid could have "drastic environmental consequences." No other consequences are mentioned in the passage, so D must be the correct answer.

> **TIP:** Base your answer only on the information in the passage. Do not rely on outside knowledge or suppositions.

42. **(E)** Inference *Common* means occurring frequently, but the passage says that such collisions are frequent or "common" only in the context of billions of years. So the word is being used in a different or special context, and E is the correct answer. F is incorrect; the word is not used earlier in the passage, and there is no indication that the author is quoting anyone. G might possibly be an acceptable choice if E were not clearly correct. H is incorrect according to grammar and context.

43. **(B)** Detail Although it is stated that a big collision could cause environmental change, there is no mention of such change except in this one statement. There is no statement or suggestion that they have caused most of Earth's environmental changes. A, C, and D are directly stated in the passage.

44. **(F)** Detail It is stated that people worry about a collision because of a possible "shift in the asteroid's path" or an "error in calculation." In other words, such events are not entirely predictable. The other choices are not stated or suggested in the passage.

Passage V

45. **(C)** Main Idea This item is an example of the need sometimes to recognize tone in determining main idea. A and B are too narrow. D is inaccurate, as none of the methods are presented as being desirable. Only C is acceptable since the entire passage focuses on various detrimental effects of building on the beach.

46. **(G)** Inference The passage says that hard devices block the sand flow to other areas and cause erosion (lines 42–44), this is the most likely reason for banning the devices. The other choices are not suggested or stated in the passage.

47. **(A)** Main Idea The topic of the paragraph in which the bulkhead is mentioned is that technology cannot control the ocean; the bulkhead is used as an example of this concept. B, C, and D are not mentioned or suggested in connection with the bulkhead.

48. **(H)** Detail The first paragraph states this idea (lines 11–12). E and F are not stated or suggested in the passage, and G contradicts the information in the first paragraph.

49. **(B)** Main Idea Again, tone is important. The author paints a negative picture of the results of building on the beach. Thus A is not a good choice. Nowhere are federal subsidies supported in the text; they are mentioned only once, in the last paragraph (line 63) and in a negative context, so C is incorrect. Nothing in the passage supports D as a good choice.

50. **(H)** Detail Dunes are called "protective" of the beach. All the other choices are presented in the passage as harmful.

Passage VI

51. **(B)** Main Idea A mentions it, but the passage is more about a discovery to eradicate it. Choice C is too broad. Choice D builds off a minor detail in the last paragraph.

52. **(G)** Detail Details in lines 1–2 suggest the parasite's significance.

53. **(B)** Detail Lines 15–17 says "Currently," which links with the question stem word "as of today."

54. **(F)** Inference The second paragraph introduces the key members in "the research" (lines 10–15). The third paragraph elaborates on "The research" (line 21).

55. **(B)** Inference Lines 43–48 suggest that CIS43 can be combined with antimalarial drugs to eliminate malaria, the inference being that CIS43 alone cannot do it.

56. **(G)** Main Idea The topic sentence of the paragraph in lines 49–52 introduces epitopes. The following sentences explain its properties as significant.

57. **(D)** Inference The last paragraph discusses the importance of collaborators (helpers) because of the size of the research. They will be testing CIS43's safety and effectiveness, which means that it is not ready yet.

Mathematics

58. **(3.5)** Since P is located at -3 and R is located at 7, S, the midpoint of $\overline{PR}$, is located at $\frac{-3+7}{2} = \frac{4}{2} = 2$. Since Q is located at 5, the midpoint of $\overline{SQ}$ is therefore located at $\frac{2+5}{2} = \frac{7}{2} = 3.5$.

59. **(5.76)** Note that $\frac{3.6}{0.2} = \frac{36}{2} = 18$ and $0.32 = \frac{32}{100}$. So $\frac{3.6}{0.2} \times 0.32 = 18 \times \frac{32}{100}$. Since $18 \times 32 = 576$, we have $18 \times \frac{32}{100} = \frac{576}{100} = 5.76$.

60. **(63)** Let x and $x + 1$ be two consecutive integers. So $x + (x + 1) = -17$. We can solve this equation to find that $x = -9$. So the two consecutive integers are -9 and -8. (The integers could also be determined via thoughtful guessing and checking.) Since -9 is the smaller, the product we seek is $(-9 + 2)(-8 - 1) = (-7)(-9) = 63$.

61. **(158)** Since $\angle ABC$ forms a line with a $68°$ angle, $m\angle ABC = 180° - 68° = 112°$. In a parallelogram, opposite angles are congruent, so $m\angle ADC = m\angle ABC = 112°$. Since the measures of the angles about a point must sum to $360°$, we have $x + 90 + 112 = 360$, and so $x = 360 - 90 - 112 = 158$.

62. **(96)** To create our five-digit number, we have four options for the first digit: 2, 4, 6, and 8. Since no digit can be repeated, only three of these digits will be available for the next choice, but since 0 is now an option, we will have four options for the second digit. Once a second digit is selected, we will have three options for our third choice, then two, and then only one option for the last choice. The total number of such numbers then is $4 \times 4 \times 3 \times 2 \times 1 = 96$.

63. **(A)** Multiplying $\frac{1}{2}$ by $\frac{1}{6}$ produces $\frac{1}{12}$. That is the same as $\frac{1}{3}$ times $\frac{1}{4}$.

64. **(G)** Adding the areas of the two large triangles ($= 20$) counts the overlapped region twice. Subtracting that region once must produce 14, so its area is 6.

65. **(D)** Adding, $1.1 + 2.11 + 3.111 = 6.321$.

66. **(E)** One approach is to try values for x. When $x = 6$, $x^2 + x = 36 + 6 = 42$, so 6 is too small. Letting $x = 7$ turns out to be too large, so x is between 6 and 7.

67. **(B)** Since the triangle is isosceles, angle BCA must be $80°$. Then angle $BCE = 100° = 4x°$, so $x = 25$ and $3x = 75$.

68. **(H)** Start with Katie's age $= 16$. That makes Carole 32, so Barbara is 39.

> **TIP:** When simple but specific numerical values are given in a problem, that is often a good starting point for analysis.

69. **(A)** If we think of 3.4 as p and 10^2 as q, we have $pq + pq$. This is $2pq$, or $2 \times 3.4 \times 10^2 = 6.8 \times 10^2$. It is sometimes easier to manipulate letters (symbols) than numbers.

70. **(G)** The area of $SXRD$ is 12, so $SD = 4$. The area of $PBQX$ is 27, so $PB = 9$. Then $AD + AB = 7 + 12 = 19$, and the perimeter of $ABCD$ is 38.

71. **(D)** Start to test the choices. If Kobi has 208 pennies, the remaining $7.75 must be made up of nickels. This is certainly possible. So long as the difference between $9.83 and the number of pennies is a multiple of 5, that difference can be made up of nickels. Only 85 pennies will not work.

72. **(F)** $2x - 3 = 32$. Rather than solve for x, we can add 6 to both sides producing $2x + 3 = 38$. Notice that you do not always have to solve for x (although that would be another way to do the problem).

73. **(B)** We wish to compare pears with bananas, knowing that 1 apple = 2 pears. Putting this information into the first sentence (and using letters to represents the fruits) produces $10p + 6b = 8b + 9p$. Therefore, $1p = 2b$, and the answer is 2. Another approach would be to set a price for one pear. For example, if one pear costs 10¢, then one apple costs 20¢, and so on.

74. **(H)** We have $R = 2^3 \cdot 3^2 \cdot 7 \cdot 13$ and $S = 2^3 \cdot 3 \cdot 7^2 \cdot 11$. The greatest common factor (sometimes called the greatest common divisor) must contain every prime that is in *both* R and S, and each of those primes must be raised to the smallest exponent that it originally had in either R or S. Therefore, the greatest common factor is $2^3 \cdot 3 \cdot 7 = 168$.

75. **(C)** Substitution produces $4 \mid -5 - 2\mid -3 \mid -10 \mid = 4 \mid -7 \mid -3 \mid -10 \mid = 4(7) - 3(10) = 28 - 30 = -2$.

> **TIP:** Combine the terms inside the absolute value signs before you compute the absolute value.

76. **(F)** List the numbers vertically. There are eight 2s in the units column, for a total of 16. Thus, we must carry 1 into the tens column. There are seven 1s in that column, for a total (including the "carry") of 8. There are six 1s in the hundreds column (and no "carry"), so that total is 6.

77. **(D)** If we let g represent the number of girls, we can express everything in terms of g. There would be $2g$ boys and g girls, so the class has $3g$ members. Half of the boys plus all of the girls would be $g + g$, so $2g$ students are in the math club. Changing this to a percent, we have $\frac{2g}{3g} \cdot 100 = \frac{2}{3} \cdot 100 = 66\frac{2}{3}\%$.

78. **(H)** Removing all parentheses produces $16 + 5x - 8 + 2x$, so the answer is $8 + 7x$.

79. **(B)**

> **FACT:** When two straight lines intersect, the "vertical angles" formed are equal.

We can fill in the values of all the vertical angles, producing $x + 40 + 60 + x + 40 + 60 = 360$, leading to $x = 80$. If you prefer, just add the angles on one side of a straight line, getting $x + 40 + 60 = 180$. This also produces $x = 80$.

80. **(G)** Each half hour we are losing 100 people. To lose 350 people would take three half-hours plus another 15 minutes. That is 1 hour and 45 minutes. Measuring from noon, this would bring us to 1:45 P.M.

81. **(D)** Draw triangle PXQ. Each side is actually a radius of one of the circles. Since the circles are congruent, all three sides are equal. That makes this an equilateral triangle, so each of its angles is 60°.

82. **(H)** Since Andrew has d dollars, Bruce must have $3d$ dollars. Carlos has $80 less than half of $(d + 3d)$, so Carlos has 80 less than $2d$, or $2d - 80$ dollars.

83. **(B)** If six of the integers are as small as possible, the seventh would have to be as large as possible. Since the integers must be positive and unequal, let the first six be 1, 2, 3, 4, 5, and 6. Their sum is 21, so the seventh integer would be 40.

84. **(G)** Using algebra would give us $\frac{1 + 5 + x + 10 + 15}{5} = x - 1$. That means $31 + x = 5(x - 1)$, leading to $x = 9$. Another method would be to use "trial and error." That is, try each choice until you find the correct answer. Note that since x is supposed to be an integer, the mean (which is 1 less than x) must also be an integer. For example, if $x = 6$, the mean would be $\frac{31 + 6}{5}$. That is not 1 less than 6 (and isn't even an integer).

85. **(B)**

> **FACT:** For positive numbers a, b, c, and d, $\frac{a}{b} < \frac{c}{d}$ if and only if $ad < bc$.

$\frac{7}{50} < \frac{1}{x}$ tells us that $7x < 50$ so $x < 7\frac{1}{7}$. Also,

$\frac{1}{x} < \frac{8}{51}$ tells us that $51 < 8x$, so $6\frac{3}{8} < x$.

Putting these together produces $6\frac{3}{8} < x < 7\frac{1}{7}$.

Since x is an integer, it can only be 7.

86. **(E)** $\frac{2^8}{2} = 2^7$ Remember that 2 is the same as 2^1. Notice how choice H is testing whether anyone would try to cancel the 2s. That choice is a wonderfully absurd answer since 1^8 is simply 1, which is certainly not half of 2^8.

87. **(C)** Each choice must be tested. Since x is between $\frac{1}{2}$ and 1, $2x - 1$ is between 0 and 1. x^2 is between $\frac{1}{4}$ and 1. $\frac{1}{x}$ is between 2 and 1. $1 - x$ is between $\frac{1}{2}$ and 0. The largest value occurs for $\frac{1}{x}$. The problem does not actually allow x to have the value $\frac{1}{2}$ or the value 1. Another approach would be to choose an appropriate number for x (such as $\frac{3}{4}$) and evaluate each choice.

88. **(E)** In eight years, the sum of their three ages will be $49 + 24$. Ten years ago, the sum of their three ages was $49 - 30$. Then $F - P = (49 + 24) - (49 - 30) = 54$.

89. **(C)** Clearly $\frac{1}{x} = \frac{3}{4}$, so $x = \frac{4}{3}$.

90. **(H)** $N = 7Q + 5$. Then $N + 24 = 7Q + 29$, which is 1 more than a multiple of 7.

91. **(B)**

> **FACT:** An exterior angle of a triangle is equal to the sum of the two remote interior angles.

Angle $DBE = 70 + 50 = 120$, so the third angle of triangle DBE is 40°.

92. **(G)** Since $\frac{3}{2}$ is $2 \times \frac{3}{4}$, the answer is $2L$.

93. **(D)** The numerator 18 is divisible by the positive integers 1, 2, 3, 6, 9, and 18. The only positive integer values of N that produce any of these are $N = 1$, 4, 7, and 16. The *number* of values is 4.

94. **(F)** To find x, we must fill in several other boxes first. Since the "constant sum" is 33, the center box must be 11. Then the upper right box must be 12, so x must be 7.

95. **(D)** We must locate the approximate position on the horizontal axis where the height of the coffee graph is twice the height of the sugar graph. At the start of June, the coffee graph is $5\frac{1}{2}$ boxes high, while the sugar graph is only $2\frac{2}{3}$ boxes high. By July, the coffee graph is too low. The correct heights occurred during June.

96. **(E)** "Other" occupies 20% of the pie chart. The correct bar graph must have the same heights for F and R, the same (but lower) heights for C and O, and a still lower height for T.

97. **(D)** Start with a post at one corner. We have 4 more posts along the 20 foot side, then 7 more along the 35 foot side, then 5 more along the 25 foot side. However, that final post is the same as the starting post. Therefore the answer is $1 + 4 + 7 + (5 - 1) = 16$. A carefully drawn picture is very helpful.

98. (E)

> **FACT:** The longest side of a triangle is opposite the largest angle of the triangle.

In triangle ABD, $\overline{BD}$ is the longest side. Now in triangle BCD, $\overline{BC}$ is the longest side, making it longer than $\overline{BD}$. The longest side of the figure is $\overline{BC}$.

99. (D) Remember the rules of exponents for multiplication, and that multiplication can be done in any order. Then we have $x^2 \cdot x \cdot y^3 \cdot y^2 = x^3 \cdot y^5$.

100. (G) $\dfrac{12n}{56} = \dfrac{3n}{14}$. For this fraction to be an integer, 14 must exactly divide n. The smallest n that works is 14.

101. (D) Dividing both sides of the first equation by 2 and then replacing $x + y$ with 11, we have $11 + z = 55$. Then $z = 44$.

102. (F) The easiest way to test each choice is to first rewrite $a^2 - ab$ as $a(a - b)$. Then, for example, choice F equals $15 \cdot 1 = 15$. We quickly find that F is the answer.

103. (D) An even sum comes from two odd or two even numbers. The 3, 5, or 9 could each go with the 1 or 7; that produces six possibilities. The 6 could only go with the 4, producing one more possibility. Therefore there are seven satisfactory pairs. Since there are 12 possible pairings all together, the probability is $\dfrac{7}{12}$.

104. (E) Distance = rate × time, or $t = \dfrac{D}{r}$.

Therefore Larry will make up the 80 miles in $\dfrac{80}{5}$ hours.

105. (D) Dividing each term in the numerator by 3 produces $x + 1 = 2.5$, so $x = 1.5$.

106. (H) It is easiest to consider how much value remains each day. If we started with N worth of stock, at the end of the first day we have 40% of N, or $\dfrac{40}{100}N$, left. At the end of the second day we have $\dfrac{40}{100} \cdot \dfrac{90}{100} N$ left. That is 36% of N. If $y\%$ were to *remain* each day, we would have $\dfrac{y}{100} \cdot \dfrac{y}{100} N$ left. Thus $\dfrac{y^2}{10000} = \dfrac{36}{100}$, so $y^2 = 3600$ and $y = 60$. Retaining 60% each day is equivalent to losing 40% each day.

107. (B) When using the formula Area $= \dfrac{1}{2}hb$ to get the area of a triangle, any side of the triangle can be considered its base, so long as the altitude goes to that base. For triangle AOE, let $\overline{OA}$ be the base and draw an altitude from E to that base. Since point E is 1 unit to the right of the y-axis, the length of that altitude is 1. Base $\overline{OA}$ is 4, so the area of the triangle is $\dfrac{1}{2} \cdot 1 \cdot 4 = 2$. There is no need to find the y-coordinate of point E. Do not let yourself be distracted by that missing coordinate.

108. (H) In triangle DEB, angle EBD must be 80°. Now look at triangle ABC.

> **FACT:** An exterior angle of a triangle is equal to the sum of the two remote interior angles.

$x = y + 80$, so $y = x - 80$.

109. (D) Sequence F contains every 5th integer after 17. Sequence S contains every 7th integer after 17. Therefore both will contain every 35th integer after 17. The next common number will be $17 + 35 = 52$.

110. (F) We must figure out how many times $\dfrac{5}{8}$ goes into 40. That is $\dfrac{40}{\frac{5}{8}} = 40 \cdot \dfrac{8}{5} = 64$.

111. **(A)** This is $5 \times 5^4 = 5^5$.

112. **(G)** Let $AH = p$ and $HG = q$. Note that $p + q = 15$. Also notice that the altitude for each triangle is equal to 8 $(= AB)$. The three areas are $\frac{1}{2} \cdot 8 \cdot 15$, $\frac{1}{2} \cdot 8 \cdot p$, and $\frac{1}{2} \cdot 8 \cdot q$.

Then their mean is $\dfrac{60 + 4p + 4q}{3}$. Since $p + q = 15$, $4p + 4q = 60$. The mean is now

$\dfrac{60 + 60}{3} = 40$.

113. **(B)** When two lines intersect, the vertical angles formed are equal. In the small right triangle formed, the lower left angle and the given 30° angle are vertical angles, so the lower left angle is also equal to 30°. Consequently, the third angle of that right triangle is 60°. That "third angle" and the angle whose size measures x are vertical angles. Therefore, $x = 60$. Note that the 40° angle is not needed for this solution and is given as a "distractor."

114. **(E)** If none of the consecutive integers is greater than 9, the maximum possible sum would be $5 + 6 + 7 + 8 + 9 = 35$. Therefore, at least one of the integers must be greater than 9 (for example, $6 + 7 + 8 + 9 + 10 = 40$). Thus, choice E is correct. This example also shows that none of the integers need be greater than 10.

ANSWER SHEET
Practice Test 3

Part I   English Language Arts

Revising/Editing Part A

1. Ⓐ Ⓑ Ⓒ Ⓓ
2. Ⓔ Ⓕ Ⓖ Ⓗ
3. Ⓐ Ⓑ Ⓒ Ⓓ
4. Ⓔ Ⓕ Ⓖ Ⓗ
5. Ⓐ Ⓑ Ⓒ Ⓓ
6. Ⓔ Ⓕ Ⓖ Ⓗ

Revising/Editing Part B

7. Ⓐ Ⓑ Ⓒ Ⓓ
8. Ⓔ Ⓕ Ⓖ Ⓗ
9. Ⓐ Ⓑ Ⓒ Ⓓ
10. Ⓔ Ⓕ Ⓖ Ⓗ
11. Ⓐ Ⓑ Ⓒ Ⓓ
12. Ⓔ Ⓕ Ⓖ Ⓗ
13. Ⓐ Ⓑ Ⓒ Ⓓ
14. Ⓔ Ⓕ Ⓖ Ⓗ
15. Ⓐ Ⓑ Ⓒ Ⓓ
16. Ⓔ Ⓕ Ⓖ Ⓗ
17. Ⓐ Ⓑ Ⓒ Ⓓ
18. Ⓔ Ⓕ Ⓖ Ⓗ
19. Ⓐ Ⓑ Ⓒ Ⓓ
20. Ⓔ Ⓕ Ⓖ Ⓗ

Reading

21. Ⓐ Ⓑ Ⓒ Ⓓ
22. Ⓔ Ⓕ Ⓖ Ⓗ
23. Ⓐ Ⓑ Ⓒ Ⓓ
24. Ⓔ Ⓕ Ⓖ Ⓗ
25. Ⓐ Ⓑ Ⓒ Ⓓ
26. Ⓔ Ⓕ Ⓖ Ⓗ
27. Ⓐ Ⓑ Ⓒ Ⓓ
28. Ⓔ Ⓕ Ⓖ Ⓗ
29. Ⓐ Ⓑ Ⓒ Ⓓ
30. Ⓔ Ⓕ Ⓖ Ⓗ
31. Ⓐ Ⓑ Ⓒ Ⓓ
32. Ⓔ Ⓕ Ⓖ Ⓗ
33. Ⓐ Ⓑ Ⓒ Ⓓ
34. Ⓔ Ⓕ Ⓖ Ⓗ
35. Ⓐ Ⓑ Ⓒ Ⓓ
36. Ⓔ Ⓕ Ⓖ Ⓗ
37. Ⓐ Ⓑ Ⓒ Ⓓ
38. Ⓔ Ⓕ Ⓖ Ⓗ
39. Ⓐ Ⓑ Ⓒ Ⓓ

40. Ⓔ Ⓕ Ⓖ Ⓗ
41. Ⓐ Ⓑ Ⓒ Ⓓ
42. Ⓔ Ⓕ Ⓖ Ⓗ
43. Ⓐ Ⓑ Ⓒ Ⓓ
44. Ⓔ Ⓕ Ⓖ Ⓗ
45. Ⓐ Ⓑ Ⓒ Ⓓ
46. Ⓔ Ⓕ Ⓖ Ⓗ
47. Ⓐ Ⓑ Ⓒ Ⓓ
48. Ⓔ Ⓕ Ⓖ Ⓗ
49. Ⓐ Ⓑ Ⓒ Ⓓ
50. Ⓔ Ⓕ Ⓖ Ⓗ
51. Ⓐ Ⓑ Ⓒ Ⓓ
52. Ⓔ Ⓕ Ⓖ Ⓗ
53. Ⓐ Ⓑ Ⓒ Ⓓ
54. Ⓔ Ⓕ Ⓖ Ⓗ
55. Ⓐ Ⓑ Ⓒ Ⓓ
56. Ⓔ Ⓕ Ⓖ Ⓗ
57. Ⓐ Ⓑ Ⓒ Ⓓ

ANSWER SHEET
Practice Test 3

Part II   Mathematics

58.

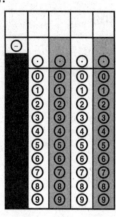

59.

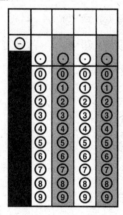

60.

61.

62.

63. Ⓐ Ⓑ Ⓒ Ⓓ	89. Ⓐ Ⓑ Ⓒ Ⓓ
64. Ⓔ Ⓕ Ⓖ Ⓗ	90. Ⓔ Ⓕ Ⓖ Ⓗ
65. Ⓐ Ⓑ Ⓒ Ⓓ	91. Ⓐ Ⓑ Ⓒ Ⓓ
66. Ⓔ Ⓕ Ⓖ Ⓗ	92. Ⓔ Ⓕ Ⓖ Ⓗ
67. Ⓐ Ⓑ Ⓒ Ⓓ	93. Ⓐ Ⓑ Ⓒ Ⓓ
68. Ⓔ Ⓕ Ⓖ Ⓗ	94. Ⓔ Ⓕ Ⓖ Ⓗ
69. Ⓐ Ⓑ Ⓒ Ⓓ	95. Ⓐ Ⓑ Ⓒ Ⓓ
70. Ⓔ Ⓕ Ⓖ Ⓗ	96. Ⓔ Ⓕ Ⓖ Ⓗ
71. Ⓐ Ⓑ Ⓒ Ⓓ	97. Ⓐ Ⓑ Ⓒ Ⓓ
72. Ⓔ Ⓕ Ⓖ Ⓗ	98. Ⓔ Ⓕ Ⓖ Ⓗ
73. Ⓐ Ⓑ Ⓒ Ⓓ	99. Ⓐ Ⓑ Ⓒ Ⓓ
74. Ⓔ Ⓕ Ⓖ Ⓗ	100. Ⓔ Ⓕ Ⓖ Ⓗ
75. Ⓐ Ⓑ Ⓒ Ⓓ	101. Ⓐ Ⓑ Ⓒ Ⓓ
76. Ⓔ Ⓕ Ⓖ Ⓗ	102. Ⓔ Ⓕ Ⓖ Ⓗ
77. Ⓐ Ⓑ Ⓒ Ⓓ	103. Ⓐ Ⓑ Ⓒ Ⓓ
78. Ⓔ Ⓕ Ⓖ Ⓗ	104. Ⓔ Ⓕ Ⓖ Ⓗ
79. Ⓐ Ⓑ Ⓒ Ⓓ	105. Ⓐ Ⓑ Ⓒ Ⓓ
80. Ⓔ Ⓕ Ⓖ Ⓗ	106. Ⓔ Ⓕ Ⓖ Ⓗ
81. Ⓐ Ⓑ Ⓒ Ⓓ	107. Ⓐ Ⓑ Ⓒ Ⓓ
82. Ⓔ Ⓕ Ⓖ Ⓗ	108. Ⓔ Ⓕ Ⓖ Ⓗ
83. Ⓐ Ⓑ Ⓒ Ⓓ	109. Ⓐ Ⓑ Ⓒ Ⓓ
84. Ⓔ Ⓕ Ⓖ Ⓗ	110. Ⓔ Ⓕ Ⓖ Ⓗ
85. Ⓐ Ⓑ Ⓒ Ⓓ	111. Ⓐ Ⓑ Ⓒ Ⓓ
86. Ⓔ Ⓕ Ⓖ Ⓗ	112. Ⓔ Ⓕ Ⓖ Ⓗ
87. Ⓐ Ⓑ Ⓒ Ⓓ	113. Ⓐ Ⓑ Ⓒ Ⓓ
88. Ⓔ Ⓕ Ⓖ Ⓗ	114. Ⓔ Ⓕ Ⓖ Ⓗ

Practice Test 3

PART 1—ENGLISH LANGUAGE ARTS

57 QUESTIONS

SUGGESTED TIME: 90 MINUTES

Revising/Editing

QUESTIONS 1–20

IMPORTANT NOTE: The Revising/Editing section (Questions 1–20) is in two parts: Part A and Part B.

Revising/Editing Part A

Directions: Read and answer each of the following questions. You will be asked to recognize and correct errors in sentences or short paragraphs. Mark the **best** answer for each question.

1. Read this paragraph.

   (1) A contagious respiratory infection, people infected with the seasonal flu virus feel miserable with fever, chills, muscle aches, and fatigue. (2) Within two weeks, the symptoms of the flu disappear, and most people get better. (3) However, some people may develop serious complications, such as pneumonia. (4) Each year, seasonal influenza sickens millions and causes thousands of hospitalizations and flu-related deaths.

   Which sentence should be revised to correct a misplaced modifier?

   A. sentence 1
   B. sentence 2
   C. sentence 3
   D. sentence 4

2. Read this sentence.

> The heavy, bulky box contained an invaluable relic that could be traced to the ancient Egyptians but John, unaware of its contents, broke it by sitting on the box.

Which edit should be made to correct this sentence?

E. delete the comma after *heavy*
F. insert a comma after *relic*
G. insert a comma after *Egyptians*
H. delete the comma after *John*

3. Read this paragraph.

> (1) Redfish Lake is located in central Idaho, where the majestic Sawtooth Range provides beautiful scenery. (2) The shores of Redfish Lake are filled with picnic areas and campsites with beach access and fantastic views. (3) The Redfish Lake Lodge offers overnight lodging, cabin options, a dining facility, bike and canoe rentals, public showers, and more, making this a great mountain beach destination. (4) You deserve some peace, this is the best place to get it.

Which sentence should be revised to correct a run-on?

A. sentence 1
B. sentence 2
C. sentence 3
D. sentence 4

4. Read this paragraph.

> (1) With a rover named Curiosity, Mars Science Laboratory is part of NASA's Mars Exploration Program. (2) They are a part of a long-term effort of robotic exploration of the red planet. (3) Curiosity was designed to assess whether Mars ever had an environment able to support small life forms called microbes. (4) In other words, its mission is to determine the planet's "habitability."

Which sentence should be revised to correct an inappropriate shift in pronoun?

E. sentence 1
F. sentence 2
G. sentence 3
H. sentence 4

5. Read this paragraph.

> (1) Jupiter is the fifth planet from our Sun and the largest planet in the solar system. (2) Its stripes and swirls are cold windy clouds of ammonia and water. (3) The atmosphere is mostly hydrogen and helium, and its iconic Great Red Spot is a giant storm bigger than Earth that has raged for hundreds of years. (4) Scientist have observed, however, that the Great Red Spot is shrinking in length but growing in height.

Which edit should be made to correct this paragraph?

A. add a comma after *Sun* in sentence 1
B. add a comma after *cold* in sentence 2
C. delete the comma after *helium* in sentence 3
D. delete the comma after *however* in sentence 4

6. Read this paragraph.

> (1) Fossils are the remains or traces of organisms that were once alive. (2) From the massive bones of dinosaurs to the delicate impression of a fern frond, fossils come in all shapes and sizes. (3) The remains of an actual organism, such as a shell, leaf, or bone, are known as body fossils, while fossils that record the action of an organism, such as a footprint or burrow, are known as trace fossils. (4) Paleontologists studied fossils to help understand the evolution and the history of life on Earth.

Which sentence should be revised to correct an inappropriate shift in verb tense?

E. sentence 1
F. sentence 2
G. sentence 3
H. sentence 4

> **Directions:** Read the passage below and answer the questions following it. You will be asked to improve the writing quality of the passage and to correct errors so that the passage follows the conventions of standard written English. You may reread the passage if you need to. Mark the best answer for each question.

Managing Wasted Food

(1) Wasted food is a growing problem today. (2) In 2014 alone, over 40 million tons of food waste was produced. (3) The Food and Agriculture Organization estimates that approximately a third of all food produced for human consumption worldwide is wasted. (4) Reducing waste can trim our waistlines and bulk up our wallets.

(5) When we waste food, we're not just creating a problem, we're also missing an opportunity to save money. (6) First, by keeping wasted food out of the garbage, homeowners may be able to save money by paying less for trash pickup. (7) Secondly, donating healthy, safe, and edible food to hungry people can have tax benefits in the form of charitable deductions. (8) Thirdly, many people, not only the well-to-do, but those in moderate circumstances, throw out a ridiculous amount of food. (9) Finding ways to prevent waste in the first place can lead to money saved, as well as reduction of energy and labor costs associated with food waste.

(10) Reducing wasted food can also be good for the environment. (11) When food goes to the landfill, it's no different from throwing out food in a plastic bag. (12) The nutrients in the food never return to the soil. (13) The wasted food rots and produces methane, which contributes to climate change. (14) Reducing food waste can not only mitigate global warming, but it saves water, gasoline, energy, labor, pesticides, land, and fertilizers used to make the food.

(15) If you can't prevent, reduce, or donate wasted food, consider composting. (16) Composting is an eco-friendly alternative to throwing out food. (17) By sending food scraps to a composting facility instead of to a landfill or composting at home, you're helping make healthy soils. (18) Compost processing typically costs less than recycling plastics or cans. (19) Properly composted organics improve soil health and structure, improve water retention, support more native plants, and reduce the need for fertilizers and pesticides.

(20) This is not to say that composting is a magic bullet, but it is one out of many tactics that we must use in order to conserve and reuse our resources.

7. Which sentence should replace sentence 4 to best introduce the main claim of the passage?

    A. One of the largest waste management companies derives a large part of its revenue from restaurant waste disposal.

    B. It is important to note that with wasted food also comes wasted opportunity.

    C. The problem of food waste is compounded by our demand for ethanol, a corn-based fuel.

    D. While the USDA recommends that we watch what we eat, the EPA tells us to watch what we don't eat.

8. Which of the following revisions should be made to sentence 5?

    E. When we waste food, we're not only creating a problem but also missing an opportunity to save money.

    F. When we waste food, we are not just creating a problem but also an opportunity to save money.

    G. We waste food, we create a problem, and we save money.

    H. Wasting food, we are not just creating a problem, but we miss opportunities to save money also.

9. Which revision of sentence 8 best maintains the formal style of the passage?

    A. Thirdly, many people, not only the well-to-do, but those in moderate circumstances, waste tons of food.

    B. Thirdly, many people, not only the well-to-do, but those in moderate circumstances, blow all their dough on food.

    C. Thirdly, many people, not only the well-to-do, but those in moderate circumstances, use needless quantities of food.

    D. Thirdly, many people, not only the well-to-do, but those in moderate circumstances, eat like a savage.

10. Which transition word or phrase should be added to the beginning of sentence 9?

    E. Due to this fact,
    F. In contrast,
    G. More importantly,
    H. Finally,

11. What is the best way to combine sentences 11 and 12 to clarify the relationship between the ideas?

    A. When food goes to the landfill, it's no different from throwing out food in a plastic bag since the nutrients in the food never return to the soil.

    B. When food goes to the landfill, it's no different from throwing out food in a plastic bag, but the nutrients in the food never return to the soil.

    C. Despite the food going into the landfill, it's no different from throwing out food in a plastic bag because the nutrients in the food never return to the soil.

    D. While food goes to the landfill, it's no different from throwing out food in a plastic bag, and the nutrients in the food never return to the soil.

12. Which sentence is irrelevant and should be removed?

    E. sentence 9

    F. sentence 14

    G. sentence 17

    H. sentence 18

13. Which concluding sentence should be added after sentence 20 to support the main claim presented in the passage?

    A. Another problem with food waste is the pollution, resulting from corporate agriculture.

    B. With the aid of science, waste management should soon be a problem of the past.

    C. We must find a way to encourage the conservation of resources or suffer the consequences.

    D. After all, the American public is notorious for waste and cannot be expected to change its behavior.

Graphene from Lingin

(1) Measuring one million times less than the width of a human hair, graphene is harder than diamonds and 200 times stronger than steel. (2) Small, strong, and flexible, they are the most conductive material on Earth. (3) Graphene has the potential to charge a cell phone in just five seconds or to upload a terabit of data in one. (4) It can be used to filter salt from water, develop bullet-stopping body armor, and create biomicrorobots. (5) They are all seeking to harness graphene's potential for applications in electronics, energy, composites and coatings, biomedicine, and other industries.

(6) Derived from graphite, the same graphite used in pencils and many other common-use products, graphene is, ironically, one of the most expensive materials on the planet. (7) The process of chemically peeling off, or exfoliating, a single layer of graphene from graphite ore is cost-prohibitive on an industrial scale. (8) Most labs and industries, recognizing that graphene is unprofitable, refuse to use it in their production process.

(9) A group of United States Department of Agriculture (USDA) scientists has developed a more cost-effective way to produce graphene from lignin rather than graphite. (10) Considered very lowly by the paper-making industry, lignin is what makes plants both strong and flexible, which contributes to making graphene so remarkable. (11) It is also an abundant source of renewable organic fertilizer. (12) USDA scientists have been working with lignin since 2010, when they were awarded a Biomass Research and Development Initiative grant. (13) The pilot project has produced a small quantity of graphene that will be shared with university and industry collaborators for further testing. (14) The USDA scientists are now working to further characterize lignin-graphene properties, including electronic/thermal conductivity, and streamlining the lignin-to-graphene conversion process. (15) They will also thoroughly analyze the safety of lignin-to-graphene production.

(16) The availability of large quantities of graphene will have a huge impact upon the development of lighter and stronger structural materials for the automotive, aerospace, and building industries, among others. (17) That's the hope anyway. (18) There is a good chance that it will take about twenty years.

14. Which sentence in paragraph 1 (sentences 1–5) should be revised to correct an inappropriate shift in pronoun?

    E. sentence 2
    F. sentence 3
    G. sentence 4
    H. sentence 5

15. Read this sentence.

> These incredible properties have captured the attention of scientists and industry specialists around the world.

Where should this sentence be added to best support the ideas in the first paragraph (sentences 1–5)?

    A. between sentences 1 and 2
    B. between sentences 2 and 3
    C. between sentences 3 and 4
    D. between sentences 4 and 5

16. Which transition word or phrase should be added to the beginning of sentence 8?

    E. As a result,
    F. However,
    G. Unfortunately,
    H. In other words,

17. Which sentence should be added before sentence 9 to help develop ideas in the third paragraph (sentences 9–15)?

    A. Most companies will continue to neglect this promising technological innovation.

    B. Scientists are a stubborn bunch, who will never give up on their research.

    C. Many scientific advances have been made by accident, and graphene is no outlier.

    D. This situation may change as the government takes the lead on graphene research.

18. Which sentence is irrelevant to the ideas presented in the third paragraph (sentences 9–15) and should be deleted?

    E. sentence 10

    F. sentence 11

    G. sentence 12

    H. sentence 13

19. Which revision of sentence 10 uses the most precise language?

    A. Considered a low-value byproduct of the paper-making industry, lignin is what gives plants their characteristics, thereby making graphene so remarkable.

    B. Considered a low-value byproduct of the paper-making industry, lignin is what gives plants their characteristics, thereby making graphene so strong.

    C. Considered a low-value byproduct of the paper-making industry, lignin is what makes the cell walls of plants rigid and woody, thereby making it both strong and flexible.

    D. Considered a low-value byproduct of the paper-making industry, lignin is what makes the cell walls of plants rigid and woody, thereby contributing to its tensile strength.

20. Which sentence could best replace sentence 18 and support the main point of the fourth paragraph (sentences 16–18)?

    E. Affordable industrial production of graphene has the potential to boost innovation and reduce costs of consumer goods.

    F. Graphene is typically translucent, but interaction with hydrogen and oxygen changes its color.

    G. Despite its promise, graphene still faces some regulatory hurdles that require extensive testing to ensure that it is safe for human use.

    H. The greatest inventions were made in a leap in the dark, but graphene is making solid strides toward the next step in our technological world.

Directions: Read each passage and answer the questions that follow it. Base your answers **only on the material contained in the passage**. Select the one **best** answer for each question. Bubble in the letter corresponding to that answer on the answer sheet.

I. The English language has undergone many changes in its long history and in fact is still evolving, although more slowly now *Line* than it did in the past. Its story began in (5) the fifth century C.E. when tribesmen later called Anglo-Saxons brought their dialects to the island now named England.

Anglo-Saxon, or Old English, was an inflected language—that is, one in which (10) the endings of words indicate grammatical function. For example, the Old English word meaning *stones* would be spelled *stanas* if it were the subject, but *stanum* if it were the direct object. Between the fifth and (15) fourteenth centuries, most of these endings disappeared.

Another major way in which the language has changed is in its vocabulary. The original inhabitants of England, the Celts, contrib- (20) uted only a few words to English, as did the eighth- and ninth-century Danish invaders, who spoke Old Norse. But after the Anglo-Saxons were converted to Christianity, many Latin words entered the language, and (25) scholars continued to add Latin words for several hundred years. The major change in English vocabulary, however, came with the Norman Conquest of 1066. The Normans brought their Norman French dialect with (30) them, and in the three hundred years following the Conquest thousands of French words entered the English language.

The most mysterious development in English had to do with pronunciation. Between the (35) late fourteenth and the late sixteenth century, English speakers, for some reason, began to pronounce their long vowels differently. This phenomenon is called the Great Vowel Shift, and it radically changed the sound of spo- (40) ken English. The word sheep, for example, formerly had a sound closer to the modern shape, while the word mouse used to sound somewhat like moose.

Our language has altered much less in (45) the last five hundred years than it did in the previous five hundred. The spelling of English is now standardized, and there have been no dramatic changes in vocabulary or pronunciation. But the language does (50) continue to develop. Although the rules of grammar are established, those rules are not immutable, and some formerly "unbreakable" laws have changed in recent years. For example, sentences may now end in prepo- (55) sitions, and infinitives may be split.

Vocabulary is still a factor in the ongoing evolution of our language. *Macho* from Latin America and *blitz* from Germany show that English remains hospitable to outside influ- (60) ences. Another important influence is technology. The familiar *laptop* does not appear in fifteen-year-old dictionaries, and the noun *mouse* appears, but only as a rodent or an undereye bruise. Our fifteen-hundred-year- (65) old language continues to grow.

21. Which of the following best tells what this passage is about?

   A. The reason why English is the earth's most influential language

   B. The evolution of the English language

   C. How new words come into a language

   D. Grammar and vocabulary changes in English from the beginning to the present

22. What is the meaning of "immutable" (line 52)?

   E. Contradictory

   F. Unacceptable

   G. Flexible

   H. Unchangeable

23. Which of the following is true of an inflected language?

   A. It has a varying pronunciation.

   B. Professional grammarians determine the endings of its words.

   C. Words have varying meanings depending on their spellings.

   D. The endings of some words change according to how they are used in a sentence.

24. According to the passage, which of the following has had the most influence on English vocabulary?

   E. Latin

   F. French

   G. Old Norse

   H. Modern technology

25. Why does the author call the Great Vowel Shift "mysterious"?

   A. No one knows why it happened.

   B. No one knows how the different vowel sounds are produced.

   C. There are no recordings to indicate the earlier sounds.

   D. No one knows when it happened.

26. Which of the following is an example of what the author of the passage calls the English language's being "hospitable to outside influences"?

   E. The English word *futon*, adopted from the Japanese language

   F. The word *pulsar*, introduced by astronomers in the late 1960s

   G. The Great Vowel Shift

   H. The dropping of inflections

II. A Greek myth tells of the engineer Daedalus, who used wax and feathers to fashion wings for himself and his son Icarus.
Line According to the story the two were able to
(5) escape from the island where they were held prisoner by flapping their wing-enhanced arms. In the fifteenth or sixteenth century, the great Leonardo da Vinci, perhaps intrigued by the Daedalus myth, investi-
(10) gated the possibility of human flight. His notebooks and sketches indicate that he studied aerodynamics and learned much about the design requirements of a workable wing.

(15) Earthbound human beings have always been fascinated by the bird's ability to fly. No one knows how many other inventors like Daedalus and Leonardo thought that they might be able to figure out the mysteries of
(20) successful wing design for human flight. But even if Leonardo or some other genius had designed the perfect wing, the human body's bulky, uneven shape and cumbersome weight would have kept it on the ground.

(25) A bird's body, unlike a human's, is a true marvel of aerodynamic engineering. Unlike the denser bones of Homo sapiens, many of the bones of a bird are hollow, and thus the bird's body is light enough to be wing
(30) borne. It is also designed for maximum flight efficiency, with most of the weight carried below the wings and a tapered shape that minimizes air resistance.

The wings of a bird are aerodynamic won-
(35) ders. A complex muscle system makes the
essential flapping motion possible, and the
shape of the wing makes it an excellent air-
foil. The forward part of the wing is curved
in such a way that air is pushed downward
(40) with each wing stroke, increasing the air
pressure under the wing. At the same time,
the air moving across the upper part of the
wings flows freely, decreasing the pressure
above the wing. The pressure differential
(45) creates the lift needed for flight. Once aloft,
birds can decrease drag, or air resistance, by
altering their angle of flight.

Feathers are another bird exclusive that
contribute to flight. The tapered lines of a
(50) bird's body are accentuated by the smooth
surface of its contour feathers, and the tail
and wings have flight feathers that assist in
taking off, navigation, and landing. On the
wings' downstroke, the wing flight feathers
(55) move in such a way that they provide a
propeller-like effect for thrust and maneu-
verability. Tail feathers act as rudders,
steering the bird in the direction it wishes
to go as it flies. For the complicated task of
(60) landing, the bird raises its body until it is
almost vertical and fans out its tail feathers.
As its rate of motion slows, feathers (called
the alula), folded back until now, move
forward to act as stabilizers, producing a
(65) smooth landing.

27. Which of the following best states the
author's purpose?

   A. To explain why flight has always
   fascinated humankind
   B. To explain why the Daedalus myth
   cannot be true
   C. To create a feeling of admiration for
   the wonders of the animal world
   D. To explain the complex design that
   makes bird flight possible

28. According to the passage, why could
a human body not fly even with well-
designed wings?

   E. Its muscles are not strong enough.
   F. It does not have feathers.
   G. It is too heavy and awkward.
   H. It is too large.

29. How do contour feathers assist flight?

   A. They make the bird's body lighter.
   B. They provide insulation.
   C. They help reduce air resistance.
   D. They assist in takeoff, navigation, and
   landing.

30. What is the function of the wing's curved
shape?

   E. It creates lift by altering the angle of
   flight.
   F. It increases pressure under the wing
   and lessens the pressure above.
   G. It directs the faster-moving air above
   the wing downward.
   H. It makes the flapping motion possible.

31. Which of the following is **not** given as part
of the landing maneuver?

   A. Decrease in speed
   B. "Rudder" action of the tail feathers
   C. Change in the position of the bird's
   body
   D. Movement of tail feathers

32. What does the passage suggest about
Leonardo da Vinci?

   E. His notebooks were hard to decipher.
   F. He tried unsuccessfully to build a flying
   machine.
   G. He did not understand the importance
   of feathers.
   H. He did not master all the principles of
   aerodynamics.

III. In 1969 scientists made a discovery destined to revolutionize the medical world's thinking about disease and its causes. The *Line* discovery was a copper protein that makes (5) possible the body's use of oxygen. Further study identified many substances of this type, whose interactions with other molecules in the body trigger a variety of useful reactions. Some, for example, stimulate (10) hormones active in fighting harmful bacteria and viruses. Free radicals, as these substances are called, had been identified before 1969, but until this time their functions had not been thoroughly understood.

(15) Ironically, this biochemical group also includes molecules that trigger harmful reactions. Today's medical experts are accusing the harmful free radicals of biological mayhem ranging from wrinkled skin to (20) cancer and Alzheimer's disease. And a problem is that some of the same processes that produce the helpful molecules also create their harmful opposites.

A free radical is a molecule with a free or (25) unpaired electron. The unpaired electron seeks a stable bond with available molecules. If it finds and bonds with a molecule in a nearby cell, it causes cell injuries including damaged walls, weakened DNA, (30) and altered chemistry. Thus crippled, cells can no longer function adequately to maintain the body's health. A host of illnesses that used to be considered a natural part of aging are now known to be associated with (35) the action of free radicals.

Fortunately, human beings can defend their bodies against the ravages of free radicals. It is known that many external factors are linked to free radical damage: cigarette (40) smoke, alcohol, ultraviolet light, and pesticides are some examples. Obviously, then, one thing people can do for the health of their bodies is to avoid substances and radiation that lead to the production of these

(45) harmful particles. At this time, though, total protection is not possible. Is the body, then, helpless against attack?

The welcome answer is "no." In addition to maintaining a healthful lifestyle, (50) people can fight free radical damage with a group of chemicals called antioxidants. Antioxidants are able to make free radicals harmless by altering their molecular structure. Nutritionists therefore recom- (55) mend a diet high in vitamins A, C, and E. Furthermore, some experts also recommend supplemental doses of these as well as of melatonin and selenium.

As scientists learn more about free radical (60) harm and antioxidant protection, some are predicting that medicine will change course in the next century. The treatment and prevention of disease, say these experts, will rely heavily on the use of antioxidants to (65) control free radicals. Drugs, which now lead the fight against illness, will be relegated to a secondary role.

33. Which of the following best expresses the author's purpose?

   A. To give medical advice on a little-known problem in the area of disease prevention

   B. To explain the difference between similar molecules produced in the human body

   C. To inform the reader of relatively recent discoveries concerning disease and its prevention

   D. To explain why medicine will be revolutionized in the near future

34. Which of the following is **not** true concerning free radicals?

   E. A healthful lifestyle will prevent the formation of free radicals in the human body.

   F. They are attracted to other molecules or atoms.

   G. Some are important to the body's healthy functioning.

   H. Antioxidants prevent them from attacking other cells.

35. What are the harmful opposites mentioned in (line 23)?

   A. Molecules that cause cell damage

   B. Harmful external factors such as smoking

   C. Diseases caused by free radicals

   D. Antioxidants

36. How do free radicals cause disease?

   E. They cripple the disease-fighting "good" free radicals.

   F. They stimulate hormones that strengthen bacteria and viruses.

   G. They increase the intensity of ultraviolet light.

   H. They weaken the cells that they attack.

37. What does the passage suggest about antioxidants?

   A. They destroy free radicals in the human body.

   B. They can eliminate disease in human beings by controlling the action of free radicals.

   C. They will completely destroy the pharmaceutical industry.

   D. They can eliminate some of the ills of aging.

38. What aspect of the molecular structure of a free radical causes its damaging effects?

   E. One of its components causes it to invade nearby cells.

   F. It contains environmental toxins.

   G. Its free electron upsets the hydrogen balance in the body.

   H. The unpaired electron results in electrolyte imbalance within the healthy cell.

IV. Light pollution is not new, but it has been widely recognized as a serious problem only in recent years. With the spread
Line of urban areas has come the invasion of
(5) nighttime lighting in areas that used to be dark after sundown. In the suburbs, too, the night is brighter, lit by glaring street lights, home security lamps, and massive shopping centers beaming upward at the sky. It is
(10) harder and harder to find a spot where a person can gaze upward at a star-filled sky.

Environmentalists worry because too much nighttime light can upset natural patterns in both plant and animal life. For example,
(15) endangered sea turtles will not lay their eggs on brightly lit beaches. Cultures such as the Inuit, to whom the constellations have strong significance, find the transmission of their legends hampered. Amateur
(20) skygazers can see little because the ambient light is brighter than all but the brightest stars. Even professional astronomy, with all its advanced technology, is suffering from the interference of this noxious pollution.
(25) Important observatories such as Mount Wilson and Goethe Link can no longer see as much as they did in former years, and in fact the earth's light is so strong that it actually interferes with signals from space.

(30) The earth is not doomed, however, to live with an orange night sky. Shielding the upper regions from unwanted light is not forbiddingly difficult. One simple approach is to design fixtures so that their light is

(35) directed downward, adequately illuminating the target area without spilling unwanted brightness outward and upward. Lamps that produce excessive glare, like mercury vapor fixtures, can be replaced by less glar-
(40) ing appliances. Such measures are practical as well as being environmentally friendly. Experts argue that much home-security lighting is poorly designed in that it is too diffuse and inappropriately directed, some-
(45) times actually providing handy shadows for a lurking burglar! More careful design and placement not only avoid polluting the sky but offer better protection. Also, since better-designed systems for every purpose
(50) would put light only where it is needed, they would be economical and energy efficient.

Action is being taken to deal with the situation. Some state and local governments have passed antilight-pollution laws. Maine and
(55) New Mexico are leading the way for other states, and counties and cities across the nation are following suit. Environmental and astronomical groups such as the International Dark-Sky Association are working to restore
(60) a more natural night. And in July 1999, the International Astronomical Union convened in Austria to consider the extent of the problem and possible solutions. Perhaps in the next millennium, Earth dwellers will
(65) once again have a night sky brightened only by celestial lights.

39. Which of the following best tells what this passage is about?

  A. A serious technological problem for astronomers
  B. A new form of pollution
  C. Improvements in lighting design and how to implement them
  D. Causes, results, and possible solutions of a problem

40. All of the following are mentioned in the passage as effects of light pollution **except**

  E. interference in astronomical studies.
  F. negative impact on biological processes.
  G. fewer opportunities for watching the night sky.
  H. closing down of some important observatories.

41. According to the passage, which of the following is true about the reduction of light pollution?

  A. It is expensive but worth the investment.
  B. It yields significant incidental benefits.
  C. It requires technology not presently available.
  D. It results in an orange night sky.

42. In what sense is light pollution a penalty paid for growth?

  E. It encourages urban sprawl by providing well-lighted areas
  F. Light pollution exists only in densely populated regions.
  G. It mainly develops because of security concerns.
  H. It tends to increase as populated areas grow.

43. What is the meaning of the word "noxious" (line 24)?

  A. Harmful
  B. Unusual
  C. Subtle
  D. Urban

44. How do brightly lit beaches threaten the survival of the sea turtle?

  E. They force female sea turtles to lay eggs in dangerous open water.
  F. They prevent the sea turtles from mating.
  G. They interfere with reproduction.
  H. They interrupt the balance between time in the ocean and time on dry land.

V. Even before her death in September 1997, it was widely assumed that Mother Teresa of Calcutta was destined for official
Line sainthood in the Roman Catholic Church.
(5) She had become a worldwide hero through her dedication to the poor. Moreover, her prayerful lifestyle and adherence to Catholic teaching marked her as a true daughter of her Church.

(10) Mother Teresa was born in 1910 of Albanian parents in the town of Shkup, in what is now the Former Yugoslav Republic of Macedonia. At the age of eighteen she joined the Sisters of Loreto and was sent
(15) to Darjeeling, India, to serve her years as a novice. In 1931 she began teaching at Loreto House, a Calcutta girls' school for the daughters of the elite. But Sister Teresa was drawn to a different kind of ministry,
(20) and fifteen years later she left the upper-class world for the slums of Calcutta. In the next four years she recruited others—Indian women—to assist her in her work on the streets, and in 1950 the Missionaries of
(25) Charity was given official recognition by the Vatican.

It took the citizens of Calcutta several years to trust this woman who, by Indian standards, behaved so strangely. One of her
(30) special ministries was to the dying poor and homeless who, in "normal" circumstances, would die alone, without care or comfort. The 1952 opening of the Nirmal Hriday ("Pure Heart") Home for Dying Destitutes
(35) was a puzzle for Hindus. They did not understand why Mother Teresa was so determined to soften what they saw as a welcome escape from earthbound existence. They were also cynical about her
(40) interest in destitute children. The order called itself "Missionaries," after all, and sheltering ignorant children could be seen as an easy way to pick up converts to Christianity. Furthermore, with India so
(45) plagued by overpopulation, her teachings against abortion and birth control seemed both wrong-headed and subversive.

Mother Teresa proved her sincerity when she opened a facility to provide care for
(50) lepers, the outcasts of India. Skeptics finally acknowledged that the Missionaries of Charity were indeed dedicated to the service of the destitute and abandoned.

Mother Teresa's stature grew both in
(55) Calcutta and throughout India. In 1963 the government of India recognized her work with an official award, the Padmashri. Her fame spread until she achieved worldwide recognition as a holy person devoted to
(60) the service of God and others. The Nobel Peace Prize in 1979 seemed a fitting reward for such a woman. In later life, until her health began to fail, Mother Teresa traveled widely, establishing her ministry on other
(65) continents. She was welcomed with honor wherever she went, and when she died, the world mourned the loss of a holy person.

45. Which of the following best tells what this passage is about?

   A. How Mother Teresa won the hearts of the people of India
   B. The wretched conditions of the poor of Calcutta
   C. A change of direction in the life of a nun
   D. The life of a twentieth-century holy woman

46. Why were the people of Calcutta skeptical about Mother Teresa's work?

   E. They didn't like Roman Catholics.
   F. They doubted that her main goal was to serve the poor.
   G. They thought that her attentions to the dying were insincere.
   H. They thought that her work with lepers was a scheme to gain converts.

47. What does the passage suggest about Mother Teresa?

    A. She disliked working with children.

    B. She was reluctant to leave the comforts of "upper-class" life.

    C. She thought that overpopulation was manageable without resorting to artificial birth control.

    D. She was ambitious for fame and honor.

48. Which of the following is the meaning of the word "novice" as it is used in line 16?

    E. Servant of the poor and destitute

    F. Citizen of Calcutta

    G. Child

    H. New member of a religious order

49. Which of the following is not stated in the passage?

    A. Mother Teresa was publicly honored by her adopted country.

    B. As a young woman Mother Teresa joined an order of nuns.

    C. Mother Teresa was officially named a saint of her Church.

    D. Mother Teresa extended her missionary work beyond India.

50. Which of the following most closely parallels the work of Mother Teresa?

    E. Providing free medical care to the poor

    F. Establishing a religious school for young children

    G. Operating a health education clinic

    H. Campaigning for population control

VI. A few days before Woodrow Wilson took office as president of the United States in 1913, Mexico's General Victoriano Huerta overthrew the Mexican government (5) of President Francisco Madero and installed himself as its new leader. Wilson wanted to focus on issues at home, and since this event had the potential to distract from domestic reform measures he wanted Congress to (10) pass, Mexico became one of Wilson's main foreign policy concerns.

Developing a foreign policy toward Mexico was not an easy process for Wilson and his administration as they struggled to learn (15) what was happening during Mexico's revolution. Their primary source of information, the Department of State, was unreliable, so Wilson pulled together a network of formal and informal sources to observe and report (20) on events occurring in Mexico.

Wilson's attempts to acquire information about Mexico's revolution demonstrate the difficulties presidents often encountered before there was a government intelligence (25) agency in the United States. Until the office of Coordinator of Information was established in 1941, many presidents faced similar problems in gathering information.

Prior to the 1950s, collecting intelligence (30) on people, places, and events was severely restricted. Today's advanced computer and satellite technology, used to gather imagery, intercept communications, and parse data wasn't available during the early 1900s. (35) Instead, Wilson had to rely on simpler sources of information, such as reports from diplomats or newspapers. However, these sources presented many conflicting perspectives of the situation in Mexico, and (40) President Wilson was wary of relying upon them for policy-making decisions.

Presented with conflicting information, Wilson looked for more reliable sources. First he turned to a reporter, William (45) Bayard Hale. Hale was a trustworthy writer who worked for a progressive publication. Hale was delegated to tour the Latin America states, get a firm grasp of the situation, and report back to Wilson.

(50) Hale spent a month in Mexico before he sent his first report to President Wilson. Hale's comprehensive reports and analytical conclusions confirmed Wilson's worst fears. President Madero had been overthrown in a (55) coup begun by Huerta, who was opposed to his reforms. To make matters worse, Huerta staged the coup only because the U.S. ambassador to Mexico promised support. Because of Hale's reports, President Wilson (60) recalled the ambassador and excluded him from further engagements with Mexico.

Wilson continued to use the information he received from Hale and other assigned reporters to find the truth and eliminate (65) his own uncertainties about which Mexican revolutionary group to aid. Wilson believed that pieces of truth had to be put together in order to get a bigger picture—the trick was to separate the facts from the propa- (70) ganda and mistruths.

51. Which of the following best tells what this passage is about?

  A. a collapse of the Mexican government
  B. the victory of General Victoriano Huerta
  C. the advances in intelligence collection
  D. the attempts of Woodrow Wilson to gain more information

52. Why did Wilson want to focus on the revolt in Mexico?

  E. He wanted to strengthen relations between the United States and its neighbors.
  F. He felt that it was America's responsibility.
  G. He saw that it could endanger his agenda.
  H. He felt Mexicans could provide more information about the world.

53. The author refers to the office of the Coordinator of Information to

  A. emphasize Wilson's struggles in collecting usable information.
  B. highlight the advances made in the intelligence community.
  C. identify the first attempt at collecting intelligence.
  D. provide information on the history of the Mexican revolution.

54. Which evidence best supports the idea that Wilson did not trust the government as a source of information?

  E. the details about Victoriano Huerta's revolt
  F. the details about the State Department
  G. the details about William Bayard Hale
  H. the details about other Mexican revolutionary groups

55. How does the fourth paragraph contribute to the passage?

  A. It describes an important turning point in intelligence collection.
  B. It highlights Wilson's role as an important figure in history.
  C. It promotes the adoption of technology.
  D. It provides a contrast to justify Wilson's actions.

56. Why was the ambassador to Mexico recalled?

   E. He brought valuable information to Wilson.

   F. He failed to bring valuable information to Wilson.

   G. He did not take his job seriously.

   H. He was instrumental in the Mexican revolution.

57. What evidence does the author provide to support the last sentence of the passage?

   A. Victoriano Huerta became leader.

   B. Wilson established the Coordinator of Information.

   C. Today's technology has advanced greatly.

   D. Wilson used Hale and other reporters to gain information.

PART 2—MATHEMATICS

QUESTIONS 58–114

SUGGESTED TIME: 90 MINUTES

Grid-In Problems

Directions: Solve each problem. On the answer sheet, write your answer in the boxes at the top of the grid. Start on the left side of each grid. Print only one number or symbol in each box. **DO NOT LEAVE A BOX BLANK IN THE MIDDLE OF AN ANSWER.** Under each box, fill in the circle that matches the number or symbol you wrote above. **DO NOT FILL IN A CIRCLE UNDER AN UNUSED BOX.**

58. What is the solution to the equation below?

$$\frac{0.42}{0.63} = \frac{x}{1.23}$$

59. Point C is to be placed one-third of the way from point A to point B. What number will be at the midpoint of $\overline{AC}$?

60. If $\frac{a}{b} = 15$ and $a = 3$, what is the value of

$4b + a^2$?

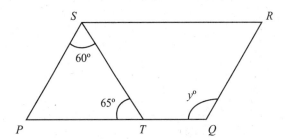

61. In the figure above, $PQRS$ is a parallelogram. The measure of $\angle PST$ is 60°, and the measure of $\angle PTS$ is 65°. What is the value of y?

62. Jane is now 18 years old. In 8 years, she will be twice as old as her nephew will be at that time. How old is her nephew now?

Multiple-Choice Problems

Directions: For each of the following questions, select the **best** answer from the given choices. Bubble in the letter corresponding to your answer on the answer sheet. **DO NOT PUT ANY OTHER WORK ON THE ANSWER SHEET.** All necessary work can be done in your test booklet or on scrap paper that is provided.

NOTE: Diagrams other than graphs might not be drawn to scale. Do not assume any relationships that are not specifically stated unless they are implied by the given information.

63. $\dfrac{3^3 + 3^2 + 3}{3} =$

    A. 9
    B. 12
    C. 13
    D. 18

64. After Richard gave 10% of his money to charity, he had $180 left. How much money did he have originally?

    E. $216
    F. $200
    G. $195
    H. $172

65. $(a - 1) - (a - 2) + (a - 3) =$

    A. $-a + 4$
    B. $a + 4$
    C. $a - 6$
    D. $a - 2$

66. $.\overline{3} + \dfrac{1}{6} =$

    E. .4
    F. .6

    G. $\dfrac{2}{3}$

    H. $\dfrac{1}{2}$

67. In Mr. Chin's math class there were g girls and b boys. The number of girls was 5 less than twice the number of boys. Which of the following represents the value of g in terms of b?

    A. $5 + 2b$
    B. $5 - 2b$
    C. $2b - 5$
    D. $b + 10$

68. On line segment $\overline{AB}$, $AY = XB = 30$ and $XY = 7$. What is the length of $\overline{AB}$?

    E. 44
    F. 53
    G. 60
    H. 67

69. If $4(x - 3) = 3(x - 4)$, then $x =$

    A. 0
    B. -24
    C. 24

    D. $\dfrac{24}{7}$

70. The least common multiple of 2, 3, 4, 5, and 6 is

   E. $2 \times 3 \times 4 \times 5 \times 6$
   F. $2 \times 3 \times 4 \times 5$
   G. $2 \times 3 \times 5$
   H. $3 \times 4 \times 5$

71. $(6)(6) + (-6)(-6) =$

   A. 0
   B. 24
   C. 72
   D. none of these

72. A room is 20 feet long, 15 feet wide, and 12 feet high. If it costs 20¢ per square foot to paint walls, 30¢ per square foot to paint a ceiling, and 10¢ per square foot to paint a floor, how much does it cost to paint just the four walls of the room?

   E. $48
   F. $84
   G. $96
   H. $168

73. $.26 \times .37$ is closest to

   A. $\dfrac{1}{4}$

   B. $\dfrac{3}{32}$

   C. $\dfrac{3}{5}$

   D. $\dfrac{2}{3}$

74. The mean of a, b, and c is 80. The mean of a, b, c, d, and e is 84. What is the mean of d and e?

   E. 87
   F. 88
   G. 89
   H. 90

75. As shown in the straight line graph, the ABC Telephone Company charges an initial fee of $5 per month and then charges a fixed amount for each minute of phone call time. *What is that fixed amount charge* for each minute of phone call time?

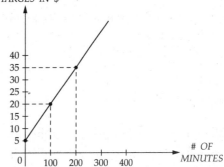

   A. 20¢
   B. 15¢
   C. 10¢
   D. 7.5¢

76. The area of square *ABCD* is 9. The area of trapezoid *CDEF* is 24. The area of square *EFGH* is 81. Then the height of the trapezoid is

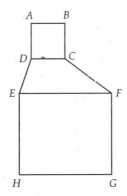

   E. 4
   F. 5
   G. 6
   H. 7

77. During a dull football game, $\frac{1}{4}$ of the spectators left after 1 hour. During the next hour another 20,000 spectators left. There were now $\frac{1}{12}$ of the original number of spectators still watching the game. How many spectators were originally present?

A. 120,000
B. 60,000
C. 40,000
D. 30,000

78. What is the smallest prime number that is 2 more than a positive multiple of 7?

E. 9
F. 19
G. 23
H. 37

79. One-third of the sum of P, Q, and R is 21. If $P + Q = 46$, then $R =$

A. −25
B. 17
C. 25
D. 50

80. In the figure, point B is on line segment $\overline{AC}$ and point D is on line segment $\overline{AE}$. The value of $x + y$ is

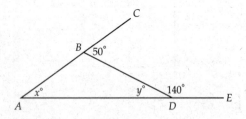

E. 50°
F. 70°
G. 75°
H. 90°

81. If $709 - x = 199$, then the value of $720 - x$ is

A. 520
B. 510
C. 210
D. 189

82. The figure shows two circles, one entirely within the other. The area of the entire large circle is 9 times the area of the small circle. Then the ratio of the *shaded* area to the *unshaded* area is

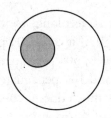

E. 1:9
F. 1:8
G. 1:18
H. 1:16

83. Let x represent a positive integer. Which of the following *must* be true?

A. If $5x$ is even, then x must be even.
B. If $5 + x$ is odd, then x must be odd.
C. If $3x + 7$ is even, then x must be even.
D. If $x + 1$ is even, then $x + 12$ must be even.

84. For any positive integer n, let $\Diamond n \Diamond$ represent the *number of odd factors* of n. For example, $\Diamond 15 \Diamond = 4$ because 15 has exactly 4 odd factors [1, 3, 5, and 15]. Which of the following has the largest value?

E. $\Diamond 10 \Diamond$
F. $\Diamond 12 \Diamond$
G. $\Diamond 25 \Diamond$
H. $\Diamond 27 \Diamond$

85. In the figure, rectangle $ABCD$ is drawn in the coordinate plane with its sides parallel to the axes. The area of $ABCD$ is

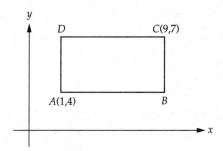

A. 4
B. 6
C. 24
D. 30

86. In a scale diagram, 1 inch represents 5 feet. On the same diagram, how many square inches would represent 1 square foot?

E. 25
F. 4
G. .4
H. .04

87. On the number line, point R (not shown) is to the right of Q, and PQ is $\frac{1}{5}$ of PR. What is the coordinate of R?

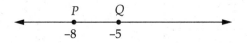

A. 7
B. 15
C. 23
D. 25

88. $-3x(7y-5) =$

E. $21xy - 15x$
F. $-10xy + 8x$
G. $-21xy + 15x$
H. $10xy + 8x$

89. In writing the integers from 1 to 50 inclusive, how many times is the digit "2" written?

A. 5
B. 13
C. 14
D. 15

90. Let $x = 3y$ and $y = 3z$. If $y = 30$, then the value of $(x + y + z)$ is

E. 390
F. 130
G. 90
H. $43\frac{1}{3}$

91. If M and N are positive integers, then the statement "One-ninth of M is greater than one-eighth of N" is equivalent to

A. $\dfrac{N}{M} > \dfrac{8}{9}$

B. $MN > 72$
C. $N - M > 1$
D. $8M > 9N$

92. The sum $2^{10} + 1^{10} + \left(\frac{1}{2}\right)^{10} + \left(\frac{1}{3}\right)^{10} + \left(\frac{1}{4}\right)^{10}$ is closest to

E. 21
F. 32
G. 513
H. 1,025

93. If $2x(x - y) = 54$ and $x = 9$, then $y =$

A. 6
B. 3
C. 2
D. 1

94. What is the acute angle formed by the hands of a clock at 2:00?

E. 30°
F. 36°
G. 45°
H. 60°

95. In the figure, the area of the entire circle is twice the area of the entire rectangle. If the shaded area is removed, then the remaining area of the circle would be 9 more than the remaining area of the rectangle. The area of the rectangle

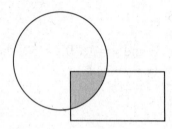

A. is 6
B. is 9
C. is 12
D. cannot be determined from the given information

96. In rectangle *ABCD, E* is a point on $\overline{DC}$. The area of rectangle *ABCD* is 120. The area of triangle *AEB*

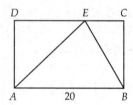

E. is 30
F. is 50
G. is 60
H. cannot be determined from the given information

97. In the following pattern, each letter represents some number:
P Q 6 *R S T* 10
The sum of any three consecutive numbers in the pattern is 21. Then

A. *Q* is 11
B. *Q* is 10
C. *Q* is 5
D. there is more than one possible value for *Q*

98. Six bleeps equal 13 floops, and 2 floops equal 5 geebles. Based on this, 1 bleep is equal to *N* geebles. The integer closest to *N* is

E. 2
F. 3
G. 4
H. 5

99. If the base and the height of a rectangle are each doubled, the area of the original rectangle will be multiplied by

A. 2
B. 4
C. 8
D. The answer depends on the lengths of the sides of the original rectangle.

100. Alan ran $\frac{5}{6}$ the distance run by Ilayne.

Alan ran $8\frac{1}{3}$ miles. How many miles did Ilayne run?

E. $6\frac{17}{18}$

F. 7

G. $7\frac{5}{18}$

H. 10

101. If $\frac{a}{b} = \frac{1}{3}$, where *a* and *b* are each greater than 3, which one of the following must also equal $\frac{1}{3}$?

A. $\frac{3ab}{a+b}$

B. $\frac{a+b}{3ab}$

C. $\frac{a+b}{3a}$

D. $\frac{b}{9a}$

102. The probability that Roberto wins is $\frac{1}{3}$ the probability that Roberto loses.

What is the probability that Roberto loses?

E. $\frac{1}{4}$

F. 1

G. $\frac{1}{3}$

H. $\frac{3}{4}$

103. x and y are positive integers and $x + y = 11$. What is the largest possible value of

$$\frac{1}{x} - \frac{1}{y} ?$$

A. $\frac{1}{30}$

B. $\frac{9}{10}$

C. 1

D. 9

104. What is the *smallest* prime p such that one-fifth of p is greater than 12?

E. 3
F. 13
G. 49
H. 61

105. Express the product of 8×10^2 and 8×10^4 in scientific notation.

A. 6.4×10^7
B. 64×10^6
C. 6.4×10^6
D. 6.4×10^5

106. In the figure, a square with perimeter 20 is contained within a square of perimeter P. The area of the shaded region is 56. Then the *perimeter* of the larger square is

E. 81
F. 76
G. 36
H. 32

107. The table shows what two different companies charge for shipping packages, based on the weight of the package. How many pounds does a package weigh if the charge for shipping that package is the same by both companies?

SHIPPING COMPANY	FIRST POUND	EACH ADDITIONAL POUND
AERO FREIGHT	$9.50	$3.95
BETTER EXPRESS	$8.00	$4.10

A. 101
B. 51
C. 31
D. 11

108. The total value of some coins is $1.20. The coins contain nickels, dimes, and quarters only (*at least one of each kind*). What is the fewest number of coins possible?

E. 5
F. 6
G. 7
H. 8

109. It takes 12 men 4 hours to do a certain job. Working at the same rate, how many hours would it take 8 men to do that job?

A. 2

B. $\frac{8}{3}$

C. 3

D. 6

110. In the diagram, O is the center of the circle. What is the area of the shaded region?

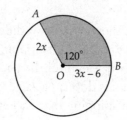

E. 48π

F. 12π

G. 8π

H. Cannot be determined from the given information.

111. Which of the following points is closest to the point $(4, 5)$?

A. $(4, 0)$

B. $(0, 5)$

C. $(0, 0)$

D. $(-4, 5)$

112. Which one of the following *cannot* be the product of two consecutive integers?

E. 9,900

F. 15,750

G. 20,448

H. 38,612

113. The mean of x and y is 6. The mean of 1, 3, $5x$, and $5y$ is

A. 8.5

B. 12

C. 16

D. 32

114. Lily is unable to solve two multiple-choice questions, each having exactly four answer choices. She decides to randomly guess. Each choice has the same chance of being selected, and her choice selection on one question does not influence her choice selection on the other question. What is the probability that Lily answers at least one of the two questions correctly?

E. $\frac{7}{16}$

F. $\frac{1}{2}$

G. $\frac{9}{16}$

H. $\frac{15}{16}$

Revising/Editing Part A

1. **A**   3. **D**   5. **B**
2. **G**   4. **F**   6. **H**

Revising/Editing Part B

7. **B**   10. **H**   13. **C**   16. **E**   19. **D**
8. **E**   11. **A**   14. **E**   17. **D**   20. **E**
9. **C**   12. **H**   15. **D**   18. **F**

Reading

21. **B**   29. **C**   37. **D**   45. **D**   53. **A**
22. **H**   30. **F**   38. **E**   46. **F**   54. **F**
23. **D**   31. **B**   39. **D**   47. **C**   55. **D**
24. **F**   32. **H**   40. **H**   48. **H**   56. **H**
25. **A**   33. **C**   41. **B**   49. **C**   57. **D**
26. **E**   34. **E**   42. **H**   50. **E**
27. **D**   35. **A**   43. **A**   51. **D**
28. **G**   36. **H**   44. **G**   52. **G**

Mathematics

58. **0.82**   70. **H**   82. **F**   94. **H**   106. **G**
59. **−5.5**   71. **C**   83. **A**   95. **B**   107. **D**
60. **9.8**   72. **H**   84. **H**   96. **G**   108. **G**
61. **125**   73. **B**   85. **C**   97. **C**   109. **D**
62. **5**   74. **H**   86. **H**   98. **H**   110. **E**
63. **C**   75. **B**   87. **A**   99. **B**   111. **B**
64. **F**   76. **E**   88. **G**   100. **H**   112. **G**
65. **D**   77. **D**   89. **D**   101. **D**   113. **C**
66. **H**   78. **G**   90. **F**   102. **H**   114. **E**
67. **C**   79. **B**   91. **D**   103. **B**
68. **F**   80. **E**   92. **H**   104. **H**
69. **A**   81. **C**   93. **A**   105. **A**

Revising/Editing Part A

1. **(A)** Examine the pairings of <u>modifiers</u> and *modified object*s below.

    Incorrect: <u>A contagious respiratory infection,</u> *people infected with the seasonal flu virus*

    Correct: <u>A contagious respiratory infection,</u> *the seasonal flu virus*

2. **(G)** Rule number 1: FANBOYS clause: *but John, unaware of the box's contents, broke it by sitting on the box* is a FANBOYS clause. Therefore, a comma is necessary to split it with the independent clause before it.

3. **(D)** Sentence 1 contains an independent clause and a dependent clause. This is not a run-on.

Redfish Lake is located in central Idaho	where the majestic . . .
Independent Clause	Dependent Clause

    Sentence 2 contains an independent clause and a prepositional phrase. This is not a run-on.

The shores of Redfish . . . campsites	with beach access . . .
Independent Clause	Independent Clause

    Sentence 3 contains an independent clause and a modifier.

The Redfish Lake Lodge offers . . . and more	makes this a great . . .
Independent Clause	Prepositional Phrase

    Sentence 4 contains two independent clauses joined by a comma. This is a run-on.

You deserve some peace	this is the best place to get it
Independent Clause	Independent Clause

    Correction: You deserve some peace, *and* this is the best place to get it.

4. **(F)** Examine the pairings of <u>antecedents</u> and *pronouns* below.

    (1) With a rover named Curiosity, <u>Mars Science Laboratory</u> is part of NASA's Mars Exploration Program. (2) *They* are a part of a long-term effort of robotic exploration of the red planet. (3) <u>Curiosity</u> was designed to assess whether Mars ever had an environment able to support small life forms called microbes. (4) In other words, *its* mission is to determine the planet's "habitability."

    Sentence 1: Does not contain a pronoun.

    Sentence 2: The plural pronoun *they* is an inappropriate replacement for the antecedent <u>Mars Science Laboratory.</u> *They* should be revised to *It*.

    Sentence 3: Does not contain a pronoun.

    Sentence 4: The singular pronoun *its* properly replaces the antecedent *Curiosity*.

5. **(B)** The adjectives *cold* and *windy* are coordinate adjectives, meaning they can be used interchangeably with the word *and* to describe clouds. A comma is necessary to indicate that.

    Choice A is wrong because there are only two characteristics that the word AND connects: the fifth planet . . . and the largest planet.

    Choice C is wrong because the comma is necessary for the FANBOYS clause. And yes—you can have two *ands* in a sentence. The first *and* is used to complete a list. The second *and* is used to start a FANBOYS clause.

    Choice D is wrong because the commas are necessary around the word *however* to indicate a pause.

6. **(H)** Examine all the predicate verbs underlined below.

    (1) Fossils <u>are</u> the remains or traces of organisms that <u>were</u> once alive. (2) From the

massive bones of dinosaurs to the delicate impression of a fern frond, fossils <u>come</u> in all shapes and sizes. (3) The remains of an actual organism, such as a shell, leaf, or bone, <u>are known</u> as body fossils, while fossils that record the action of an organism, such as a footprint or burrow, <u>are known</u> as trace fossils. (4) Paleontologists <u>studied</u> fossils to help understand the evolution and the history of life on Earth.

The paragraph is written in the present tense and the predicate verb that doesn't agree is the past tense verb *studied.*

Revising/Editing Part B

7. **(B)** The phrase *wasted opportunity* best links with the phrase *an opportunity to save money* in sentence 5.

8. **(E)** The sentence is a run-on consisting of a dependent clause, an independent clause, and an independent clause. To fix this, one of the independent clauses needs to be changed to a dependent clause or a phrase.

   Choice F is wrong because *not just . . . but also* is awkward. Typically, the phrase should be *not only . . . but also.* Secondly, the wording after *not just* should be similar to the wording after *but also.* For example, *not just <u>creating a problem</u> but also <u>solving a problem</u>* would be similar.

   Choice G is wrong because there are three independent clauses listed unnecessarily.

   Choice H is wrong because the wording after *not just . . . but* is not similar.

9. **(C)** The passage uses formal language (like a textbook). Wording that uses informal choices (words and phrases you would normally see in casual conversation) should be removed.

   Choice A is wrong because *tons of food* is informal.

   Choice B is wrong because *blow all their dough* is informal.

Choice D is wrong because *eat like a savage* is informal.

10. **(H)** Sentences 6 through 8 all introduce their ideas in order. The transition word *Finally* best fits in with *First* of sentence 6, *Secondly* of sentence 7, and *Thirdly* of sentence 8.

11. **(A)** Choices B, C, and D are wrong because they all create contrasts with the words *but, Despite,* and *While.*

12. **(H)** The passage discusses the eco-friendly alternative rather than the cost benefits.

13. **(C)** The passage deals with the harms of wasted food and one possible solution. Choice C best addresses that idea.

    Choice A is wrong because it begins a new topic of agricultural pollution.

    Choice B is wrong because it contradicts sentence 20.

    Choice D is wrong because its negative outlook contradicts the hopeful tone in sentence 20.

14. **(E)** The plural pronoun *they* replaces the singular *graphene* in sentence 1. The pronoun should therefore be the singular *it.*

15. **(D)** The phrase *These incredible properties* links with the characteristics of graphene outline in sentence 4. The phrase *scientists and industry specialists* connects with the pronoun *They* in sentence 5.

16. **(E)** Sentence 7 mentions that graphene is costly. Sentence 8 explains the effect of the *cost-prohibitive* aspect of graphene. The best transition is the causal transition *As a result.*

17. **(D)** Sentence 9 identifies a particular government agency, the USDA, with regard to developing research on graphene.

18. **(F)** The passage discusses the USDA's research on graphene, but sentence 11 goes off topic and discusses other uses for lignin.

19. (D)

Least Precise (cross out)	Most Precise
their characteristics strong and flexible	the cell walls of plants rigid and woody,
making graphene so remarkable	contributing to its tensile strength
making it both strong and flexible	

20. (E) The paragraph discusses the possibilities of graphene in the industrial sector. Choice E introduces the positive aspects of those possibilities.

Reading

Passage I

21. (B) Main Idea This question requires a broad answer that incorporates all the information in the passage. A involves information that is neither stated nor implied in the passage. While it may be true that the changes English has undergone contribute to its influence, you must base your answer only on the information given. B is correct because the entire passage is about changes in the language from its beginning to the present, and the word *evolution* is general enough to include all the changes. C involves only part of the passage. D involves most of the passage but does not cover the paragraph on pronunciation changes.

22. (H) Inference Questions on word meanings will ask you to rely on the context in which the word is used. E is incorrect because there is no idea of contradiction in the context. F is wrong because the context concerns grammar development, and the sentence containing the word *immutable* is followed by examples of development or change, not of acceptance. G is incorrect because the context actually suggests some flexibility in the rules. H is correct because the context shows that

the grammar rules do change and thus are not unchangeable.

23. (D) Detail A is an example of the need to rely on the context. Inflection, which involves tone or pitch, may seem to involve pronunciation; however, the sentence gives a definition of an inflected language that clearly limits the term to grammar.

> **FACT:** When a word has more than one meaning, context determines meaning.

B is wrong because there is no statement or implication about professional grammarians deciding upon word endings. C might possibly be an acceptable answer if the word *meanings* is interpreted very loosely, however, D is clearly the best answer because grammar, as the example involving *stanas* clearly illustrates, involves how words are used in a sentence.

24. (F) Detail F is the only possible correct response because the passage clearly states that the "major change in English vocabulary" occurred when the Normans brought French to England.

25. (A) Inference A is the correct answer because the sentence following the one that calls the Great Vowel Shift "mysterious" says that "for some reason" people started changing their pronunciation. B is incorrect because there is no statement or suggestion about how vowel sounds are produced. C is true, but it provides a good example of why you must base your answers on the content of the passage. There are, of course, no recordings of speech that were made at that time, but the passage does not mention or suggest this fact.

> **FACT:** An answer may be true but incorrect.

26. (E) Inference E is correct because the Japanese language is an "outside" factor and "hospitable" implies giving a welcome; so the English language welcomed this "outsider," a Japanese word. Furthermore, the sentence involved gives two examples of this hospitality, and they are both foreign words. F gives an example of a new word from technology, which the passage identifies as a separate category of influence on vocabulary. G and H are incorrect because nothing in the passage states or suggests that outside influences affected the Great Vowel Shift or the dropping of inflections.

Passage II

27. **(D)** Main Idea Determining the author's purpose can be difficult because it involves recognizing the main idea of a passage and, in some cases, the author's attitude as well. A is a tempting response because the second paragraph states that human beings are fascinated by birds' flying ability. The passage, however, does not dwell on this idea of fascination or even mention it again after this paragraph. B is true for the same reason; the information probably does show that Daedalus could not have flown, but the passage does not stress this idea. C is too broad; birds are the only animals discussed. D is correct because most of the passage carries out the purpose of explaining how a bird can fly. Paragraphs one and two, while not giving such explanation, lead up to it, and both mention the form requirements of flight.

28. **(G)** Detail The correct answer is stated clearly in the last sentence of paragraph two.

29. **(C)** Detail The correct answer is clearly stated, but in two different places in the passage. It is stated in lines 50–51 that contour feathers accentuate the bird's tapered shape. In line 33 it is stated that the bird's tapered body minimizes air resistance.

30. **(F)** Detail E is incorrect because nothing in the passage connects angle of flight to wing shape. The fourth paragraph states that the curved shape of the wing creates the air-pressure difference, so F is correct. G is incorrect because while the shape of the wing does push air downward, the air pushed is not the air above the wing. H is incorrect because it

contradicts the second sentence of paragraph four.

31. **(B)** Detail The last two sentences in the passage explain landing. The rudder action of tail feathers is not mentioned in these sentences, but in the sentence just before, which explains steering, not landing.

32. **(H)** Inference Although an inference question requires you to understand ideas or facts that are suggested rather than stated, you still must base your response on the passage. You cannot rely on anything you know or think unless it is stated in the passage. H is correct because the passage states (line 12) that Leonardo learned "much" about the requirements of a wing. The word "much" indicates that there are things he did not learn. None of the other choices are mentioned in connection with Leonardo.

Passage III

33. **(C)** Main Idea Although the passage does suggest ways of avoiding free radical damage, A is too narrow. Most of the passage does not involve advice. B and D are also too narrow. Only the first two paragraphs consider the similarity and difference of the molecules, so B is incorrect. Only the last three sentences in the passage mention the revolutionizing of medicine, making D incorrect. Only C covers all the information in the passage.

34. **(E)** Detail A question asking what is *not* true requires you to locate details in the passage.

> **TIP:** The correct answer choice may be worded differently from the wording in the passage.

E is correct because the passage states (line 46) that a healthful lifestyle cannot offer "total protection" against free radicals. F is given in the words "seeks a stable bond with available molecules" (lines 26–27). G summarizes information given in the first paragraph. H is stated in lines 52–53, in the words "able to make free radicals harmless."

Since the radicals harm cells by attacking them, this statement about antioxidants is true.

35. **(A)** Detail   A is correct because the pronoun *their* (line 23) refers to helpful molecules. The opposite of helpful molecules is harmful molecules—the free radicals that damage cells.

36. **(H)** Detail   The third paragraph describes cells attacked by free radicals as "crippled" (line 30). Thus H is correct.

37. **(D)** Inference   A is incorrect because the passage states that antioxidants make free radicals "harmless" (line 53). This language does not suggest destruction of the free radicals. B and C are both too exaggerated. The passage states that many illnesses (line 32) are caused by free radicals, not all illnesses. Thus controlling the free radicals will not eliminate all disease.

> **TIP:** Be very careful about choosing an answer including "all," "every," "always," and so on. Such an answer may be correct, but it may well be a trap.

The word "completely" in C makes it too extreme. Drugs will still have a "secondary" role, and so the pharmaceutical industry will still be in existence. D is correct; the suggestion is made in two different sentences. The passage states (lines 52–53) that antioxidants make free radicals harmless and also (line 34) that free radicals "are associated" with illness of aging. It can be inferred that antioxidants can "eliminate some of the ills of aging."

38. **(E)** Detail The correct answer is found in the third paragraph. The "component" mentioned is the free radical's unpaired electron.

Passage IV

39. **(D)** Main Idea

> **FACT:** The correct answer to a main idea question must be broad enough and also accurate.

A is too narrow, as the passage discusses light pollution as a problem in several areas, not just astronomy. B is broad enough but not accurate, as the word "new" contradicts the first sentence of the passage. D is correct because it names every topic covered in the passage.

40. **(H)** Detail   The other choices are all mentioned in the second paragraph. H is inaccurate as the passage mentions problems of two observatories but not their being closed down.

41. **(B)** Detail   This question requires you to summarize details. The third paragraph discusses the reduction of light pollution. B is correct because the paragraph mentions as incidental benefits better security, economy, and energy efficiency. A contradicts the paragraph's statement (line 51) that such measures are economical. C contradicts the information given in the paragraph. D is inaccurate as the "orange sky" (line 31) is the light-polluted sky.

42. **(H)** Inference   E is not stated in the passage; the passage says (lines 4–5) that urban sprawl produces light, not that light produces or encourages urban sprawl. F is too extreme. The word "only" contradicts the information (line 6) that suburbs, which are not always densely populated, can also be light polluted. G is also too extreme; security lighting is mentioned as being polluting, but not as a *main* cause of light pollution. H is correct according to the information on the growth of urban areas (lines 3–4) and its effect on lighting.

43. **(A)** Inference   You must depend on the context to determine a word's definition. The passage says that astronomy suffers from "noxious" (line 24) light pollution. A factor that causes suffering can be called "harmful." You should check the other choices, however. B is wrong because the passage make it clear that light pollution is common today. C is wrong because it is unrelated to the context, which involves a problem. D is too limited,

as light pollution has been stated as involving the suburbs also (line 6).

44. **(G)** Detail. The passage states that light pollution affects egg-laying. Only G refers to egg-laying.

Passage V

45. **(D)** Main Idea   A, B, and C are all too narrow because they each involve only one part of the passage. D is the only choice both broad enough and accurate.

46. **(F)** Inference   G is wrong because it is not stated or suggested in the passage. F is correct because the passage states that the citizens were cynical about Mother Teresa's work with children because such work could result in converts (line 43). In other words, that she had an ulterior motive for working with the poor. G is inaccurate because the passage states that the citizens did not understand her work with the dying, but does not suggest that they thought it was insincere. H is also inaccurate because Mother Teresa's work with lepers is what finally convinced the citizens of her sincerity.

47. **(C)** Inference   A is not supported by the passage. Mother Teresa left her teaching job because she was "drawn to a different kind of ministry"; furthermore, this new ministry involved working with children. B contradicts the statement that she was "drawn," attracted away, from the upper-class life. C is correct although the inference is subtle. Mother Teresa preached against abortion and artificial birth control, and yet she was deeply concerned for the welfare of the people; therefore, she must have thought that the problem of overpopulation was somehow manageable by other means. D is incorrect because while she gained fame and honor, nothing in the passage states or suggests that she sought it or even enjoyed it.

48. **(H)** Inference   The second paragraph states (line 14) that Mother Teresa joined the religious order and was sent to India for her years as a novice. The suggestion is that she went to India right after joining; this context clue implies that a novice must be a new member of an order. E is wrong because she was not yet serving the poor. F contradicts the information given, as she went to Darjeeling. G is wrong because she was eighteen at the time, not a child.

49. **(C)** Detail   All of the other choices are stated in the passage. C is correct because while it is stated that she was expected to be made an official saint, it is not stated that this has happened.

> **TIP:** Marking details as you read can help you locoate the correct answer.

50. **(E)** Main Idea   E is the best choice because the main idea in the description of Mother Teresa's work is that she cared for the poor. None of the other choices are parallel to anything stated in the passage about Mother Teresa's work, and H actually contrasts her teachings against abortion and artificial birth control.

Passage VI

51. **(D)** Main Idea   Choices A and B provide the context in which Wilson began his mission, but neither choice is what the entire passage is about. Choice C is wrong because the passage describes advances in intelligence collection only as they affect President Wilson and not in an overall general sense.

52. **(G)** Detail   Lines 6–11 clearly show why he was interested in Mexico.

53. **(A)** Detail   The first sentence of the paragraph introduces Wilson's difficulties. The mention of the office of the Coordinator of Information emphasizes those difficulties by way of contrast.

54. **(F)** Inference   Line 17 clearly states that for reporting primary information, Wilson found the State Department "unreliable."

55. **(D)** Main Idea   This paragraph provides a contrast between the period before the 1950s

and today to show that Wilson had reasons to look for another way to collect information.

56. **(H)** Detail   Lines 56–58 provide information that clearly supports H.

57. **(D)** Inference   The last sentence states that he needed "pieces of truth." Choice D best describes Hale and the other reporters, who can be considered "pieces of truth."

Mathematics

58. **(0.82)** Multiply the numerator and denominator of both fractions by 100 to get $\frac{42}{63} = \frac{100x}{123}$. The left side can be simplified, since $\frac{42}{63} = \frac{6 \times 7}{9 \times 7} = \frac{6}{9} = \frac{2}{3}$, so $\frac{2}{3} = \frac{100x}{123}$. Multiplying both sides of the equation by 123 yields $\frac{2}{3}(123) = 100x$. Now:

$$\frac{2}{3}(123) = 2\left(\frac{123}{3}\right) = 2(41) = 82$$

Thus $100x = 82$, and so $x = \frac{82}{100} = 0.82$.

59. **(–5.5)** Since A is located at –8 and B is located at 7, the distance from point A to point B is 15 units. One-third of 15 is 5, so point C is located five units to the right of A, which is –3. The midpoint of A and C is therefore:

$$\frac{-8 + -3}{2} = \frac{-11}{2} = -5.5$$

60. **(9.8)** Since $a = 3$, we can solve for b. Since $\frac{a}{b} = 15$, we have $b = \frac{a}{15} = \frac{3}{15} = \frac{1}{5}$. Thus:

$$4b + a^2 = 4\left(\frac{1}{5}\right) + 3^2 = \frac{4}{5} + 9 = 0.8 + 9 = 9.8$$

61. **(125)** The measures of the three interior angles in any triangle sum to 180°, so we know that the measure of $\angle SPT$ is:

$$180° - 60° - 65° = 55°$$

Since adjacent angles in a parallelogram are supplementary, we know that $y + 55 = 180$, so $y = 125$. Alternately, we know that

the measure of $\angle TSR$ is 65°, since $\overline{SR} \parallel \overline{PQ}$ and $\angle TSR$ and $\angle PTS$ are alternate interior angles. Thus, the measure of $\angle PSR$ is $60° + 65° = 125°$, and since opposite angles in a parallelogram are congruent, $y = 125$.

62. **(5)** In 8 years, Jane will be $18 + 8 = 26$ years old, and her nephew will be half that age, or 13 years old. The nephew's current age is thus $13 - 8 = 5$.

63. **(C)** Divide each term of the numerator by 3, getting $3^2 + 3 + 1 = 13$. Alternatively, combine the terms of the numerator first, getting 39, then divide by 3.

64. **(F)** \$180 must be 90% of what he started with. Dividing both numbers by 9, we see that \$20 is 10% of his starting money, so he started with $10 \times \$20 = \$200$.

65. **(D)** Removing parentheses produces $a - 1 - a + 2 + a - 3 = a - 2$.

66. **(H)** This is $\frac{1}{3} + \frac{1}{6} = \frac{3}{6} = \frac{1}{2}$.

67. **(C)** Twice the number of boys is represented by $2b$, so 5 less than that is $2b - 5$.

68. **(F)** Subtracting 7 from 30 shows that $AX = 23$ and $YB = 23$. Then $AB = 23 + 7 + 23 = 53$. Another approach would be to add AY and $XB = 60$, then realize that XY was counted twice. Subtracting 7 once produces the correct answer.

69. **(A)** Multiplying out, we have $4x - 12 = 3x - 12$, so $x = 0$.

70. **(H)** These numbers, expressed in terms of their prime factors, are 2, 3, 2^2, 5, and $2 \cdot 3$. The least common multiple is $2^2 \cdot 3 \cdot 5$.

71. **(C)** The sum is $36 + 36 = 72$.

72. **(H)** The total area of the four walls is $12 \cdot 15 + 12 \cdot 20 + 12 \cdot 15 + 12 \cdot 20 = 840$ square feet. The cost of painting is $840 \cdot 20¢ = \$168$.

73. **(B)** This product is a little more than $\frac{1}{4} \times \frac{1}{3}$, which is $\frac{1}{12}$. The respective choices are approximately (or exactly) $\frac{1}{4}$, $\frac{1}{10}$, $\frac{1}{2}$, $\frac{2}{3}$, and $\frac{1}{5}$. The closest to $\frac{1}{12}$ is B.

74. **(H)**

> **TIP:** If the mean of n numbers is A, then the numbers add up to $n \times A$.

$a + b + c + d + e = 5 \times 84 = 420$, while $a + b + c = 3 \times 80 = 240$. Subtracting these equations produces $d + e = 180$, so the mean of d and e is $\frac{180}{2} = 90$.

75. **(B)** Eliminating the initial $5 fee, we see that 100 minutes of phone call time costs $15. Therefore each minute of phone call time costs 15¢.

76. **(E)**

> **FACT:** The area of a trapezoid is $\frac{1}{2}h(b_1 + b_2)$, where h is its height, and b_1 and b_2 are the lengths of its bases.

From the areas of the squares, we see that DC must be 3 and EF must be 9. Applying the formula for the area of a trapezoid, we have $24 = \frac{1}{2} \cdot h(3 + 9) = 6h$. Therefore, $h = 4$.

77. **(D)** $\frac{11}{12}$ of the spectators left during the first two hours. Since $\frac{1}{4}(=\frac{3}{12})$ left during the first hour, the other $\frac{8}{12}$ left during that second hour. Therefore, $\frac{8}{12}(=\frac{2}{3})$ of the spectators is 20,000. Then $\frac{1}{3}$ is 10,000 and

$\frac{3}{3}$ is 30,000. If you prefer, you can use algebra as follows: If x is the original number of spectators, then $\frac{x}{4} + 20{,}000 = \frac{11}{12}x$. Multiplying both sides of this equation by 12 produces $3x + 240{,}000 = 11x$, leading to $x = 30{,}000$. A third approach would be to try each of the choices.

78. **(G)** Trying small multiples of 7 and adding 2 to each quickly produces $21 + 2 = 23$, which is a prime.

79. **(B)** $P + Q + R = 3 \times 21 = 63$. Subtracting $46 (= P + Q)$ from both sides of the equation produces $R = 17$.

80. **(E)**

> **FACT:** An exterior angle of a triangle is equal to the sum of the two remote interior angles.

The fact above immediately produces the answer 50. The 140° is not needed.

81. **(C)** Instead of solving for x, just add 11 to both sides of the equation. This produces $720 - x = 210$.

82. **(F)** If the area of the small circle is x, then the area of the large circle is $9x$. The unshaded area is $9x - x = 8x$. Then the ratio of the shaded area to the unshaded area is $x : 8x$, which is 1:8.

83. **(A)** This is the type of problem where you examine each choice. However, it is immediately clear that choice A is correct!

> **FACT:** If the product of two integers is even, at least one of them must be even.

There is no need to waste time looking at the other choices. You should go right on to the next problem.

84. **(H)** Here we *must* examine all of the choices. The number 10 has two odd factors (1 and 5). The number 12 also has two. The number 27 has four (1, 3, 9, and 27). The answer is H.

85. **(C)** The height (above the x axis) of point D is the same as the height of point $C\ (= 7)$, so $AD = 7 - 4 = 3$. The length of $\overline{AB}$ is $9 - 1 = 8$. Therefore the area of the rectangle is $3 \times 8 = 24$.

86. **(H)** If 1 inch represents 5 feet, then 1 square inch represents 25 square feet. Therefore $\frac{1}{25}\ (= .04)$ square inches represents 1 square foot. Did you spend too much time on this problem?

> **TIP:** If a problem gives you too much trouble, move on!

87. **(A)** $PQ = 3$, so PR must equal 15. Now 15 more than -8 is $+7$.

88. **(G)** Multiplying, and being careful of signs, we get $-21xy + 15x$.

89. **(D)** Writing the integers from 1 through 9 requires writing the digit "2" only 1 time. The same is true each time when we write the integers from 10 through 19, 30 through 39, and 40 through 49. So far we have written the digit "2" 4 times all together. The tricky part is counting the digit "2" when we write the integers from 20 through 29. This requires writing that digit 11 times (try it). The final total is $11 + 4 = 15$.

90. **(F)** If $y = 30$, then $x = 90$ and $z = 10$. The value of $x + y + z$ is 130.

91. **(D)** The statement, when written in symbols, says $\frac{M}{9} > \frac{N}{8}$.

> **FACT:** For positive numbers a, b, c, and d,
> $\frac{a}{b} > \frac{c}{d}$, if and only if $ad > bc$.

Then $8M > 9N$. That is choice D.

92. **(H)** The first two terms add up to 1,025. The other three terms are extremely small [for example, $\left(\frac{1}{2}\right)^{10} = \frac{1}{1024}$] and barely affect the total. The correct choice is H.

93. **(A)** Substituting $x = 9$ into the equation, we have $18(9 - y) = 54$. Therefore $9 - y = 3$, so $y = 6$.

94. **(H)** At 3:00, the hands form a 90° angle. The angle at 2:00 is $\frac{2}{3}$ of $90° = 60°$, so the answer is H. A much harder problem is to find the angle between the hands at 2:05 or 2:15. For example, at 2:05 the minute hand would be on the 1, but the hour hand would have gone *past* the 2! That hour hand would have traveled $\frac{1}{12}$ of the distance from the 2 to the 3, which is $\frac{1}{12}$ of 30°. The angle between the hands at 2:05 would be $32\frac{1}{2}°$.

95. **(B)** If the area of the rectangle is R, then the area of the circle is given to be $2R$. If the shaded area is x, then we have $2R - x = (R - x) + 9$. This is $2R - x = R - x + 9$, so $R = 9$.

96. **(G)** Since the area of the rectangle is 120, its height must be 6. But in triangle AEB, that would be the same as the length of an altitude from point E to base $\overline{AB}$. The area of a triangle is $\left(\frac{1}{2}\right)$(height)(base) $= \left(\frac{1}{2}\right)(6)(20) = 60$. No matter where E is located along $\overline{DC}$, the area of triangle AEB will be half the area of the rectangle.

97. **(C)** The sum of R, S, and T is the same as the sum of S, T, and 10. Therefore R must equal 10. Then $Q + 6 + R = Q + 6 + 10 = 21$, so $Q = 5$.

98. **(H)** Using single letters to stand for the "nonsense words," we have $6b = 13f$ and $2f = 5g$. We can relate b and g if we can

eliminate the *f*s. One easy way to do this is to change each equation to an equivalent one. Multiplying each side of the first equation by 2, and each side of the second equation by 13, we get $12b = 26f$ and $26f = 65g$.

Therefore $12b = 65g$, so $1b = \dfrac{65}{12}g$. That means $N = \dfrac{65}{12} = 5\dfrac{5}{12}$. The integer closest to N is 5.

99. **(B)** If the base and height of the original rectangle are *b* and *h,* then its area is $(b)(h)$. The base and height of the new rectangle are $2b$ and $2h$, so its area is $(2b)(2h)$, which equals $4bh$. Thus the new area is 4 times the original area.

100. **(H)** If the distance run by Ilayne is *D*, then $8\dfrac{1}{3} = \dfrac{25}{3} = \dfrac{5}{6}D$. Multiplying each side of this equation by 6 produces $50 = 5D$, so $D = 10$.

101. **(D)** If $\dfrac{a}{b} = \dfrac{1}{3}$, then $b = 3a$. Replacing *b* with $3a$ in each of the choices allows us to evaluate them more easily. The choices become $\dfrac{9a^2}{4a}$, $\dfrac{4a}{9a^2}$, $\dfrac{4a}{3a}$, and $\dfrac{3a}{9a}$. The last choice is the only one that must equal $\dfrac{1}{3}$. This problem can also be done by choosing a simple value for *a*, such as 4. Then $b = 12$, and only the last choice equals $\dfrac{1}{3}$ (if more than one choice became $\dfrac{1}{3}$ you must try another value for *a*).

102. **(H)**

Let *L* be the probability that Roberto loses. The probability that he wins is given as $\dfrac{1}{3}L$. Then $\dfrac{1}{3}L + L = 1$. Multiplying each side of

this equation by 3, we get $L + 3L = 3$. Then $4L = 3$, so $L = \dfrac{3}{4}$.

103. **(B)** The fraction $\dfrac{1}{x}$ will be largest when the positive integer *x* is as small as possible. Similarly, $\dfrac{1}{y}$ will be smallest when the positive integer *y* is as large as possible. Therefore the greatest difference will occur when $x = 1$ and $y = 10$.

That difference will be $\dfrac{1}{1} - \dfrac{1}{10} = 1 - \dfrac{1}{10} = \dfrac{9}{10}$.

104. **(H)** Since one-fifth of *p* is greater than 12, then *p* is greater than $(5)(12) = 60$. The smallest prime greater than 60 is 61.

105. **(A)** The product is $(8)(10^2)(8)(10^4)$. Rearranging terms before multiplying, we get $(8)(8)(10^2)(10^4) = (64)(10^6) = 6.4 \times 10^7$.

106. **(G)** The side of the smaller square is 5, so its area is 25. Adding on the shaded area produces the area of the larger square. Therefore the area of the larger square is $25 + 56 = 81$. Then the side of the larger square must be 9, so its perimeter is 36.

107. **(D)** If the package weighs $x + 1$ pounds, then the first company will charge (in dollars) $9.50 + 3.95x$. The second company will charge $8.00 + 4.10x$. Setting these expressions equal to one another, we have $9.50 + 3.95x = 8.00 + 4.10x$. The easiest

way to solve for x is to first multiply both sides by 100 to eliminate all decimal points. We then solve $950 + 395x = 800 + 410x$. This leads to $150 = 15x$, so $x = 10$. *But this is not the final answer to the problem.* The weight of the package is $x + 1 = 11$ pounds.

> **TIP:** The value of x is not always the answer to the problem!

Trying choices and finding out what the companies would charge in each case is very time consuming, and not an efficient way to do this problem.

108. **(G)** We are required to have at least one nickel, one dime, and one quarter. These 3 coins total 40¢. We still have 80¢ to go. The fewest coins that total 80¢ would be 3 quarters and 1 nickel. That makes a total of 7 coins needed.

109. **(D)** The job takes $12 \times 4 = 48$ man-hours to do. If there are only 8 men, they must work for 6 hours (because $8 \times 6 = 48$) to get the job done.

110. **(E)** The angle at the center of the circle is $\frac{1}{3}$ of 360°, so the shaded region is $\frac{1}{3}$ of the entire circle. We must find the area of the circle. All radii of a circle are equal, so we set $2x = 3x - 6$. This produces $x = 6$, so the radius $(= 2x)$ is 12.

> **TIP:** The value of x is not always the answer to the problem!

The area of the circle is equal to πr^2, which is 144π. Therefore the shaded area is $\frac{1}{3}(144\pi) = 48\pi$.

111. **(B)** The distance between $(4, 5)$ and $(4, 0)$ is 5 units. The distance between $(4, 5)$ and $(0, 5)$ is 4 units. Now consider the rectangle with vertices $(0, 0)$, $(4, 0)$, $(4, 5)$, and $(0, 5)$. We have already found that the lengths of two sides of that rectangle are 5 and 4. The line segment joining $(0, 0)$ and $(4, 5)$ is a

diagonal of the rectangle, so it is longer than either side. The final two choices are clearly more than 4. The answer is B.

112. **(G)** This is an unusual problem. When two consecutive integers are multiplied, the product can only end in 0×1, 1×2, 2×3, 3×4, 4×5, 5×6, 6×7, 7×8, 8×9, or 9×0 (those are the possible final digits of the numbers we are multiplying together). These products only end in 0s, 2s, or 6s! Therefore such a product cannot end in an 8 (that is choice G). What can the product of three consecutive integers end in? How about four consecutive integers?

113. **(C)** We have $\frac{(x + y)}{2} = 6$, so $x + y = 12$. Now $\frac{5(x + y) + 4}{4} = \frac{5(12) + 4}{4} = \frac{64}{4} = 16$.

Also, if averaged numbers are unknown and not needed specifically, you can say each number equals the average. If $x = 6$ and $y = 6$ then:
$$\frac{1 + 3 + 5(6) + 5(6)}{4} = \text{new average}$$

114. **(E)** Note that p, the probability of guessing a correct answer to a question having four answer choices, is $\frac{1}{4}$. The probability of getting a question wrong is $\frac{3}{4}$. We may approach this problem first by computing the probability that Lily answers *both questions incorrectly*. This is computed by multiplying $\frac{3}{4}$ by $\frac{3}{4}$, since the events are independent. Thus, the probability that Lily answers *both questions incorrectly* is $\frac{9}{16}$. Subtracting $\frac{9}{16}$ from 1 gives us the probability that Lily does *NOT answer both questions incorrectly*, meaning that she had to answer at least one of the two questions correctly. The correct answer to the problem is $1 - \frac{9}{16} = \frac{7}{16}$. Try doing this problem directly by listing all possible favorable outcomes or by making a tree diagram.

Ninth-Grade Mathematics Supplement

Practice Problems

This section provides a brief sampling of some of the types of problems that can appear on the ninth-grade form of the admissions test.

Topics covered on the 9th-year test may vary as curricula change. Problems marked with an asterisk (*) represent topics that have not appeared recently.

1. If $6! + 7! + 8! = (n)(6!)$, then the value of n is

    A. 15
    B. 16
    C. 63
    D. 64

2. $\dfrac{x \cdot x^2 \cdot x^3 \cdot x^4 \cdot x^5}{x^8 \cdot x^{15}} =$

    E. x
    F. x^{-8}
    G. x^8
    H. $\dfrac{5}{2}$

3. The volume of a cube is 64. What is its total surface area?

    A. 128
    B. 96
    C. 72
    D. 64

4. Which of the following ordered pairs (x, y) satisfies *both* of the inequalities $y \geq 3x + 8$ and $y < x$?

    E. $(2, 1)$
    F. $(2, -1)$
    G. $(8, -1)$
    H. $(-8, -9)$

5. The value of $\dfrac{12!}{9!}$ is

    A. $\dfrac{4}{3}$
    B. 3
    C. 3!
    D. 1320

6. Which of the following is the only one that can be (and is) the sum of 5 consecutive integers?

    E. 43,210
    F. 43,211
    G. 43,212
    H. 43,213

*7. In right triangle ABC, hypotenuse $AB = 25$. If $\cos A = .28$, then $AC =$

    A. 2.4
    B. 7
    C. 15
    D. 24

8. For which of the following values of L will the lines whose equations are $3x + 4y = 10$ and $12x + 16y = L$ be parallel?

   I. $L = 0$
   II. $L = 10$
   III. $L = -10$

   E. I only
   F. II only
   G. III only
   H. I, II, and III

9. The product of the ages of three teenagers is 3705, and their ages are integers. The sum of their ages

   A. is less than 45
   B. is 47
   C. is 51
   D. cannot be determined from the information given

10. What is the smallest integer x for which the sides of a triangle can be $2x$, $4x + 10$, and $6x - 21$?

   E. 1
   F. 2
   G. 7
   H. 8

11. A jar contains only white and black marbles. The probability of picking a black marble is $\frac{1}{10}$. One red marble is added to the original jar. Now the probability of picking a black marble

   A. is $\frac{1}{3}$

   B. is $\frac{1}{10}$

   C. is $\frac{1}{11}$

   D. cannot be determined from the information given

12. In the diagram, the lines $y = ax - 10$ and $x + 3y = 20$ intersect at the point (n, n). What is the value of a?

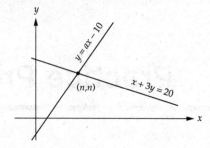

   E. 1
   F. 2
   G. 3
   H. 4

13. A pyramid has a triangular base whose sides are 3, 4, and 5 meters. If the volume of the pyramid is 24 cubic meters, what is the height (to that base) of the pyramid, in meters?

   A. 12
   B. 8
   C. 6
   D. 2

*14. A polyhedron is made up of 10 triangular faces. How many vertices does the polyhedron have?

   E. 7
   F. 10
   G. 15
   H. 22

*15. In right triangle ABC, $AC = 6$ and $BC = 8$. The sine of angle y is

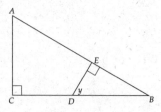

   A. .6
   B. .75
   C. .8
   D. 1

16. The measure of each interior angle of a regular polygon is 156°. How many sides does the polygon have?

    E. 12
    F. 15
    G. 24
    H. cannot be determined from the information given

17. If $x + y = 10$ and $xy = 20$, then $\dfrac{1}{x} + \dfrac{1}{y} =$

    A. $\dfrac{1}{10}$
    B. 10
    C. $\dfrac{1}{2}$
    D. 2

18. Let x be a number greater than 10. Which of the following is closest to $x(x-1)$?

    E. x^2
    F. $(x-1)^2$
    G. x
    H. $x-1$

19. Two vertices of a square are $(12, 0)$ and $(12, 12)$. What is the smallest possible area the square can have?

    A. $24\sqrt{2}$
    B. 36
    C. 48
    D. 72

20. In triangle ABC, $AB = AC = 18$, and $BC = 10$. If $\overline{PQ} \parallel \overline{AC}$ and $\overline{RQ} \parallel \overline{AB}$, then the perimeter of quadrilateral $APQR$ is

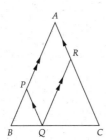

    E. 18
    F. 20
    G. 23
    H. 36

21. If $\dfrac{a}{b} = -6$, then $\dfrac{a+b}{a-b}$

    A. $-\dfrac{7}{6}$
    B. -1
    C. $\dfrac{5}{7}$
    D. $\dfrac{7}{6}$

22. Let x, y, and z be positive numbers such that $5x = 3y = 7z$. Which one of the following inequalities must be true?

    E. $x < y < z$
    F. $x < z < y$
    G. $y < x < z$
    H. $z < x < y$

23. In the diagram, line segment $\overline{AC}$ is a diagonal of square $ABCD$ and triangle ABE is equilateral. What is the measure of $\angle AFE$?

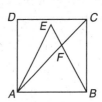

    A. 120°
    B. 105°
    C. 75°
    D. 60°

24. An equivalent value of $\left(4\dfrac{1}{4}\right)^2$ is

    E. $8\dfrac{1}{2}$
    F. $16\dfrac{1}{16}$
    G. $16\dfrac{1}{4}$
    H. $18\dfrac{1}{16}$

25. Let $M = .\overline{35} + \dfrac{1}{11}$. The value of M may

also be expressed as

A. $.\overline{36}$

B. $.\overline{46}$

C. $\dfrac{4}{99}$

D. $\dfrac{4}{9}$

26. The point $A(3,4)$ is rotated about the origin to point $A'(x,y)$. Which one of the following **cannot** be a possible value for x?

E. 6

F. 4

G. 2

H. −3

27. The original price of an item is discounted by 30%. In order to restore this discounted price to the original price, the discounted price must be increased by x%, where x is **closest** to

A. 23

B. 30

C. 35

D. 43

28. If $\dfrac{4^4 + 4^4}{4} = 2^x$, then $x =$

E. 7

F. 14

G. 16

H. 20

29. Line segment $\overline{AB}$ in the *xy*-coordinate plane has endpoints $A(1,1)$ and $B(9,13)$. *How many* points, **both** of whose coordinates are integers, are on segment $\overline{AB}$? Include points A and B in the total count.

A. 2

B. 3

C. 5

D. 8

30. A formula for converting temperature from degrees Centigrade (Celsius) to degrees Fahrenheit is $F = \dfrac{9}{5}C + 32$. Which of the following graphs *best* represents this relation?

E.

F.

G.

H.

31. The sum of two nonnegative numbers A and B is 20. Let P represent the product of A and B. Which one of the following graphs best represents the relationship between A and P?

A.
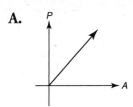

B.
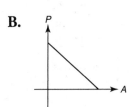

C.
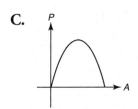

D.
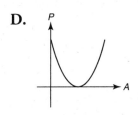

32. In how many different ways can a team of 3 boys and 2 girls be formed if there are 4 boys and 5 girls from which to select and Robert (one of the boys) **must** be on the team?

E. 6
F. 20
G. 30
H. 40

33. The graph of a certain relation is known to be symmetric about the line $x = 3$. If the point $A(8,7)$ is on this graph, which one of the following points **must** also be on the graph?

A. (–8,7)
B. (–2,7)
C. (–3,7)
D. (3,7)

34. In $\triangle ABC$, altitudes $\overline{BD}$ and $\overline{CE}$ intersect at F as shown in the figure. $\angle ABD$ is labeled 1, $\angle CBD$ is labeled 2, $\angle BCE$ is labeled 3, $\angle ACE$ is labeled 4, and $\angle CFD$ is labeled 5. Which one of the following pairs of angles **must** be congruent?

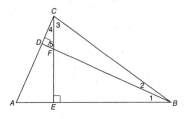

E. 1 and 4
F. 2 and 3
G. 3 and 4
H. 3 and 5

35. Each edge of a rectangular box has integer length. If the volume of the box is 72 cubic inches and one face is a square, what is the *smallest* possible total surface area of the box (in square inches)?

A. 100
B. 114
C. 120
D. 152

ANSWER KEY
Practice Problems

1. **D**	8. **H**	15. **C**	22. **H**	29. **C**
2. **F**	9. **B**	16. **F**	23. **B**	30. **H**
3. **B**	10. **H**	17. **C**	24. **H**	31. **C**
4. **H**	11. **D**	18. **F**	25. **D**	32. **G**
5. **D**	12. **G**	19. **D**	26. **E**	33. **B**
6. **E**	13. **A**	20. **H**	27. **D**	34. **E**
7. **B**	14. **E**	21. **C**	28. **E**	35. **B**

ANSWER EXPLANATIONS

1. **(D)** Factoring out 6! from each term produces $6!(1 + 7 + 7 \cdot 8) = 6!(64)$. Therefore $n = 64$.

2. **(F)** Applying the laws of exponents, we get $\dfrac{x^{15}}{x^{23}}$, which equals x^{-8}.

3. **(B)** The edge of the cube must be 4. Therefore each face has an area of 16. Since there are six congruent faces, the total surface area is $6(16) = 96$.

4. **(H)** Substituting each pair of values into the first inequality shows that only choice H works: $-9 \geq 3(-8) + 8 = -16$.

5. **(D)** The numerator is $12 \cdot 11 \cdot 10 \cdot 9 \cdot 8 \cdots 3 \cdot 2 \cdot 1$. Dividing by 9! leaves us with $12 \cdot 11 \cdot 10$, which equals 1320.

6. **(E)** If the smallest integer is represented by x, then the others are $x + 1$, $x + 2$, $x + 3$, and $x + 4$. The sum of these five numbers is $5x + 10$, which must be a multiple of 5. The only choice that is a multiple of 5 is E. An alternate representation for a set of five consecutive integers is $x - 2$, $x - 1$, x, $x + 1$, and

$x + 2$. Their sum is $5x$, which is also a multiple of 5. It is usually easier to use a representation similar to this second set when dealing with consecutive integers.

7. **(B)** $\mathrm{Cos}\, A = \dfrac{AC}{AB} = \dfrac{AC}{25} = .28$. Then $AC = (25)(.28) = 7$.

8. **(H)**

> **FACT:** The slope of the line whose equation is $y = mx + b$ is the number m. If two lines have the same slope, the lines are parallel.

If we solve each equation for y, the equations become $y = -\dfrac{3}{4}x + \dfrac{10}{4}$ and $y = -\dfrac{12}{16}x + \dfrac{L}{16}$. Each of these lines has a slope of $-\dfrac{3}{4}$, so they are parallel regardless of the value of L. Thus, the lines are parallel for all three given values for L.

9. **(B)** Since the product of the ages is 3705, we must factor that number. Clearly 5 and 3 are factors, producing $3705 = 5 \times 3 \times 247$. To factor 247, we try dividing by prime numbers: 2, 3, 5, 7, and 11 don't work (you should know divisibility tests for 2, 3, 4, 5, 9, 10, and 11; for 7, just do the division). But 13

does, giving $247 = 13 \times 19$. Thus $3705 = 3 \times 5 \times 13 \times 19$. The teenagers must be 15, 13, and 19 years old, so the sum of their ages is 47. If they did not have to be teenagers, then the three ages (and their sum) would not have been uniquely determined.

10. **(H)**

> **FACT:** The sum of the lengths of two sides of a triangle is greater than the length of the third side.

Adding different pairs of sides and making each sum greater than the third side produces three different inequalities, each of which must be true. These inequalities are $6x + 10 > 6x - 21$, $8x - 21 > 4x + 10$, and $10x - 11 > 2x$. The first inequality, when simplifed, becomes $10 > -21$; this is always true. The second inequality becomes $4x > 31$; the smallest integer x for which this is true is $x = 8$. The third inequality becomes $8x > 11$; the smallest integer x for which this is true is $x = 2$. The smallest x that works for all three inequalities is $x = 8$.

11. **(D)** If there are n black marbles, then there are $9n$ white marbles, for a total of $10n$ marbles to start with. After adding a red marble, the probability of picking a black marble becomes $\frac{n}{10n + 1}$. The value of this fraction depends on the value of n, so the answer is D.

12. **(G)** The point (n, n) is on both lines, so the ordered pair (n, n) must satisfy both equations. Substituting n for both x and y in the second equation, we get $4n = 20$, so $n = 5$. Substituting 5 for both x and y in the first equation produces $5 = 5a - 10$, so $a = 3$.

13. **(A)**

> **FACT:** The volume of a pyramid is given by $V = \frac{1}{3} Bh$, where B represents the area of the base of the pyramid, and h represents the length of the altitude to that base.

The base is a right triangle whose area is $\frac{1}{2}(3)(4) = 6$. Therefore we have $24 = \frac{1}{3}(6)(h)$, so $h = 12$.

14. **(E)**

> **FACT:** Euler's Formula states that $V - E + F = 2$, where V is the number of vertices the figure has, E is the number of edges, and F is the number of faces.

Clearly $F = 10$. Each triangular face has three edges (total = 30). However, each edge is shared by exactly two faces; therefore every edge has been counted twice. There are really only 15 different edges, so $E = 15$. The formula gives us $V = 7$.

15. **(C)** Using the Pythagorean theorem in triangle ABC, we find that $AB = 10$. Now notice that angle y and angle A must be equal since each is the complement of angle B.

Therefore, $\sin y = \sin A = \frac{8}{10} = .8$.

16. **(F)** Method 1.

> **FACT (Method 1):** The measure of each interior angle of a regular polygon of n sides is equal to $\frac{(n - 2) \cdot 180}{n}$ degrees.

$\frac{(n - 2) \cdot 180}{n} = 156$. Then $(n - 2) \cdot 180 = 156n$, leading to $24n = 360$. Thus, $n = 15$.

Method 2.

> **FACT (Method 2):** The sum of the measures of the exterior angles of *any* polygon is $360°$.

Since each interior angle is $156°$, then each exterior angle must be $24°$. Then $24n = 360$, so $n = 15$.

17. **(C)** $\frac{1}{x} + \frac{1}{y} = \frac{x + y}{xy} = \frac{10}{20} = \frac{1}{2}$.

18. **(F)** Method 1.   Trying choice E, we see that the difference between x^2 and $x(x-1)$ is $x^2 - (x^2 - x) = x$. Trying choice F, we see that the difference between $x(x-1)$ and $(x-1)^2$ is $x-1$. Thus choice F is closer to the original expression. The other choices are much further away, especially when x is a large number.

Method 2.   The problem implies that the result will be true for any value of x that is greater than 10. Choose a value for x, such as $x = 11$. Then $x(x-1) = 110$. Trying the choices quickly leads to F as the closest.

19. **(D)** The given vertices are either consecutive vertices of the square or opposite vertices of the square. Draw a figure for each case. If the two given vertices are consecutive vertices of the square, then the side of the square is 12. Its area would be 144. But if the given vertices are opposite vertices of the square, we can connect both pairs of opposite vertices, forming four congruent right triangles. Each leg of each right triangle is 6, so the area of each right triangle is $\frac{1}{2}(6)(6) = 18$. That produces $(4)(18) = 72$ for the area of the square. That is the smallest possible area the square can have.

20. **(H)** Triangle ABC is isosceles, so angle $B \cong$ angle C.

> **FACT:** If two parallel lines are crossed by a transversal, the "corresponding angles" formed must be equal.

Since $\overline{PQ} \parallel \overline{AC}$, angle C = angle PQB. But that means that angle B = angle PQB. This tells us that triangle PBQ is isosceles. Thus, $PQ = PB$. We now see that $PQ + PA = PB + PA = AB = 18$. By similar reasoning, we find that $RQ + RA = RC + RA = AC = 18$. Therefore, the perimeter of quadrilateral $APQR$ is $18 + 18 = 36$. The length of $\overline{BC}$ has no bearing on the solution, and is simply a "distracter" that the student must pay no attention to.

21. **(C)** Method 1.   If $\frac{a}{b} = -6$, then $a = -6b$.

Therefore $a + b = -6b + b = -5b$ and $a - b = -6b - b = -7b$. Then $\frac{a+b}{a-b} = \frac{-5b}{-7b} = \frac{5}{7}$.

Method 2.   Choose suitable values for a and b that reflect the given condition. For example, choose $a = -6$ and $b = 1$. Then $\frac{a+b}{a-b} = \frac{-6+1}{-6-1} = \frac{-5}{-7} = \frac{5}{7}$.

22. **(H)** Method 1.   Let $5x = 3y = 7z = T$ and notice that T is positive. Thus $x = \frac{1}{5}T$, $y = \frac{1}{3}T$, and $z = \frac{1}{7}T$. Since $\frac{1}{7} < \frac{1}{5} < \frac{1}{3}$, we have $z < x < y$.

Method 2.   Since $z = \frac{5}{7}x$, that means $z < x$. Since $x = \frac{3}{5}y$, that means $x < y$. Thus $z < x < y$.

23. **(B)** Equilateral $\triangle ABE$ is also equiangular, so $\angle BAE = \angle AEB = 60°$. Notice that $\triangle ABC$ is an isosceles right triangle, so $\angle BAC = 45°$. Thus in $\triangle AEF$, $\angle EAF = 60° - 45° = 15°$ and $\angle AEB = 60°$. Thus $\angle AFE = 180° - (15° + 60°) = 180° - 75° = 105°$.

24. **(H)** One approach is to express $4\frac{1}{4}$ as $\frac{17}{4}$. Then $\left(4\frac{1}{4}\right)^2 = \left(\frac{17}{4}\right)^2 = \frac{289}{16} = 18\frac{1}{16}$.

25. **(D)** Let us first consider $x = .\overline{35} = .353535\ldots$ After multiplying both sides of this equation by 100, we get:

$$100x = 35.3535\ldots = 35.\overline{35}$$

Since $x = .3535\ldots = .\overline{35}$, subtracting $100x - x$ produces $99x = 35$. So $x = \frac{35}{99}$.

Notice that multiplication by 100 $(= 10^2)$ shifts the decimal point 2 places to the right. The number of digits in the repeating part of the decimal, in this case 2, motivates the choice of 10^2 as the multiplier.

> **FACT:** If a and b represent any of the digits 0, 1, 2, ..., 9, then $.\overline{a} = \dfrac{a}{9}$ and $.\overline{ab} = \dfrac{ab}{99}$, where "$ab$" represents a two-digit number.

However, we want the value of $M = .\overline{35} + \dfrac{1}{11}$. By expressing $\dfrac{1}{11}$ as $\dfrac{9}{99}$, we have $M = \dfrac{35}{99} + \dfrac{9}{99}$ $= \dfrac{44}{99}$. After looking at the choices, we see that $\dfrac{44}{99}$ does not appear in this form. Be careful to consider the choices! Note that $\dfrac{44}{99} = \dfrac{4 \times 11}{9 \times 11} = \dfrac{4}{9}$. (Alternatively, using the FACT shown above, $\dfrac{44}{99} = .\overline{44} = .444444... = .\overline{4} = \dfrac{4}{9}$.) You can gain much understanding from carefully reviewing this problem.

26. **(E)** First observe that as point A is rotated about the origin, its distance from the origin remains the same. Point $A(3,4)$ is 5 units from the origin. To see this, let d be the distance from A to the origin. Drawing a perpendicular from A to the x-axis creates a right triangle with hypotenuse d and legs 3 and 4. By the Pythagorean theorem, $d^2 = 3^2 + 4^2 = 25$, so $d = 5$. Thus all possible images of $A(3,4)$, when rotated about the origin, lie on a circle of radius 5 and center $(0,0)$, which is the origin. Any point whose x-coordinate is 6 would lie *outside* of this circle.

27. **(D)** Choosing a specific number for the original price will not affect the answer. For ease of computation, choose \$100 as the original price. The discounted price is then $(\$100) - (30\% \text{ of } \$100) = \$100 - \$30 = \$70$. You must now increase \$70 by \$30 to obtain the original price. Therefore you need to find what percent of \$70 is \$30. Thus $x\% = \dfrac{x}{100}$ $= \dfrac{30}{70}$. Solving for x gives $x = \dfrac{300}{7} = 42\dfrac{6}{7}$, which is closest to choice D.

28. **(E)** Express 4^4 and 4 as powers of 2. Since $4 = 2^2$, the value of $4^4 = (2^2)^4 = 2^8$. (Note that $(2^2)^4 = 2^2 \times 2^2 \times 2^2 \times 2^2 = 2^8$.) Therefore $\dfrac{4^4 + 4^4}{4} = \dfrac{2^8 + 2^8}{2^2} = \dfrac{2 \cdot 2^8}{2^2} = \dfrac{2^9}{2^2}$ $= 2^7$, so $x = 7$.

29. **(C)** The slope of $\overline{AB}$ is $\dfrac{13-1}{9-1} = \dfrac{12}{8} = \dfrac{3}{2}$. This tells us that on this line, 2 units of motion in the positive x direction corresponds to 3 units of motion in the positive y direction. Starting at $A(1,1)$, the next "integer" point is $(1 + \mathbf{2}, 1 + \mathbf{3})$, which is $(3,4)$. Continuing, we reach $(5,7)$, then $(7,10)$, and then $(9,13)$, for a total of 5 such points. (Making a good sketch would be quite helpful.)

30. **(H)** When $C = 0$, $F = 32$. Therefore the point $(0,32)$ is on the graph. Notice from the formula that if C increases, F also increases. You could use many other approaches to solve this problem.

31. **(C)** Making a brief table of selected values is quite revealing.

A	B	P
0	20	0
2	18	36
4	16	64
6	14	84
8	12	96
10	10	100
12	8	96
14	6	84
16	4	64
18	2	36
20	0	0

Notice that as A increases, P increases and then decreases. (The values of P are symmetric about $A = 10$.) Choice C "best" illustrates this behavior.

32. **(G)** From 5 girls (*a, b, c, d, e*) we can select 2 girls in 10 different ways: *ab, ac, ad, ae, bc, bd, be, cd, ce,* and *de*. Since Robert must be on the team, we must select 2 more boys from the remaining 3 boys (*x, y, z*). This can be done in 3 different ways: *xy, xz,* and *yz*. Selecting the girls is independent of selecting the boys. So the total number of different team selections is $10 \times 3 = 30$.

33. **(B)** The sketch reveals the solution quite clearly.

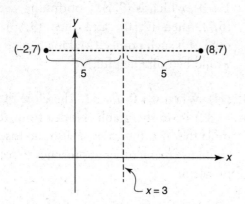

34. **(E)** Triangle *ACE* and triangle *ABD* are right triangles. Therefore $\angle 4 + \angle A = 90°$ and $\angle 1 + \angle A = 90°$. Thus $\angle 1$ and $\angle 4$ must be congruent. The word **must** rules out cases in which a pair of angles **may** be congruent but do not have to be congruent. Can you show why $\angle 5$ cannot be congruent to $\angle 3$?

35. **(B)** Let the dimensions of the square face be *x* by *x*. Without loss of generality, let this face be the base of the box. Let *y* represent the height. The volume of a rectangular box is $V = $ length $\times$ width $\times$ height, which leads to $72 = x^2 y$. Remember that *x* and *y* are integers, so x^2 must be a factor of 72. The only possible square factors of 72 are 1, 4, 9, and 36, leading to $x = 1, 2, 3,$ or 6. The total surface area is $4xy + 2x^2$. Compute the value of this expression for each *x*. If $x = 1$, $y = 72$, so the surface area would be 290. If $x = 2$, $y = 18$; if $x = 3$, $y = 8$; and if $x = 6$, $y = 2$. The corresponding surface areas are, respectively, 152, 114, and 120. The answer is 114.

Appendix:
Progress on Math Workouts and Follow-Ups

Date	Workouts (15-minute time limit) and Follow-Ups	Number Correct	Circle Number of Each Incorrect Problem (compare results of <u>same</u> tests; work on problems gotten wrong both times)
3-8-19	Workout A	7	①②③ 4 5 6 7 8 9 10
3-8-19	Follow-Up A	10	1 2 3 4 5 6 7 8 9 10
	Workout B		1 2 3 4 5 6 7 8 9 10
	Follow-Up B		1 2 3 4 5 6 7 8 9 10
	Workout C		1 2 3 4 5 6 7 8 9 10
	Follow-Up C		1 2 3 4 5 6 7 8 9 10
	Workout D		1 2 3 4 5 6 7 8 9 10
	Follow-Up D		1 2 3 4 5 6 7 8 9 10
	Workout E		1 2 3 4 5 6 7 8 9 10
	Follow-Up E		1 2 3 4 5 6 7 8 9 10
	Workout F		1 2 3 4 5 6 7 8 9 10
	Follow-Up F		1 2 3 4 5 6 7 8 9 10
	Workout A		1 2 3 4 5 6 7 8 9 10
	Follow-Up A		1 2 3 4 5 6 7 8 9 10
	Workout B		1 2 3 4 5 6 7 8 9 10
	Follow-Up B		1 2 3 4 5 6 7 8 9 10
	Workout C		1 2 3 4 5 6 7 8 9 10
	Follow-Up C		1 2 3 4 5 6 7 8 9 10
	Workout D		1 2 3 4 5 6 7 8 9 10
	Follow-Up D		1 2 3 4 5 6 7 8 9 10
	Workout E		1 2 3 4 5 6 7 8 9 10
	Follow-Up E		1 2 3 4 5 6 7 8 9 10
	Workout F		1 2 3 4 5 6 7 8 9 10
	Follow-Up F		1 2 3 4 5 6 7 8 9 10

Really. This isn't going to hurt at all . . .

Learning won't hurt when middle school and high school students open any *Painless* title. These books transform subjects into fun—emphasizing a touch of humor and entertaining brain-tickler puzzles that are fun to solve.

Bonus Online Component—each title followed by (*) includes additional online games to challenge students, including Beat the Clock, a line match game, and a word scramble.

Each book: Paperback

Painless Algebra, 4th Ed.*
Lynette Long, Ph.D.
ISBN 978-1-4380-0775-5, $9.99, Can$11.99

Painless American Government
Jeffrey Strausser
ISBN 978-0-7641-2601-7, $9.99, Can$11.99

Painless American History, 2nd Ed.
Curt Lader
ISBN 978-0-7641-4231-4, $9.99, Can$11.99

Painless Chemistry, 2nd Ed.*
Loris Chen
ISBN 978-1-4380-0771-7, $9.99, Can$11.99

Painless Earth Science
Edward J. Denecke, Jr.
ISBN 978-0-7641-4601-5, $11.99, Can$14.99

Painless English for Speakers of Other Languages, 2nd Ed.
Jeffrey Strausser and José Paniza
ISBN 978-1-4380-0002-2, $9.99, Can$11.50

Painless Fractions, 3rd Ed.
Alyece Cummings, M.A.
ISBN 978-1-4380-0000-8, $10.99, Can$13.99

Painless French, 3rd Ed.*
Carol Chaitkin, M.S., and Lynn Gore, M.A.
ISBN 978-1-4380-0770-0, $9.99, Can$11.99

Painless Geometry, 3rd Ed.*
Lynette Long, Ph.D.
ISBN 978-1-4380-1039-7, $9.99, Can$12.50

Painless Grammar, 4th Ed.*
Rebecca Elliott, Ph.D.
ISBN 978-1-4380-0774-8, $9.99, Can$11.99

Painless Italian, 2nd Ed.
Marcel Danesi, Ph.D.
ISBN 978-0-7641-4761-6, $9.99, Can$11.50

Painless Math Word Problems, 2nd Ed.
Marcie Abramson, B.S., Ed.M.
ISBN 978-0-7641-4335-9, $11.99, Can$14.99

Painless Poetry, 2nd Ed.
Mary Elizabeth
ISBN 978-0-7641-4591-9, $9.99, Can$11.99

Painless Pre-Algebra, 2nd Ed.*
Amy Stahl
ISBN 978-1-4380-0773-1, $9.99, Can$11.99

Painless Reading Comprehension, 3rd Ed.*
Darolyn "Lyn" Jones, Ed.D.
ISBN 978-1-4380-0769-4, $9.99, Can$11.99

Painless Spanish, 3rd Ed.*
Carlos B. Vega and Dasha Davis
ISBN 978-1-4380-0772-4, $9.99, Can$11.99

Painless Spelling, 3rd Ed.
Mary Elizabeth
ISBN 978-0-7641-4713-5, $9.99, Can$11.99

Painless Study Techniques
Michael Greenberg
ISBN 978-0-7641-4059-4, $9.99, Can$11.99

Painless Vocabulary, 3rd Ed.*
Michael Greenberg
ISBN 978-1-4380-0778-6, $9.99, Can$11.99

Painless Writing, 3rd Ed.*
Jeffrey Strausser
ISBN 978-1-4380-0784-7, $9.99, Can$11.99

Prices subject to change without notice.

SUPPORTS STATE STANDARDS

Available at your local bookstore or visit **www.barronseduc.com**

Barron's Educational Series, Inc.
250 Wireless Blvd.
Hauppauge, N.Y. 11788
Order toll-free:
1-800-645-3476

(#79) R2/18